# Small-Batch Baking

# Small-Batch Baking

*When Just Enough for 1 or 2 . . . Is Just Enough!*

## Debby Maugans Nakos
### Illustrated by Laurie Lafrance

WORKMAN PUBLISHING • NEW YORK

Library of Congress Cataloging-in-Publication Data
Nakos, Debbie Maugans.
Small-batch baking : when just enough for 1 or 2 . . .
is just enough! / Debby Maugans Nakos ; illustrated by
Laurie Lafrance.
p. cm.
Includes index.
ISBN 0-7611-3035-7 (alk. paper)—ISBN 0-7611-3587-1
1. Baking.  2. Cookery for two.  3. Cookery for one.  I. title

TX765.N35 2004
641.8'15—dc22                           2004058895

Cover design by Paul Gamarello
Book design by Barbara Balch

Workman books are available at special discounts when
purchased in bulk for premiums and sales promotions
as well as for fund-raising or educational use. Special
editions or book excerpts can be created to specification.
For details, contact the Special Sales Director at the
address below.

Workman Publishing Company, Inc.
708 Broadway
New York, NY 10003-9555

First printing: October 2004
Printed in the United States of America

10 9 8 7 6 5 4 3 2 1

For my girls, JK and Eleni,
because my favorite job always is to be their mom.

# Acknowledgments

**I can unabashedly** say that it has been my dream to have my own
book published by Workman. I've admired the handiwork of Suzanne Rafer,
my clever editor, for many years, beginning with the Workman books I
received to review when I was food editor of *Creative Ideas for Living*
magazine. Those Workman books made an impression on me, and now
I have a good number of them (almost all of the cookbooks) on my office
bookshelves. So when my wonderful agent, Patricia Moosbrugger, told
me she was ready to shop my book proposal, I just crossed my fingers.
Thanks to the Workman family for embracing this book idea and giving
it wings. I have great respect for the publishing genius of Peter Workman.
And everything Suzanne Rafer tweaked, probed, and questioned turned
me into a better author. Those are very good hands to be in.

My unending thanks go to Patty Moosbrugger for her unselfish and
generous support and determination to see this book published in a big
way. It was her inspired vision that turned a market niche with a need
into a valid book on baking. I'll never be able to tell you what you've done
for me personally, and I thank you for trusting me with this book.

In addition to Patty, warm thanks go to Wendy Hubbert, my very first
book editor, for believing in me in the beginning. Wendy inspired me to
think outside the box and coaxed me into writing a first book that I was
proud of. It was Wendy who is responsible for recommending that Patty

and I collaborate, and I hope the three of us will continue the friendship for many years.

Completing the immediate circle of how I got around to writing this book, I have to thank Robert Barnett. That first chance meeting outside an olive grove in Seville turned into quite a productive friendship. I've enjoyed the many projects we have worked on together and sincerely hope there are more to come.

In the beginning, however, there was Martha Johnston. When I was a neophyte with the desire and ability but not the direction, Martha stepped in. As my first "boss" in the food business, Martha was not happy until I could do it all, faster, and with utmost professionalism. She gave me many opportunities to develop, test, write, produce, perform, and manage, and I give her complete credit for honing my professional skills and some of the personal ones, too. Thank you for everything, MJ.

I wouldn't be doing what I do without my family's influence. Thank you, Mama and Daddy (Aileen and Joe Maugans), for being there for me through the ages. I love you so much, and it was your delicious food that inspired me to cook. Some of my fondest childhood memories area of spending weeks during my summer vacations with my aunt, Cora Boyett Evans, learning to cook, iron, sew, pick oranges, and enjoy central Florida. Aunt Cora was a home economics professor at Rollins College, and it was largely her enthusiasm that turned me into a baker. My sister, Pam Hamby, is my best friend and confidante; thank you for being true to us and understanding me more than anyone. Many thanks to my husband, Dean, and my girls for your love and support.

While I was doing most of the recipe development, I had a teenager, Jessie Kate, going through her final year in high school and a three-year-old, Eleni, trying to help me write the book. So I've not made it to New York as of this writing to shake the hands of the people who put this all together. But I know who they are, and I want to express my gratitude for all of their efforts. Kathie Ness and Ann ffolliott were my skilled copyeditors; your job and production editor Anne Cherry's are, in the end, what make the text credible. Without your watchful eyes and Barbara Peragine's meticulous typesetting, there's no telling what those recipes would say. Many thanks to all four of you. Thanks to Doug Wolff for making sure it all gets printed on schedule, and I greatly appreciate the rest of the sales and marketing staff for taking care of getting the book out there. Thank you, Sarah O'Leary, for wanting to take on the publicity for this book. You have so many wonderful ideas and I know ours will be a dynamic and enjoyable relationship.

I must say that Anthony Loew has the best lighting technique of any photographer who has ever attempted to take my picture. I would like to look that perky all the time. Thank you, Tony, for shooting a cover shot that I'm happy to look at. I am grateful to have had Paul Gamarello and Barbara Balch designing the cover and interior, respectively; the package that a cookbook's recipes come in is supremely important and I appreciate their talented work. Thank you, Laurie Lafrance, for the lively illustrations in the book; they add such fun to the recipes.

I come from a background of working in a test kitchen, where I developed my skills of recipe testing, and now accept nothing less than professional testing of the recipes that I develop and publish. I fortunate to have found a protégée in Sarah Ott, a student at Samford University. Sarah assisted me in many hours of testing, and her questions about the recipes' methods and outcomes have ensured their quality. Thank you, Sarah, for your devotion; your enthusiasm fuels my heart.

Finally, I am humbly thankful for all of the doors that have opened for me and for the faith to step through them.

# Contents

# Cookies *and* Bars 168

All your favorite cookies in small batches—Cream-Filled Chocolate,
Oatmeal, Peanut Butter, Chocolate Chip, and two kinds of biscotti.
Plus Moist Fudgy Brownies and Cherry Macadamia Bars.

# Crumbly, Sweet, *and* Fruity: Cobblers, Crisps, Crumbles, *and* Shortcakes 216

Just enough for two—Strawberry Rhubarb Crumble,
Fig and Hazelnut Crisp, Nectarine Blueberry Buckle,
Coconut Shortcakes, a Mixed Berry Cornmeal Cobbler.
And many more to tempt the palate.

# Baked Puddings: I'd Rather Have Them *for* Supper 260

Wonderful bread puddings, warm and soothing, rich with butterscotch
or mascarpone, chocolate or pecans. Also, Lemon Pudding Cakes and
a Maple Pear Blueberry Hasty Pudding.

# Sweet *and* Savory Muffins *and* Breads 295

Sweet breakfast and tea breads, muffins, and scones. Dinner boules and
popovers, cheese bread and country-style classics. Plus a focaccia redolent
with rosemary.

## Valentine Specials 352

Perfect for the one you love: Cream Puffs with Coffee Ice Cream and Orange Mocha Sauce, Chocolate-Glazed Raspberry Cheesecakes, Apricot Meringue Cookie Tarts, or Pistachio Napoleons with Orange Mousse and Orange Caramel Sauce.

## Holiday Goodies You Can't Live Without 396

Holiday cheer the Small-Batch way includes Brandy Caramel Pumpkin Pies, Southern Pecan Pies, Fruitcake You Will Love, Cranberry Eggnog Pudding, and an Apple Walnut Crostata, to name just a few of the delicious choices.

# Introduction:
# The Small-Batch Solution

**I began dreaming** about this book when I was in college. You see, stress relief comes to me when I bake, so back then, I often felt the need to whip something up, especially the night before an important exam. But I knew I'd hate myself in the morning—as I always do when I overindulge in a temptingly good thing, and underindulge in what I really should have been doing—studying, for example.

I didn't bake only for myself. After my best friend broke up with her guy, for instance, I whipped up an incredibly rich, flourless chocolate torte to soothe her. However, pondering life's larger questions might have been better served had we nibbled on only one slice instead of devouring the entire thing. The concept of baking small batches of goodies was beginning to take hold.

When I got married and started preparing dinners for two, there were evenings my new husband and I really wanted dessert, say a couple of chocolate chip cookies, but not more. The recipes I had yielded dozens. Brownies sounded great too, but I didn't want to be dipping a knife into a pan of leftovers the next morning. As for fresh bread, we both love it and tried baking it, but an entire loaf was wasted on us. Naturally, when I wanted to bake a special dessert for our first anniversary, I couldn't find anything small enough to suit the occasion and our needs.

Writing a cookbook that enabled me and others to bake small quantities of smashing desserts, melt-in-your-mouth cookies, and individual loaves of crusty bread was sounding better and better. But other projects, including starting a family, took priority. Now that I have a teenager and a toddler (both girls), I realized it was time for me to stop dreaming about baking in small batches and start doing something about it.

My girls were especially helpful because they don't agree on what they like in the treats department. They're each into their own kind of small batch. Our three-year-old loves giant oatmeal cookies (with sprinkles) and blue-colored cupcakes, but she is completely satisfied after one. Small batches work well for her, but had I not been working on this book, we might have been stuck with a pantry full of blue food. Our teenager discovered that chocolate can soothe away boyfriend problems, school glitches, and annoying parents. Before I began working on this book, we were left with the rest of her favorite frosted fudge cake after she decided she was okay. Do I need to tell you who ate the rest of that perfectly delicious homemade chocolate cake?

Whether you're hungry for mile-high mini layer cakes, buttery pies or tarts, fruit crisps, chewy cookies or bars, easy breakfast muffins or breads, a special holiday dessert, or a Valentine's Day treat for your sweetheart, if you only need enough for one or two servings, *Small-Batch Baking* is for you. The recipes are easy, the batters come together quickly, and cleanup is a breeze. And you won't have leftovers to tempt you to eat more than you want. So enjoy treating yourself—and one other important someone—without overdoing it. You deserve dessert!

# Small-Batch Baking

# CHAPTER 1

# How *to* Bake Small Batches

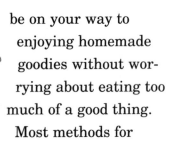

**So how can** you bake old-fashioned, "from scratch" desserts and breads just for two? With a bit of ingredient maneuvering and creativity! You are just pages away from baking small batches of spectacular desserts and fragrant breads, including crisp and flaky pie crusts that hold a wonderful assortment of fillings; tender cakes (yes, even layered ones) with creamy rich frostings; delicious buttery cookies and biscuits; and crusty French *boules*. Before you get going, I do have some tips for successful baking in small batches, so please read through this chapter and you'll be on your way to enjoying homemade goodies without worrying about eating too much of a good thing.

Most methods for baking in small batches are the same as for larger versions. But it's not always possible to divide a standard recipe by halves, thirds, or quarters and arrive at something perfectly baked. Amounts do not always reduce in straightforward proportions. These recipes were created specifically for small batches. The formulas work perfectly and will result in the quality of dessert or bread you expect from its traditional counterpart. If you are an accomplished baker, you will feel right at home with these recipes. If these are your first attempts, you'll find clear instruc-tions in the recipes that will help you feel confident about mixing and baking.

# Equipment

**While manufacturers** have yet to offer pans for baking small cakes, you can most likely use what you have in your kitchen. Below is a list of equipment needed for the recipes in this book; most recipes call for standard pans that you use in everyday cooking. Basically, if you have assorted muffin and loaf pans and a baking sheet, you need only purchase two individual tart pans in two sizes. A few delicate cakes and cheesecakes are baked in 3-inch round stainless steel rings, called mousse rings, dessert rings, or baking rings. They are available online at www.cooking.com as well as in kitchenware shops. And you'll need to save cans from standard pantry items like pineapple and tomatoes, because individual double- and single-layer cakes are baked in thoroughly cleaned 8- and 14-inch cans with one end and the label neatly removed.

You may be surprised at how easy it is to use the pans you have for baking in small batches. Included in this basic equipment list are also items you'll need for mixing the batter or dough.

*That one great bowl:* For mix-ing butter and sugar, or cake and cookie batters, beating egg whites, and whipping cream, you'll need a 1½-quart bowl that is taller than it is wide. The one I use is the small mixing bowl that came with my first stand mixer; it measures 6 inches in diameter at the top, about 3 inches in diameter at the bottom, and stands 4 inches tall. The higher sides will effectively contain the small amounts of butter, sugar, and flour, as the ingredients are beaten with a hand-held mixer (see below). If the bowl is shallow and wide at the top, those small amounts tend to fly up and around the bowl instead of collecting at the center. All-Clad makes a good-quality 1½-quart bowl with a handle; it is about 7 inches in diameter at the top and is widely available in kitchen supply stores. But any good, deep bowl will do.

*Hand-held mixer:* Both the lower speed and the ability to control the direction of the mixer make a hand-held mixer perfect for the smaller jobs in these recipes. It works better for creaming a few tablespoons of butter and sugar, aerating ½ cup of batter, and whipping 1 egg white or ¼ cup of heavy cream. Even if your stand mixer comes with a 1½-quart bowl, you'll mix the batter more efficiently if you use a hand-held mixer.

*Rubber spatulas:* When you bake small batches, you use small amounts of most ingredients, so every little bit counts toward the end results. A rubber spatula is the best tool for scraping out every smidgeon of melted chocolate into a frosting or batter, or all of the batter into the prepared baking pan, or the last morsel of cookie dough to make that sixth and final cookie. You'll need both wide and thin spatulas.

*A good-quality baking sheet:* You'll need one rimmed baking sheet for baking cookies and breads, and for conveniently transporting tart pans, custard cups, ramekins, and baking cans to and from the oven. Line it with parchment paper and you can bake six to eight cookies, two or three scones, two crostatas (or free-form tarts), and one or two small loaves of bread.

*Muffin pans:* The large Texas, or jumbo, muffin pan, with six ¾-cup-capacity cups, is just right for baking deep-dish fruit pies, large bakery-style muffins, and single-serving upside-down cakes. A regular-size muffin pan, with six ½-cup-capacity cups, is great for baking individual quick breads and cupcakes.

*Loaf pans:* A petite, or mini, loaf pan that measures 5¾ x 3⅛ inches and holds 2 cups will bake small loaves of quick breads or pound cakes that serve two or three. Most

large grocery stores and kitchen supply stores carry them. Rolled cakes that serve two or three can be baked in 9 x 5 inch loaf pans. There are no tiny jelly-roll pans on the market, but when you line the loaf pan with parchment and use the paper to lift the cake layer from the pan, it rolls beautifully over a filling to make three neat slices.

*Individual tart pans with removable bottoms:* Two sizes of tart pans are used for these recipes: 4 x 1⅜-inch tart pans and 4½ x ¾-inch. These are great sizes for individual pies and tarts. I use the 4-inch tart pan, lined with aluminum foil, for single-serving cheesecakes. (In a few recipes, I've baked cheesecakes in

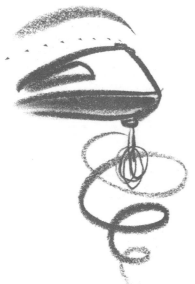

8-ounce cans lined with parchment because I wanted the cheesecake to be taller.)

*Reusable cans:* You may be surprised to know that when you cut off the tops of empty 14- to 15-ounce cans neatly with a can opener (see below), remove the labels, and wash out the cans thoroughly in the dishwasher, they make wonderful baking pans. The 14- to 15-inch cans hold just the right amount of batter for a two-layer cake, and an 8-ounce can is a good size for baking single-layer cakes. For easy removal of the

baked cakes, you simply butter the inside of the can and cut out a circle of parchment to fit snugly into the bottom. Be sure to use only cans that have no dents or nicks.

*Can openers:* These are must-haves in any kitchen, but a Small-Batch baker needs a can opener that cuts off the tops without leaving any jagged edges to tear the cakes as they are unmolded, or that will knick your hands as you prepare the cans for baking. Many manufacturers make clean-cut electric and hand-held can openers, such as the OXO Good Grips Locking Can Opener and ones from Hamilton Beach, Krups, Sunbeam, and Tupperware.

*Wire rack:* You'll only need one for these recipes, unless you are baking several small batches at one time.

*Single-serving ovenproof bowls:* These include soufflé dishes, custard cups, and ramekins. You'll only need two of each, and they'll prove very useful. Ovenproof cereal bowls and custard cups are great for baking puddings, cobblers, and crisps; soufflé dishes or ramekins hold beautiful individual soufflés.

## HOW TO BAKE IN CANS

Here are tips on getting the batter into—and out of—the cans.

- After you have removed the label, and greased and floured the can, drop small amounts of batter off the tip of a narrow rubber spatula into the center of the can. If you have dropped more batter into one can than the other, even them up by removing some of the batter with a long-handled teaspoon and dropping it into the other can. Smooth the top of the batter as best you can with the spatula tip. You can also use the spatula to scrape the drips of batter off the edge of the can and into the center.

- The batter in my recipes will only fill the can one quarter to one third full. After they bake, the cakes will appear short, rising only about halfway up the sides of the cans. After you remove the cakes from the can and fill and frost them, they will be the perfect size for individual servings.

- To test the cakes for doneness, insert the tip of a long, thin skewer halfway into the center of the cake, then withdraw it. the cake is done if there are no crumbs attached (well, one or two dry crumbs ar acceptable).

- Cool the cakes for 10 minutes in the cans, then run the tip of a narrow, sharp knife around the edges of the cakes. the cakes will slip out of the cans easily. Cool them rightside up on a wire rack.

- Remember to discard the cans after two or three uses if you see any discoloration on the cans. After all, they're a cinch to replace!

# Ingredients and Measuring Techniques

**It's much easier to** cut a stir-fry recipe down to size by dividing the ingredients in half (one onion instead of two, ½ pound instead of 1 pound of chicken), but you can't tinker with baking in the same manner and expect wonderful results. When reducing a baking recipe, leavening ingredients, such as eggs, baking powder, and baking soda, do not necessarily reduce proportionally. Here's how to measure ingredients accurately and

how to store the leftovers. This is also a good list of basic supplies to have on hand for baking the recipes in this book.

*Eggs:* Standard recipe-writing procedure calls for large eggs, and when a size is not called for, we cooks are supposed to default to the large size, not medium or jumbo. In many recipes in this book, just a portion of a large egg is the optimum amount, and using an entire large egg would adversely alter the desired taste and texture. Having said that, I feel that it is easier and more accurate to use a medium egg if it is the perfect size for the recipe. So, where medium eggs can be used, they are called for; you can substitute 3 tablespoons of a beaten large egg or 3 tablespoons of egg substitute if you would rather not buy a carton of medium eggs. Medium eggs are available in most grocery stores; small eggs are not available in most markets and are not used in this book.

To measure out a portion of a large egg to use in a recipe, crack the egg into a small bowl and use a fork to whip the egg until it is well blended but not foamy, about 30 seconds. Use a sharp-edged measuring spoon to lift the desired amount from the bowl. Any left-over egg can be stored in a covered container in the refrigerator for up to one day.

*Chocolate:* The best method for determining the precise amount of chocolate and white chocolate to put into the recipe is to weigh it on a reliable kitchen scale. Even an inexpensive one will be helpful. Measuring with a tablespoon measure is not always accurate; chopped and *finely* chopped choco-late pack into a tablespoon measure differently. But for those who don't own a scale, you should get 3 to 3½ tablespoons chopped chocolate per ounce.

Most of the recipes in this book use only a few ounces of chocolate, so it is important to know what to do with the rest of that premium-quality bar. Chocolate picks up flavors from other foods, so wrap the leftovers well in aluminum foil, then seal the wrapped package in a zip-lock plastic bag. Store it in a cool, dry place, but not in the refrigerator unless you are just going to melt it anyway, or you live in an extremely hot, humid area. When chocolate is refrigerated, the cocoa butter separates from the solids and coats the outside of the bar as a hazy film, or "bloom." (However, this does not affect the flavor of the chocolate and will disappear when the chocolate is melted.)

*Butter:* Unsalted butter produces the best flavor in cakes, cookies, pie

crusts, and sweet breads. Although sweet foods are enhanced with a bit of salt, add it from the shaker, not from the butter. That way you are better able to control the flavors of small batches of the baked dessert or bread.

Small amounts of butter need to be quite soft for creaming, especially with heavy batter and dough. When you are mixing only a couple tablespoons of butter with a hand mixer and it is still slightly chilled, you'll end up chasing the butter around the bowl with the beaters. If it is very soft, it will blend easily with the other ingredients.

*Dry ingredients:* The recipes in this book call for such small amounts of dry ingredients that it is especially important to measure them correctly. And that means loosely. One extra tablespoon of flour, for instance, will drastically alter a bread or dessert, and if you scoop the flour from the canister with the measuring cup, packing the flour down as you scoop, you'll end up with at least 1 tablespoon too much. The same with leavening ingredients; if you pack too much baking powder or soda into the measuring spoon, your baked product can become overly dry or develop an off flavor.

For ingredients that are measured in a dry measuring cup, such as flour, place the cup on a piece of waxed paper and lightly spoon the ingredient into the cup, filling it a bit high on the top. Hold the flat edge of a knife against the edge of the cup and scrape it across to top to even the flour with the top lip of the cup. You can then pour the flour that has fallen onto the waxed paper back into the canister.

For baking powder and baking soda, spoon the leavening ingredient into a measuring spoon that you hold over the carton or over a piece of waxed paper; scrape the flat edge of a knife over the spoon to even the ingredient with the top lip of the spoon.

*Leftover ingredients:* It is simply the nature of the beast that you will have leftover ingredients when you bake in small batches. The staples are easy: most dry ingredients will keep for a year in airtight containers; you probably use milk, butter, and other everyday dairy products on a regular basis; but other ingredients do not age quite so well. Here are some guidelines:

*White flour, cornstarch, unsweetened cocoa:* It is not necessary to refrigerate any of these, but you do want to keep them in a dark place, away from heat and humidity, and they will last a year.

*Whole-grain flours, including cornmeal:* These have natural oils that can make them turn rancid quickly, so store them in airtight containers in the refrigerator or freezer and let them come to room temperature after measuring. they will keep for six months.

*Dry yeast:* Yeast should be frozen to keep it fresh for six months to a year; to be safe, check the expiration date on the package. You can use it right out of the freezer; snip the package and measure what you need, then slip the rest of the yeast, still in the package, into a zip-lock freezer bag and refreeze it.

*Milk, cream, buttermilk, cottage cheese, ricotta, sour cream, yogurt:* Store these in the refrigerator and, for best quality and flavor, use by

the expiration or sell-by date. On the other hand, if it smells and tastes fresh, you can sometimes use it a few days after the date on the package. For those who use buttermilk only occasionally in baking, Saco makes a powdered variety, which is available in supermarkets in the baking aisle. If refrigerated or frozen after opening it will keep for several years.

*Cream cheese:* Usually, cream cheese will last two weeks past the expiration date on the package if it is kept in the refrigerator.

*Butter:* Leave it in the original wrapper to store it in the refrigerator for one to three months. You can freeze it for up to six to nine months; be sure to wrap it well in moisture-proof freezer packaging material. This will prevent freezer burn as

well as keep odors from other foods from leaking into the packaging and being absorbed into the butter. Thaw it in the refrigerator.

*Spices:* Store jars tightly sealed in a cool, dark, dry place, away from appliances that produce heat. Ground and whole spices will keep for a year.

*Sweetened flaked coconut and dried fruits, such as raisins, apricots, currants, cherries, and cranberries:* Store them in zip-lock bags in a cool, dark, dry place for six months.

*Jams, jellies, and preserves:* After you open them, store them in the refrigerator for four to six months.

*Homemade dessert sauces, such as caramel and chocolate sauce:* Store in a covered jar in the refrigerator for one week.

*Peanut butter:* Although refrigeration is not necessary, it will keep in the refrigerator for a couple of months longer than the two to three months it lasts on the pantry shelf.

*Vanilla and other extracts:* Keep the bottles tightly sealed so the volatile essence does not escape. Store in a cool, dark place for a year.

*Nuts and seeds, such as walnuts, almonds, pecans, sesame seeds, and almond paste:* After opening, put the leftovers in airtight freezer bags or containers and, to be safe, freeze nuts and seeds; refrigerate or freeze almond paste. All three contain oils that can turn rancid if they are not kept cold and dry.

*Canned fruits and vegetables, such as pineapple and canned unsweetened pumpkin:* After removing what you need from the can, transfer the leftover product to a clean airtight container, ziplock freezer bag, or glass jar. Do not store in the can. Refrigerate and use within five to seven days.

*Coconut milk and sweetened condensed milk:* Pour any unused portion into a glass jar, cover, and refrigerate up to a week.

## THE SKINNY ON OBLONG LOAF PANS

You may think a loaf pan is a loaf pan, but despite minute variations in sizes, many are labeled "standard." Some loaf pans have slightly rounded bottom corners and some are sharper in their shape. Some measure 9¼ x 5¼ by 3 inches, some 9 x 5 x 3 inches, some 8½ x 4½ x 3 inches, 8 x 4 x 3 inches, 7½ x 3¾ x 3 inches, and so on. All are about the same depth.

When you work with the small amounts of batter called for in the recipes in this book, it is necessary to use the correct size loaf pan. Keeping in mind that you probably have no desire to keep all those different sizes in your cabinets, I've simplified matters by calling for a 9 x 5-inch, 8 x 4-inch or 7 x 3-inch loaf pan. Don't worry if yours is ½ inch longer or wider.

# CHAPTER 2

# Beautiful Small Cakes

**When I was** a young girl, homemade cake or pie always followed the meat-and-three-sides that my mother served for dinner. Leftovers were for snacking. Back in the late 1970s, she baked on at least a biweekly basis because prepared desserts were not sold at the local supermarket. So I learned to bake and grew to love it.

The fact is, however, that what we eat today we wear tomorrow. Still, I *need* dessert. I want to savor those fondly remembered old-fashioned cakes just as much as I like to experiment with fancy new creations. But I don't want to be tempted by the leftovers tomorrow. So I've tweaked my favorite recipes and developed smaller cakes with the full flavor and soft, moist crumb you would expect from their full-blown prototypes.

The first time I baked baby layer cakes in cans was for my own baby shower. They were such a hit that I've since made them for birthdays, anniversaries, dinner parties, and as a reward for my twelve-year-old's excellent report card. When you make Small-Batch layer cakes, each person gets a two- or three-layer cake, completely frosted. (For those of you who love the icing, you'll be happy to hear that there is proportionally a bit more frosting on a Small-Batch cake serving than you would get on a slice of layer cake.)

In this chapter I've reduced every kind of cake I could think of to a small serving size. Bundt cakes, such as the densely moist Spiced Sweet Potato Bundt Cakes, are baked in miniature molds, and pineapple and blueberry upside-down cakes and angel food cakes are baked in muffin pans. Fancy pound cakes, such as the buttery-rich Raspberry Almond Butter Cakes and the moist Lemon Cornmeal Pound Cakes, are baked in metal rings or clean cans—the list goes on.

You might think it impossible to prepare a roulade for two or three people, but instead of a jelly-roll pan, Small-Batch rolled cake layers are baked using a loaf pan as a small jelly-roll pan, resulting in short roulades that serve you and a friend or two. Just wait until you try the Lemon Roulade with White Chocolate–Honey Cream and Pistachios. Or how about the Gingerbread Roulade with Rum Cream and Candied Pecans?

If cupcakes are what you crave, there are two well-loved kinds in this chapter. The Just Plain Good Cupcakes are moist with melt-in-your mouth texture. The Really Fudgy ones are—as you might guess—the fudgiest, with the rich dark flavor of brownies and a pillow-soft cake texture.

Last but not least, this chapter contains cakes, ranging from plain to fancy, made in petite loaf pans. Simply great are the Presto Pound Cake and Hazelnut Chocolate Torte with Frangelico Cream. As with all the cakes, each gives you a couple of servings, and then the temptation is gone!

If you find yourself with left-overs, I'll be a little shocked. But there may be times that you are left with an extra cake. I prefer to keep leftovers in the refrigerator; they seem to last longer that way and will be just as good two or three days later if you wrap them loosely in plastic wrap.

# Chocolate Birthday Cake

## with Double Chocolate Sour Cream Frosting

*Makes 2 cakes; serves 2*

◆◆◆◆◆◆◆◆◆

**My quest for** a chocolate layer cake recipe that would yield moist, soft cake with a lingering buttery, chocolate flavor ended when I found this one. It isn't fancy—it's just the best in its class. The frosting is made from a blend of milk and bittersweet chocolates; the better quality the chocolate, the richer the frosting will taste. These are just right for an intimate celebration of a loved one's birthday.

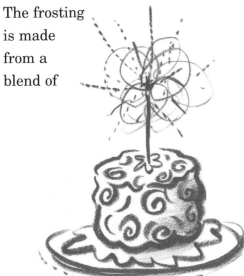

**Unsalted butter, at room temperature, for greasing the cans**

**¼ cup plus 2 tablespoons all-purpose flour, plus more for flouring the cans**

**3 tablespoons buttermilk**

**Yolk of 1 large egg**

**½ teaspoon pure vanilla extract**

**3 tablespoons unsalted butter, melted and cooled**

**2 tablespoons unsweetened cocoa powder**

**⅛ teaspoon baking soda**

$^1\!/_8$ **teaspoon salt**

$^1\!/_3$ **cup sugar**

**Double Chocolate Sour Cream
   Frosting (recipe follows)**

PANS REQUIRED:

**Two 14- or 14.5-ounce cans
   (see page 6)**

**1 baking sheet**

1. Place a rack in the center of the oven and preheat the oven to 325°F.

2. Grease the insides of the cans and lightly dust them with flour, tapping out the excess. Place the cans on a baking sheet for easier handling, and set aside.

3. Combine the buttermilk, egg yolk, and vanilla in a small bowl, and whisk to mix. Gradually pour the melted butter into the buttermilk mixture, whisking constantly.

4. Sift the flour, cocoa powder, baking soda, and salt into a medium-size mixing bowl, and then whisk to blend well. Add the sugar and whisk to combine. Add the buttermilk mixture

and whisk just until the dry ingredients are moistened.

5. Spoon the batter into the prepared cans, dividing it evenly between them. Bake the cakes until a toothpick inserted into the center of one comes out clean, 25 to 30 minutes.

6. Remove the baking sheet from the oven and transfer the cans to a wire rack to cool for 15 minutes. Then run a thin, sharp knife around the edge of each can and invert them to release the cakes. Turn the cakes upright and let them cool completely on the rack.

7. To frost the cakes, cut each cake in half horizontally. Spread a layer of Double Chocolate Sour Cream Frosting about $^1\!/_2$ inch thick on the cut side of one cake half, then stack the other half on top of it. Frost the top and sides of the cake. Repeat with the remaining cake and frosting. (The cakes can be stored in an airtight container in the refrigerator for up to 1 day. Let them stand at room temperature for 2 hours before serving.)

# Double Chocolate Sour Cream Frosting

**This frosting is** like a slather of soft fudge. I like this balance of milk and bittersweet chocolates, but you can play around with the proportions, using more bittersweet than milk or, if you prefer, all of one type. The surprising addition of sour cream provides a tangy flavor balance and makes the chocolate creamy as it sets.

**MAKES 1 CUP**

**6 ounces milk chocolate, finely chopped (about 1 cup)**

**3 ounces bittersweet or semisweet chocolate, finely chopped (about 1/2 cup)**

**1/4 cup plus 3 tablespoons sour cream, at room temperture**

**1/2 teaspoon pure vanilla extract**

**Pinch of salt**

**1.** Place both chocolates in the top of a double boiler set over simmering water, and heat, stirring occasionally, until they melt. (Or place the chocolates in a medium-size microwave-safe bowl and microwave on high power until glossy, 2 to 2 1/2 minutes, rotating the bowl after 1 1/2 minutes.)

**2.** Let the chocolate mixture cool for 5 minutes. Then add the sour cream, vanilla, and salt, and whisk to blend well. Let the frosting cool to room temperature, stirring it occasionally. When it is cool, it should be thick enough to spread. (If not, refrigerate for a few minutes to thicken.) Use immediately.

# Red Velvet Cake

*Makes 2 cakes; serves 2*

◆◆◆◆◆◆◆◆◆

**Red Velvet Cake** was my childhood favorite because it was chocolate *and* it was red like my birthstone, the ruby. It was just barely chocolate—the cake typically had only a few teaspoons of cocoa powder in it. There was nothing subtle about the color, however, because it took as much as two ounces of red food coloring to produce that shade of red. This version is a bit more subdued in color but definitely not in flavor, and it has a frosting you'll want to make again and again.

Unsalted butter, at room temperature, for greasing the cans

¼ cup plus 2 tablespoons all-purpose flour, plus more for flouring the cans

½ teaspoon red food coloring

1 recipe Chocolate Birthday Cake batter (page 17), prepared through Step 4

Boiled Cream Cheese Frosting (recipe follows)

**PANS REQUIRED:**

Two 14- or 14.5-ounce cans (see page 6)

1 baking sheet

**1.** Place a rack in the center of the oven and preheat the oven to 350°F.

**2.** Grease the insides of the cans and lightly dust them with flour, tapping out the excess. Place the cans on a baking sheet, and set aside.

**3.** Stir the red food coloring into the batter, and spoon the batter into the prepared cans, dividing it evenly between them. Place the cakes in the oven and bake until a toothpick inserted into the center of one comes out clean, 25 to 30 minutes.

**4.** Remove the baking sheet from the oven and transfer the cans to a wire rack to cool for 15 minutes. Then run a thin, sharp knife around the edge of each can and invert them to release the cakes. Set the cakes upright on the rack and let them cool completely.

**5.** To frost the cakes, cut each in half horizontally. Spread a layer of the frosting about ¼ inch thick on the cut side of one cake half, then stack the other half on top of it. Frost the top and sides. Repeat with the remaining cake and frosting. (The cakes can be stored in an airtight container in the refrigerator for up to 2 days. Let them come to room temperature before serving.)

# Boiled Cream Cheese Frosting

**When my aunt** Cora made her Red Velvet Cake, she covered it with "gravy frosting," so named because the first step in making it was to cook flour and milk, just as you would for biscuit gravy. Also called "boiled frosting," it was the most popular topping for Red Velvet Cake during the first part of the twentieth century. It is not as sweet as a buttercream and is made with granulated sugar— possibly because confectioners' sugar was so expensive in those days. Without the confectioners' sugar, cooks had to thicken the frosting, so they improvised with a cooked base. Gravy frosting was frequently made with shortening instead of butter, also most likely because of availability.

Today we see more Red Velvet Cakes with cream cheese frosting, and that is delicious too. I decided to put the two together by substituting cream cheese for some of the butter in a gravy frosting. The result is a tangy, cheesy frosting with a smooth and fluffy texture— a yummy frosting unlike any you've ever had.

**MAKES 1 CUP**

¼ **cup whole milk**

**1 tablespoon plus 1 teaspoon all-purpose flour**

**3 tablespoons unsalted butter, at room temperature**

**1½ ounces (3 tablespoons) cream cheese, at room temperature**

⅓ **cup sugar**

**Pinch of salt**

½ **teaspoon pure vanilla extract**

1. Pour the milk into a small microwave-safe bowl and add the flour, beating with a fork until it is smooth. Microwave on high power to form a thick mixture resembling a paste, about 30 seconds. Then beat the mixture with a fork until smooth. If the mixture is not thick enough, microwave for 20 seconds longer and then beat with a fork until it is smooth. Let the paste cool to room temperature, beating with a fork occasionally to prevent lumps from forming.

2. Place the butter, cream cheese, sugar, and salt in a small bowl and beat with a hand-held electric mixer until well blended, about 1 minute. Add the cooled flour mixture and vanilla, and beat the frosting until it is spreadable. Use immediately.

# Not-So-German Chocolate Cake

*Makes 2 cakes; serves 2*

◆◆◆◆◆◆◆◆

**By using the** traditional coconut and pecan filling and basically the same recipe as the Fudgy Mocha Layer Cake on page 25, you can make a layer cake reminiscent of that old classic, German chocolate cake. The cake will not be the traditional mildly sweet chocolate, but the filling will be the one you remember.

The rich chocolate buttercream adds the finishing touch.

**Unsalted butter, at room temperature, for greasing the cans**

**½ cup all-purpose flour, sifted, plus more for flouring the cans**
**¼ cup boiling water**

**1 ounce bittersweet or semisweet chocolate, chopped (3 tablespoons)**

**2 tablespoons sour cream, at room temperature**

**Yolk of 1 large egg**

**1 tablespoon vegetable oil**

**½ teaspoon pure vanilla extract**

**⅓ cup sugar**

**⅛ teaspoon baking soda**

**⅛ teaspoon salt**

3 tablespoons Rich Caramel Sauce
(page 259) or store-bought
caramel sauce

¼ cup sweetened flaked coconut,
toasted (see Notes)

3 tablespoons chopped pecans,
toasted (see Notes)

Rich Chocolate Frosting
(recipe follows)

PANS REQUIRED:

Two 14- or 14.5-ounce cans
(see page 6)

1 baking sheet

1. Place a rack in the center of the oven and preheat the oven to 350°F.

2. Grease the insides of the cans and lightly dust them with flour, tapping out the excess. Place the cans on a baking sheet for easier handling, and set aside.

3. Pour the boiling water into a small heatproof bowl, and add the chocolate. Whisk until the chocolate is melted. Let the mixture cool slightly.

4. Place the sour cream, egg yolk, oil, and vanilla in a small bowl and whisk to combine. Add the chocolate mixture and whisk to blend.

5. Place the flour, sugar, baking soda, and salt in a medium-size mixing bowl and whisk to blend well. Add the chocolate mixture and whisk just until blended and smooth.

6. Spoon the batter into the prepared cans, dividing it evenly between them. Bake the cakes until a toothpick inserted into the center of one comes out clean, 30 to 35 minutes.

7. Remove the baking sheet from the oven and transfer the cans to a wire rack to cool for 15 minutes. Then run a thin, sharp knife around the edge of each can, and invert them to release the cakes. Place the cakes upright on the rack and let them cool completely.

8. Place the caramel sauce, coconut, and pecans in a small bowl and stir to mix.

9. Cut the cakes in half horizontally. Place the bottom half of one cake, cut side up, on a serving plate and spread half of the caramel mixture over the top. Then stack the other half on top of it. Repeat with the remaining cake and caramel mixture. Frost the tops and sides of the cakes with the Rich Chocolate Frosting.

**NOTES:** To toast coconut, spread it in a shallow baking pan and place it on the middle rack of a preheated 350°F oven. Toast until golden, stirring occasionally and watching carefully to avoid burning, 10 to 12 minutes.

Transfer the coconut to a bowl and set it aside to cool.

To toast pecans, spread them in a shallow baking pan and place it on the middle rack of a preheated 350°F oven. Toast until lightly golden, 5 to 7 minutes.

# Rich Chocolate Frosting

**This scrumptious** chocolate frosting can be used whenever you're looking for something rich but simple.

**MAKES 1 CUP**

¼ cup whipping (heavy) cream

3 tablespoons unsalted butter

2 tablespoons sugar

⅛ teaspoon salt

2 ounces semisweet chocolate, finely chopped (⅓ cup)

½ teaspoon pure vanilla extract

**1.** Place the cream, butter, sugar, and salt in a heavy medium-size saucepan over medium heat and bring to a simmer, stirring, until the sugar dissolves and the butter melts. Remove from the heat and add the chocolate; whisk until it is melted and smooth. Add the vanilla and whisk to mix.

**2.** Place the frosting in a medium-size bowl and refrigerate, whisking it several times as it chills, until it is thick enough to spread, 1½ to 2 hours. Use immediately.

# Fudgy Mocha Layer Cake

*Makes 2 cakes; serves 2*

**Mocha, the name** of a Yemeni port on the Red Sea where a superior coffee was grown, entered the food world as a term indicating that something was coffee-flavored. Now it usually refers to a luscious combination of coffee and chocolate, two flavors that complement each other perfectly. This layer cake is rich and the texture is soft as a pillow.

Unsalted butter, at room temperature,
   for greasing the pans
1/2 cup all-purpose flour, sifted,
   plus more for flouring the cans
1/4 cup boiling water
3/4 teaspoon instant espresso powder
1 ounce bittersweet or semisweet
   chocolate, chopped
2 tablespoons sour cream,
   at room temperature

Yolk of 1 large egg
1 tablespoon vegetable oil
1/2 teaspoon pure vanilla extract
1/3 cup sugar
1/8 teaspoon baking soda
1/8 teaspoon salt
**Mocha Fudge Frosting**
   **(recipe follows)**

PANS REQUIRED:
**Two 14- or 14.5-inch cans
   (see page 6)
1 baking sheet**

1. Place a rack in the center of the oven and preheat the oven to 350°F.

2. Grease the insides of the cans and lightly dust them with flour, tapping out the excess. Place the cans on a baking sheet for easier handling, and set aside.

**3.** Pour the boiling water into a small heatproof bowl, and add the espresso powder and the chocolate. Whisk until the chocolate is melted and smooth. Let the mixture cool slightly.

**4.** Place the sour cream, egg yolk, oil, and vanilla in a small bowl and whisk to combine. Add the chocolate mixture and whisk to blend.

**5.** Place the flour, sugar, baking soda, and salt in a medium-size mixing bowl and whisk to blend well. Add the chocolate mixture and whisk just until blended and smooth.

**6.** Spoon the batter into the prepared cans, dividing it evenly between them. Bake the cakes until a toothpick inserted into the center of one comes out clean, 30 to 35 minutes.

**7.** Remove the baking sheet from the oven and transfer the cans to a wire rack to cool for 15 minutes. Then run a thin, sharp knife around the edge of each can, and invert them to release the cakes. Place the cakes upright on the rack and let them cool completely.

**8.** To frost the cakes, cut each in half horizontally. Spread a layer of the Mocha Fudge Frosting about ¼ inch thick on the cut side of one cake half, and then stack the other half on top of it. Frost the top and sides of the cake. Repeat with the remaining cake and frosting.

# Mocha Fudge Frosting

**Double your** pleasure with this sophisticated espresso-flavored fudge frosting. Not overly sweet, it's good on the Really Fudgy Cupcakes (page 64), too.

**MAKES 1 CUP**

¼ **cup whipping (heavy) cream**

**3 tablespoons unsalted butter**

**2 tablespoons sugar**

½ **teaspoon instant espresso powder**

⅛ **teaspoon salt**

**2 ounces semisweet chocolate, finely chopped**

**¹⁄₂ teaspoon pure vanilla extract**

1. Place the cream, butter, sugar, espresso powder, and salt in a heavy medium-size saucepan over medium heat and bring to a simmer, stirring, until the sugar dissolves and the butter melts, about 4 minutes.

Remove from the heat and add the chocolate; then whisk until it is melted and smooth. Add the vanilla and whisk to mix.

2. Place the frosting in a medium-size bowl and refrigerate, whisking it several times as it chills, until it is thick enough to spread, 1¹⁄₂ to 2 hours. Use immediately.

# Mississippi Mud Cake

*Makes 1 cake; serves 2 or 3*
◆◆◆◆◆◆◆◆◆

**Named for a** river famed for its mud, this rich chocolate cake may look dark and dense enough to be confused with something dug up along the Mississippi, but it doesn't taste like it! It's a perennial favorite in the South. Normally a sheet cake, the standard version features the flavors of coffee and bourbon in both the cake and rich glaze, and it is sometimes studded with marshmallows. The Small-Batch version contains all three, along with toasted pecans for opulent texture. Servings are dramatically reduced because the single layer cake is baked in a loaf pan.

**FOR THE CAKE:**

Unsalted butter, at room temperature, for greasing the pan

½ cup all-purpose flour, plus more for flouring the pan

½ cup sugar

⅛ teaspoon baking soda

¼ teaspoon salt

¼ cup whole milk

2 tablespoons unsweetened cocoa powder

1 teaspoon instant coffee powder

3 tablespoons unsalted butter, melted

Yolk of 1 large egg

½ teaspoon pure vanilla extract

¼ cup semisweet chocolate chips

¼ cup miniature marshmallows

¼ cup coarsely chopped pecans, toasted (see Note)

**FOR THE GLAZE:**

1½ tablespoons whipping (heavy) cream

2 teaspoons dark corn syrup

2 teaspoons bourbon

¼ cup semisweet chocolate chips

**PAN REQUIRED:**

1 standard loaf pan
(8 x 4 or 9 x 5 inches)

**1. MAKE THE CAKE:** Place a rack in the center of the oven and preheat the oven to 350°F.

**2.** Grease the loaf pan. Cut a strip of waxed or parchment paper long enough to fit down the length and up the short sides of the loaf pan, allowing extra length to extend over the edges. Now cut a strip of paper to fit the width of the loaf pan and up the long sides, allowing extra length to extend over the edges. Fit the strips into the pan, and grease and lightly flour the waxed paper. Set the pan aside.

**3.** Place the flour, sugar, baking soda, and salt in a medium-size mixing bowl and whisk to blend well.

**4.** Place the milk, cocoa powder, and coffee powder in a small bowl and whisk until smooth. Add the melted butter, egg yolk, and vanilla, and whisk to mix. Add the milk mixture to the flour mixture and whisk just until the dry ingredients are moistened. Spoon the batter into the prepared loaf pan.

**5.** Bake the cake until a toothpick inserted in the center comes out with a few moist crumbs attached to it, about 15 minutes.

**6.** Remove the pan from the oven (leave the oven on), and sprinkle the chocolate chips and the marshmallows evenly over the top. Return the cake to the oven and bake until the marshmallows and chocolate chips start to melt, 2 minutes. Remove the cake from the oven and sprinkle the pecans evenly over the top. Let the cake cool in the loaf pan on a wire rack.

**7. MAKE THE GLAZE:** Pour the cream, corn syrup, and bourbon into a small microwave-safe bowl and microwave on high power until the mixture is very hot, about 45 seconds. Remove the bowl from the microwave and add the chocolate chips. Wait a minute for the chips to soften; then stir the glaze until it is smooth. Let the glaze cool to lukewarm; then drizzle it evenly over the cooled cake in the pan. Place the pan in the refrigerator, uncovered, for at least 1 hour or as long as 4 hours. Then carefully remove the cake from the pan, using the waxed paper strips to lift it so the top of the cake is not disturbed.

**NOTE:** Toast the pecans in a 350°F oven until they are lightly browned, 5 to 7 minutes.

# Hazelnut Chocolate Torte

## *with* Frangelico Cream

*Makes 1 cake; serves 2 or 3*

◆◆◆◆◆◆◆◆◆

**This intensely flavored** dessert is a guaranteed hit for lovers of chocolate and hazelnut, a time-honored combination, especially in Italy. It's perfect for special occasions. Four delicate layers of hazelnut cake—sandwiched with chocolate-flavored whipped cream sweetened with Frangelico, an Italian hazelnut liqueur—are enrobed in a rich chocolate ganache. How can you go wrong?

**FOR THE CAKE:**

**Unsalted butter, at room temperature, for greasing the loaf pan**

**1/4 cup plus 2 tablespoons cake flour, sifted, plus more for flouring the loaf pan**

**2/3 cup hazelnuts plus 6 whole hazelnuts, toasted and husked (see Note)**

**4 tablespoons sugar**

**1/8 teaspoon salt**

**2 large eggs, at room temperature**

**1/2 teaspoon pure vanilla extract**

**2 tablespoons Frangelico**

**FOR THE FRANGELICO CREAM:**
**3 ounces bittersweet chocolate,**
**    finely chopped**
**½ cup cold whipping (heavy) cream**
**2 tablespoons Frangelico**

**Frangelico Ganache**
**    (see Step 11; recipe follows)**

**PAN REQUIRED:**
**1 standard loaf pan**
**    (8 x 4 or 9 x 5 inches)**

**1. MAKE THE CAKE:** Place a rack in the center of the oven and preheat the oven to 375°F.

**2.** Grease and lightly flour the loaf pan. Line the bottom of the pan with parchment paper, then grease and lightly flour the paper. Set the pan aside.

**3.** Set aside the 6 whole hazelnuts. Place the ⅔ cup hazelnuts and 1 tablespoon of the sugar in a food processor and process until finely ground. Place ½ cup of the ground hazelnuts in a small bowl; add the flour and salt, and whisk to blend well. Set the remaining ground nuts aside.

**4.** Warm a small bowl by letting hot tap water run into and over it. Dry the bowl thoroughly and add the remaining 3 tablespoons of sugar. Stir 2 teaspoons of hot water into the sugar. Add the eggs and beat with a hand-held electric mixer on high speed until the mixture is pale in color and thick; when you lift the beaters, a ribbon of egg mixture should drizzle back onto the remainder in the bowl, leaving a "track" that sits on the top before it sinks in.

**5.** Add the vanilla to the egg mixture. Sift one third of the flour mixture over the top. Using a whisk, gently fold the flour mixture into the egg mixture. Repeat twice more with the remaining flour mixture.

**6.** Spoon the batter into the prepared loaf pan. Bake the cake until the top is golden and a toothpick inserted in the center comes out clean, about 12 minutes.

**7.** Remove the pan from the oven and place it on a wire rack to cool for 10 minutes. Then run a thin, sharp knife around the sides and turn the cake out onto the rack. Turn the cake upright and allow it to cool completely.

**8.** Cut the cake vertically into two 4-inch halves, then slice each half horizontally into 2 even layers. You should have 4 roughly equal-sized layers. Arrange the layers, cut side up, on a work surface. Trim the sides and ends of each layer, then brush the tops with the Frangelico.

**9. MAKE THE FRANGELICO CREAM:** Place the chocolate in a small microwave-safe bowl and microwave on medium power until it is very glossy, 1 to 1½ minutes. Stir the chocolate until it is smooth; then let it cool to room temperature. The chocolate should still be soft.

**10.** Place the cream and Frangelico in a small bowl and beat with a hand-held electric mixer on high speed until firm peaks form, about 2 minutes. Beat in the chocolate.

**11.** Place the bottom half of one piece of cake, cut side up, on a serving plate and spread one third of the Frangelico Cream over it, covering the top completely. Top this with a second piece of cake and another third of the Frangelico Cream. Repeat the layers once more, then top with the remaining layer. Cover the cake with plastic wrap and refrigerate it while you prepare the ganache.

**12.** Remove the cake from the refrigerator, unwrap it, and immediately spread the ganache on the top and sides. Sprinkle the reserved ground hazelnuts over the top of the cake and press them into the ganache. Then arrange the whole hazelnuts around the top of the cake, spacing them evenly. Refrigerate the cake for 1 hour to set the ganache before cutting it

into thin slices and serving. (After the ganache has set, you can wrap the cake in plastic wrap and store it in the refrigerator for up to 1 day. Remove it from the refrigerator 1 hour before slicing and serving.)

**NOTE:** To toast hazelnuts, spread them out on a baking sheet and bake at 400°F until golden, about 8 minutes. Remove the nuts, place on a towel, and fold the towel over them. Rub the towel between your hands to remove the outer skins.

# Frangelico Ganache

## The chocolate chills as you beat it into the whipped cream, giving the chocolate cream a firm texture much like frosting. Hazelnut liqueur adds a sweet, nutty taste to the filling.

**MAKES ¾ CUP**

½ **cup whipping (heavy) cream**

2 **tablespoons Frangelico (hazelnut liqueur)**

4 **ounces bittersweet chocolate, finely chopped**

Pour the cream and Frangelico into a small microwave-safe bowl and microwave on high power until the mixture simmers, about 1 minute. Add the chocolate and stir until smooth. Pour the ganache into a pie plate and refrigerate it until it is thick enough to spread, 5 to 10 minutes; it will resemble thick pudding.

# Classic Chocolate Truffle Soufflé Cakes

*Makes 3 cakes; serves 3*

**◆◆◆◆◆◆◆◆◆**

**These cakes come** close to delivering an overdose of chocolate, but you can stand it! They are more flourless soufflés than cakes; they rise in the oven, then fall, forming a fudgy layer with a sugary, crisp crust. The hint of liqueur is divine. For a particularly intense flavor treat, serve the orange or raspberry liqueur–flavored cakes with a matching flavored whipped cream. Or use Kahlùa in the cake and serve it with the cappuccino-flavored whipped cream.

2¹/₂ tablespoons melted unsalted butter, plus more for greasing the baking rings

All-purpose flour for flouring the rings

4 ounces bittersweet chocolate or semisweet chocolate, chopped

1 tablespoon Grand Marnier (orange liqueur), Chambord (raspberry liqueur), or Kahlùa (coffee liqueur)

1 large egg, at room temperature

Yolk of 1 large egg, at room temperature

3 tablespoons sugar

Plain or flavored Sweetened Whipped Cream (page 36), for serving

**PANS REQUIRED:**

3 baking rings (about 3 x 1¹/₂-inches)

1 baking sheet

**1.** Place a rack in the center of the oven and preheat the oven to 350°F.

**2.** Cut four 5-inch squares of heavy-duty aluminum foil and four 5-inch squares of parchment paper. Place a parchment paper square on top of each aluminum foil square. Center a baking ring on top of each square; form the edges of the foil up around the sides of each ring, bringing up the parchment with the foil. Mold the foil well to the sides of the rings to create individual baking dishes with parchment-lined foil bottoms. Brush the parchment paper bottoms and the sides of the rings with melted butter and dust them lightly with flour, tapping out the excess. Place the baking rings on a baking sheet for easier handling, and set aside.

**3.** Place the chocolate and butter in a small microwave-safe bowl and microwave on high power until they melt, 1 to 1½ minutes. Stir until the chocolate mixture is smooth. Whisk in the liqueur and let the mixture cool to lukewarm.

**4.** Place the egg, egg yolk, and sugar in a small bowl and beat with a hand-held electric mixer at high speed until tripled in volume, 4 to 5 minutes. Fold one quarter of the egg mixture into the chocolate mixture to lighten it; then fold all of the chocolate mixture into the remaining egg mixture. Spoon the batter into the prepared baking rings, dividing it evenly among them.

**5.** Bake the cakes until they have pulled away from the sides of the baking rings and a toothpick inserted into the center of one comes out clean, about 20 minutes. Remove the baking sheet from the oven and transfer the cakes to a wire rack to cool, still in the baking rings, for 10 minutes. Then loosen the cakes with a sharp knife and remove the parchment paper and foil bottoms. Gently push each cake through the baking ring onto the rack, and allow to cool completely.

**6.** Serve the cakes warm or at room temperature, with sweetened whipped cream.

# SWEET CREAMS

Most people serve a chocolate truffle soufflé cake with whipped cream in order to cut the intense chocolate flavor and make the sensational dessert last a bit longer. These fresh-tasting fruit-flavored whipped creams go a step further by bringing out the liqueur taste in the cake. Choose a flavored cream to match the liqueur you choose for the cakes.

**SWEETENED WHIPPED CREAM:**
Place ½ cup of cold whipping (heavy) cream and 2 tablespoons of confectioners' sugar in a small bowl and beat with a hand-held electric mixer on high speed until firm peaks form, about 1 minute. This makes about 1 cup of sweetened whipped cream.

**VANILLA WHIPPED CREAM:** Place ½ cup of cold whipping cream, 2 tablespoons of confectioners' sugar, and ½ teaspoon vanilla paste or pure vanilla extract in a small bowl and beat with a hand-held electric mixer on high speed until firm peaks form, about 1 minute. This makes about 1 cup of vanilla whipped cream.

**RASPBERRY WHIPPED CREAM:**
Press ¼ cup of fresh or thawed frozen raspberries through a fine-mesh sieve placed over a small bowl. Scrape off the pulp that clings to the bottom of the sieve and add it to the pulp in the bowl. Discard the seeds. Place ½ cup of cold whipping cream and 2 table-spoons of confectioners' sugar in a small bowl and beat with a

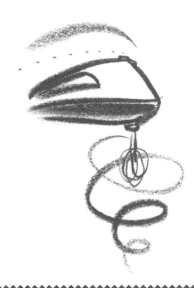

hand-held electric mixer on high speed until firm peaks form, about 1 minute. Fold the whipped cream into the raspberry puree. Use right away, or cover and store in the refrigerator for up to 2 hours. This makes about 1 cup of flavored cream.

ORANGE WHIPPED CREAM: Place $\frac{1}{2}$ cup of cold whipping cream and 1 tablespoon of Grand Marnier in a small bowl. Add 1 tablespoon of confectioners' sugar and beat with a hand-held electric mixer on high speed until firm peaks form, about 1 minute. Fold in 1 teaspoon of grated orange zest. This makes about 1 cup of flavored cream.

Strips and curls of orange zest make an attractive garnish for the cream: To make zest strips, use a citrus zester to remove thin strips of zest, and sprinkle them on the cream. To make citrus curls, use a cutting tool called a canelle knife, which has sharp grooves on the end, to remove long continu-ous strips of zest from around the orange. Curl them around a pencil and refrigerate for 10 minutes to set the curl. Remove the curls from the pencil and garnish the flavored cream.

CAPPUCCINO CREAM: In a small bowl, place 2 tablespoons of con-fectioners' sugar, 1 teaspoon of unsweetened cocoa powder, and $\frac{1}{4}$ teaspoon of instant espresso powder. Gradually whisk in $\frac{1}{2}$ cup cold whipping cream. Beat with a hand-held electric mixer on high speed until firm peaks form, about 1 minute. This makes about 1 cup of flavored cream.

Garnish the cakes with con-fectioners' sugar or cocoa: Arrange 1-inch-wide strips of waxed paper diagonally on each cake, spacing them 1 inch apart. Sift confection-ers' sugar or unsweetened cocoa powder (or a mixture of both) over the cakes; then carefully lift the strips up and off the cakes to leave a striped pattern.

# White Chocolate Layer Cake

*Makes 2 cakes; serves 2*

◆◆◆◆◆◆◆◆◆

**White chocolate adds** a subtle richness and body to the tender crumb of this cake. The white chocolate frosting enhances the cake's understated flavor, but the cake also goes well with any of the chocolate frostings and cream cheese frostings in this chapter. Use a premium-quality white chocolate—it'll melt more smoothly.

1 tablespoon unsalted butter, cut into pieces, at room temperature, plus more for greasing the cans

¹/₂ cup all-purpose flour, sifted, plus more for flouring the cans

1 ounce good-quality white chocolate, finely chopped

¹/₄ cup boiling water

2 tablespoons sour cream, at room temperature

Yolk of 1 large egg

¹/₂ teaspoon pure vanilla extract

¹/₃ cup sugar

¹/₈ teaspoon baking soda

¹/₈ teaspoon salt

White Chocolate Cream Frosting (recipe follows)

**PANS REQUIRED:**
**Two 14- or 14.5-ounce cans**
  **(see page 6)**
**1 baking sheet**

**1.** Place a rack in the center of the oven and preheat the oven to 350°F.

**2.** Grease the insides of the cans and lightly dust them with flour, tapping out the excess. Place the cans on a baking sheet for easier handling, and set aside.

**3.** Place the white chocolate in a small microwave-safe bowl and microwave on medium power until melted, about 1 minute. Let the white chocolate cool to lukewarm.

**4.** Place the butter in a small microwave-safe bowl and microwave on medium power until it melts, about 30 seconds. Let the boiling water cool slightly. Add it to bowl and whisk to blend. Add the sour cream, egg yolk, and vanilla, and whisk to combine.

**5.** Place the flour, sugar, baking soda, and salt in a medium-size mixing bowl

and whisk to blend well. Add the sour cream mixture and the melted white chocolate, and whisk until blended and smooth.

**6.** Spoon the batter into the prepared cans, dividing it evenly between them. Bake the cakes until a toothpick inserted into the center of one comes out clean, about 30 minutes.

**7.** Remove the baking sheet from the oven and transfer the cans to a wire rack to cool for 15 minutes. Then run a thin, sharp knife around the edge of each can and invert them to release the cakes. Place the cakes upright on the rack and let them cool completely.

**8.** To frost the cakes, cut each in half horizontally. Spread a layer of the White Chocolate Cream Frosting about ¼ inch thick on the cut side of one cake half, then stack the other half on top of it. Frost the top and sides of the cake. Repeat with the remaining cake and frosting. (The cakes can be stored in an airtight container in the refrigerator for up to 2 days before serving.)

# White Chocolate Cream Frosting

**White chocolate** both sweetens and adds body to this whipped cream frosting. In addition to the White Chocolate Layer Cake, it is also quite delicious on the Chocolate Birthday Cake (page 16) and the Really Fudgy Cupcakes (page 64).

**MAKES 1 CUP**

⅔ cup whipping (heavy) cream
2 ounces good-quality white
    chocolate, finely chopped
½ teaspoon pure vanilla extract

1. Place the cream in a 2-cup microwave-safe bowl and microwave on high power until just boiling, about 1½ minutes. Add the white chocolate and whisk until it melts and the mixture is smooth. Let cool; then cover and refrigerate until well chilled, 3 to 4 hours. (The frosting can be prepared up to this point 1 day ahead.)

2. Add the vanilla to the cream mixture and beat with a hand-held mixer on high speed until firm peaks form, about 2 minutes. Use immediately.

# Fresh Strawberry Cake

*Makes 2 cakes; serves 2*

◆◆◆◆◆◆◆◆◆

**This is the cake** to make when strawberry season rolls around. Strawberries and white chocolate make a perfect pair, and this cake shows them off splendidly. The cake layers soak up the sweet red berry juices, while the smooth whipped frosting gives the ensemble the taste of a strawberry shortcake.

**2 tablespoons strawberry jam**

**1/2 cup sliced fresh strawberries**

**1 recipe White Chocolate Layer Cake (page 38), baked and cooled**

**1 recipe White Chocolate Cream Frosting (page 40)**

**1.** Place the jam in a small microwave-safe bowl, and microwave on high power until it melts, about 20 seconds. Press it through a fine-mesh sieve into another bowl. Add the strawberries to the bowl. Toss gently to coat the berries with the jam, then chill for 1 hour in the refrigerator.

**2.** Cut the cakes horizontally into 3 layers each. Place the bottom cake layers on serving plates, cut side up, and spread a layer of frosting on them. Arrange about 2 tablespoons of the strawberry mixture on each frosted cake layer. Top with the middle layers, and spread a layer of frosting on them. Arrange the remaining strawberries on the frosting, dividing them evenly between the cakes, then top with another layer of frosting. Stack the remaining layers on top, cut side down, and frost the tops and sides of the cakes. Refrigerate the cakes, covered, for 1 hour before serving.

# Old-Fashioned Yellow Cake

*Makes 2 cakes; serves 2*

◆◆◆◆◆◆◆◆◆

**Just a plain** yellow cake? Maybe, but it has a fine, moist crumb and you can dress it up with your favorite frosting. I especially like it layered with a combination of Raspberry Whipped Cream and fresh raspberries, then garnished with fresh raspberries and pecans.

Unsalted butter, at room temperature, for greasing the cans

¹/₂ cup all-purpose flour, sifted, plus more for flouring the cans

3 tablespoons buttermilk

¹/₈ teaspoon baking soda

Yolk of 1 large egg

¹/₂ teaspoon pure vanilla extract

3 tablespoons unsalted butter, melted and cooled

¹/₃ cup sugar

¹/₄ teaspoon salt

Double Chocolate Sour Cream Frosting (page 18), Maple Buttercream (page 61), or Raspberry Whipped Cream (page 36)

PANS REQUIRED:

Two 14- or 14.5-ounce cans (see page 6)

1 baking sheet

1. Place a rack in the center of the oven and preheat the oven to 350°F.

**2.** Grease the insides of the cans and lightly dust them with flour, tapping out the excess. Place the cans on a baking sheet for easier handling, and set aside.

**3.** Place the buttermilk and baking soda in a small bowl, and whisk until the baking soda is dissolved. Add the egg yolk, vanilla, and melted butter, and whisk to combine.

**4.** Place the flour, sugar, and salt in a medium-size mixing bowl and whisk to blend well. Add the buttermilk mixture and whisk just until blended and smooth.

**5.** Spoon the batter into the prepared cans, dividing it evenly between them. Bake the cakes until a toothpick inserted into the center of one comes out clean, about 25 minutes.

**6.** Remove the baking sheet from the oven and transfer the cans to a wire rack to cool for 15 minutes. Then run a thin, sharp knife around the edge of each can, and invert them to release the cakes. Place the cakes upright on the rack and let them cool completely. (The unfrosted cakes can be stored in an airtight container in the refrigerator for up to 2 days; or they can be frozen, well wrapped, for up to 1 month. Let them return to room temperature before frosting.)

**7.** To frost the cakes, cut each in half horizontally. Spread a layer of the frosting about ¼ inch thick on the cut side of one cake half, then stack the other half on top of it. Frost the top and sides of the cake. Repeat with the remaining cake and frosting.

# Apricot Almond Tortes

*Makes 2 cakes; serves 2*

◆◆◆◆◆◆◆◆◆

**Here is just one** example of how you can turn plain yellow cake into a fancy dessert. Each layer is brushed with amaretto and gilded with apricot jam and a layer of marzipan before it is stacked and all lightly blanketed with whipped cream. For a beautiful presentation, dust the dessert plates with confectioners' sugar before you place the cakes on them; then scatter toasted sliced almonds around the cakes.

1 recipe Old-Fashioned Yellow Cake
   (page 42), baked and cooled
2 tablespoons amaretto (almond
   liqueur)
2 tablespoons marzipan or almond
   paste

2 tablespoons apricot jam (see Note)
⅓ cup cold whipping (heavy) cream
1 tablespoon confectioners' sugar

**1.** Cut each cake in half horizontally. Brush 1 teaspoon of the amaretto on the cut sides of each cake.

**2.** Divide the marzipan in half, and form each piece into a ball. Roll out each ball between pieces of waxed paper or plastic wrap to form a circle the same diameter as the cakes.

**3.** Press the jam through a sieve set over a small bowl, pressing down hard on the solids to extract the pulp. Discard the solids. Stir the remaining amaretto into the strained jam. Brush both cut sides of each cake with the jam mixture, dividing it evenly among them.

**4.** Place the bottom halves of the cakes on serving plates, cut side up. Top each with a circle of marzipan, and then stack the other halves on top, cut side down.

**5.** Place the cream and confectioners' sugar in a small bowl and beat with a hand-held electric mixer on high speed until firm peaks form, 1 to 1½ minutes. Frost the tops and sides of the cakes with the whipped cream. Refrigerate the cakes for 1 hour, or up to 6 hours, before serving.

NOTE: You can use raspberry jam instead of the apricot preserves, if you prefer.

# Lemon Layer Cake

*Makes 2 cakes; serves 2*

◆◆◆◆◆◆◆◆◆

**Lemon curd** and whipped cream make this a delicate layer cake that is fit for your finest tea service. If you like, stir a teaspoon of grated lemon zest into the cake batter. A small vase of lilacs, pansies, or primroses from the garden would make a lovely table decoration.

**1 recipe Old-Fashioned Yellow Cake (page 42), baked and cooled**
**3 tablespoons store-bought lemon curd**
**½ cup cold whipping (heavy) cream**
**1 tablespoon confectioners' sugar**

**1.** Cut each cake in half horizontally. Place the bottom halves of the cakes on serving plates, cut side up. Spread 1 tablespoon of the lemon curd on each of these halves, and then stack the other halves on top, cut side down.

**2.** Place the cream and confectioners' sugar in a small mixing bowl and beat with a hand-held electric mixer on high speed until firm peaks form, 1½ to 2 minutes. Add the remaining 1 tablespoon of lemon curd and beat to mix. Frost the tops and sides of the cakes with the lemon cream. (The frosted cakes can be refrigerated, loosely covered, for up to 6 hours. Let them return to room temperature before serving.)

# Coconut Layer Cake

*Makes 2 cakes; serves 2*
◆◆◆◆◆◆◆◆◆

**This one's** for my mom, who adores anything with coconut in it—especially cake. The cake contains coconut in two different forms—creamed and in flakes— and the frosting also has an intense coconut flavor. The coconut is so prominent that you'll feel like you're sitting near a palm tree in a tropical paradise.

3 tablespoons unsalted butter, at room temperature, plus more for greasing the cans

½ cup plus 2 tablespoons all-purpose flour, sifted, plus more for flouring the cans

1 medium egg

3 tablespoons well-stirred canned sweetened cream of coconut (such as Coco López); see Note

½ teaspoon pure vanilla extract

¼ cup plus 3 tablespoons sugar

⅛ teaspoon baking powder

1/8 teaspoon salt

1/2 cup sweetened flaked coconut

**Coconut Cream Frosting**
(recipe follows)

PANS REQUIRED:

**Two 14- or 14.5-ounce cans**
(see page 6)

**1 baking sheet**

1. Place a rack in the center of the oven and preheat the oven to 350°F.

2. Grease the insides of the cans and lightly dust them with flour, tapping out the excess. Place the cans on a baking sheet for easier handling, and set aside.

3. Place the egg, cream of coconut, and vanilla in a small bowl. Add 1 tablespoon of water and whisk to mix.

4. Place the flour, sugar, baking powder, and salt in a medium-size mixing bowl and whisk to blend well. Add the butter and the egg mixture. Beat with a hand-held mixer on low speed until the dry ingredients are moistened. Increase the speed to medium and beat until the mixture is lightened and increased in volume, about 1 minute.

5. Spoon the batter into the prepared cans, dividing it evenly between them. Bake the cakes until a toothpick inserted into the center of one comes out clean, about 30 minutes.

6. Remove the baking sheet from the oven and transfer the cans to a wire rack to cool for 15 minutes. (Leave the oven on.) Then run a thin, sharp knife around the edge of each can, and invert them to release the cakes. Place the cakes upright on the rack and let them cool completely.

7. While the cakes are cooling, spread the coconut on a rimmed baking sheet and bake, stirring once, until it is lightly toasted, 10 to 12 minutes.

**8.** To frost the cakes, cut each cake in half horizontally. Spread a layer of the Coconut Cream Frosting about ½ inch thick on the cut side of one cake half, then stack the other half on top of it. Frost the top and sides of the cake. Repeat with the remaining cake and frosting. Sprinkle the toasted coconut all over the frosting, pressing it into the frosting. (The cakes can be made 1 day ahead and refrigerated, covered. Let them return to room temperature before serving.)

**NOTE:** Cream of coconut is the secret flavor ingredient here. After you measure out the 3 tablespoons, pour the rest into a jar, cover it, and store it in the refrigerator for up to a month. Use it to flavor sweet and savory rice dishes and broth for Thai dishes. Substitute a tablespoon or two for whipping cream when making chocolate ganache (see page 356), or substitute some for the cream when making fudge. A little bit stirred into your morning latte is delicious—you only need a teaspoon.

# Coconut Cream Frosting

**A whipped cream** frosting is a nice finish to the coconut cake. The cake is very moist and a bit denser than most of the others here, and the light, fluffy, sweetly coconutty frosting complements it perfectly.

**MAKES ABOUT 1 CUP**

½ **cup cold whipping (heavy) cream**
1 **tablespoon confectioners' sugar**

1 **tablespoon well-stirred canned sweetened cream of coconut (such as Coco López)**
½ **teaspoon pure vanilla extract**

Place the cream, confectioners' sugar, cream of coconut, and vanilla in a small mixing bowl and beat with a hand-held electric mixer until firm peaks form, 1 to 1½ minutes. Use immediately or cover and refrigerate for up to 1 hour.

# Baby Carrot Cakes

*Makes 2 cakes; serves 2*

◆◆◆◆◆◆◆◆◆

**These miniature** carrot cakes are full of everything that makes carrot cake wonderful: raisins, coconut, nuts, and pineapple. If this were a recipe for a large layer cake, you'd have trouble cutting a clean slice because of the abundance of flavorful but chunky ingredients. Those ingredients also make this cake extremely moist. A traditional Cream Cheese Frosting adds a sweet but tangy finishing touch.

Unsalted butter, at room
   temperature, for greasing
   the cans

¾ cup plus 2 tablespoons sifted
   all-purpose flour, plus more
   for flouring the cans

¼ cup plus 2 tablespoons buttermilk

¼ cup vegetable oil

Yolk of 1 large egg

½ teaspoon pure vanilla extract

¼ cup sugar

½ teaspoon baking soda

¼ teaspoon salt

½ teaspoon ground cinnamon

½ cup grated carrots

2 tablespoons raisins

2 tablespoons chopped pecans or
   walnuts, plus more for garnish

2 tablespoons sweetened flaked
   coconut

2 tablespoons finely chopped fresh
   or canned pineapple, well drained
   (optional)

**Cream Cheese Frosting
   (recipe follows)**

PANS REQUIRED:

Two 14- or 14.5-ounce cans
   (see page 6)

1 baking sheet

1. Place a rack in the center of the oven and preheat the oven to 350°F.

2. Grease the insides of the cans and lightly dust them with flour, tapping out the excess. Place the cans on a baking sheet for easier handling, and set aside.

3. Place the buttermilk, oil, egg yolk, and vanilla in a small bowl and stir to mix.

4. Place the flour, sugar, baking soda, salt, and cinnamon in a medium-size mixing bowl and whisk to blend well. Add the buttermilk mixture and whisk just until the dry ingredients are moistened. Fold in the carrots, raisins, nuts, coconut, and pineapple if using.

5. Spoon the batter into the prepared cans, dividing it evenly between them. Bake the cakes until a toothpick inserted in the center of one comes out clean, 37 to 39 minutes.

6. Remove the baking sheet from the oven and transfer the cans to a wire rack to cool for 10 minutes. Then run a thin, sharp knife around the edge of each can, and invert the cans to

release the cakes. Turn the cakes upright and let them cool on the rack. (The cakes can be wrapped individually in plastic wrap and stored in the refrigerator for up to 3 days.)

7. To frost the cakes, cut each in half horizontally. Spread a layer of the Cream Cheese Frosting about ¼ inch thick on the cut side of one cake half, then stack the other half on top of it. Frost the top and sides of the cake. Repeat with the remaining cake and frosting. Garnish with additional nuts. (The frosted cakes can be stored, loosely but well covered with plastic wrap, in the refrigerator for up to 2 days.)

# Cream Cheese Frosting

**The luscious,** slightly tangy taste of Cream Cheese Frosting makes it the perfect complement to the sweet ingredients in carrot cake.

**MAKES 1 CUP**

**4 ounces cream cheese, cubed, at room temperature**

**2 tablespoons unsalted butter, at room temperature**

**1½ cups confectioners' sugar**

**½ teaspoon pure vanilla extract**

Place the cream cheese and butter in a medium-size bowl, and cream them with a fork or a hand-held electric mixer on medium speed until smooth, about 45 seconds. Sift the confectioners' sugar over the cream cheese mixture; then beat, using a hand-held electric mixer on medium speed, until the frosting is creamy. Stir in the vanilla. Use immediately, or cover and refrigerate. Let stand at room temperature for 1 hour before serving.

# Orange Spice Layer Cake

*Makes 2 cakes; serves 2*

◆◆◆◆◆◆◆◆◆

**When you grow** up climbing orange trees in your grandmother's front yard, as I did, you gain an insatiable thirst for all things orange. Orange zest perfumes this cake and adds a lovely balance to the spice mixture. Orange Cream Cheese Frosting further enhances the sweet citrus flavor.

4 tablespoons (1/2 stick) unsalted butter, at room temperature, plus more for greasing the cans

1/2 cup all-purpose flour, sifted, plus more for flouring the cans

1/4 cup buttermilk

Yolk of 1 large egg

2 teaspoons grated orange zest

1/2 cup sugar

1/8 teaspoon baking soda

1/4 teaspoon salt

1/4 teaspoon ground cinnamon

1/4 teaspoon ground nutmeg

1/8 teaspoon ground cardamom

1/8 teaspoon ground ginger

Orange Cream Cheese Frosting (recipe follows)

PANS REQUIRED:

Two 14- or 14.5-ounce cans (see page 6)

1 baking sheet

1. Place a rack in the center of the oven and preheat the oven to 325°F.

2. Lightly grease the insides of the cans and dust them with flour, tapping out the excess. Place the cans on a baking sheet for easier handling, and set aside.

3. Combine the buttermilk, egg yolk, and orange zest in a small bowl and whisk to mix.

4. Place the flour, sugar, baking soda, salt, cinnamon, nutmeg, cardamom, and ginger in a medium-size mixing bowl and whisk to blend well. Add the butter and half of the buttermilk mixture. Beat with a hand-held electric mixer on low speed until the dry ingredients are moistened. Increase the speed to medium and beat for 45 seconds. Scrape down the sides of the bowl. Pour in the remaining buttermilk mixture; then beat on medium speed for 20 seconds. Scrape down the sides of the bowl.

5. Spoon the batter into the prepared cans, dividing it evenly between them. Bake the cakes until a toothpick inserted into the center of one comes out clean, 30 to 35 minutes.

6. Remove the baking sheet from the oven and transfer the cans to a wire rack to cool for 15 minutes. Then run

a thin, sharp knife around the edge of each can and invert them to release the cakes. Turn the cakes upright and let them cool completely on the rack.

**7.** To frost the cakes, cut each one in half horizontally. Spread a layer of the Orange Cream Cheese Frosting about ¼ inch thick on the cut side of one cake half and then stack the other half on top of it. Frost the top and sides of the cake. Repeat with the remaining cake and frosting. (The cakes can be made 1 day ahead and refrigerated, covered. Let them return to room temperature before serving.)

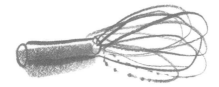

# Orange Cream Cheese Frosting

**Orange juice** concentrate gives a powerful burst of tangy, sweet citrus flavor to this frosting. Try it on Really Fudgy Cupcakes (page 64) for a chocolate-orange flavor sensation.

**MAKES 1 CUP**

**4 ounces cold cream cheese**

**2 tablespoons unsalted butter, at room temperature**

**¾ cup confectioners' sugar**

**1 teaspoon grated orange zest**

**½ teaspoon pure vanilla extract**

**1 tablespoon thawed frozen orange juice concentrate**

Place the cream cheese and butter in a medium-size mixing bowl and beat with a hand-held electric mixer on medium speed until blended, 20 seconds. Add the sugar, orange zest, and vanilla, and beat to mix. Then add the orange juice concentrate and beat until the frosting is fluffy, 1 minute. Use right away, or cover and let stand for up to 1 hour before using.

# BABY CAKE DECORATIONS

Individual cakes are even more special when you take the time to decorate them. If you're decorating cakes for children, most grocery stores sell colored sprinkles and sugars. For adults, here are some more sophisticated garnishes. When you are arranging garnishes on top of the cakes, remember the food styling trick of always using an odd number, such as one, three, or five. And matching the flavor of the garnish to that of the cake always makes for a winning combination.

**ANIMAL CRACKERS:** For children, parade animal crackers around the top of a cake, connecting them nose to tail. It will be a big hit.

**SHAVED CHOCOLATE CURLS:** This lovely garnish is easier to make when the chocolate is softened (you should be able to smudge the top with a fingertip). Put a thick bar of high-quality bittersweet or semisweet chocolate on a plate. If the temperature is above 70°F, loosely cover it and set it outside for 5 or 10 minutes, until the top is slightly softened and can be smudged, but watch it carefully. Or heat the oven to 200°F, then open the oven door and turn off the heat. Lay an oven mitt on the rack and top with the plate of chocolate. Let it stay in the oven until the top is slightly softened, about 5 minutes.

To make the curls, place a piece of waxed paper over a work surface. Drag a sharp swivel-bladed vegetable peeler across the surface of the chocolate, creating long chocolate curls. Let the curls harden a few minutes on the waxed paper, then use toothpicks to lift them onto the cake.

If you can't find a thick bar of chocolate, chop a 3- or 4-ounce bar into pieces (don't use chips) and microwave at medium power for 1½ to 2 minutes, then stir until smooth. Line the inside of a custard cup or ramekin with aluminum foil and pour in the chocolate. Let it harden (do not refrigerate); this will take an hour or two. You'll end up with a chunk of chocolate about 2 inches thick, which you can use over and over again. To use it, lift the foil and chocolate out of the custard cup and peel back the foil. Soften the top of the chocolate if necessary, then use a vegetable peeler to make the curls. Wrap any extra in the foil and store in a cool place.

**EDIBLE FLOWERS,** such as impatiens, lavender, lilac, Johnny-jump-ups, nasturtiums, pansies, primroses, and violets are a beautiful addition to any cake. Just be sure to use flowers that have been grown especially for eating (without pesticides).

**MARZIPAN FRUITS AND VEGE-TABLES:** Cake decorating shops, specialty food stores, and some bakeries sell marzipan decorations, which come in an amazing variety of forms—everything from mushrooms to mice. Tiny carrots are perfect for carrot cakes, or you can strike an autumn theme with acorns and colored leaves.

**NUTS AND SMALL FRUITS:** Whole blanched almonds, pecan halves, and small fruits such as raspberries or blueberries all make tasty decorations. So do sliced apricots. Just be sure the fruit is patted dry before you arrange it on the frosting.

**FINELY CHOPPED NUTS, TOASTED COCONUT, AND AMARETTI OR BISCOTTI COOKIE CRUMBS:** It's not hard to sprinkle nuts, coconut, or crumbs on the tops of cakes, but it can be tricky to pat them around the sides of small cakes. To make it easier, use a spatula to lift the frosted cake onto a large piece of waxed paper. Sprinkle the garnish liberally around the cake on the paper. Then lift the paper up, patting the garnish onto the sides of the cake, making sure to coat it all around.

# Jam Cakes

## *with* Molasses Caramel Frosting

*Makes 2 cakes; serves 2*

◆◆◆◆◆◆◆◆

**Blackberries are** abundant in the South. They grow in the wild and are cultivated on farms that stretch from the Smoky Mountains to the Deep South. With these juicy nuggets popping up all over the place, it didn't take long for bakers to start experimenting with the tart berries, and thus Southern jam cakes were born. Because the cakes keep well, they became a popular holiday gift. Blackberry jam makes them moist and adds a refreshing fruit flavor.

2 tablespoons unsalted butter, at room temperature, plus more for greasing the cans

½ cup all-purpose flour, sifted, plus more for flouring the cans

3 tablespoons seedless blackberry jam

3 tablespoons sour cream

Yolk of 1 large egg

½ teaspoon pure vanilla extract

⅓ cup packed light brown sugar

⅛ teaspoon baking soda

⅛ teaspoon salt

½ teaspoon apple pie spice (see Note)

3 tablespoons finely chopped walnuts (optional)

Molasses Caramel Frosting (recipe follows)

**PANS REQUIRED:**

Two 14- or 14.5-ounce cans (see page 6)

1 baking sheet

1. Place a rack in the center of the oven and preheat the oven to 350°F.

2. Lightly grease the insides of the cans and dust them with flour, tapping out the excess. Place the cans on a baking sheet for easier handling, and set aside.

3. Combine the blackberry jam, sour cream, egg yolk, and vanilla in a small bowl and whisk to mix.

4. Place the flour, brown sugar, baking soda, salt, and apple pie spice in a medium-size mixing bowl and whisk to blend well. Add the butter and the jam mixture. Beat with a hand-held electric mixer on low speed until the dry ingredients are moistened. Increase the speed to medium and beat until the batter is lightened and increased in volume, 1 minute. Stir in the walnuts, if using.

5. Spoon the batter into the prepared cans, dividing it evenly between them.

Bake the cakes until a toothpick inserted into the center of one comes out clean, about 30 minutes.

6. Remove the baking sheet from the oven and transfer the cans to a wire rack to cool for 15 minutes. Then run a thin, sharp knife around the edge of each can and invert them to release the cakes. Turn the cakes upright and let them cool completely on the rack.

7. To frost the cakes, cut each cake in half horizontally. Spread a layer of the Molasses Caramel Frosting about ¼ inch thick on the cut side of one cake half, then stack the other half on top of it. Frost the top and sides of the cake. Repeat with the remaining cake and frosting.

NOTE: If you don't have apple pie spice on hand, you can make your own: Mix together ¼ teaspoon of ground cinnamon, ⅛ teaspoon of ground nutmeg, a dash of ground allspice, and a tiny pinch of ground cardamom.

# Molasses Caramel Frosting

**Molasses is just** about as Southern a sweetener as you can find, and a mere touch of it turns this simple butterscotch-tasting frosting into a dark, rich butter-cream that makes the jam cake taste sublime.

**MAKES 1 CUP**

¼ cup plus 2 tablespoons packed dark brown sugar

3 tablespoons unsalted butter, cut into pieces

2 tablespoons whipping (heavy) cream

2 teaspoons light molasses

Pinch of salt

1¼ cups confectioners' sugar

½ teaspoon pure vanilla extract

**1.** Place the brown sugar, butter, cream, molasses, and salt in a small saucepan, and stir to combine. Cook over medium-low heat, stirring constantly, until the butter melts, the brown sugar dissolves, and the mixture is smooth. Remove the saucepan from the heat and transfer the mixture to a medium-size bowl. Let it cool to room temperature.

**2.** Sift half of the confectioners' sugar (½ cup plus 2 tablespoons) onto the cooled molasses mixture, and beat with a hand-held electric mixer at medium speed until smooth. Repeat with the remaining confectioners' sugar. Beat in the vanilla. Use right away.

# Moist Apple Cake
## *with* Maple Buttercream

*Makes 2 cakes; serves 2*

◆◆◆◆◆◆◆◆◆

I love the effect that black walnuts, a nut native to North America, have on this old-fashioned spiced apple cake. I think their strongly nutty and smoky flavor complements the sweet flavors of cinnamon and nutmeg, but they're not to everyone's taste. If you prefer, use regular walnuts or even pecans. Maple Buttercream frosting adds another indigenous North American flavor note to the cake.

Unsalted butter, at room temperature, for greasing the cans

1/2 cup all-purpose flour, sifted, plus more for flouring the cans

3 tablespoons vegetable oil

2 tablespoons buttermilk

Yolk of 1 large egg

1/2 teaspoon pure vanilla extract

1/4 cup plus 3 tablespoons sugar

1/4 teaspoon baking soda

1/8 teaspoon salt

1/2 teaspoon ground cinnamon

1/4 teaspoon ground nutmeg

3/4 cup coarsely grated peeled tart green apple (about 1 medium-size apple)

3 tablespoons finely chopped black walnuts, plus 2 tablespoons for garnish

Maple Buttercream (recipe follows)

PANS REQUIRED:

Two 14- or 14.5-ounce cans (see page 6)

1 baking sheet

1. Place a rack in the center of the oven and preheat the oven to 350°F.

2. Grease the insides of the cans and lightly dust them with flour, tapping out the excess. Place the cans on a baking sheet for easier handling, and set aside.

3. Place the oil, buttermilk, egg yolk, and vanilla in a medium-size mixing bowl, and whisk to mix.

4. Place the flour, sugar, baking soda, salt, cinnamon, and nutmeg in a medium-size mixing bowl and whisk to blend well. Add the buttermilk mixture and whisk just until the dry ingredients are moistened. Stir in the apples and the 3 tablespoons of black walnuts. (The batter will be thick.)

5. Spoon the batter into the prepared cans, dividing it evenly between them.

Smooth the tops with the back of a teaspoon. Bake the cakes until a toothpick inserted into the center of one comes out clean, 30 to 35 minutes.

6. Remove the baking sheet from the oven and transfer the cans to a wire rack to cool for 5 minutes. Then run a thin, sharp knife around the edge of each can and invert them to release the cakes. Turn the cakes upright on the wire rack and allow to cool completely.

7. To frost the cakes, cut each cake in half horizontally. Spread a layer of the Maple Buttercream about ¼ inch thick on the cut side of one cake half, then stack the other half on top of it. Frost the top and sides of the cake. Repeat with the remaining cake and frosting. Garnish the cakes with the remaining 2 tablespoons of black walnuts.

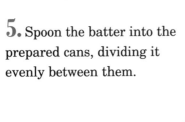

# Maple Buttercream

**Maple syrup, dark** brown sugar, and espresso powder give an earthy dimension to this buttercream frosting. Its rich flavor complements the spices and black walnuts in the apple cake. This frosting is wonderful on carrot cake, too.

**MAKES ABOUT 1 CUP**

1 tablespoon pure maple syrup

2 teaspoons packed dark brown
   sugar

1/8 teaspoon instant espresso powder

5 tablespoons plus 1 teaspoon
   unsalted butter, at room
   temperature

1 cup confectioners' sugar

1. Place the maple syrup, brown sugar, and espresso powder in a small bowl and stir until the espresso powder dissolves and the mixture is smooth.

2. Place the butter in a medium-size bowl and beat with a hand-held electric mixer at high speed until it is fluffy, about 30 seconds. Sift the confectioners' sugar into the bowl and beat until the mixture is smooth, about 1 minute. Scrape down the sides of the bowl and add the maple syrup mixture. Beat the frosting at high speed until it is fluffy, about 1 minute, scraping down the sides of the bowl as often as you need to.

3. Spread the frosting on the cakes. (You can store the frosting in an airtight container in the refrigerator for up to 1 day. Let it stand at room temperature for 2 hours before spreading it on the cakes.)

# Just Plain Good Cupcakes

*Makes 4 cupcakes; serves 2 to 4*

◆◆◆◆◆◆◆◆◆

**With these** simple cupcakes, you just can't go wrong. They are personal favorites—not just any old yellow cake. Buttermilk in the batter makes them taste rich, slightly tangy, and buttery, with a dense but tender crumb. They are delicious with the frostings suggested here, or you can top them with the Orange Cream Cheese Frosting on page 53. During the summer, when peaches, plums, and nectarines are at their peak, I slice the fruit over a serving dish to collect the juices, then put a plain cupcake in the middle of the fruit to soak up the delicious flavor. Add a bit of whipped cream and you have a heavenly concoction.

**2 tablespoons unsalted butter,** at room temperature, plus more for greasing the muffin cups

**1/2 cup all-purpose flour, sifted,** plus more for flouring the muffin cups

**1/4 cup buttermilk**

**1/8 teaspoon baking soda**

**Yolk of 1 large egg,** at room temperature

**1/2 teaspoon pure vanilla extract**

**1/4 cup plus 2 tablespoons sugar**

**1/8 teaspoon salt**

**Quick Fudge Frosting (page 66) or Peanut Butter Frosting (page 67),** optional

**PAN REQUIRED:**

**1 standard muffin pan** (1/2-cup capacity)

**1.** Place a rack in the center of the oven and preheat the oven to 350°F.

Grease and lightly flour 4 of the muffin cups, or fit paper liners into the cups; set the muffin pan aside.

2. Combine the buttermilk and baking soda in a small bowl, and stir to mix. Gently whisk in the egg yolk and vanilla.

3. Place the flour, sugar, and salt in a medium-size mixing bowl and whisk to blend well. Add the butter and half of the buttermilk mixture. Beat with a hand-held mixer on low speed until the dry ingredients are moistened. Increase the speed to medium and beat until the mixture is lightened and has slightly increased in volume, about 45 seconds. Scrape down the sides of the bowl. Pour in the remaining buttermilk mixture and beat on medium speed until well blended, 20 seconds. Scrape down the sides of the bowl.

4. Spoon the batter into the prepared muffin cups, dividing it evenly among them. Fill the empty muffin cups half-way with water to prevent them from scorching. Bake the cupcakes until a toothpick inserted in the center of one comes out clean, 20 to 23 minutes. The tops will be just beginning to brown.

5. Remove the muffin pan from the oven and place it on a wire rack to cool for 10 minutes. Then remove the cupcakes from the pan and transfer them to a wire rack to cool completely. (If you did not use paper liners, care-fully pour the water out of the extra muffin cups. Place a large plate over the muffin pan and, using potholders to hold the plate securely, invert the cupcakes onto the plate. Then transfer them to the wire rack.)

6. Frost the cupcakes with Quick Fudge Frosting or Peanut Butter Frosting, if desired. (You can store the frosted cupcakes in an airtight container in the refrigerator for up to 2 days.)

# Really Fudgy Cupcakes

*Makes 4 cupcakes; serves 2 to 4*

◆◆◆◆◆◆◆◆◆

**When you crave** a chocolate cupcake, this is the one. With deep chocolate flavor and a moist texture, Really Fudgy Cupcakes are especially good when you top them with either Fudge Frosting or Peanut Butter Frosting. They make great lunchbox treats. Or for an "I Love You" surprise, use store-bought sprinkles or icing to draw a heart or write a message to that special person.

4 tablespoons (½ stick) unsalted butter, at room temperature, plus more for greasing the muffin cups

½ cup all-purpose flour, sifted, plus more for flouring the muffin cups

½ ounce bittersweet or semisweet chocolate, chopped (about 2 tablespoons)

1 tablespoon buttermilk

¼ teaspoon baking soda

Yolks of 2 medium eggs, at room temperature

½ teaspoon pure vanilla extract

¼ cup plus 2 tablespoons sugar

2 tablespoons unsweetened cocoa powder

¼ teaspoon salt

Quick Fudge Frosting or Peanut Butter Frosting (recipes follow)

PAN REQUIRED:

1 standard muffin pan (½-cup capacity)

**1.** Place a rack in the center of the oven and preheat the oven to 350°F. Grease and lightly flour 4 of the muffin cups, or fit paper liners into the cups; set the pan aside.

**2.** Place the chocolate in a small microwave-safe bowl and microwave on high power until it is glossy, 1 to 1½ minutes. Stir the chocolate until it is smooth; then let it stand until it is cool but still soft, 10 minutes.

**3.** Combine the buttermilk and baking soda in a small bowl and stir to mix. Gently whisk in the egg yolks and vanilla.

**4.** Place the flour, sugar, cocoa powder, and salt in a medium-size mixing bowl and whisk to blend well. Add the butter and half of the buttermilk mixture. Beat with a hand-held electric mixer on low speed until the dry ingredients are moistened. Increase the speed to medium and beat until the mixture is lightened and slightly increased in volume, about 30 seconds. Scrape down the sides of the bowl. Pour in the remaining buttermilk mixture and the melted chocolate, and beat on medium speed until well blended,

15 seconds. Scrape down the sides of the bowl.

**5.** Spoon the batter into the prepared muffin cups, dividing it evenly among them. Fill the empty cups halfway with water to prevent them from scorching. Bake the cupcakes until a toothpick inserted in the center of one comes out clean, 18 to 20 minutes.

**6.** Remove the muffin pan from the oven and place it on a wire rack to cool for 5 minutes. Then remove the cupcakes from the pan and transfer them to the wire rack to cool completely. (If you did not use paper liners, carefully pour the water out of the extra muffin cups. Place a large plate over the muffin pan, and using pot holders to hold the plate securely, invert the cupcakes onto the plate. Then transfer them to the wire rack.)

**7.** Frost the cupcakes with Quick Fudge Frosting or Peanut Butter Frosting. (You can store the frosted cupcakes in an airtight container in the refrigerator for up to 2 days.)

# Quick Fudge Frosting

**For me,** this is the supreme fudge frosting, and luckily it is very quick and easy to make. I love to frost brownies with it, too (see page 204). For a bit of adventure, you can substitute one tablespoon of your favorite liqueur for one tablespoon of the cream. Yummy!

**MAKES ⅔ CUP**

**2 tablespoons unsalted butter**

**1½ ounces bittersweet chocolate, chopped**

**1½ tablespoons sugar**

**Pinch of salt**

**¼ cup whipping (heavy) cream**

**½ teaspoon pure vanilla extract**

**1.** Combine the butter and chocolate in a small saucepan over low heat, and stir until melted. Stir in the sugar and salt; then gradually whisk in the cream. Cook over medium heat, stirring constantly, until the mixture is hot and smooth, but do not let it boil.

**2.** Remove the saucepan from the heat and stir in the vanilla. Let the chocolate mixture cool slightly, and then use it warm as a glaze for cupcakes; or let it cool until it thickens to the consistency of frosting and then spread it on the cupcakes. (Refrigerate any leftover frosting in a covered jar for up to 1 week. Bring it to room temperature before using.)

# Peanut Butter Frosting

**This frosting** tastes like peanut butter fudge! It is quite creamy and turns a chocolate cupcake into a superindulgence. For the smoothest frosting, use a commercial brand of creamy peanut butter, not one that says "all natural" on the jar. (The latter will not yield as smooth a result.)

**MAKES ½ CUP**

⅓ **cup confectioners' sugar**
¼ **cup creamy peanut butter**
1 **tablespoon plus 1 teaspoon**
   **unsalted butter, at room**
   **temperature**
¼ **teaspoon pure vanilla extract**

**1.** Place the confectioners' sugar, peanut butter, butter, and vanilla in a small mixing bowl and beat with a hand-held electric mixer on low speed until well blended, 1 minute. Raise the speed to high and beat until the mixture is fluffy, about 1 minute.

**2.** Spread the frosting on the cupcakes. (You can store the frosting in a covered jar in the refrigerator for up to 1 week. Bring it to room temperature before using.)

# Pineapple Upside-Down Cake

*Makes 2 cakes; serves 2*

◆◆◆◆◆◆◆◆◆

**This pineapple** upside-down cake, an old-fashioned dessert favorite, tastes just like the one you remember, but with a twist. A tablespoon of light rum in the cake batter adds a bit of tropical flavor that complements the pineapple. If you don't want to use rum, you can substitute a tablespoon of buttermilk and add a drop of rum extract to achieve a similar tang.

**3 tablespoons unsalted butter, at room temperature**

**1/3 cup canned pineapple tidbits in juice or syrup, well drained**

**1 tablespoon packed light brown sugar**

**3 tablespoons buttermilk**

**1 tablespoon light rum**

**Yolk of 1 large egg**

**1/2 teaspoon pure vanilla extract**

**1/3 cup all-purpose flour**

**1/3 cup granulated sugar**

**1/8 teaspoon baking soda**

**1/8 teaspoon salt**

**Vanilla ice cream, for serving (optional)**

**PAN REQUIRED:**

**1 jumbo muffin pan (3/4-cup capacity)**

1. Place a rack in the center of the oven and preheat the oven to 375°F.

2. Place 1 1/2 teaspoons of the butter in each of 2 muffin cups. Bake until the

butter is bubbly and beginning to turn golden, 1 minute.

**3.** Meanwhile, mix the pineapple with the brown sugar in a small bowl. Remove the muffin pan from the oven and spoon the pineapple mixture over the butter in the muffin cups, dividing it evenly between them. Set the muffin pan aside.

**4.** Place the buttermilk, rum, egg yolk, and vanilla in a small bowl and whisk to mix.

**5.** Sift the flour, granulated sugar, baking soda, and salt together into a medium-size mixing bowl. Add the remaining 2 tablespoons of butter and half of the buttermilk mixture. Beat with a hand-held electric mixer on low speed until the dry ingredients are moistened. Increase the mixer speed to medium and beat until the batter is lightened and has slightly increased in volume, 45 seconds. Scrape down the sides of the bowl. Pour in the remaining buttermilk mixture and beat on medium speed until well blended, 20 seconds. Scrape down the sides of the bowl.

**6.** Spoon the batter over the pineapple in the muffin cups, dividing it evenly between them, and then smooth the tops. Fill the empty muffin cups halfway with water to prevent them from scorching. Bake the cakes until a toothpick inserted in the center of one comes out clean, 20 to 24 minutes.

**7.** Remove the muffin pan from the oven and place it on a wire rack to cool for 5 minutes. Carefully pour the water out of the muffin cups. Place a large plate over the muffin pan, and using potholders to hold the plate securely, invert the cakes onto the plate. Transfer the cakes to serving plates. Serve the cakes warm, with vanilla ice cream if desired.

# Blueberry Upside-Down Cake

## *with* Vanilla Crème Fraîche

*Makes 2 cakes; serves 2*

◆◆◆◆◆◆◆◆◆

**A variation on** traditional pineapple upside-down cake, this version uses intensely colored, juicy blueberries, which makes it somewhat messier than the classic dessert. But you will love the fresh berry flavor that seeps through the tender and tasty yellow cake, made with buttermilk. Serve warm with Vanilla Crème Fraîche, which picks up the tangy buttermilk flavor, and you will have a special summertime treat. If you line the muffin tin cups with parchment, you will avoid having the blueberries stick.

(For a Small-Batch version of pineapple upside-down cake, see page 68.)

2 tablespoons unsalted butter, at room temperature, plus more for greasing the muffin cups

1/3 cup all-purpose flour, plus more for flouring the muffin cups

1/2 cup fresh or thawed frozen blueberries

1/3 cup plus 1 teaspoon sugar

1/4 cup buttermilk

Yolk of 1 large egg

1/2 teaspoon pure vanilla extract

1/8 teaspoon baking soda

1/8 teaspoon salt

**Vanilla Crème Fraîche**
   **(recipe follows)**

PAN REQUIRED:

**1 jumbo muffin pan**
   **(¾-cup capacity)**

**1.** Place a rack in the center of the oven and preheat the oven to 375°F. Place the muffin pan on a piece of parchment paper and, using a pencil, trace around the bottom of one of the cups. Cut out 4 parchment paper rounds.

**2.** Grease and lightly flour 2 muffin cups. Fit 2 of the parchment rounds into each of the prepared muffin cups, making a double layer. Grease and lightly flour the top pieces of parchment paper.

**3.** Place the blueberries and 1 teaspoon of the sugar in a small bowl, and stir to mix. Spoon the berries into the prepared muffin cups, dividing them evenly between them. Set the muffin pan aside.

**4.** Place the buttermilk, egg yolk, and vanilla in a small bowl and whisk to mix.

**5.** Sift the flour, baking soda, and salt into a medium-size mixing bowl; add the remaining ⅓ cup sugar and whisk to combine. Add the butter and half of the buttermilk mixture. Beat with a hand-held electric mixer on low speed until the dry ingredients are moistened. Increase the mixer speed to medium and beat until the batter is lightened and has slightly increased in volume, about 45 seconds. Scrape down the sides of the bowl. Pour in the remaining buttermilk mixture and beat on medium speed until well blended, about 20 seconds. Scrape down the sides of the bowl.

**6.** Spoon the batter over the blueberries in the muffin cups, dividing it evenly between them, and then smooth the tops. Fill the empty muffin cups halfway with water to prevent them from scorching. Bake the cakes until a toothpick inserted in the center of one comes out clean, 20 to 24 minutes.

**7.** Remove the muffin pan from the oven and place it on a wire rack to cool for 5 minutes. Carefully pour the water out of the muffin cups. Place a large plate over the muffin pan, and using potholders to hold the plate securely, invert the cakes onto the plate. Transfer the cakes to serving plates, and peel off and discard the parchment paper. Serve the cakes warm, with a bowl of Vanilla Crème Fraîche to spoon over.

# Vanilla Crème Fraîche

**Creamy ice cream** loaded with vanilla acts as the flavoring in this sauce. It's an easy and delicious topping for cobblers, crisps, and bread pudding.

**MAKES ABOUT ⅓ CUP**

¼ **cup premium-quality vanilla bean ice cream, softened**

3 **tablespoons crème fraîche or sour cream**

Place the soft ice cream and the crème fraîche in a small bowl, and whisk just to mix. Serve immediately.

# Angel Food Cake

*Makes 2 cakes; serves 2*
◆◆◆◆◆◆◆◆◆

**These cakes have** authentic homemade flavor and are low-fat, just like the full-size versions. So when you are watching your weight, these little angels will become your standby dessert. You can dress them up by serving fresh berries with them instead of a glaze—or use both.

The standard angel food cake, cooked in a tube pan, is placed upside down over a bottle to cool so it will maintain its height while it cools. We do the same thing here with the muffin pan, so you'll need to position two or three soft drink or water bottles on the counter to hold the inverted pan as the cakes cool.

**3 tablespoons sifted cake flour**

**4 tablespoons superfine sugar (see Note)**

**Dash of ground nutmeg**

**Whites of 2 large eggs, at room temperature**

**⅛ teaspoon salt**

**¼ teaspoon pure vanilla extract**

**¼ teaspoon cream of tartar**

**Chocolate Glaze or Tangerine Glaze (recipes follow; optional)**

**PAN REQUIRED:**

**1 jumbo muffin pan (¾-cup capacity; don't use a nonstick pan)**

**1.** Place a rack in the center of the oven and preheat the oven to 350°F. Set aside an ungreased jumbo muffin pan.

**2.** Place the flour, 2 tablespoons of the superfine sugar, and the nutmeg in a small bowl and whisk to blend well.

**3.** Place the egg whites, salt, and vanilla in a medium-size mixing bowl and beat with a hand-held electric mixer on medium speed until the whites are frothy, about 5 seconds. Sprinkle the cream of tartar over the whites and beat until soft peaks fold over when the mixer is turned off and the beaters are lifted, 20 to 30 seconds. With the mixer running, gradually sprinkle the remaining 2 tablespoons of superfine sugar over the whites and beat on high speed until the egg whites are glossy, about 45 seconds; they should form stiff peaks when the mixer is turned off and the beaters are lifted.

**4.** Sift half of the flour mixture over the egg whites and fold it in gently with a rubber spatula. Fold in the remaining flour mixture. Spoon the batter into 2 of the ungreased muffin cups, dividing it evenly between them. The cups will be completely filled. Fill the empty muffin cups halfway with water to prevent them from scorching.

**5.** Bake the cakes for 15 minutes. Then drape a piece of aluminum foil over the cakes to prevent them from browning too much, and continue baking until the tops are golden and spring back when lightly touched in the center, another 5 to 10 minutes.

**6.** Remove the muffin pan from the oven. Carefully pour the water out of the muffin cups, and then turn the pan upside down, and place it on bottles to cool completely (place the tops of a couple of liter bottles into empty muffin cups so that the pan is balanced). Since the muffin pan wasn't greased, the cakes won't fall out.

**7.** To remove the cakes from the muffin pan, loosen the edges with a small rubber spatula or a table knife, pulling the edges away from the sides of the muffin cups. Place the cakes on serving plates and drizzle the glaze over them, if desired.

**NOTE:** If you can't find superfine sugar in your supermarket, you can easily make it: Simply process about $1/3$ cup granulated sugar in a blender or mini food processor until it is ground superfine, pulsing it about 6 times. Then measure out $1/4$ cup.

# Chocolate Glaze

The angel food cakes are good plain, but they become heavenly when drizzled with this glaze. Yes, it contains a bit of fat, but it's spectacular and worth a mini splurge.

**MAKES ½ CUP**

1 tablespoon unsalted butter

1 ounce unsweetened chocolate, chopped (3 tablespoons)

1 cup sifted confectioners' sugar

1 teaspoon pure vanilla extract

1. Place the butter and chocolate in a small microwave-safe bowl and add 2 tablespoons of water. Microwave on medium power until the butter melts and the chocolate is glossy, 1 to 1½ minutes. Whisk until smooth. Add the confectioners' sugar and vanilla, and whisk until smooth and blended.

2. Use right away, drizzling the glaze on the cakes with a teaspoon, or cover and let stand at room temperature for up to 1 hour before using.

# Tangerine Glaze

Tangerines have a bright citrus flavor that adds a clean finish to the delicate Angel Food Cakes. If tangelos are available, their juice will substitute nicely.

**MAKES ½ CUP**

¼ cup fresh tangerine juice

1 tablespoon whipping (heavy) cream

1 cup sifted confectioners' sugar

1. Pour the tangerine juice into a small saucepan and bring to a boil over medium-high heat. Let boil until it is reduced to 2 tablespoons, 3 to 5 minutes. Remove from the heat and stir in the cream and confectioners' sugar.

2. Use right away, drizzling the glaze on the cakes with a teaspoon, or cover and let stand at room temperature for up to 1 hour before using.

# Dulce de Leche Cheesecakes

## *with* Candied Pecans

*Makes 2 cheesecakes; serves 2*

◆◆◆◆◆◆◆◆◆

*Dulce de leche,* a caramel made from the sugars that occur in milk (it means "milk jam" or "milk candy"), is a specialty of Argentina that has been adopted throughout Latin America. It is frequently made by caramelizing sweetened condensed milk and used as a spread for bread. A few years ago, a major U.S. manufacturer decided to produce *dulce de leche* ice cream for the Hispanic market and was astonished to find that it became the company's most popular flavor. This rich cheese-cake has the authentic south of the border flavor.

**Unsalted butter, at room temperature, for greasing the pans**

**FOR THE CRUST:**
**Candied Pecans (page 99)**
**²/₃ cup shortbread cookie crumbs**
**1 tablespoon unsalted butter, melted**

**FOR THE FILLING:**
**4 ounces cream cheese, at room temperature**
**¼ cup canned sweetened condensed milk**
**1 tablespoon all-purpose flour**

½ teaspoon pure vanilla extract

¼ teaspoon fresh lemon juice

1 large egg, at room temperature

FOR THE CARAMELIZED MILK SAUCE:

½ cup whipping (heavy) cream

½ cup firmly packed dark brown sugar

Cinnamon stick (1½ inches)

2 tablespoons canned sweetened condensed milk

PANS REQUIRED:

Two 4½ x 1⅜-inch tart pans with removable bottoms

1 baking sheet

1. Place a rack in the center of the oven and preheat the oven to 325°F. Line the tart pans with aluminum foil, pressing the foil into the grooves of the pans. Grease the foil. Place the tart pans on a baking sheet for easier handling, and set it aside.

2. MAKE THE CRUST: Place ⅓ cup of the candied pecans, the shortbread crumbs, and the melted butter in a food processor and process until the pecans are finely ground. (Reserve the remaining candied pecans for garnish.) Press the cookie mixture on the bottom and up the sides of the prepared tart pans, dividing it evenly between them, pressing it firmly into the fluted sides of the pans. Bake the crusts until they are lightly browned, 12 to 15 minutes. Remove the baking sheet from the oven and transfer the tart pans to a wire rack to cool completely. Keep the oven on.

3. MAKE THE FILLING: Place the cream cheese, condensed milk, flour, vanilla, and lemon juice in a small bowl. Beat with a hand-held electric mixer on medium speed just until the batter is smooth. Add the egg, reduce the mixer speed to low, and beat just until the batter is blended, about 10 seconds.

4. Return the tart pans to the baking sheet. Pour the batter into the crusts, dividing it evenly between them. Bake until the filling is set, 20 to 25 minutes. Then remove the baking sheet from the oven and transfer the cheesecakes to a wire rack to cool completely. Cover and refrigerate 6 hours or overnight.

**5.** MAKE THE SAUCE: Place the cream, brown sugar, and cinnamon stick in a small, heavy saucepan over medium heat and bring to a boil, stirring constantly until the sugar dissolves. Continue to boil, stirring occasionally, until the mixture reduces to $\frac{1}{2}$ cup, about 5 minutes. Remove the cinnamon stick and stir in the condensed milk and lemon juice.

**6.** To serve, unmold the cheesecakes by pushing up on the bottom of the tart pans. Carefully remove the aluminum foil, and place the cheesecakes on serving plates. Sprinkle them with the remaining candied pecans, and spoon the sauce over the cheesecakes.

# Mini Génoises

*Makes 4 cakes; serves 2 to 4*

◆◆◆◆◆◆◆◆◆

**Génoise is an** Italian sponge cake that was adopted by the French. Because it includes a bit of melted butter and the whole egg, this light, airy cake is tastier than American sponge cake, but it's not as sweet. It makes a good base for many desserts, because the individual cake can be split into layers that greedily absorb the juices of sweetened fruits, flavored sugar syrups, and liqueurs. Because génoise is leavened only with eggs, you must be careful not to deflate the batter when folding in the flour and melted butter.

**2 tablespoons unsalted butter, plus
more for greasing the baking rings**

**⅓ cup all-purpose flour, sifted twice,
plus more for flouring the rings**

**¼ cup sugar**

**1 large egg, at room temperature**

**Yolk of 1 large egg, at room
temperature**

**¼ teaspoon pure vanilla extract**

**Pinch of salt**

**PANS REQUIRED:**

**4 baking rings (about 3 x ½-inch)**

**1 baking sheet**

**1.** Place a rack in the center of the oven and preheat the oven to 350°F.

**2.** Cut out four 5-inch squares of heavy-duty aluminum foil. Center a baking ring on top of each square; form the edges of the foil up around the sides of each ring. Mold the foil well to the sides of the rings to create individual baking dishes with foil bottoms. Carefully grease and lightly flour the foil bottoms only. Place the rings on a baking sheet for easier handling, and set aside.

**3.** Place the butter in a small microwave-safe bowl and microwave on medium power until the butter

melts, 50 to 65 seconds. Set the melted butter aside to cool.

**4.** Warm a small bowl by letting hot tap water run into and over the bowl. Dry the bowl thoroughly and add the sugar. Stir 2 teaspoons of hot tap water into the sugar. Add the egg and egg yolk, and beat with a hand-held electric mixer on high speed until the mixture is thick and pale in color, about 5 minutes; when you lift the beaters out of the bowl, a ribbon of egg mixture should drizzle back onto the bowl, leaving a "track" that sits on the top before it sinks in.

**5.** Fold the vanilla into the egg mixture, and sift the flour and salt over the top. Using a whisk, gently fold in the flour. Whisk 3 tablespoons of the batter into the melted butter, then fold that butter mixture into the remaining batter just until blended.

**6.** Spoon the batter into the prepared baking rings, dividing it evenly among them. Bake the cakes until they have pulled away from the sides of the baking rings and the centers are springy when lightly touched with a finger, about 15 minutes.

**7.** Remove the baking sheet from the oven, and immediately run the tip of a sharp knife around the edge of each cake (this will prevent the crust from sticking to the top edge of the ring as it cools and shrinks). Let the cakes cool, still in the rings, for 10 minutes on a wire rack. Then remove them from the baking rings and let them cool, upright, on the rack. (The cakes can be wrapped individually in plastic wrap and stored at room temperature for up to 2 days.)

## FINISHING TOUCHES

Classic génoise is a versatile cake that will thirstily soak up flavorful liquids—making it suitable for many different desserts. Here are a few ideas to spark your or imagination.

**MAKE A GENOISE SHORTCAKE:** Split the cakes in half horizontally. Spoon slices of fresh fruit and Vanilla Whipped cream (page 36) on top of the bottom halves, then cover each with a cake top.

**SERVE THEM WITH LIQUEUR-SOAKED FRUITS:** Combine 1 cup sliced strawberries, sliced peeled peaches, sliced apricots, orange segments, or another fruit with ¼ cup of your favorite liqueur or brandy in a small bowl. Soak 2 hours in the refrigerator. Sift confectioners' sugar over the cakes and serve with the fruit and juices.

**FROST THE CAKES WITH GANACHE:** Prepare the ganache as described on page 356, and let it cool until it is just slightly warm. Spread the ganache on the tops and sides of the cakes. If you like, sprinkle finely chopped nuts on top before the ganache sets. Refrigerate the cakes 30 minutes to set the ganache. After the ganache has set, you can wrap the cakes in plastic wrap and refrigerate up to 24 hours before serving.

# Tiramisù

*Makes 4 desserts; serves 4*

◆◆◆◆◆◆◆◆◆

**Tiramisù is also** known as "Tuscan trifle," although it's much lighter than an English trifle. I like to use génoise instead of the traditional ladyfingers or sponge cake because I prefer the texture and flavor of a butter cake in this heavenly dessert. Because the cake is home baked, I've taken a short-cut by using store-bought pudding instead of the classic custard. It comes in conveniently small serving sizes and is delicious, so it just seemed a natural step saver.

Sprinkle confectioners' sugar or grated chocolate—or both— on dessert plates, then place the individual desserts on them for a deluxe dinner party presentation. If you're only serving two, the extras will keep for two days wrapped in plastic.

1 recipe Mini Génoises (page 78), baked, at room temperature

¼ cup brewed espresso or extra-strong coffee at room temperature

2 tablespoons rum or brandy

2 teaspoons sugar

¼ cup whipping (heavy) cream

¼ cup mascarpone or cream cheese, at room temperature

¼ cup prepared vanilla pudding (such as Jell-O refrigerated pudding)

1½ ounces bittersweet chocolate, grated or very finely chopped

**PAN REQUIRED:**

One 14- or 14.5-ounce can (see page 6)

1 baking sheet

**1.** Lay a génoise on its side on a cutting board and, using a sharp serrated knife, cut it horizontally into 3 equal layers. Set the layers aside and repeat with the remaining génoises.

**2.** To make molds for the tiramisù, tear off a 12-inch-long piece of heavy-duty aluminum foil and lay it on a countertop. Tear off a 12-inch-long piece of plastic wrap and lay it on top of the foil. Center the can on top of the plastic wrap, and mold the foil up and around the can's sides, smoothing the foil and plastic wrap snugly against the can to form a mold. Fold the edges of the foil and plastic wrap out away from the top of the can. Carefully remove the can. Repeat the process to form 3 additional molds. Set the molds aside.

**3.** Place the coffee, rum, and sugar in a small bowl, and stir until the sugar dissolves.

**4.** Place the heavy cream in a small bowl and beat with a hand-held electric mixer at high speed until soft peaks form, about 1 minute.

**5.** Place the mascarpone in a small bowl and beat with a hand-held electric mixer on medium speed until fluffy, 20 to 30 seconds. Add the pudding and beat on low speed until smooth and blended. Fold in the whipped cream.

**6.** To assemble the tiramisùs, place a bottom cake layer in each of the 4 foil molds, and brush each with the some of the coffee mixture. Using a long-handled teaspoon, spoon about one third of the pudding mixture over the layers in the molds, dividing it evenly among them. Sprinkle 1 teaspoon of the grated chocolate into each mold. Repeat the layers once, and then top with the final cake layer. Brush the remaining coffee mixture evenly over the cakes, and sprinkle the remaining chocolate over them. Place the tiramisùs on a baking sheet for easier handling. Fold the plastic wrap in over the layers to cover them loosely, leaving the foil edges out. Refrigerate the tiramisùs for at least 6 hours or up to 2 days.

**7.** To serve, pull the foil down gently to expose the plastic-wrapped tiramisùs. Gently remove the plastic wrap and using a spatula, lift the tiramisùs onto serving plates.

# Presto Pound Cake

*Makes 1 cake; serves 2 or 3*

❖❖❖❖❖❖❖❖❖

**I love rich,** dense, buttery pound cakes with crunchy sugar crusts. This little gem is a prime example, and by baking it in a small loaf pan, there is even more crust per serving than usual. For extra sweetness, add a spoonful or two of your favorite jam to the batter. Because this one bakes in less time than a normal-size pound cake, you could be enjoying a piece of warm homemade cake about fifty minutes from now. For suggested embellishments that transform simple pound cake into elegant desserts, see page 86.

3 tablespoons unsalted butter,
    at room temperature, plus more
    for greasing the pan

1/2 cup all-purpose flour, plus more
    for flouring the pan

3 tablespoons buttermilk

1/8 teaspoon baking soda

Yolk of 1 large egg

1/2 teaspoon pure vanilla extract

1/3 cup sugar

1/8 teaspoon salt

**PAN REQUIRED:**

1 petite loaf pan (2-cup capacity,
    about 5 x 3 x 2 inches)

1. Place a rack in the center of the oven and preheat the oven to 350°F. Grease and lightly flour the loaf pan, tapping out the excess; then set it aside.

2. Place the buttermilk and baking soda in a small bowl and stir to mix. Gently whisk in the egg yolk and vanilla.

3. Place the flour, sugar, and salt in a medium-size mixing bowl and whisk to blend well. Add the butter and half of the buttermilk mixture. Beat with a hand-held electric mixer on low speed until the dry ingredients are moistened. Increase the speed to medium and beat until the batter is lightened and has slightly increased in volume, about 45 seconds. Scrape down the sides of the bowl. Pour in the remaining buttermilk mixture and beat on medium speed until well blended, 20 seconds. Scrape down the sides of the bowl.

4. Spoon the batter into the prepared loaf pan. Bake the cake until a toothpick inserted in the center comes out clean, about 30 minutes.

## variation

# Almond Pound Cake

Substitute 2 tablespoons of amaretto for 2 tablespoons of the buttermilk, and add ½ teaspoon almond extract to the batter of the Presto Pound Cake. Sprinkle the bottom of the prepared loaf pan with 1 tablespoon sliced almonds before adding the batter. For a special breakfast, toast a piece and butter it.

5. Remove the pan from the oven and place it on a wire rack to cool for 10 minutes. Then remove the cake from the pan. Serve the cake warm or let it cool, upright, on the rack.

# Presto Chocolate Pound Cake

*Makes 1 cake; serves 2 or 3*

◆◆◆◆◆◆◆◆◆

**I'm a morning** sweet-aholic, and there's nothing like a piece of chocolate pound cake and a tall glass of iced caffè latte to perk me up around 10:00 A.M. And because I work at home, I'm temptingly close to the kitchen and a snack like this cake. It has a light chocolate flavor, akin to German's Sweet Chocolate, with a meltingly moist texture that prolongs the chocolate experience.

3 tablespoons unsalted butter, at room temperature, plus more for greasing the pan

¼ cup plus 2 tablespoons all-purpose flour, plus more for flouring the pan

3 tablespoons buttermilk

⅛ teaspoon baking soda

Yolk of 1 large egg

½ teaspoon pure vanilla extract

⅓ cup sugar

2 tablespoons unsweetened cocoa powder

⅛ teaspoon salt

**PAN REQUIRED:**

1 petite loaf pan (2-cup capacity, about 5 x 3 inches)

**1.** Place a rack in the center of the oven and preheat the oven to 350°F. Grease and lightly flour the loaf pan, tapping out the excess; then set it aside.

**2.** Place the buttermilk and baking soda in a small bowl and stir to mix. Gently whisk in the egg yolk and vanilla.

**3.** Place the flour, sugar, cocoa powder, and salt in a medium-size mixing bowl and whisk to blend well. Add the butter and half of the buttermilk mixture. Beat with a hand-held electric mixer on low speed until the dry ingredients are moistened. Increase the speed to medium and beat until the batter is lightened and has nearly doubled in volume, about 45 seconds. Scrape down the sides of the bowl. Pour in the remaining buttermilk mixture and beat for 20 seconds on medium speed. Scrape down the sides of the bowl.

**4.** Spoon the batter into the prepared loaf pan. Bake the cake until a toothpick inserted in the center comes out clean, about 30 minutes.

**5.** Remove the pan from the oven and place it on a wire rack to cool for 10 minutes. Then remove the cake from the pan and serve it warm or let it cool, upright, on the rack.

## FANCY THAT POUND CAKE

A simple pound cake can be the base for any number of sensational desserts. Here are just a few suggestions for embellishing plain or chocolate slices. Let them inspire some toppings of your own.

**SERVE POUND CAKE WITH COFFEE RUM MASCARPONE CREAM:** Beat ¼ cup cold whipping (heavy) cream until medium-firm peaks form. Fold in 2 tablespoons mascarpone (the rich Italian cream cheese used in tiramisù), ¼ teaspoon of instant espresso powder, 1 tablespoon of sugar, and 1 tablespoon of dark rum.

**MAKE IT JAMAICAN:** Serve the pound cake with a scoop of coffee or vanilla bean ice cream, and spoon a warm coconut topping over all: Mix ¼ cup of moist, flaked, sweetened coconut with 1 packed teaspoon of light brown sugar and 1 teaspoon of melted unsalted butter in a small heatproof dish. Bake in a preheated 375°F oven, stirring twice, until the coconut is golden, 8 to 10 minutes. Remove from the oven and stir in 2 to 3 teaspoons of rum, or to taste.

**TOP IT WITH BROILED FRUIT:** Preheat the broiler. Spread a little butter on one side of a slice of pound cake and place the slice, buttered side up, on a baking sheet. Arrange sliced peeled peaches, plums, or bananas over the slice, covering it completely so the cake will not burn when it is broiled. Sprinkle 1 teaspoon of sugar over the fruit and dot it with 1 teaspoon of butter, cut into bits. Broil 6 inches from the heat until the top of the fruit is slightly caramelized, about 1½ to 2 minutes. Serve warm with crème fraîche, sour cream, or ice cream.

**SERVE IT WITH STRAWBERRIES ROMANOFF:** Toss 1 cup of sliced hulled strawberries, 1 tablespoon confectioners' sugar, and 1 tablespoon Grand Marnier in a small bowl. Cover and refrigerate for 1 hour. Spoon the strawberry mixture on slices of pound cake, letting the juices pool on the plate. Dollop with sweetened whipped cream; or use a melon baller to make small scoops of orange sherbet and arrange them around the cake slices.

**MAKE A LEMON BLUEBERRY TRIFLE:** Dissolve 2 tablespoons sugar in 2 tablespoons of boiling water in a small bowl. Stir in ½ cup fresh blueberries, and set aside. Beat ⅓ cup of whipping cream until stiff peaks form; then beat in 2 tablespoons store-bought lemon curd. Arrange slices of pound cake on plates and spoon the blueberries over them. Top with the lemon cream.

# Lemon Cornmeal Pound Cakes

## *with* Raspberry Coulis

*Makes 4 cakes; serves 2 to 4*

◆◆◆◆◆◆◆◆◆

**This lemony, sweet** pillow of a cake soaks up fresh raspberry syrup to make a sensational dessert. I have doubled the recipe for dinner parties, and I have prepared it for just two to celebrate a friend's birthday. The small cakes are garnished with stenciled confectioners' sugar designs. I frequently cut out a small heart from a 4-inch piece of heavy paper, place the paper on top of the cake, and sift the sugar over it. Once the stencil is removed (lift it straight up), a sugar heart is revealed. For a lacy pattern, lay a small doily on the cake and sift the sugar over it.

3 tablespoons unsalted butter, at room temperature, plus more for greasing the baking rings

1/2 cup all-purpose flour, plus more for flouring the rings

1/4 cup whole milk

1 medium egg

1/2 teaspoon pure vanilla extract

1 teaspoon grated lemon zest

1/2 cup sugar

1/4 cup cornmeal

1/2 teaspoon baking powder

1/4 teaspoon salt

**Raspberry Coulis (recipe follows)**
**Fresh raspberries, for garnish**

PANS REQUIRED:
**4 baking rings (about 3 x ½-inch)**

1. Place a rack in the center of the oven and preheat the oven to 350°F.

2. Cut out four 5-inch squares of heavy-duty aluminum foil. Center a baking ring on top of each square and press the edges of the foil up firmly around the sides of each ring, forming individual baking dishes with foil bottoms. Carefully grease and lightly flour the foil bottoms only. Place the baking rings on a baking sheet for easier handling, and set aside.

3. Combine the milk, egg, vanilla, and lemon zest in a small bowl and whisk to mix.

4. Place the flour, sugar, cornmeal, baking powder, and salt in a medium-size mixing bowl and whisk to blend well. Add the butter and the milk mixture to the flour mixture. Beat with a hand-held electric mixer on low speed until the dry ingredients are moistened. Increase the speed to medium and beat until the batter is lightened and increased in volume, about 1 minute.

5. Spoon the batter into the prepared molds, dividing it evenly among them. Bake the cakes until a toothpick inserted into the center of one comes out clean, about 25 minutes.

6. Remove the baking sheet from the oven and transfer the cakes to a wire rack to cool, still in the baking rings, for 15 minutes. Then loosen the edges of the cakes with a sharp knife and remove them from the cans. Let the cakes continue to cool, upright, on the rack. The cakes can be served warm or at room temperature. Right before serving, drizzle Raspberry Coulis over the tops and garnish with raspberries.

# Raspberry Coulis

**This fruit sauce** makes the cakes look like little jewels and gives them a very sophisticated flavor. The sauce, however, is simple—nothing more than sieved berries with a bit of sugar added to balance the tartness. Drizzle the sauce over pound cake, ice cream, and bread pudding. For breakfast, warm it and drizzle it over waffles, followed by a drizzle of maple syrup—a combination of flavors that's a true indulgence.

**MAKES ABOUT ½ CUP**

**1½ cups fresh or thawed frozen unsweetened raspberries**
**2 tablespoons sugar**

Press the raspberries through a fine-mesh sieve placed over a small bowl. Scrape off the pulp that clings to the outside bottom of the sieve and add it to the pulp in the bowl. Discard the seeds. Add the sugar to the strained pulp and stir until it is dissolved. (The sauce can be stored in a jar in the refrigerator for up to 1 week.)

# DESIGNING CIRCLES

Lemon Cornmeal Pound Cakes (page 88) have a delicate lemon-vanilla flavor that goes well with many fruits and sauces. Here are some pairings that will add pizzazz to the cakes and color to the plates.

**DRIZZLE ON PRESERVES:** Warm ¼ cup of strained apricot preserves with 1 tablespoon of Grand Marnier, then drizzle the sauce over and around the pound cakes. Arrange fresh or thawed frozen blackberries around the cakes.

**SERVE THEM WITH BLUEBERRY CREME FRAICHE:** Fold about ½ cup of fresh or thawed frozen blueberries into Vanilla Crème Fraîche (page 72) and dollop it on the pound cakes.

**TOP THE CAKES WITH HONEY MINT SYRUP AND FRUIT:** Place ½ cup of honey, 2 tablespoons of sugar, 2 tablespoons of water, and ¼ cup of packed fresh mint leaves in a small saucepan and bring to a boil over medium heat until the sugar melts, 3 to 5 minutes. Remove the sauce from the heat and let it cool to room temperature, about 30 minutes; then strain out the mint leaves. Spoon the strained mint sauce over the cakes, add some sliced fresh peaches or strawberries, and garnish with a few fresh mint leaves.

**ADD SOME ORANGE:** Spoon Orange Caramel Sauce (page 383) over and around the pound cakes; then arrange fresh orange sections alongside.

**DON'T OVERLOOK THE STANDARDS:** Scoops of your favorite ice cream, frozen yogurt, sherbet, or sorbet are never out of place on slices of this pound cake. Lemon is a natural, but so is a good-quality vanilla, coconut, mocha, or raspberry. The same, too, with Sweetened Whipped Cream (see page 36). A hearty dollop, topped with grated lemon zest, makes a beautiful accompaniment.

# Spiced Sweet Potato Bundt Cakes

*Makes 2 cakes; serves 2*

◆◆◆◆◆◆◆◆◆

**I grew up** in a household where sweet potatoes routinely found their way into breads and desserts—they weren't reserved just for Thanksgiving dinner. Here they make a very moist and flavorful cake with a beautiful color. The brown-sugar icing adds

the perfect finish. Baked in miniature Bundt pans, they look, as a friend suggested, like doll's cakes. I sometimes garnish them with organically grown pansies, which are abundant in pots on my front porch during the fall. They are just beautiful.

Since the sweet potato needs to bake for about an hour before you can use it in the cake, you might want to bake it ahead. Or bake an extra if they are on the menu for dinner. If you remove the skin, the flesh can be stored in an airtight container in the refrigerator for three days before you use it.

## FOR THE CAKES:

1 small sweet potato
   (about 8 ounces)

Unsalted butter, at room temperature,
   for greasing the molds

1/4 cup plus 3 tablespoons
   all-purpose flour, plus more
   for flouring the molds

1/8 teaspoon baking powder

1/8 teaspoon baking soda

1/2 teaspoon ground cinnamon

1/8 teaspoon ground ginger

1/8 teaspoon salt

1/3 cup granulated sugar

3 tablespoons vegetable oil

Yolk of 1 large egg

1/4 teaspoon pure vanilla extract

## FOR THE ICING:

1/2 cup confectioners' sugar

1/4 cup plus 2 tablespoons packed
   dark brown sugar

1/4 cup whipping (heavy) cream

2 tablespoons unsalted butter

1/4 teaspoon pure vanilla extract

## PAN REQUIRED:

1 mini Bundt pan with six
   1-cup molds

**1. MAKE THE CAKES:** Place a rack in the center of the oven and preheat the oven to 350°F.

**2.** Rinse the sweet potato well and pat it dry with paper towels, then prick it several times with a fork. Place the sweet potato in a baking dish and bake until it is very tender, about 1 hour. Transfer the sweet potato to a wire rack to cool completely. Leave the oven on.

**3.** Peel the sweet potato and mash the flesh until it is free of lumps. Measure 1/4 cup plus 2 tablespoons of mashed sweet potato and place it in a medium-size mixing bowl. If there is any remaining nibble on it while you prepare the cakes.

**4.** Thoroughly grease 2 miniature Bundt molds (see Note) and dust them with flour, tapping out the excess. Set the Bundt pan aside.

**5.** Sift the flour, baking powder, baking soda, cinnamon, ginger, and salt together into a small bowl. Set aside.

**6.** Add the sugar, oil, egg yolk, and vanilla to the mashed sweet potato and whisk until the mixture is smooth. Add the flour mixture to the sweet potato mixture, and whisk just until the dry ingredients are moistened.

**7.** Spoon the batter into the prepared Bundt molds, dividing it evenly between them. Fill the empty Bundt molds halfway with water to prevent them from scorching. Bake the cakes until a toothpick inserted into one of them, between the center and the outside of the mold, comes out clean, 15 to 20 minutes.

**8.** Remove the Bundt pan from the oven and place it on a wire rack to cool for 15 minutes. Then carefully pour the water out of the extra Bundt molds. Place a large plate over the Bundt pan, and using potholders to hold the plate securely, invert the Bundt cakes onto the plate. Transfer the cakes to the rack to cool completely.

**9. MAKE THE ICING:** Sift the confectioners' sugar into a medium-size mixing bowl. Place the brown sugar, cream, and butter in a small saucepan and bring to a boil over medium heat, stirring constantly until the butter melts and the sugar dissolves. Let the mixture boil for 2 minutes, stirring occasionally. Remove the saucepan from the heat and pour the mixture over the confectioners' sugar. Whisk in the vanilla, and continue whisking until the icing is light in color and smooth. Let the icing cool, whisking it often, until it is lukewarm and thick enough to fall from a spoon in ribbons, about 20 minutes.

**10.** Spoon the icing thickly over the cakes, allowing it to drip down the sides. Let the cakes rest until the icing is firm, about 1 hour.

NOTE: Miniature Bundt molds come in pans of 6, like a jumbo muffin pan. They are available at kitchenware stores.

# Lemon Roulade

## *with* White Chocolate–Honey Cream and Pistachios

*Makes 1 cake; serves 2 or 3*

◆◆◆◆◆◆◆◆◆

**Roulade is** always an elegant dessert, and this version, with its filling of delicately but deeply flavored honey cream (it contains both white chocolate and mascarpone) is especially so. A light layer of lemon curd adds depth, and pistachios give it texture and color as well as a touch of sophistication. It is a light dessert that would be an appropriate ending to either a summer meal or a heavier cold-weather dinner.

The cake for a roulade is usually baked in a jelly-roll pan, but they don't make one small enough for a Small-Batch version. Never mind. A loaf pan works well baking a thin cake that you can roll; the pan is lined so you can easily get the cake out.

## FOR THE CAKE:

Unsalted butter, at room temperature, for greasing the pan

1 tablespoon plus 2 teaspoons cake flour, plus more for flouring the pan

1/8 teaspoon salt

Yolk of 1 large egg, at room temperature

1/4 cup confectioners' sugar, sifted, plus more for rolling the cake

1 teaspoon grated lemon zest

1/2 teaspoon fresh lemon juice

1/2 teaspoon pure vanilla extract

Whites of 2 large eggs, at room temperature

1/8 teaspoon cream of tartar

## FOR THE WHITE CHOCOLATE–HONEY CREAM:

1 ounce high-quality white chocolate (such as Lindt, Baker's, or Ghirardelli), chopped

3/4 cup plus 1 tablespoon cold whipping (heavy) cream

1/4 cup mascarpone cheese

1/4 cup honey (see Note)

1 teaspoon fresh lemon juice

## FOR ASSEMBLING THE CAKE:

2 tablespoons store-bought lemon curd

1/2 cup finely chopped shelled unsalted pistachios

## PAN REQUIRED:

1 standard loaf pan (9 x 5 inches)

1. MAKE THE CAKE: Place a rack in the center of the oven and preheat the oven to 350°F.

2. Grease the loaf pan and line the bottom with parchment paper. Grease the parchment and dust it lightly with flour, tapping out the excess. Set the loaf pan aside.

3. Place the flour and salt in a small bowl and whisk to blend well.

4. Place the egg yolk and 3 table-spoons of the confectioners' sugar in a small mixing bowl, and beat with a hand-held electric mixer on high speed until the mixture is thick and pale in

color, 1½ to 2 minutes. When you lift a beater out of the bowl, a ribbon should drizzle back onto the rest, leaving a "track" that sits on the top before it sinks in. Stir in the lemon zest, lemon juice, and vanilla. Fold the flour mixture into the batter in two batches, mixing it gently but thoroughly.

**5.** Place the egg whites and cream of tartar in a medium-size mixing bowl and beat with a hand-held electric mixer on medium speed until foamy, about 10 seconds. Sprinkle the remaining 1 tablespoon of confectioners' sugar over the egg whites and beat until stiff peaks form, 1 to 1½ minutes. Fold the beaten whites into the batter mixture in two batches, making sure no streaks of egg white remain.

**6.** Spoon the batter into the prepared loaf pan and smooth the top with a rubber spatula. Bake until a toothpick inserted in the center comes out clean, 8 to 10 minutes.

**7.** Meanwhile, spread a clean kitchen towel on a work surface and sift confectioners' sugar over an area the size of the loaf pan. As soon as the cake has finished baking, invert the loaf pan over the sugared area of the towel. Remove the loaf pan and peel off the parchment paper. Fold one end of the towel over a short end of the cake, and roll up the cake in the towel. Place the rolled cake, seam side down, on a wire rack to cool.

**8.** MAKE THE WHITE CHOCOLATE–HONEY CREAM: Place the white chocolate and 1 tablespoon of the cream in a small microwave-safe bowl. Microwave on medium power until the white chocolate is very soft, 1½ to 2 minutes; then stir until smooth. Let the mixture cool to room temperature.

**9.** Place the mascarpone, honey, and lemon juice in a small bowl and whisk to mix. Add the white chocolate mixture and whisk to blend.

**10.** Place the remaining ¾ cup of cream in a small bowl and beat with a hand-held electric mixer on high speed until firm peaks form, 1½ minutes. Add the mascarpone mixture and beat to mix.

**11.** When the cake has cooled, unroll it. Spread the lemon curd over the top of the cake to within ½ inch of the edges. Then spread ½ cup of the White Chocolate–Honey Cream over the lemon curd. Sprinkle ¼ cup of the pistachios over the cream. Roll up the cake, using the towel to help. Place the rolled cake, seam side down, on a serving platter and frost it with the remaining White Chocolate–Honey Cream. Then garnish it with the remaining ¼ cup of pistachios. When ready to serve, cut the cake with a serrated knife.

NOTE: If you can find it, lavender honey is particularly good with this cake. It's available at specialty food stores.

# Gingerbread Roulade

## *with* Rum Cream and Candied Pecans

*Makes 1 cake; serves 2 or 3*

◆◆◆◆◆◆◆◆◆

This roulade takes the best quality of gingerbread—its flavor— and gives it a new delicate texture, one that I much prefer to the heavier original version. A cream-cheese filling, flavored with rum and lightened with whipped cream, brings out all the complex gingerbread flavors. A sprinkle of candied pecans elevates it to a five-star dessert.

As with Lemon Roulade on page 95, a loaf pan works perfectly for baking this thin gingerbread cake.

## FOR THE CANDIED PECANS:

1/2 cup finely chopped pecans

1 1/2 teaspoons light corn syrup

1 tablespoon granulated sugar

## FOR THE CAKE:

Unsalted butter, at room temperature, for greasing the pan

1 tablespoon cake flour, plus more for flouring the pan

1/8 teaspoon salt

1/2 teaspoon ground ginger

1/2 teaspoon ground cinnamon

1/8 teaspoon ground cloves

1/8 teaspoon ground nutmeg

Yolk of 1 large egg, at room temperature

4 tablespoons confectioners' sugar, sifted, plus more for rolling the cake

1 1/2 teaspoons molasses

Whites of 2 large eggs, at room temperature

1/8 teaspoon cream of tartar

## FOR THE RUM CREAM:

2 ounces (1/4 cup) cream cheese, at room temperature

1/4 cup confectioners' sugar

1 tablespoon spiced or dark rum

1/2 cup cold whipping (heavy) cream

## PANS REQUIRED:

1 standard loaf pan (9 x 5 inches)

1 baking sheet

**1. MAKE THE CANDIED PECANS:** Place a rack in the center of the oven and preheat the oven to 325°F. Line a rimmed baking sheet with aluminum foil.

**2.** Place the pecans and corn syrup in a small bowl and stir to mix. Add the sugar and toss to coat the pecans well. Working quickly so the sugar does not dissolve, spread the pecans on the baking sheet and bake until they are golden, 10 minutes. Remove the pecans from the oven and increase the oven temperature to 350°F. Stir to loosen the pecans from the foil; let them cool completely. Set the pecans aside. (The candied pecans can be made 1 day ahead; store them in an airtight container.)

**3. MAKE THE CAKE:** Grease the loaf pan and line the bottom with parchment paper. Grease the parchment and sprinkle it lightly with flour, tapping out the excess. Set the pan aside.

**4.** Sift the flour, salt, ginger, cinnamon, cloves, and nutmeg into a small bowl and whisk to blend well.

5. Place the egg yolk, 3 tablespoons of the confectioners' sugar, and the molasses in a small mixing bowl. Beat with a hand-held electric mixer on high speed until the mixture is pale in color, 1½ to 2 minutes. When you lift the beaters out of the bowl, a ribbon of the yolk mixture should drizzle back, leaving a "track" that sits on the top before it sinks in. Fold the flour mixture into the yolk mixture in two batches, mixing it gently but thoroughly.

6. Wash the mixer beaters well and dry them thoroughly. Place the egg whites and cream of tartar in a medium-size mixing bowl and beat on medium speed until foamy, 10 seconds. Sprinkle the remaining 1 tablespoon of confectioners' sugar over the egg whites and beat until stiff peaks form,

1 to 1½ minutes. Fold the beaten whites into the batter mixture in two batches, making sure no streaks of egg white remain.

7. Spoon the batter into the prepared loaf pan and smooth the top with a rubber spatula. Bake the cake until a toothpick inserted in the center comes out clean, 8 to 10 minutes.

8. Meanwhile, spread a clean kitchen towel on a work surface and sift confectioners' sugar over an area the size of the loaf pan. As soon as the cake has finished baking, invert the loaf pan over the sugared area of the towel. Remove the pan and peel off the parchment paper. Fold one end of the towel over a short end of the cake, and roll up the cake in the towel. Place the rolled cake, seam side down, on a wire rack to cool.

9. MAKE THE RUM CREAM: Place the cream cheese, confectioners' sugar, and rum in a small bowl and beat with a hand-held mixer on high speed until smooth and creamy, about 1 minute. Wash the mixer beaters well and dry them thoroughly. Place the cream in another small bowl and beat on high

speed until firm peaks form, 1 minute. Add the cream cheese mixture to the whipped cream and beat just until blended.

**10.** When the cake has cooled, unroll it. Spread ½ cup of the Rum Cream over the top of the cake. Roll up the cake, using the towel to help. Place the rolled cake, seam side down, on a serving platter and frost it with the remaining Rum Cream. Sprinkle the candied pecans over the cake. Refrigerate the cake for 1 hour before serving. When ready to serve, cut the cake with a serrated knife.

# Raspberry Almond Butter Cakes

*Makes 3 cakes; serves 3*

**◆◆◆◆◆◆◆◆**

This is one of my very favorite desserts—I have made the full-size version since I developed the recipe about fifteen years ago. The cakes are very richly flavored with both ground almonds and almond paste, which also give them a denser crumb than a regular butter cake.

They are brushed with raspberry syrup and jam and then covered in warm chocolate ganache and garnished with sliced almonds and drizzles of white chocolate. It's a pull-out-all-the-stops dessert.

Pulling out all the stops, however, takes time. This recipe

uses more ingredients and has more steps than most in this book. Luckily, these cakes can be made in steps and prepared ahead of time—even several days before you want to serve them. They just get more moist and rich and are completely worth the effort to make them.

**FOR THE CAKES:**

2½ tablespoons unsalted butter, at room temperature, plus more for greasing the baking rings

¼ cup plus 1 tablespoon cake flour, plus more for flouring the rings

¼ cup (2 ounces) sliced almonds

⅛ teaspoon baking powder

⅛ teaspoon salt

3 tablespoons plus 1 teaspoon sugar

2 packed tablespoons (1½ ounces) almond paste, crumbled (see Note), at room temperature

Yolks of 2 medium eggs

½ teaspoon pure vanilla extract

White of 1 medium egg

**FOR THE SYRUP:**

2 tablespoons sugar

2 tablespoons raspberry liqueur (such as Chambord)

**FOR THE GANACHE:**

¼ cup whipping (heavy) cream

1 tablespoon unsalted butter

1 tablespoon light corn syrup

3½ ounces semisweet or bittersweet chocolate, chopped

**FOR ASSEMBLING THE CAKES:**

2 tablespoons raspberry jam

Sliced almonds

Fresh raspberries

**PANS REQUIRED:**

Three 3 x 1½-inch baking rings

1 baking sheet

1. **MAKE THE CAKES:** Place a rack in the center of the oven and preheat the oven to 325°F.

**2.** Cut out three 5-inch squares of heavy-duty aluminum foil. Center a baking ring on top of each square; fold the edges of the foil up around the sides of each ring. Mold the foil well to the sides of the rings to create individual baking dishes with foil bottoms. Carefully grease and lightly flour the foil bottoms only. Place them on a baking sheet for easier handling, and set aside.

**3.** Finely grind the almonds in a food processor. Add the flour, baking powder, and salt to the processor and pulse to blend well.

**4.** Place the butter, 3 tablespoons of the sugar, and the almond paste in a medium-size mixing bowl and beat with a hand-held electric mixer on low speed until the mixture begins to hold together, about 1½ minutes (it will take a while to break up the almond paste). Increase the speed to medium and beat until smooth, about 2 minutes. Add the egg yolks and vanilla, and beat on high speed until the mixture is light in texture and color, about 1 minute.

**5.** Sift the flour mixture over the butter mixture and beat on low speed just until the dry ingredients are blended into the batter.

**6.** Wash the mixer beaters well and dry them thoroughly. Place the egg white and the remaining 1 teaspoon of the sugar in a small bowl, and beat on high speed until stiff peaks form when the mixer is turned off and the beaters are lifted, about 1 minute. Fold the beaten egg white into the batter in two batches.

**7.** Spoon the batter into the prepared baking rings, dividing it evenly among them. Bake the cakes until a toothpick inserted near the center of one comes out clean, 25 to 28 minutes.

**8.** Remove the baking sheet from the oven and transfer the cakes to a wire rack to cool, still in the baking rings, for 10 minutes. Then loosen the edges of the cakes with a sharp knife and remove the cakes from the baking rings. Place the cakes upright on the rack and let them cool.

**9.** MAKE THE SYRUP: Place the sugar and 2 tablespoons of water in a small microwave-safe bowl and microwave on high power for 30 seconds. Stir, and microwave on high power until the sugar is dissolved, 10 to 20 seconds longer. Let the syrup cool; then stir in the raspberry liqueur. (The syrup can be made up to 1 week ahead and refrigerated in a covered jar.)

**10.** MAKE THE GANACHE: Place the cream, butter, and corn syrup in a small saucepan over medium heat and bring to a boil. Remove the saucepan from the heat and add the chocolate, swirling the pan to immerse the chocolate in the hot cream. Stir until smooth; then pour the ganache into a small bowl. Refrigerate the ganache, covered, stirring it occasionally, until it is stiff enough to spread, about 1 hour. (The ganache can be refrigerated for up to 3 days.)

**11.** ASSEMBLE THE CAKES: Place the raspberry jam in a small microwave-safe bowl, and microwave on high power until it melts, about 20 seconds. Press it through a fine-mesh sieve into another bowl. Line a baking sheet with waxed paper and arrange the cakes on top, spacing them far enough apart that you can frost around the sides. Poke holes all over the cakes with a toothpick, and then brush

the syrup over the cakes. Continue brushing the cakes with the syrup until it is all used up. When the cakes have absorbed all the syrup, brush the strained jam all over them. Spread the ganache all over the cakes. Press sliced almonds around the sides of the cakes, and then refrigerate the cakes until the ganache is set, about 30 minutes. (The cakes can be assembled up to this point, wrapped in plastic wrap, and refrigerated for 2 days.) Once the ganache has set and you are ready to serve the cakes, garnish them with fresh raspberries.

NOTE: To crumble the almond paste, rub teaspoonfuls of it between your fingers to make pieces no larger than petite peas.

# FINISHING TOUCHES

You can omit the raspberries and sliced almonds and decorate the tops of the Raspberry Almond Butter Cakes (page 101), before the ganache has set, with candied violets or other edible flowers (see page 55), or with chocolate-dipped whole almonds. As the chocolate hardens around the garnish, it will hold it in place. Or you can make a garnish of white chocolate drizzle:

Place a few ounces of chopped high-quality white chocolate, such as Lindt, Baker's, or Ghirardelli, in a small microwave-safe bowl and microwave on high power until it is glossy, 30 to 60 seconds. Stir the white chocolate until it is smooth. Let it cool slightly, then scrape it into a heavy-duty plastic bag and seal the bag. Using scissors, snip off a tiny corner of the bag to make an instant piping bag.

Line a baking sheet with waxed paper. Drizzle the melted white chocolate in a decorative pattern covering a 2-inch square area; the white chocolate should be about $1/16$ inch thick. Repeat, making 3 drizzle garnishes in all (this will use up about half of the white chocolate). Place the baking sheet in the refrigerator until the white chocolate has almost hardened, 3 to 5 minutes. Then remove the baking sheet from the refrigerator and drizzle a second layer of white chocolate on top of the first ones. Refrigerate until the garnishes are solid, about 20 minutes.

Carefully peel the waxed paper off each garnish and discard it. Refrigerate the garnishes between layers of waxed paper until you are ready to use them.

When ready to use, stand the garnishes on edge in the ganache before it sets. Then refrigerate the cakes until ready to serve. The garnished cakes will keep 2 days in the refrigerator.

# Sherry-Soaked Almond Cakes

*Makes 3 cakes; serves 3*

◆◆◆◆◆◆◆◆◆

**Almond cakes are** so good when they are soaked in a sweet sherry syrup. Serve these with lightly sweetened whipped cream and blackberries or strawberries.

½ cup cream sherry
3 tablespoons sugar
1 tablespoon unsalted butter
Drop of pure almond extract
Raspberry Almond Butter Cakes
   (page 101), baked and cooled

**1.** Combine the sherry, sugar, and butter in a small saucepan over medium heat. Bring to a boil, stirring constantly until the sugar dissolves. Reduce the heat to medium-low and let the mixture simmer until it is reduced to ¼ cup, 15 to 20 minutes. Remove from the heat and stir in the almond extract.

**2.** Poke holes all over the cakes with a toothpick and brush the syrup over the cakes. Continue brushing the cakes with the syrup until it is all used up. Place the cakes on plates and let them stand for 1 hour before serving.

# Rum Cakes

*Makes 4 cakes; serves 4*
◆◆◆◆◆◆◆◆◆

**My mother made** glorious rum cakes, crusted with almonds and wet with sugar syrup that was laced with a substantial amount of rum, but today I usually prefer something lighter and less filling after a meal. These are not as heavy as her tipsy cake—they are light and moist, with just the right amount of rum flavor and a delicate almond crust.

**Unsalted butter, at room temperature, for greasing the baking rings**

**All-purpose flour, for flouring the rings**

**4 teaspoons sliced almonds**

**1 recipe Mini Génoises batter (page 78), prepared through Step 5**

**2 tablespoons sugar**

**1 tablespoon dark rum**

**PANS REQUIRED:**
**4 baking rings (3 x ½-inch)**
**1 baking sheet**

**1.** Place a rack in the center of the oven and preheat the oven to 350°F.

**2.** Cut out four 5-inch squares of heavy-duty aluminum foil. Center a baking ring on top of each square; form the edges of the foil up around the sides of each ring. Mold the foil well to the sides of the rings to create individual baking dishes with foil bottoms. Carefully grease and lightly flour the foil bottoms only. Place the rings on a baking sheet for easier handling.

**3.** Sprinkle 1 teaspoon of the sliced almonds in the bottom of each prepared baking ring. Then spoon the batter into the rings, dividing it evenly among them. Bake the cakes until they have pulled away from the sides of the baking rings and the centers are springy when lightly touched with a finger, about 15 minutes.

4. Meanwhile, combine the sugar with 1 tablespoon water in a small microwave-safe bowl. Microwave on high power for 45 seconds; then stir until the sugar dissolves. Stir in the rum.

5. Remove the baking sheet from the oven and let the cakes, still in the baking rings, cool on a wire rack for 10 minutes. Then poke 4 to 6 holes in each cake with a thin skewer, penetrating to the bottom of the cake. Brush the rum syrup over the cake tops, dividing it evenly among them. Let the cakes cool completely in the baking rings. (The cakes can be wrapped individually in plastic wrap and refrigerated for up to 2 days. Bring to room temperature before unmolding.) Then carefully remove cakes from the rings and set them upright on serving plates.

# Baklava

*Makes 8 small pieces; serves 2 or 3*
◆◆◆◆◆◆◆◆◆

**Baklava, perhaps the** best-known Greek sweet, is festive enough to make any day a holiday. The basic ingredients—phyllo, ground nuts, honey—are standard in most recipes, but a cook can create his or her own special version by flavoring the syrup that is poured over the pastry. I prefer a stronger orange flavor than is typical, so I add a bit of orange extract, along with a drop of almond extract for balance, when the syrup has finished boiling.

In order for the baklava to soak up the syrup fully, either the baklava has to be hot and the syrup cold or vice versa. Here we do the former.

**FOR THE SYRUP:**

⅓ cup sugar

⅓ cup honey

1 cinnamon stick (3 inches)

½ teaspoon pure vanilla extract

⅛ teaspoon pure orange extract (see Note)

Drop of pure almond extract

**FOR THE PASTRY:**

Unsalted butter, at room temperature, for greasing the pan

¼ cup plus 2 tablespoons chopped almonds

¼ cup plus 2 tablespoons chopped walnuts

2 tablespoons sugar

¼ teaspoon ground cinnamon

¼ teaspoon ground allspice

7 sheets frozen phyllo dough, thawed

4 tablespoons (½ stick) unsalted butter, melted

**PAN REQUIRED:**

1 small standard loaf pan (8 x 4 inches)

1. **MAKE THE SYRUP:** Place the sugar, honey, cinnamon stick, and 1/3 cup of water in a small saucepan, and stir to mix. Bring the mixture to a boil over medium-high heat, stirring constantly until the sugar melts. Then boil for 1 minute without stirring. Remove the pan from the heat and let the syrup stand at room temperature until it is cool. Stir in the vanilla, orange extract, and almond extract, and pour the syrup into a glass jar or measuring cup. Cover and refrigerate the syrup until it is cold, 1 1/2 to 2 hours.

2. **MAKE THE PASTRY:** Place a rack in the center of the oven and preheat the oven to 325°F. Line the loaf pan with aluminum foil and grease the foil.

3. Place the almonds, walnuts, sugar, cinnamon, and allspice in a small bowl, and whisk to blend.

4. Stack the sheets of phyllo on a work surface and cut them in half crosswise, making 14 half-sheets. Stack the two halves together. Using a ruler and a sharp knife, trim the stack to form an 8-inch square. Keep the phyllo covered with a piece of plastic wrap and then a clean kitchen towel to prevent it from drying out as you work.

5. Fold 1 sheet of phyllo in half to form an 8 x 4-inch rectangle. Place the folded sheet in the prepared loaf pan and brush it lightly with melted butter. Repeat the folding with 4 more sheets, brushing the top of each folded sheet with butter. Sprinkle half of the nut mixture over the top sheet. Add another folded sheet of phyllo and brush it with butter; repeat with 3 more folded sheets, brushing the top of each folded sheet with butter. Sprinkle the remaining nut mixture over this top sheet. Add 5 more folded sheets, brushing the top of each one with butter.

6. Using a sharp knife, make 3 diagonal cuts across the width of the phyllo, cutting through just the top layers and spacing the cuts evenly. Make 1 cut down the length of the phyllo, resulting in diamond pieces in the center and 4 odd-shaped pieces at the ends. Bake the baklava until it is golden brown, about 30 minutes.

7. Strain the cold syrup, and spoon it evenly over the hot baklava. Using a sharp knife, deepen the earlier cut

lines to reach all the way through the layers. Cover the baklava and let it stand at room temperature for 4 hours for the syrup to soak through the layers.

**8.** To serve, use the foil to help you lift the baklava from the loaf pan and place it on a work surface. Using a thin metal spatula, lift the pieces onto a serving platter or individual plates.

Pour the accumulated syrup over the pieces of baklava. (The baklava can be made 2 days in advance. Bring it to room temperature, which takes about 2 hours; then remove it from the pan and serve it.)

**NOTE:** If you don't have orange extract, add four 2 x ½-inch strips of orange zest to the syrup along with the cinnamon stick.

# CHAPTER 3

# Pies *and* Tarts

**The recipes in** this chapter have put pies back into my life. For a long time I didn't make pie for dessert because I knew that I wouldn't be able to resist nibbling the crust off the leftovers. But now I make enough for two servings and when it's gone, it's gone.

It really isn't necessary to buy any cute little 3- or 4-inch pie plates to bake the pies. Just do what I do—improvise. A few of the fruit pies bake in a crust without a pan; the crust is folded up to encase the fruit loosely in a free-form manner. When a pie plate is needed, deep-dish single servings are baked in jumbo muffin cups or deep 4-inch tart pans. Other recipes call for shallow 4½-inch tart pans.

For me, a pie is not a pie unless the pastry is homemade. So many cooks are fearful of failure on the flakiness front that they resort to refrigerated or frozen pie crusts. Small-Batch pie crusts are not daunting to make. In fact, cutting the butter into the flour for these small pies takes less time than for larger ones, so the butter stays chilled, thereby ensuring a flakier baked pastry.

There are three basic pie crust recipes here that are matched to the fillings: Basic Pastry is a tender, savory foil for the sweet fruit filling in Apple Crumble Pies and New-Fashioned Cherry Pies, as well as both the Chocolate Cream Meringue Pies and the Bake Sale Lemon Meringue Pies. Basic Sweet

Pastry has an egg yolk added to make the crust a bit sturdier, plus some sugar for tenderness and taste. It is a perfect crust for the Pear Almond Custard Tarts, which are not quite as sweet as the meringue pies. In contrast, the rich filling in the Warm Chocolate Tarts is nicely complemented by the buttery, tender texture of Rich Sweet Pastry. That cookie-like texture is also perfectly suited to the Blueberry Lattice Tarts, where the thin layer of intense blueberry filling needs a rich crust.

There is a pie in here for all tastes and occasions. The jewel colors and vibrant flavors of the fresh fruit in the Apricot and Blackberry Crostatas make it perfectly suited for an alfresco early summer meal. Celebrate a Kentucky Derby afternoon with Triple Crown Tarts—pecan pies that have bourbon

## THE BIG CHILL

Chilling the uncooked, rolled-out pie crust until it is firm ensures that it will hold its shape when baking. An hour in the refrigerator is ideal, however, if your filling is made and you need to bake the crust sooner, chill it, fitted in its pan, in the freezer for about fifteen minutes. Bake it cold, right from the fridge or freezer.

and chocolate in them. Make the Banana Cream Pies with Chocolate Chip Pastry when you really need a treat, and save the Pecan Meringue Tarts with Caramel Latte Mousse for a special dinner. I've tried to include versions of everyone's favorite pies, with a few surprises added.

# Apple Crumble Pies

*Makes 2 pies; serves 2*
◆◆◆◆◆◆◆◆◆

**These delicious** apple pies are thickly layered with sweetened tart apples and topped with a spiced walnut crumb mixture. Serve them warm from the oven with a scoop of ice cream, or sprinkle the warm pies with shavings of sharp Cheddar cheese. I also like them drizzled with warm caramel sauce. You can bake them in 4-inch tart pans or jumbo muffin cups with equal success.

**2 partially baked Basic Pastry shells (page 159), baked in 4 x 1⅜-inch tart pans with removable bottoms, or in 2 jumbo muffin cups (¾-cup capacity), lined with aluminum foil, still in the pans**

FOR THE CRUMB MIXTURE:

**¼ cup walnut halves**

**2 tablespoons packed light brown sugar**

**1 tablespoon all-purpose flour**

**¼ teaspoon ground cinnamon**

**Pinch of salt**

**1 tablespoon cold unsalted butter, cut into small pieces**

FOR THE FILLING:

**1 teaspoon fresh lemon juice**

**1½ medium-size tart apples, preferably Granny Smith**

**2 tablespoons unsalted butter**

**2 tablespoons sugar**

**¼ teaspoon ground cinnamon**

**2 tablespoons apple cider or juice**
**1 teaspoon cornstarch**
**Pinch of salt**

PAN REQUIRED:
**1 baking sheet, if using tart pans**

1. Place a rack in the center of the oven and preheat the oven to 375°F. Place the tart pans on a baking sheet for easier handling, and set it aside.

2. MAKE THE CRUMB TOPPING: Place the walnuts, brown sugar, flour, cinnamon, salt, and butter in a food processor, and process until the walnuts are chopped. Transfer the mixture to a bowl and refrigerate until you are ready to bake the pie. (The crumb topping can be made 1 day ahead; cover and refrigerate.)

3. MAKE THE FILLING: Pour the lemon juice into a medium-size mixing bowl and set it aside.

4. Peel the apples, and cut the whole apple in half. Remove the cores and place the halves, cut side down, on a cutting board. Cut each half in half lengthwise and then cut the wedges crosswise into 1/2-inch-thick slices. Add the apples to the lemon juice and toss well to coat the slices with the juice.

5. Melt the butter in a medium-size skillet over medium-high heat. Stir in the sugar and cinnamon. Add the apples and sauté until they are crisp-tender, about 5 minutes.

6. Meanwhile, place the cider, cornstarch, and salt in a small bowl and whisk until smooth.

7. Add the cornstarch mixture to the apples and cook, stirring constantly, until the mixture boils and thickens, about 1 minute. Transfer the apples to a small bowl and let them cool completely.

8. Pour the apple filling into the pastry shells, dividing it evenly between them, and sprinkle with the crumb topping. Bake until the topping is golden brown and the filling is hot, 20 to 22 minutes. Let cool slightly, then unmold and serve.

# Apple Walnut Crostatas

*Makes 2 tarts; serves 2*

◆◆◆◆◆◆◆◆◆

**To make one** of these rustic tarts, all you do is roll out the dough, layer on the all-American apple filling, and pleat the edges up around the fruit, leaving part of the filling exposed. The crust is not prebaked, yet it remains flaky and crisp, with walnuts under the juicy cinnamon-apple filling. These are anytime treats for when you just get a craving for pie.

**FOR THE PASTRY:**
Yolk of 1 large egg
⅓ cup walnuts
½ cup all-purpose flour
2 teaspoons granulated sugar
Pinch of salt
3 tablespoons cold unsalted butter,
   cut into small pieces
1 teaspoon ice water, or more as
   needed

**FOR FILLING AND SERVING:**
1½ large apples, preferably
   Golden Delicious or Braeburn
1 teaspoon fresh lemon juice
2 tablespoons firmly packed light
   brown sugar
¼ teaspoon all-purpose flour
¼ teaspoon ground cinnamon
Pinch of salt
1 teaspoon milk
½ teaspoon granulated sugar
Vanilla ice cream, for serving

**PAN REQUIRED:**
1 baking sheet

**1. MAKE THE PASTRY:** Put the egg yolk in a small bowl and beat it lightly with a fork. Measure out 1 teaspoon of the yolk and set it aside for preparing the pastry. Reserve the remaining yolk for brushing on the outside of the pastry before baking.

**2.** Place the walnuts in a food processor and pulse until most pieces are coarsely ground, 20 to 25 pulses. Transfer the walnuts to a small bowl.

**3.** Place the flour, sugar, and salt in the food processor and pulse to blend, 3 or 4 pulses. Sprinkle the butter pieces evenly over the flour mixture and pulse until the lumps are no larger than small peas, about 15 pulses. Return the walnuts to the food processor, and sprinkle the 1 teaspoon of egg yolk and 1 teaspoon of the ice water over the flour mixture. Process just until small, moist clumps of dough begin to form, about 8 seconds, adding more water by teaspoonfuls if the dough is dry.

**4.** Tear off 2 sheets of waxed paper and gather the dough onto one of the sheets. Form the dough into a mass and divide it in half. Form each half

## WHAT EXACTLY IS A CROSTATA?

A crostata is a rustic Italian dessert—a simple fruit tart that was probably first created in countryside kitchens. The tart is free-form, made with a sweet pastry that is sturdy enough to be folded over the fruit. The look of a crostata is relaxed and casual, making it an enticing alfresco summertime dessert.

I don't always have the patience to make beautiful trims around the edges of pies, so this type of tart is just what I like to make—in large *and* miniature sizes. You don't prebake the crust—just roll out the dough, lay the fruit on it, and then fold in the edges of the crust toward the center and over the fruit. For an attractive presentation, leave an uncovered space in the middle so you can see the fruit.

into a disk and wrap them individually in the pieces of waxed paper. Refrigerate until chilled, 30 minutes.

**5.** Place a rack in the center of the oven and preheat the oven to 400°F. Line a baking sheet with parchment paper.

**6.** Roll out each disk of dough on a lightly floured surface to form a 6-inch round. Lay the rounds on the prepared baking sheet and refrigerate them while you prepare the filling.

**7. MAKE THE FILLING:** Peel and halve the apples and remove the cores. Cut each half into thirds lengthwise, then cut the wedges crosswise into thin slices. Place the lemon juice in a medium-size bowl, add the apples, and toss to mix. Add the brown sugar, flour, cinnamon, and salt, and toss to coat the apples with the mixture. Let the mixture stand until juices form, about 15 minutes.

**8.** Spoon the apple mixture onto the center of the pastry rounds, dividing it evenly between them and leaving a 1-inch border all around. Fold the borders up over the filling and pleat the edges, pinching them to seal any cracks. (The center of the apples will remain uncovered by the pastry.)

**9.** Place the egg yolk reserved in Step 1 and the milk in a small bowl, and whisk to blend. Brush the beaten egg mixture over the pastry, and then sprinkle the $\frac{1}{2}$ teaspoon sugar over the pastry (not on the open center). Bake until the pastry is golden brown and the apple mixture is bubbling, about 25 minutes. Remove the baking sheet from the oven and slide the tarts on the parchment to a wire rack. Let the tarts cool and serve warm or at room temperature, with ice cream.

# Apricot and Blackberry Crostatas

*Makes 2 tarts; serves 2*
◆◆◆◆◆◆◆◆◆

**The fruit in** these jewel-colored tarts makes a lot of juice when baked, so I've added a bit of cornmeal to the crust to keep it firm and crisp. The tart crust is formed around the fruit, not baked in tart pans, which gives it an informal look—perfect for summer.

**FOR THE PASTRY:**

1/3 cup all-purpose flour

1 tablespoon plus 1 teaspoon yellow cornmeal

1 teaspoon sugar

1/4 teaspoon salt

2 1/2 tablespoons cold unsalted butter, cut into small pieces

1 tablespoon plain whole-milk yogurt

1 tablespoon plus 2 teaspoons ice water, or more as needed

**FOR THE FILLING:**

2 tablespoons sugar

1 1/4 teaspoons cornstarch

2 fresh apricots, peeled, halved, pitted, and sliced

1/2 cup fresh blackberries or drained thawed frozen blackberries

1 tablespoon Cointreau, brandy, or orange juice

1 medium egg, lightly beaten

1 to 2 tablespoons coarse sugar crystals or granulated sugar

3 tablespoons melted and sieved apricot or peach preserves

**PAN REQUIRED:**

1 baking sheet

1. **MAKE THE PASTRY:** Combine the flour, cornmeal, sugar, and salt in a food processor and process until blended, about 3 seconds. Sprinkle the butter pieces over the mixture and pulse about 10 times, until the butter is reduced to pea-size pieces.

2. Place the yogurt and ice water in a small bowl and stir to blend. Add the yogurt mixture to the ingredients in the processor and pulse until the dough just comes together in moist clumps; if the dough is dry, add more ice water by teaspoonfuls. Gather the dough on a piece of plastic wrap, and

divide it in half. Form each half into a 1-inch-thick disk and wrap it separately in plastic wrap. Refrigerate for at least 1 hour, or up to 24 hours.

3. Place a 14-inch-long piece of parchment paper on a cutting board, and roll out each portion of the dough to form a 9- to 10-inch round. Trim the edges of the rounds as necessary to make them even. Slide a rimless baking sheet under the parchment, and cover the baking sheet with the pastry rounds with plastic wrap and place in the refrigerator for 30 minutes.

4. **MAKE THE FILLING:** Place the sugar and cornstarch in a medium-size mixing bowl and whisk to blend. Mix in the apricots, blackberries, and Cointreau. Let the mixture stand at room temperature, stirring it occasionally, until the juices release, 30 minutes.

5. Place a rack in the center of the oven and preheat the oven to 375°F.

6. Remove the baking sheet from the refrigerator. If the dough is too firm to fold, let it stand for a few minutes to soften. Spoon the fruit and juices onto

## CROSTATA FRUIT COMBOS

Once you've seen how easy it is to make a free-form crust to show off fresh fruit, you'll want to try these variations.

**CINNAMON PEACH AND BLUEBERRY CROSTATAS** Substitute ½ cup of blueberries for the blackberries. Substitute 1 large peach, peeled and pitted, for the apricots. Cut the peach into thin slices, then cut the slices in half. Add ⅛ teaspoon of ground cinnamon to the sugar and cornstarch mixture before you toss it with the fruit.

**NECTARINE RASPBERRY CROSTATAS** Substitute ½ cup of raspberries for the blackberries. Substitute 2 nectarines, peeled and pitted, for the apricots. Cut the nectarines into thin slices, then cut the slices in half.

the center of the pastry rounds, dividing the filling evenly between them and leaving a 1-inch border all around. Brush the borders with half of the beaten egg. Then fold the borders up over the filling and pleat the edges, pinching them to seal any cracks. (The center of the fruit will remain uncovered by the pastry.) Brush the outside of the folded borders with some of the remaining beaten egg, and sprinkle them with the coarse sugar.

7. Place the baking sheet in the oven, and bake until the crusts are golden brown and the fruit filling is bubbling, 30 to 35 minutes.

8. Remove the baking sheet from the oven and slide a large metal spatula under each tart to loosen it from the parchment. Brush the exposed fruit with the preserves and slide the tarts onto a wire rack to cool. Serve warm or at room temperature. (The tarts can be prepared up to 1 day ahead. Let them cool completely, then cover and refrigerate. Before serving, reheat them in a preheated 350°F oven for 10 minutes and serve.)

# New-Fashioned Cherry Pies

*Makes 2 pies; serves 2*
◆◆◆◆◆◆◆◆◆

**This is an** easy way to make a delicious favorite, a cherry pie filled with old-fashioned flavor. Pastry circles are piled with fresh cherry filling, then the edges are folded up around the fruit, revealing a bit of the sweet-tart cherry filling at the center. The resulting pies are a bit rustic, but still make an elegant dessert. I serve them every year to celebrate fresh cherry season, which is always too short for me.

1 recipe Basic Pastry dough
    (page 159), prepared through
    Step 2

1¹⁄₂ cups pitted fresh cherries, or
    1 bag (10 ounces) frozen pitted
    cherries, thawed and drained
3 tablespoons sugar, plus more for
    sprinkling on the tarts
2 tablespoons fresh tangerine,
    blood orange, or orange juice
2 teaspoons quick-cooking tapioca
¹⁄₈ teaspoon salt
¹⁄₄ teaspoon ground cinnamon
¹⁄₂ teaspoon pure vanilla extract
Vanilla ice cream, for serving

PAN REQUIRED:
1 baking sheet

1. Line the baking sheet with parchment paper and set it aside.

2. Prepare the pastry dough as described. When the disks of dough

have chilled for 30 minutes, roll each one out on a lightly floured surface to form a 6-inch round. Lay the rounds on the prepared baking sheet and place in the freezer while you prepare the filling, 15 minutes.

**3.** Place the cherries in a medium-size saucepan and add 1 tablespoon of water. (If you are using thawed frozen cherries, drain them in a sieve or colander, reserving 1 tablespoon of the cherry juice. Place the drained cherries and the reserved juice in the saucepan.) Stir in the sugar, tangerine juice, tapioca, salt, and cinnamon. Cook over medium-high heat, stirring constantly, until the mixture is thick and bubbling, about 5 minutes. Remove the saucepan from the heat. Stir in the vanilla, and let the mixture cool completely.

**4.** Place a rack in the center of the oven and preheat the oven to 400°F.

**5.** Remove the dough from the freezer and, if it is too firm to fold, let it stand for a few minutes at room temperature to soften. Spoon the cherries and sauce onto the center of the pastry rounds, dividing the filling evenly between

them and leaving a 1-inch border all around. Then fold up the borders of the pastry edges completely to enclose the cherry mixture, pleating the edges over the fruit. Do not twist the edges together; they will separate during baking and leave the cherry mixture uncovered. Brush the pastry with water and sprinkle about 1 teaspoon sugar over each tart. Bake until the pastry is golden brown, about 35 minutes.

**6.** Remove the baking sheet from the oven and transfer it to a wire rack. Let the tarts cool on the baking sheet. Remove the tarts from the baking sheet and serve warm or at room temperature, with vanilla ice cream.

# Peach Pies

## *with* Toffee Streusel

*Makes 2 pies; serves 2*

◆◆◆◆◆◆◆◆◆

## To this Southerner,

nothing beats a summer peach dessert. We live just up the road from Durbin Farms in Clanton, Alabama, where the peaches grow as juicy sweet as they are said to do in Georgia. The anticipation of how they will taste and what we will cook with them each year fills our heads the entire drive to the farm stand. Other than creamy peach ice cream, these little tarts are my favorites. Their sweet juices are subtly thickened with pearly tapioca, a gentle starch. The toffee streusel topping smartly sets off the soft ripe peaches.

**2 partially baked Basic Pastry shells (page 159), baked in 4 x 1⅜-inch tart pans with removable bottoms or in a jumbo muffin pan (¾-cup capacity), still in the pans**

FOR THE FILLING:

**1 teaspoon fresh lemon juice**

**3 medium-size fresh peaches, peeled, pitted, and diced, or 1½ cups frozen sliced peaches, thawed and diced**

**1½ tablespoons sugar**

**2 teaspoons quick-cooking tapioca**

FOR THE TOPPING:

**2 tablespoons all-purpose flour**

**1½ tablespoons packed light brown sugar**

**Pinch of salt**

**1 tablespoon cold unsalted butter, cut into pieces**

3 tablespoons English toffee bits (such as Skor) or almond toffee bits (such as Heath)

Ice cream, for serving

PAN REQUIRED:

1 baking sheet, if using tart pans

1. Place a rack in the center of the oven and preheat the oven to 350°F. If you used tart pans, place them on a baking sheet for easier handling and set it aide. If you used a muffin pan, simply set it aside.

2. MAKE THE FILLING: Place the lemon juice in a small bowl, add the peaches, and toss to mix. (If using frozen peaches, just place them in a bowl.) Place the sugar and tapioca in a small bowl and stir to mix. Then add the tapioca mixture to the peaches and stir to mix well. Spoon the peach filling into the tart shells, dividing it evenly between them, and refrigerate them while you prepare the topping.

3. MAKE THE TOPPING: Place the flour, brown sugar, and salt in a small bowl, and whisk to mix. Add the butter pieces and rub the mixture with your fingertips, or cut the butter in with a pastry blender, until the topping is blended and crumbly. Stir in the toffee bits. Spoon the topping evenly over the peach filling. If you used a muffin pan, fill the empty cups halfway with water to prevent them from scorching.

4. Bake until the topping is golden brown and the filling is bubbling, 30 to 40 minutes. Remove the baking sheet or muffin pan from the oven. Transfer the tarts, or the muffin pan, to a wire rack and allow to cool for at least 20 minutes. Then remove the pies from the tart pans. If you used a muffin pan, carefully pour the water out of the empty muffin cups; then run a knife around the edges and tip the pan to nudge them out. Serve the pies warm, with ice cream if desired.

# MATCHING PIES AND ICE CREAM

Although vanilla is still the leading favorite according to the International Ice Cream Association, there are so many unruly names and nutty combinations of flavors that I thought it would be nice to know which ice creams, frozen yogurts, and sorbets work for the pies in this chapter.

There is an amazing variety of flavors to choose from out there! And a lot of the wildest flavors are made only in pint size—perfect for the portions in this book. My suggestions are for flavors you should be able to find in larger grocery stores. But don't forget you can get take-home pints packed for you at "scoop shops," so look for complementary ice cream flavors there, too.

**APPLE CRUMBLE PIES (page 114):**
Toffee bar, apple, or butter pecan ice cream

Vanilla, toffee, or caramel-praline frozen yogurt

**APRICOT AND BLACKBERRY CROSTATAS (page 119):**
Orange, passion fruit, boysenberry, lemon, blueberry, or raspberry, or rainbow sherbet
Mango or blueberry ice cream

**CINNAMON PEACH AND BLUEBERRY CROSTATAS (page 121):**
Blueberry, mango, or praline ice cream
Lemon sorbet
Peach frozen yogurt

**NECTARINE RASPBERRY CROSTATAS (page 121):**
Vanilla anything or raspberry sorbet, ice cream, or frozen yogurt, plain, swirled, or with chocolate

**NEW-FASHIONED CHERRY PIES (page 122):**
Cherry vanilla, Cherry Garcia (Ben & Jerry's), or

vanilla ice cream (stick with a best-quality brand)

**PEACH PIES WITH TOFFEE STREUSEL (page 124):**
You can't go wrong with any of the vanillas here, either.
Also try caramel-pecan, macadamia nut, or toffee bar
Peach, caramel-praline, or toffee frozen yogurt
Peach sorbet

**RHUBARB PIES WITH ALMOND CRUMBLE (page 128):**
Strawberry ice cream
Strawberry frozen yogurt

**BANANA CREAM PIES WITH CHOCOLATE CHIP PASTRY (page 135):**
Pecan or banana ice cream or frozen yogurt

**BLUEBERRY LATTICE TARTS (page 140):**
Blueberry, cherry vanilla, or crème brûlée ice cream
Raspberry and vanilla frozen yogurt

**APRICOT LATTICE TARTS (page 142):**
Crème brûlée, vanilla, macadamia nut, or pecan ice cream
Peach or lemon sorbet
Lemon frozen yogurt

**PLUM TARTS WITH OATMEAL COOKIE CRUST (page 146):**
Dulce de Leche (Häagen-Dazs), vanilla, butter pecan, orange swirl, apple, or cookie chunk ice cream

**PEAR ALMOND CUSTARD TARTS (page 148):**
Pistachio or pistachio almond ice cream
Coconut sorbet

**TRIPLE CROWN TARTS (page 154):**
Vanilla or any combination of pecan and caramel ice cream

# Rhubarb Pies

## *with* Almond Crumble

*Makes 2 pies; serves 2*

◆◆◆◆◆◆◆◆◆

**Today it's easy** to find rhubarb during its springtime season, but during the Depression it was hard to get in mid-south Florida, where my grandparents lived. Because it was one of my grandfather's favorite things, my grandmother would go straight home and make him a pie whenever she found it in the market.

Rhubarb becomes quite soft and juicy when it is baked, so the thick almond crumble plays an important role by soaking up the sweet-tart juices. Part of the attraction of this dessert is that each layer has a distinct texture. The thick layer of crumb topping provides two layers, because the bottom remains soft and moist while the top becomes crunchy and sweet.

**2 partially baked Rich Sweet Pastry shells (page 165), baked in 4 x 1⅜-inch tart pans with removable bottoms or in a jumbo muffin pan (¾-cup capacity), still in the pans**

**FOR THE FILLING:**
**¼ cup granulated sugar**
**1 tablespoon quick-cooking tapioca**
**1 cup finely diced (¼-inch), trimmed fresh rhubarb (about 4 medium stalks) or thawed frozen rhubarb**
**2 teaspoons unsalted butter, cut into bits**

**FOR THE CRUMBLE:**
**3 tablespoons all-purpose flour**
**2 tablespoons packed almond paste**

1 tablespoon packed light brown
   sugar
1 tablespoon cold unsalted butter,
   cut into ½-inch pieces
2 tablespoons sliced almonds

**PAN REQUIRED:**
1 baking sheet, if using tart pans

1. Place a rack in the middle of the oven and preheat the oven to 325°F. If you are using tart pans, place them on a baking sheet for easier handling and set it aside. If you use a muffin pan, simply set it aside.

2. **MAKE THE FILLING:** Place the sugar, tapioca, rhubarb, and butter in a medium-size bowl and stir well. Let the mixture stand, stirring it occasionally, until the juices are released, 15 minutes.

3. **MAKE THE CRUMBLE TOPPING:** Place the flour, almond paste, and brown sugar in a food processor and process until the almond paste is finely ground, 10 to 20 seconds. Sprinkle the butter pieces over the flour mixture and process until coarse crumbs form, about 5 seconds. Transfer the crumble to a small bowl and use a fork to mix in the almonds.

4. Spoon the rhubarb mixture into the pastry shells, dividing it evenly between them. Sprinkle the crumble topping evenly over the rhubarb. If you are using a muffin pan, fill the empty muffin cups halfway with water to prevent them from scorching. Bake until the filling is bubbling and the topping is golden brown, 30 to 35 minutes.

5. Remove the baking sheet or muffin pan from the oven. Transfer the tarts, or the muffin pan, to a wire rack and allow to cool. Then remove the pies from the tart pans. If you used a muffin pan, carefully pour the water out of the empty muffin cups and tip the pies out of the cups. Serve warm or at room temperature.

# Bake Sale Lemon Meringue Pies

*Makes 2 pies; serves 2*

◆◆◆◆◆◆◆◆◆

**In my area** of the country, we save our most special cake and pie recipes to make for school and charity bake sales. This smaller version of my favorite and best lemon meringue pie has just the right balance of sweet and tart, with a high crown of fluffy meringue. It needs to be eaten the day it is baked, because if it's

kept any longer, the meringue will absorb moisture from the filling—or from the air—and turn soggy.

**2 partially baked Basic Pastry shells (page 159), baked in 4 x 1⅜-inch tart pans with removable bottoms, still in the pans**

**FOR THE FILLING:**

**⅓ cup sugar**

**2 tablespoons plus 1 teaspoon cake flour**

**Pinch of salt**

**2 tablespoons plus 1 teaspoon fresh lemon juice**

**Yolk of 1 large egg**

**1 tablespoon unsalted butter, cut into small pieces**

**¼ teaspoon pure vanilla extract**

**FOR THE MERINGUE:**

**Whites of 2 large eggs, at room temperature**

**1/8 teaspoon cream of tartar**

**1/4 teaspoon pure vanilla extract**

**Pinch of salt**

**1 1/2 tablespoons sugar**

**PAN REQUIRED:**

**1 baking sheet**

**1.** Place a rack in the center of the oven and preheat the oven to 375°F. Put the tart pans on a baking sheet for easier handling and set it aside.

**2. MAKE THE FILLING:** Place the sugar, flour, and salt in a small sauce pan and whisk to blend well. Whisk in 1/3 cup of water, the lemon juice, and the egg yolk. Place the saucepan over medium heat and cook, whisking constantly, until the mixture is bubbling and thick, about 5 minutes. Remove the saucepan from the heat and add the butter pieces and vanilla; whisk until the butter melts and the mixture is smooth.

**3. FOR THE MERINGUE:** The filling needs to be as hot as possible when you spread the meringue on top, so prepare the meringue immediately. Place the egg whites in a medium-size mixing bowl and beat with a hand-held electric mixer on medium speed until foamy. Add the cream of tartar, vanilla, and salt, and increase the mixer speed to high. Beat until soft peaks form, 10 seconds. With the mixer running on high speed, slowly pour in the sugar. Beat until stiff peaks form, 30 seconds more.

**4.** Pour the filling into the pie crusts, dividing it evenly between them. Mound the meringue over the filling in high peaks, making sure to seal the meringue to the edges of the tart pans. Bake until the meringue is golden brown, 10 minutes.

**5.** Remove the baking sheet from the oven and transfer the tart pans to a wire rack. Let the pies cool completely, away from drafts. Remove the pies from the tart pans before serving.

# Chocolate Cream Meringue Pies

*Makes 2 pies; serves 2*
◆◆◆◆◆◆◆◆◆

**Now *this* is** a chocolate cream pie: pudding-like, smooth, chocolatey custard topped with tender, fluffy meringue that has a lightly toasted marshmallow flavor on its very top. As with the Bake Sale Lemon Meringue Pies, serve it the day it is baked.

**2 partially baked Basic Pastry shells (page 159), baked in 4 x 1⅜-inch tart pans with removable bottoms, still in the pans**

**FOR THE FILLING:**

⅓ **cup sugar**

**1 tablespoon plus 2 teaspoons cake flour**

**1 tablespoon unsweetened cocoa powder**

**Pinch of salt**

⅓ **cup whole milk**

**Yolk of 1 large egg**

**1 ounce bittersweet or semisweet chocolate, finely chopped**

**1 tablespoon unsalted butter, cut into small pieces**

¼ **teaspoon pure vanilla extract**

## Don't Weep for Me, Meringue

When a meringue "weeps," a syrup forms between the filling and the meringue, and it runs out when you tilt the pie or cut into it. That syrup forms because the meringue was not spread on filling that was still hot, so the bottom of the meringue never heated up during the baking. The meringue is undercooked on the bottom and some of the moisture in the egg whites seeps out all over the filling.

To make sure your meringue doesn't weep, spread the beaten egg whites on hot filling, anchoring it to the edges of the tart pan or muffin cup. Then bake the pies immediately. Let them cool in a draft-free area.

**FOR THE MERINGUE:**
**Whites of 2 large eggs,**
 **at room temperature**
**1/8 teaspoon cream of tartar**
**1/4 teaspoon pure vanilla extract**
**Pinch of salt**
**1 1/2 tablespoons sugar**

**PAN REQUIRED:**
**1 baking sheet**

1. Place a rack in the center of the oven and preheat the oven to 375°F. Place the tart pans on a baking sheet for easier handling, and set it aside.

2. **MAKE THE FILLING:** Place the sugar, flour, cocoa powder, and salt in a small saucepan and whisk to blend well. Whisk in the milk and egg yolk. Place the saucepan over medium heat and cook, whisking constantly, until the mixture is bubbling and thick, 5 minutes. Remove the saucepan from the heat and add the chocolate and butter. Then return the pan to the heat for a moment, whisking until the butter and chocolate melt and the mixture is smooth. Remove from the heat and whisk in the vanilla. (Alternatively, whisk all the filling ingredients except the chocolate, butter, and vanilla in a 4-cup microwave-safe bowl and microwave, uncovered, at high power for 1 minute. Stir, and

microwave until the filling has thick-ened, 25 to 30 seconds; then stir and microwave again until it is very thick, 10 to 20 seconds. Whisk in the choco-late, butter pieces, and vanilla.)

**3.** FOR THE MERINGUE: The filling needs to be hot when you spread the meringue on top, so prepare the meringue immediately. Place the egg whites in a medium-size mixing bowl and beat with a hand-held electric mixer on medium speed until they are foamy. Add the cream of tartar, vanilla, and salt, increase the mixer speed to high, and beat until soft peaks form. With the mixer

running on high speed, slowly pour in the sugar. Beat until stiff peaks form.

**4.** Pour the filling into the pie crusts, dividing it evenly between them. Mound the meringue over the fillings in high peaks, making sure to seal the meringue to the edges of the tart pans. Bake until the meringue is golden brown, 10 minutes.

**5.** Remove the baking sheet from the oven and transfer the tart pans to a wire rack. Let the pies cool completely, away from drafts. Remove the tarts from the pans before serving.

# Banana Cream Pies

## *with* Chocolate Chip Pastry

*Makes 2 pies; serves 2*

◆◆◆◆◆◆◆◆◆

**This delicious tart** is a perfect combination of banana and chocolate. Chocolate chips and walnuts in the pastry make it more like a flaky cookie than a crust. The optional banana liqueur in the filling intensifies the banana flavor, but the tart is delicious without it.

Unsalted butter, at room temperature, for greasing the tart pans

FOR THE PASTRY SHELLS:
1 recipe Rich Sweet Pastry dough (page 165), prepared through Step 2

1/2 ounce bittersweet or semisweet chocolate, finely chopped

2 tablespoons finely chopped walnuts

FOR THE CUSTARD FILLING:
2 tablespoons granulated sugar

1 tablespoon plus 2 teaspoons all-purpose flour

Pinch of salt

Yolk of 1 large egg

1/4 cup plus 2 tablespoons whole milk

1 1/2 teaspoons banana-flavored liqueur (optional)

1/2 teaspoon pure vanilla extract

1/2 medium banana

FOR THE TOPPING AND GARNISH:
1/4 cup whipping (heavy) cream

1 tablespoon confectioners' sugar

1/4 teaspoon pure vanilla extract

Grated chocolate or chocolate curls (see page 54, optional)

PANS REQUIRED:
Two 4 x 1 3/8-inch tart pans with removable bottoms

1 baking sheet

1. Lightly grease the tart pans. Place the tart pans on a baking sheet for easier handling, and set it aside.

2. Prepare the pastry dough as directed. Remove the dough from the processor bowl, place it in a shallow dish, and knead in the chopped chocolate and nuts. Divide the dough in half, and while it is still soft, press it into the bottom and sides of the prepared tart pans, dividing it evenly between them. Pierce the bottom of the tart shells with a fork, and freeze the shells until firm, 15 minutes.

3. Meanwhile, place a rack in the center of the oven and preheat the oven to 325°F.

4. Remove the tart shells from the freezer and line them with aluminum foil. Fill them to the top with pie weights or dried beans. Place the tart shells, on the baking sheet, in the oven and bake for 20 minutes. Remove the baking sheet from the oven and carefully remove the foil and weights. Return the baking sheet to the oven and bake until the tart shells are lightly browned and dry, 13 to 15 minutes. Remove the baking sheet from the oven and transfer the tart pans to a wire rack. Let them cool completely.

5. MAKE THE FILLING: Place the sugar, flour, and salt in a small saucepan and whisk to blend well. Add the egg yolk and milk, and whisk until the mixture is smooth. Cook over medium heat, whisking constantly, until the custard thickens and just begins to boil, 3 to 5 minutes. Remove the saucepan from the heat and whisk in the liqueur, if desired, and the vanilla. (Alternatively, whisk all the filling ingredients in a 4-cup microwave-safe bowl until smooth. Microwave on high power for 1 minute. Whisk, and then microwave until the custard is thickened, 30 seconds. Whisk, and microwave again until the custard is thick, 10 to 20 seconds.)

6. Transfer the custard to a small bowl and let it cool to lukewarm, whisking it occasionally.

7. Spread half of the custard in the bottoms of the tart shells, dividing it evenly between them. Peel and slice the banana and arrange the slices evenly over the custard. Cover the

banana slices with the remaining custard, dividing it evenly between the tarts. Cover the tarts and refrigerate until they are cold, at least 2 hours.

**8. MAKE THE TOPPING:** When you are ready to serve, remove the tarts from the pans. Place the cream, confectioners' sugar, and vanilla in a small bowl and beat with a hand-held electric mixer on high speed until firm peaks form. Spread the whipped cream over the tarts, dividing it evenly. Refrigerate the tarts for 30 minutes before serving. Garnish with grated chocolate or curls, if desired.

# Dr. Robert's Coconut Cream Pies

*Makes 2 pies; serves 2*
◆◆◆◆◆◆◆◆

**My children's** pediatrician considers himself a pie expert. When Dr. Robert Levin pointed out to me that my brother-in-law, Sam Nakos, didn't have a coconut pie on the menu at Demetri's, his barbecue restaurant, I set out to help him develop one.

The pie crust contains ground coconut, which lightly toasts as the crust bakes and keeps it crisp and flaky under the filling. The coconut-flavored custard is creamy smooth, and the whipped cream on top is capped with a sprinkling of toasted coconut. It is one of my favorites.

FOR THE FILLING:

¼ cup sweetened flaked coconut

¼ cup whole milk

2 tablespoons sugar

1 tablespoon all-purpose flour

Pinch of salt

Yolk of 1 large egg

⅛ teaspoon pure vanilla extract

Drop of coconut extract

FOR THE CRUST:

Unsalted butter, at room temperature, for greasing the muffin cups

½ cup all-purpose flour

2½ tablespoons sweetened flaked coconut

1 teaspoon sugar

⅛ teaspoon salt

2 tablespoons cold unsalted butter, cut into ½-inch cubes

3 to 5 teaspoons ice water

FOR THE TOPPING:

¼ cup sweetened flaked coconut

¼ cup cold whipping (heavy) cream

1 tablespoon confectioners' sugar

Drop of pure coconut extract

PAN REQUIRED:

1 jumbo muffin pan (¾-cup capacity), preferably nonstick

1. MAKE THE FILLING: Place the coconut, milk, sugar, flour, salt, and egg yolk in a small nonreactive saucepan, and whisk until no lumps of flour remain and the egg yolk is blended into the mixture. Then cook over medium heat, stirring constantly, until the pastry cream is thick and bubbly, about 5 minutes. Remove the saucepan from the heat and stir in the vanilla and coconut extracts.

2. Transfer the filling to a small bowl and press a piece of plastic wrap directly onto the surface (this prevents a skin from forming on the top). Refrigerate until cold, at least 2 hours.

3. Lightly grease 2 of the muffin cups, and set the muffin pan aside.

4. MAKE THE CRUST: Combine the flour, coconut, sugar, and salt in a food processor, and process until the coconut is finely minced. Add the butter pieces and pulse the processor to cut the butter into the flour mixture until it resembles coarse meal, about 24 pulses. Add 3 teaspoons of the ice water and blend until the dough begins to clump together, a few seconds; add more ice water, by teaspoonfuls, if the dough is dry. Gather up the dough and divide it in half. Flatten each half into

a disk and wrap them individually in plastic wrap; refrigerate for 30 minutes.

**5.** Working with one piece of the dough at a time, roll out each disk between 2 pieces of plastic wrap to form a 6-inch round. Fit the dough into a prepared muffin cup, folding it to fit the curve of the cup. Gently smooth the top of the dough with your fingertip so it is even with the rim of the muffin cup, and tuck the overhang to the inside for reinforcement. Pierce the bottom of each crust all over with a fork, and freeze the crusts until firm, 15 minutes. (You can wrap and freeze these for up to 1 day ahead; thaw for 30 minutes before using.)

**6.** Meanwhile, place a rack in the center of the oven and preheat the oven to 375°F.

**7.** Line the crusts with aluminum foil, and fill them to the tops with pie weights or dried beans. Fill the empty muffin cups halfway with water to prevent them from scorching. Bake for 18 minutes. Remove the muffin pan from the oven and remove the foil and weights. Return the muffin pan to the oven and bake until the pastry shells are lightly browned, 10 to 12 minutes. Remove the muffin pan from the oven and let it cool completely on a wire rack. (You can prepare these up to 1 day ahead; cover the muffin pan and let it stand at room temperature.)

**8.** Remove the pastry crusts from the muffin pan and place them on dessert plates. Pour the filling into the crusts, dividing it evenly between them. Cover and refrigerate the pies while you prepare the topping. (The pies can be refrigerated, covered, for up to 24 hours before adding the topping and serving.)

**9.** MAKE THE TOPPING: Sprinkle the coconut in a heavy skillet and place it over medium heat. Cook, stirring frequently, until the coconut is toasted, 2 to 3 minutes. Transfer the coconut to a small bowl and let it cool completely.

**10.** Place the cream, confectioners' sugar, and coconut extract in a medium-size mixing bowl and beat with a hand-held electric mixer on high speed until firm peaks form. Spread the whipped cream over the filling, and sprinkle with the toasted coconut.

# Blueberry Lattice Tarts

*Makes 2 tarts; serves 2*

◆◆◆◆◆◆◆◆◆

**Dried blueberries** intensify the fruit flavor of these tarts, but much of their charm lies in the delicious pastry. The buttery, shortbread-like crust is a nice complement to the thin layer of flavor-packed fruit. Dried blueberries can be hard to find, depending on the success of the year's blueberry crop. If you can't find them in your market, you can make the tarts using drained canned wild blueberries, which are smaller than cultivated blueberries and more concentrated in flavor.

**Unsalted butter, at room temperature, for greasing the tart pans**

**2 recipes Rich Sweet Pastry dough (page 165), prepared through Step 2**

**Flour, for rolling out the dough**

**¼ cup plus 2 tablespoons blueberry preserves**

**3 tablespoons dried blueberries**

**¼ teaspoon grated lemon zest**

**¼ teaspoon pure almond extract**

**2 tablespoons slivered almonds (optional)**

**White of 1 large egg**

**2 teaspoons whole milk or half-and-half**

**2 teaspoons sugar**

PANS REQUIRED:

**Two 4¹/₂ x ³/₄-inch tart pans
   with removable bottoms**

**1 baking sheet**

**1.** Place a rack in the center of the oven and preheat the oven to 325°F. Lightly grease the tart pans and set them aside.

**2.** Prepare the pastry dough as directed, doubling the recipe. Turn the dough out on a piece of plastic wrap and divide it into 4 equal portions. Shape each portion into a disk and wrap them individually in plastic wrap. Refrigerate the dough for at least 15 minutes, or until ready to roll out.

**3.** Remove 2 of the disks from the refrigerator and roll each one out on a lightly floured surface to form a 5¹/₂-inch round. Fit the pastry rounds into the tart pans, pressing them into the sides and bottom edges; prick the bottoms with a fork. Freeze the tart shells while you prepare the filling, 15 minutes.

**4.** Place the preserves, dried blueberries, lemon zest, and almond extract in a small bowl and stir to mix. Spoon the filling over the bottoms of the tart shells, dividing it evenly between them. Sprinkle with the slivered almonds if using.

**5.** Roll out the remaining 2 dough disks on a lightly floured surface to form two 5¹/₂-inch squares. Cut each square of dough into ¹/₂-inch-wide strips. Arrange several strips on top of each filled pastry shell, spacing them ¹/₂ inch apart. Top with more strips at a 90-degree angle to the first ones, forming a lattice pattern. Press the ends of the strips to the edges of the tart pans, and trim off the overhang.

**6.** Place the egg white and milk in a small bowl and beat lightly with a fork. Brush some of the egg white mixture over the lattice. Sprinkle the sugar over the tarts. Place the tart pans on a baking sheet for easier handling and bake until the tart crust is golden and the filling is bubbling, 40 to 43 minutes.

**7.** Remove the baking sheet from the oven and transfer the tarts to a wire rack. Let them cool completely, remove from their pans, and serve. (The tarts can be wrapped and stored at room temperature for up to 24 hours.)

# Apricot Lattice Tarts

*Makes 2 tarts; serves 2*

◆◆◆◆◆◆◆◆◆

**Instead of blueberries,** you can make equally intense fruit tarts using dried apricots, which also set off the delicious pastry to perfection. I like to serve them with a dollop of plain crème fraîche or with Sweetened Almond Crème Fraîche (see Note).

Unsalted butter, at room temperature, for greasing the tart pans

2 recipes Rich Sweet Pastry dough (page 165), prepared through Step 2

Flour, for rolling out the dough

¼ cup dried apricots

2 tablespoons plus 2 teaspoons sugar

1 tablespoon amaretto (almond liqueur) or brandy

2 tablespoons apricot preserves

2 tablespoons slivered almonds

White of 1 large egg

2 teaspoons whole milk or half-and-half

**PANS REQUIRED:**

Two 4½ x ¾-inch tart pans with removable bottoms

1 baking sheet

**1.** Place a rack in the center of the oven and preheat the oven to 325°F. Lightly grease the tart pans. Place the tart pans on a baking sheet for easier handling, and set the pans aside.

**2.** Prepare the pastry dough as directed, doubling the recipe. Turn the dough out on a piece of plastic wrap and divide it into 4 equal portions. Shape each portion into a disk and wrap them individually in plastic wrap. Refrigerate the dough for at least 15 minutes, or until ready to roll out.

**3.** Remove 2 of the disks from the refrigerator and roll each one out on a lightly floured surface to form a 5½-inch round. Fit the pastry rounds into the tart pans, pressing them into the sides and bottom edges; prick the bottoms with a fork. Freeze the tart shells while you prepare the filling, 15 minutes.

**4.** Place the apricots, ⅓ cup of water, and 2 tablespoons of the sugar in a small saucepan over medium-high heat. Bring to a boil, stirring until the sugar is dissolved. Continue boiling until the liquid is reduced by half, 8 to 12 minutes. Remove the pan from the heat and transfer the mixture to a food processor or blender. Add the liqueur and puree until smooth. Add the preserves and process until the filling is almost smooth. Spoon the filling over the bottoms of the pastry shells, dividing it evenly between them. Sprinkle with the slivered almonds.

**5.** Roll out the remaining 2 dough disks on a lightly floured surface to form two 5½-inch squares. Cut each square of dough into ½-inch-wide strips. Arrange several strips on top of each filled tart shell, spacing them ½ inch apart. Top with more strips at a 90-degree angle to the first ones, forming a lattice pattern. Press the ends of the strips to the edges of the tart pans, and trim off the overhang.

**6.** Place the egg white and milk in a small bowl and beat lightly with a fork. Brush some of the egg white mixture over the lattice strips. Sprinkle the remaining 2 teaspoons sugar over the tarts. Bake until the tart crust is golden and the filling is bubbling, 40 to 43 minutes. Remove the baking sheet from the oven and transfer the tarts to a wire rack. Let them cool completely. Remove from their pans and serve. (The tarts can be wrapped and stored at room temperature for up to 24 hours.) Remove the bottoms of the pans before serving.

**NOTE:** To make Sweetened Almond Crème Fraîche: Fold together 3 tablespoons crème fraîche, 1 tablespoon confectioners' sugar, and 1 tablespoon amaretto.

# Blood Orange Tarts

## *with* Raspberry Orange Sauce

*Makes 2 tarts; serves 2*

◆◆◆◆◆◆◆◆◆

## Blood oranges contain

dark red pigments that give them a "bloody" appearance and a more complex flavor than other sweet oranges, such as Valencia or navel. They are everyday fare in Italy— even the frozen orange juice concentrate is red—but have only recently become available in U.S. markets during their spring season.

The distinctive color of blood orange juice makes the custard in these tarts a lovely pastel pink-orange, and they have a fragrantly orange tang. The deeply colored Raspberry Orange Sauce provides a pleasant color contrast as well as intense flavor.

For this recipe, you need to fill the pastry shells in two steps. If you filled them completely before putting them in the oven, they would be so full that the filling might spill.

**2 partially baked Rich Sweet Pastry shells (page 165), baked in 4 x 1⅜-inch tart pans with removable bottoms, still in the pans**

1 large egg

Yolk of 1 large egg

¼ cup whipping (heavy) cream

¼ cup sugar

3 tablespoons freshly squeezed
blood orange juice

1 teaspoon cornstarch

Raspberry Orange Sauce
(recipe follows)

Fresh raspberries, for garnish

Sifted confectioners' sugar,
for garnish

PAN REQUIRED:

1 baking sheet

1. Place a rack in the center of the oven and preheat the oven to 300°F. Place the tart pans on a baking sheet for easier handling, and set it aside.

2. Place the egg, egg yolk, cream, sugar, blood orange juice, and cornstarch in a small bowl and whisk until combined (do not beat). Pour three quarters of the filling into the tart shells, dividing it evenly between them, and carefully place the baking sheet in the oven. Using a small cup, pour the remaining filling into the tart shells.

3. Bake until the tarts are just set in the center, 35 to 38 minutes. Remove the baking sheet from the oven and transfer the tarts to a wire rack. Let them cool completely. Cover and refrigerate the tarts until they are cold, at least 2 hours and up to 24 hours. Remove the tarts from their pans.

4. Just before serving, swirl Raspberry Orange Sauce on 2 serving plates. Decorate the tarts with raspberries and place them on the plates. Dust the tarts and plates with sifted confectioners' sugar.

## variation

# A Citrus Duo

## Lime Custard Tarts

Replace the blood orange juice with fresh lime juice. Serve and garnish as directed.

## Tangerine Custard Tarts

Replace the blood orange juice with fresh tangerine juice. Serve and garnish as directed.

# Raspberry Orange Sauce

**MAKES ABOUT ⅔ CUP**

¾ cup fresh or thawed frozen
   unsweetened raspberries

3 tablespoons raspberry jam,
   warmed

2 tablespoons fresh blood orange or
   tangerine juice

Place the raspberries, jam, and juice in a small bowl and stir to mix. Set a fine-mesh sieve over a bowl, and press the mixture through the sieve. Scrape the pulp off the bottom of the sieve and add it to the pulp in the bowl. Discard the seeds. (The sauce may be made up to 2 days in advance, and refrigerated in a covered jar.)

# Plum Tarts
## *with* Oatmeal Cookie Crust

*Makes 2 tarts; serves 2*
◆◆◆◆◆◆◆◆◆

**These tarts make** a great impromptu dessert, because plums are so easy to bake with—they don't need to be peeled—and the crushed oatmeal cookie crust is a snap to throw together. For best results, use firm but ripe dark purple plums, but any other ripe variety will also work well.

Unsalted butter, at room temperature, for greasing the tart pans

**FOR THE CRUST AND TOPPING:**
$2/3$ cup plus $1/4$ cup crushed oatmeal cookies

3 tablespoons unsalted butter, melted

2 tablespoons all-purpose flour

1 tablespoon packed light brown sugar

**FOR THE FILLING:**
3 plums, unpeeled, pitted and diced

2 tablespoons granulated sugar

2 teaspoons cornstarch

$1/4$ teaspoon ground cinnamon

Pinch of salt

**PANS REQUIRED:**
Two $4^{1}/_{2}$ x $3/4$-inch tart pans with removable bottoms

1 baking sheet

**1.** Place a rack in the center of the oven and preheat the oven to 350°F. Grease the tart pans and place them on a baking sheet for easier handling; set it aside.

**2. MAKE THE CRUSTS:** Place $2/3$ cup of the cookie crumbs and 2 tablespoons of the melted butter in a small bowl and stir to mix well. Firmly press the mixture onto the bottoms and up the sides of the prepared tart pans, dividing it evenly between them. Bake the tart crusts until they are lightly browned, 8 to 10 minutes. Remove the baking sheet from the oven and let the tarts cool on a wire rack. Increase the oven temperature to 375°F.

**3. MAKE THE TOPPING:** Place the remaining $1/4$ cup of cookie crumbs, the flour, brown sugar, and remaining 1 tablespoon of melted butter in a small bowl, and stir to blend well. Refrigerate the mixture for 15 minutes.

**4. MAKE THE FILLING:** Combine the plums, sugar, cornstarch, cinnamon, and salt in a medium-size mixing bowl and toss well. Spoon the plum mixture into the tart crusts, dividing it evenly between them, and sprinkle the topping over the filling.

**5.** Bake until the topping is browned and the filling is bubbling, 20 to 22 minutes. Remove the baking sheet from the oven, transfer the tarts to a wire rack, and allow to cool. Remove the tarts from the pans and serve warm.

# Pear Almond Custard Tarts

*Makes 2 tarts; serves 2*
◆◆◆◆◆◆◆◆◆

**This is an** elegant little tart like one that you might find in a sophisticated pastry shop. A sweet crust encases first a thin layer of custard flavored with ground almonds, then lightly baked pears and more ground almonds. Garnish the tarts with a sprig of mint for color.

**2 partially baked Basic Sweet Pastry shells (page 165), baked in 4¹/2 x ³/4-inch tart pans with removable bottoms, still in the pans**

**¹/2 cup slivered almonds**

**2 tablespoons unsalted butter, at room temperature**

**5 tablespoons sugar**

**Yolk of 1 large egg**

**2 teaspoons all-purpose flour**

**1 firm ripe pear, such as Bosc**

**1 teaspoon unsalted butter, melted**

**PAN REQUIRED:**

**1 baking sheet**

1. Place a rack in the center of the oven and preheat the oven to 375°F. Place the tart pans on a baking sheet for easier handling, and set it aside.

2. Place the almonds in a food processor and process until they are finely ground.

3. Place the butter, 3 tablespoons of the sugar, and the egg yolk in a small bowl, and beat with a hand-held electric mixer at low speed until blended,

about 30 seconds. Increase the mixer speed to medium and beat, scraping down the sides of the bowl from time to time, until the mixture is fluffy, about 2 minutes. Then beat in the flour and ¼ cup of the ground almonds until just blended, about 10 seconds. Spread the almond cream over the bottom of the pastry shells, dividing it evenly between them.

**4.** Peel and core the pear, then cut it into ½-inch cubes. Pile the pear cubes on top of the almond cream in the pastry shells.

**5.** Place the melted butter, the remaining 2 tablespoons of sugar, and the remaining ground almonds in a small bowl, and stir to mix. Spoon the mixture evenly over the pears.

**6.** Bake until the crusts and the pear topping are nicely browned, about 35 minutes. Remove the baking sheet from the oven and transfer the tarts to a wire rack to cool. Remove the tarts from the pans and serve slightly warm or at room temperature, the same day they are baked.

# Warm Chocolate Tarts

*Makes 2 tarts; serves 2*
◆◆◆◆◆◆◆◆◆

**If you're a** chocolate pie fan, you will love the rich brownie flavor of this warm fluffy baked custard. The tarts are easy to put together and will fix that chocolate craving in a jiffy. Serve them warm with ice cream or flavored whipped cream.

2 fully baked Rich Sweet Pastry
    shells (page 165), baked in 4 x 1⅜-
    inch tart pans with removable
    bottoms, still in the pans
¼ cup plus 2 tablespoons whipping
    (heavy) cream
3 tablespoons whole milk
3 ounces bittersweet or semisweet
    chocolate, chopped
Yolk of 1 large egg
1 tablespoon sugar
Pinch of salt

Vanilla ice cream, Raspberry Whipped
    Cream (page 36), or Cappuccino
    Cream (page 37), optional

**PAN REQUIRED:**
**1 baking sheet**

**1.** Place a rack in the center of the oven and preheat the oven to 350°F. Put the tart pans on a baking sheet for easier handling, and set it aside.

**2.** Pour the cream and milk into a small saucepan and bring to a boil over medium heat. Remove the saucepan from the heat and add the chocolate, swirling the pan to submerge the chocolate in the hot cream mixture. Let it stand for 1 minute to soften the chocolate; then stir until the mixture is smooth.

**3.** Place the egg yolk, sugar, and salt

in a small bowl and beat with a whisk until blended. Gradually pour ¼ cup of the chocolate mixture into the egg yolk mixture, stirring constantly with the fork so the egg will not "cook." Add the remaining chocolate mixture to the yolk mixture, whisking while you pour. Pour the filling into the tart crusts, dividing it evenly between them.

**4.** Bake the tarts until the filling is set in the center, about 16 minutes. Remove the baking sheet from the oven and transfer the tarts to a wire rack to cool for 15 minutes. Then carefully remove the tarts from the pans and place them on individual serving plates. Serve warm, with your choice of topping. (The tarts can be prepared up to 1 day ahead. Let them cool completely and, leaving them in their pans, cover and refrigerate. Before serving, reheat them in a pre-heated 350°F oven for 10 minutes. Then take them out of the pans and serve.)

# Pecan Meringue Tarts

## *with* Caramel Latte Mousse

*Makes 2 tarts; serves 2*

**◆◆◆◆◆◆◆◆◆**

**When you want** a light, ener-gizing, sophisticated dessert, this is it. Crisp and tender meringue shells—studded with toasted pecans and flavored with vanilla—make a celestial container for a filling that tastes like the best caramel latte you've ever had. It is a rich yet never heavy dessert. The meringue shells can be made a day in advance and stored in an airtight container at room temperature. Prepare the mousse a couple of hours before serving so it has time to set properly.

### FOR THE MERINGUE:

½ cup very finely chopped pecans

White of 1 large egg, at room temperature

¼ teaspoon cornstarch

¼ teaspoon pure vanilla extract

⅛ teaspoon cream of tartar

Pinch of salt

¼ cup superfine sugar (see Note, page 74)

### FOR THE MOUSSE:

½ teaspoon instant espresso powder

½ teaspoon unflavored gelatin

¼ cup Rich Caramel Sauce (page 259) or good-quality store-bought caramel sauce

⅔ cup cold whipping (heavy) cream

1 tablespoon confectioners' sugar

### PAN REQUIRED:

2 baking sheets

1. Place a rack in the center of the oven and preheat the oven to 350°F. Line a baking sheet with parchment paper and set it aside.

2. MAKE THE MERINGUE SHELLS: Spread the pecans on an unlined baking sheet and bake until they are toasted, 4 to 5 minutes. Remove the pecans from the oven and let them cool completely. Keep the oven on.

3. Place the egg white in a small bowl and beat with a hand-held electric mixer on medium speed until foamy, 10 seconds. Add the cornstarch, vanilla, cream of tartar, and salt and beat on high speed until the whites begin to hold soft peaks, 20 seconds. With the mixer running, slowly pour in the superfine sugar, beating until stiff peaks form, 30 seconds. Then fold in ¼ cup plus 2 tablespoons of the toasted pecans. (Reserve the remaining 2 tablespoons of pecans for the garnish.)

4. Spoon the meringue into 2 equal mounds on the prepared baking sheet, spacing them at least 6 inches apart. Using the back of a spoon and pushing from the center out, smooth the meringues out to form 3-inch rounds with raised edges (the cavities will be 2 to 2½ inches in diameter). Place the baking sheet in the oven and immediately reduce the oven temperature

to 300°F. Without opening the oven door, bake the meringues until they are dry and crisp on the outside and just cooked through on the inside, 20 minutes.

**5.** Turn the oven off and leave the meringues in the oven for 1 hour. Then remove the baking sheet from the oven and let the meringues cool completely on the sheet. (The meringue shells can be made a day in advance; store them in an airtight container at room temperature.)

**6. MAKE THE MOUSSE:** Combine the espresso powder and the gelatin in a small microwave-safe bowl. Stir in 1 tablespoon of water, and let the mixture stand for 1 minute to soften the gelatin. Then microwave on high power for 30 seconds. Stir to dissolve the gelatin. Mix the gelatin mixture into the caramel sauce, stirring well.

Refrigerate until the caramel mixture is chilled and slightly thickened, about 20 minutes.

**7.** Place the cream and confectioners' sugar in a medium-size mixing bowl and beat with a hand-held electric mixer on high speed until firm peaks form, 30 seconds. Fold ½ cup of the whipped cream into the caramel mixture. (You can prepare the mousse and the whipped cream, cover, and refrigerate up to 2 hours before serving.)

**8.** Gently pry the meringues from the parchment paper with a spatula and place on dessert plates. Spread the caramel mousse into the meringue tart shells, dividing it evenly between them. Spread the remaining whipped cream over the mousse, and sprinkle the remaining 2 tablespoons of pecans over the whipped cream. Refrigerate for 30 minutes, or up to 2 hours, before serving.

# Triple Crown Tarts

*Makes 2 tarts; serves 2*
◆◆◆◆◆◆◆◆◆

**These rich** and extremely sweet tarts are small versions of a Kentucky specialty called Derby Pie. They are too good to be saved for Derby Day, so I've renamed them to honor all three major spring horse races in the United States.

2 partially baked Basic Pastry shells
   (page 159), baked in 4 x 1⅜-inch
   tart pans with removable bottoms,
   still in the pans
1 ounce unsweetened chocolate,
   chopped
1 teaspoon unsalted butter
1 large egg
⅓ cup sugar
3 tablespoons corn syrup
1 tablespoon bourbon, plus more
   for topping the whipped cream
½ teaspoon pure vanilla extract

Pinch of salt
⅓ cup chopped pecans, toasted
   (see page 195)
Sweetened Whipped Cream
   (page 36; optional)

**PAN REQUIRED:**
**1 baking sheet**

1. Place a rack in the center of the oven and preheat the oven to 350°F. Place the tart pans on a baking sheet for easier handling, and set it aside.

2. Place the chocolate and butter in a small microwave-safe bowl and microwave on medium power until the chocolate is glossy and the butter is mostly melted, 1 to 1½ minutes. Stir the mixture until it is smooth. Let it cool.

3. Place the egg, sugar, corn syrup, bourbon, vanilla, and salt in a medium-

size mixing bowl and whisk to blend. Whisk about ¼ cup of the egg mixture into the melted chocolate mixture; then whisk the chocolate mixture into the remaining egg mixture. Pour the filling into the pastry shells, dividing it evenly between them, and sprinkle with the pecans. Bake until the edges of the pies are slightly puffed and the centers are soft but set, about 30 minutes.

4. Remove the baking sheet from the oven and transfer the tarts to a wire rack. Let them stand until they are cool enough to handle. Then remove the tart shells from the tart pans. Serve them warm or at room temperature. If desired, spoon sweetened whipped cream on the tarts and then, making an indentation in the whipped cream, add a spoonful of bourbon.

# Ashley's Cappuccino Crème Brûlée Tarts

*Makes 2 tarts; serves 2*

◆◆◆◆◆◆◆◆◆

**This recipe was** created for Ashley, one of my youngest daughter's loyal babysitters. She and her college friends frequently study over cups of their favorite fancy coffee and she made a special request for a coffee-flavored tart to go alongside. These taste like great cappuccino with a texture like crème brûlée. They're easy to make, but need plenty of time to chill, so you might want to prepare them the day before serving.

2 Rich Sweet Pastry shells (page 165), partially baked without pricking the bottoms in 4 x 1⅜-inch tart pans with removable bottoms, still in the pans

¼ cup plus 3 tablespoons whipping (heavy) cream

¼ teaspoon instant espresso powder

1½ ounces imported white chocolate (such as Lindt), finely chopped

Yolk of 1 large egg

1 teaspoon all-purpose flour

¼ teaspoon pure vanilla extract

⅛ teaspoon pure almond extract

2 teaspoons sugar

Chocolate-covered coffee beans, for garnish (optional)

PAN REQUIRED:

1 baking sheet

1. Place a rack in the center of the oven and preheat the oven to 350°F. Put the tart pans on a baking sheet for easier handling, and set it aside.

2. Place the cream and espresso powder in a small saucepan over medium-high heat and bring to a simmer, stirring to dissolve the espresso powder. Remove the pan from the heat and whisk in the white chocolate until smooth.

3. Place the egg yolk, flour, and vanilla and almond extracts in a medium-size bowl and whisk to blend well. Slowly pour the white chocolate mixture into the egg mixture, whisking constantly. Pour the custard into the pastry shells, dividing it evenly between them. Bake until the centers of the tarts are just set, about 15 minutes.

4. Remove the baking sheet from the oven and transfer the tarts to a wire rack. Let them cool completely; then cover and refrigerate the tarts for 4 hours or overnight.

5. Place a rack in the top third of the oven and preheat the broiler.

6. Return the tarts to the baking sheet and sprinkle each one with 1 teaspoon of the sugar. Cover the tart crusts with strips of aluminum foil to prevent browning. Broil just until the sugar melts and browns, 2 minutes. Remove the tarts from the broiler and refrigerate them until cold, at least 2 hours and up to 1 day.

7. Remove the tarts from the pans and place them on serving plates; arrange the chocolate-covered coffee beans around the edges of the tarts, if using.

# Strawberry Mascarpone Cheesecake Tarts

*Makes 2 cheesecakes; serves 2*

◆◆◆◆◆◆◆◆◆

**Every bite of** this cheesecake is divine. The topping will remind you of a strawberry pie, and the filling is wonderfully creamy. To me, cheesecakes made with mascarpone (the Italian cream cheese) taste much richer and seem a bit more sophisticated than the usual ones made with cream cheese.

Unsalted butter, at room temperature, for greasing the tart pans

**FOR THE CRUST:**
⅓ cup vanilla wafer or graham cracker crumbs

1 teaspoon sugar

⅛ teaspoon ground cinnamon

1 tablespoon unsalted butter, melted

**FOR THE GLAZE AND THE FILLING:**
Half a 10-ounce package frozen strawberries in syrup, thawed, with their juices (see Note)

⅔ cup mascarpone cheese, at room temperature

¼ cup sugar

2 teaspoons all-purpose flour

Yolks of 2 large eggs

½ teaspoon pure vanilla extract

Pinch of salt

6 to 8 fresh strawberries, hulled and sliced

**PANS REQUIRED:**
Two 4 x 1⅜-inch tart pans with removable bottoms

1 baking sheet

1. Place a rack in the center of the oven and preheat the oven to 325°F. Grease the tart pans and place them on a baking sheet for easier handling; set it aside.

2. MAKE THE CRUST: Place the vanilla wafer crumbs, sugar, cinnamon, and melted butter in a medium-size bowl and whisk until well blended. Press the mixture firmly into the bottom of the prepared tart pans, dividing it evenly between them. Bake until the crusts are just set, 8 to 10 minutes. Remove the baking sheet from the oven (leave the oven on), transfer the tarts to a wire rack, and let the tarts cool to room temperature.

3. MAKE THE GLAZE: Set a fine-mesh sieve over a small saucepan, and press the thawed strawberries and their juices through the sieve, pressing down hard on the solids to extract all the juice. Scrape the bottom of the sieve to extract any pulp clinging it, and add it to the pulp in the saucepan. Bring the strained pulp to a boil over high heat. Then reduce the heat to medium and boil until reduced to 3 tablespoons, 15 to 20 minutes. Remove the syrup from the heat and let it cool completely.

4. MAKE THE FILLING: Place the mascarpone and sugar in a medium-size mixing bowl and beat with a hand-held electric mixer on medium speed just until smooth. Reduce the mixer speed to low and mix in the flour. Then add the egg yolks, 1 teaspoon of the strawberry syrup, the vanilla, and the salt. Beat just until the filling is blended, about 10 seconds. Take care not to overbeat it. Pour the filling into the tart pans, dividing it evenly between them. Cover and set aside the remaining strawberry syrup.

5. Bake the cheesecakes until they appear dry and have begun to brown, about 28 minutes. Remove the baking sheet from the oven, transfer the cheesecakes to a wire rack, and let them cool completely. Cover and refrigerate for 4 hours or overnight.

**6.** Remove the cheesecakes from the tart pans and place them on serving plates. Heat the remaining strawberry syrup until it is liquid again, and brush a little on each cheesecake. Arrange the sliced strawberries on top of the cheesecakes, and brush the remaining syrup all over the cheesecakes. Refrigerate for 1 hour before serving.

NOTE: You only need to use half a package of frozen strawberries in syrup. Because it comes in a box, you can just slice through the frozen block and put the rest of the strawberries in a zip-lock freezer bag and pop them back into the freezer. Or, for total recipe accuracy, you can thaw all the berries, drain and reserve the syrupy juices, and measure out half of each. Then store the remaining half of the strawberries and syrup in a covered container in the refrigerator to serve with Classic Vanilla Shortcakes (page 243) or to spoon over the Presto Pound Cake (page 83) or Angel Food Cakes (page 73).

# Basic Pastry

*Makes enough pastry for 2 single-crust pies or tarts*

◆◆◆◆◆◆◆◆◆

I am one of those people who love pie crust. Actually, I sometimes eat the filling first and save the crust for last. And I always make enough crust to roll out a "pastry cookie" for my daughter to eat. It is so very easy to mix together the crust—no more trouble than making biscuits. You just measure the flour, mix in the cold butter, and toss in the chilled water. Once you get the hang of it, the crust is the part that will garner the most compliments. You won't believe how many people are impressed by homemade crust!

Speaking of mixing in the cold butter, it doesn't matter which fat you use for tenderizing the pastry—go with your own preferences. I like the flavor of butter; if you wish to substitute vegetable shortening, make sure to chill it before using.

½ **cup all-purpose flour**

¼ **teaspoon salt**

¼ **teaspoon sugar**

**3 tablespoons cold unsalted butter, cut into small pieces**

**4 teaspoons ice water, or more as needed**

**Unsalted butter, at room temperature, for greasing the pans**

PANS REQUIRED:

**Two 4 x 1⅜ -inch tart pans with removable bottoms, two 4½ x ¾-inch tart pans with removable bottoms, or 1 jumbo muffin pan (¾-cup capacity)**

**1 baking sheet**

**1.** Place the flour, salt, and sugar in a food processor and pulse to blend.

Sprinkle the butter pieces evenly over the flour mixture and pulse until the lumps of butter are reduced to the size of small peas, about 15 pulses. Sprinkle the ice water over the flour mixture and process lightly until small, moist clumps of dough begin to form; you can add up to 2 teaspoons more ice water, 1 teaspoon at a time, if the dough is dry.

**2.** Tear off 2 sheets of waxed paper and gather the dough onto one of the sheets. Form the dough into a mass and then divide it in half. Form each half into a disk, and wrap them individually in the pieces of waxed paper. Refrigerate for 30 minutes.

**3.** Place a rack in the center of the oven and preheat the oven to 375°F.

**4.** Lightly grease the tart pans, and place them on a baking sheet for easier handling; set it aside. If you are using the jumbo muffin pan, line 2 muffin cups with aluminum foil and lightly grease the foil; set the pan aside.

**5.** Roll out each disk of pastry on a lightly floured surface to form a 6-inch round.

*If you are using tart pans,* fit each pastry round into a prepared tart pan, pressing the pastry into the grooves of the pan's sides. Smooth the top edge with your fingertip and tuck the overhang to the inside for reinforcement.

*If you are using a muffin pan,* fit the pastry rounds into the prepared cups, pressing it into the bottom edges and along the sides, pleating the dough in even folds to fit it to the cup. Smooth the top edge with your fingertip and tuck the overhang to the inside for reinforcement.

**6.** Prick the bottom of the pastry all over with a fork. Gently place the baking sheet with the tart pans, or the muffin pan, in the freezer and chill until firm, 15 minutes.

**7.** Line the chilled pastry shells with aluminum foil, pressing it into the corners and edges, and fill them to the top with pie weights or dried beans. Fill the empty muffin cups halfway with water to prevent them from warping. Place the baking sheet or muffin pan in the oven and bake for 15 minutes.

**8.** Remove the baking sheet or muffin pan from the oven and carefully remove the foil and weights. Return the baking sheet or muffin pan to the oven.

*For partially baked crusts,* bake until the crusts are just dry and set, 4 to 5 minutes.

*For fully baked crusts,* bake until they are light golden brown, 8 to 10 minutes.

# Foolproof Pie Pastry Tips

The first commandment for making great pie shells is to decide that you will roll up your sleeves and measure out that flour instead of relying on a store-bought crust. The second is to keep a positive attitude; tasty pie crusts are easier to make than you might think. I don't buy into the whole it's-got-to-be-flaky-or-dump-it thing with pastry; even if you overwork yours a little when you first start making pie crusts, it still tastes better than store-bought!

Here are some tips for making great-tasting *and* flaky pie crusts:

- Measure the flour exactly: spoon the flour into the measuring cup and level it off with the flat edge of a knife. If you pack the flour, the dough will be too dry and will end up heavy, not light and crisp.

- Use ice-cold butter and water. I cut butter into small pieces and put them on a plate in the freezer for five minutes to make sure they are good and cold. Put ice in a glass of water for two or three minutes to make sure it is chilled. Remove the cubes before using.

- To help your pie crust retain its shape during baking, freeze or refrigerate the pie shells until they are very cold and firm before you bake them. And to prevent the pastry from drooping during baking, fill the pie shells all the way to the top of the pan with pie weights (little round metal weights found in cookware stores), dried beans, or even rice.

# Basic Sweet Pastry

*Makes enough pastry for 2 pies or tarts*
◆◆◆◆◆◆◆◆◆

**This pastry makes** a tender pie crust, but the little bit of egg yolk makes it a bit sturdier so it can hold heavier fillings. It is a great pastry to use for free-form tarts: Roll each portion out to form a six-inch round. Slice two or three pieces of seasonal fruit (peaches, plums, apricots, pears), and toss the fruit with a few tablespoons of sugar and a dash of cinnamon. Then arrange the fruit in the center of each pastry round. Fold up the edges of the pastry over the fruit, leaving 1½ to 2 inches exposed in the center, and put them on a parchment-lined baking sheet. Bake in a preheated 375°F oven until the fruit is bubbling and the crust is browned, 30 to 35 minutes.

Yolk of 1 large egg

½ cup all-purpose flour

2 teaspoons sugar

Pinch of salt

3 tablespoons cold unsalted butter, cut into small pieces

2 teaspoons ice water, or more as needed

Unsalted butter, at room temperature, for greasing the tart pans

**PANS REQUIRED:**

Two 4½ x ¾-inch tart pans with removable bottoms, two 4 x 1⅜-inch tart pans with removable bottoms, or 1 jumbo muffin pan (¾-cup capacity)

1 baking sheet

1. Put the egg yolk in a small bowl and beat it lightly with a fork. Measure out 2 teaspoons of the yolk and set it aside for the pastry. Reserve the remaining yolk for another use.

**2.** Place the flour, sugar, and salt in a food processor and pulse to blend. Sprinkle the butter pieces evenly over the flour mixture and pulse until the lumps of butter are reduced to the size of small peas, about 15 pulses. Sprinkle the ice water and egg yolk over the flour mixture and process just until small, moist clumps of dough begin to form, 6 to 10 seconds; add up to 2 teaspoons more ice water 1 teaspoon at a time if the dough is dry.

**3.** Tear off 2 sheets of waxed paper and gather the dough onto one of the sheets. Form the dough into a mass and then divide it in half. Form each half into a disk, and wrap them individually in the pieces of waxed paper. Refrigerate for 30 minutes.

**4.** Place a rack in the center of the oven and preheat the oven to 375°F.

**5.** Lightly grease the tart pans, and place them on a baking sheet for easier handling; set it aside. If you are using the jumbo muffin pan, line 2 muffin cups with aluminum foil and lightly grease the foil; set the pan aside.

**6.** Roll out each disk of pastry on a lightly floured surface to form a 6-inch round.

*If you are using tart pans,* fit each pastry round into a prepared tart pan, pressing the pastry into the grooves of the pan's sides. Smooth the top edge with your fingertip and tuck the overhang to the inside for reinforcement.

*If you are using a muffin pan,* fit the pastry rounds into the prepared cups, pressing it into the bottom edges and along the sides, pleating the dough in even folds to fit it to the cup. Smooth the top edge with your fingertip and tuck the overhang to the inside for reinforcement.

**7.** Pierce the bottom of the pastry all over with a fork. Gently place the baking sheet with the tart pans, or the muffin pan, in the freezer and chill until firm, 15 minutes.

**8.** Line the chilled pastry shells with aluminum foil, pressing it into the corners and edges, and fill them to the top with pie weights or dried beans. Fill the empty muffin cups halfway with water to prevent them from scorching. Place the baking sheet or muffin pan in the oven and bake for 15 minutes.

**9.** Remove the baking sheet or muffin pan from the oven and carefully remove the foil and weights. Return the baking sheet or muffin pan to the oven.

*For partially baked crusts,* bake until the crusts are just dry and set, 3 to 5 minutes.

*For fully baked crusts,* bake until they are light golden brown, 8 to 10 minutes.

# Rich Sweet Pastry

*Makes enough pastry for 2 pies or tarts*
◆◆◆◆◆◆◆◆◆

This is an excellent tart pastry—it's sweet, buttery, and stays crisp under a cream, custard, or fruit filling. To change the flavor of the pastry, mix a tablespoon of grated lemon or orange rind into the flour mixture, or two teaspoons of finely minced candied ginger. If there are leftover scraps, I press them out into a cookie on an ungreased baking sheet and sprinkle it with cinnamon sugar, then bake it at 375°F until it is golden and crisp; my daughter loves this impromptu snack.

**Yolk of 1 egg**

**¼ cup confectioners' sugar**

**½ cup plus 1 tablespoon all-purpose flour, plus more for rolling out the dough**

**Pinch of salt**

**2 tablespoons plus 1 teaspoon Unsalted butter, at room temperature, plus more for greasing the pans**

PANS REQUIRED:

**Two 4½ x ¾-inch tart pans with removable bottoms, two 4 x 1⅜-inch tart pans with removable bottoms, or 1 jumbo muffin pan (¾-cup capacity)**

**1 baking sheet**

**1.** Place the egg yolk in a small bowl and beat it lightly with a fork. Measure out 2 teaspoons of the yolk for the pastry and set it aside for the pastry. Reserve the remaining yolk for another use.

**2.** Sift the confectioners' sugar, flour, and salt into the bowl of a food processor. Add the butter and 2 teaspoons of egg yolk, and pulse until the dough just begins to clump together.

**3.** Turn out the dough on a piece of plastic wrap and divide it in half.

Shape each half into a disk, and wrap them individually in plastic wrap. Refrigerate for at least 1 hour and up to 24 hours.

**4.** Place a rack in the center of the oven and preheat the oven to 325°F.

**5.** Lightly grease the tart pans, and place them on a baking sheet for easier handling; set it aside. If you are using the jumbo muffin pan, line 2 muffin cups with aluminum foil and lightly grease the foil; set the pan aside.

**6.** Dust a work surface lightly with flour. Working with one at a time, lightly dust a disk of dough with flour, and using a floured rolling pin, roll it out to form a 5½- to 6-inch round. (Lift the dough several times while you roll it out, making sure that the work surface and the dough are lightly floured at all times.)

*If you are using tart pans,* fit each pastry round into a prepared tart pan, pressing the pastry into the grooves of the pan's sides. Roll the pin over the top of each pan to cut away the excess dough, or tuck the overhang to the inside of the pan for reinforcement.

*If you are using a muffin pan,* fit the pastry rounds into the prepared cups, pressing the pastry into the bottom edges and along the sides, pleating the dough in even folds to fit it to the cup. Roll the pin over the top of each cup to cut away the excess dough, or tuck the overhang to the inside of the pan for reinforcement.

7. Prick the bottoms of the tart shells all over with a fork. Gently place the baking sheet with the tart pans, or the muffin pan, in the freezer and chill until firm, 15 minutes. (Or you can refrigerate them, covered, for 24 hours.)

8. Line the chilled pastry shells with aluminum foil, pressing it into the corners and edges, and fill them to the top with pie weights or dried beans. Fill the empty muffin cups halfway with water to prevent them from scorching. Place the baking sheet or muffin pan in the oven and bake for 20 minutes.

9. Remove the baking sheet or muffin pan from the oven and carefully remove the foil and weights. Return the baking sheet or muffin pan to the oven.

*For partially baked crusts,* bake until the crusts are just dry and set, 5 to 8 minutes.

*For fully baked crusts,* bake until they are light golden brown, 10 to 12 minutes.

# CHAPTER 4

# Cookies *and* Bars

**Though baking** cookies was one of my favorite things to do as a child, somewhere during the process I found myself getting impatient. After all, the whole batch invariably was six dozen, and that meant hours, and hours, setting up the cookie sheets and baking and cooling the cookies. I admit to occasionally throwing away some of the dough, and I've also been known to freeze part of the dough for later batches of cookies. But that lump of dough often got buried under other frozen things and forgotten.

Now, however, I've devised recipes for small batches and I'm a cookie-baking fool. I can make a different batch every day, if persuaded, because it takes so much less time to make *and* bake the dough for just six to eight cookies.

It takes a lot less time to bring a couple of tablespoons of butter to room temperature than two sticks. And only one baking sheet goes into the oven!

These Small-Batch recipes allow you to fit in the time to bake, so it'll be less daunting to prepare cookies you can take to work or school, or cookies to munch while you are out for a day's hike. Cookie baking with your children can be the cherished ritual it should be. There are brownies, oatmeal cookies, peanut butter cookies, chocolate candy bar cookies, and all kinds of child-pleasers in this chapter. The batters are easy for small hands to mix up, the cookies are done before their attention spans flag, and the batches are small, so there's no chance of overdoing the sweets.

When you've invited a friend to come for coffee, you may decide to make cookies to accompany it. For those times, you'll find biscotti (fancy bars made of lemon and oats and chocolate and more), rolled cookies, cream-filled wafers, and shortbread. When you're not in the mood for company, forgo fancy and simply indulge in the pleasure of a few hot-out-of-the-oven gooey chocolate chip wonders or Chunky Peanut Butter Cookies.

The techniques for making small batches of cookies are the same as for preparing dozens, except that you need less equipment (cleanup is a breeze). A hand-held mixer is perfect for mixing the dough, and you need just one baking sheet to do the job. You'll find that when you are beating a small amount of heavy cookie dough, you have to hold the mixing bowl tightly while you beat with the mixer—that bowl wants to move in all kinds of directions. The trick: Make sure

## MEASURING EGGS

For Small-Batch cookies, small eggs are more in line with the amount of egg required, but mediums are the smallest size you'll find in these large, extra large, and jumbo times. So you'll have to use part of the egg; just beat it with a fork, a whisk, or an egg whip in a custard cup or small bowl until it is liquefied and less gloppy, 45 seconds to a minute. Then measure out the amount called for. (One medium egg equals about 3 tablespoons of beaten egg; if you have extra, you can save it for another use by storing it in a covered container in the refrigerator for up to 1 day.)

You can also use egg substitute in place of a whole or partial egg. A medium egg would equal about 3 tablespoons of egg substitute.

your butter is very soft; it will be easier to incorporate the other ingredients.

Small batches make any time cookie time.

# JK's Favorite Chocolate Chip Cookies

*Makes 6 cookies; serves 2 or 3*
◆◆◆◆◆◆◆◆◆

**My teenager, Jessie Kate,** gets a chocolate craving every time she has friends for sleepovers. So she and the friend make either these cookies or a big bowl of chocolate icing, and sometimes both. Thank goodness it's a small batch, or they would never go to sleep.

¼ **cup plus 2 tablespoons all-purpose flour**

⅛ **teaspoon baking soda**

⅛ **teaspoon salt**

**3 tablespoons plus 1 teaspoon unsalted butter, at room temperature**

¼ **cup firmly packed light brown sugar**

**2 tablespoons granulated sugar**

½ **teaspoon pure vanilla extract**

**1 tablespoon plus 1 teaspoon well-beaten egg or egg substitute**

½ **cup semisweet chocolate chips**

**PAN REQUIRED:**
**1 baking sheet**

**1.** Place a rack in the center of the oven and preheat the oven to 350°F. Set aside an ungreased baking sheet.

**2.** Place the flour, baking soda, and salt in a small bowl and whisk to blend.

**3.** Place the butter, brown sugar, granulated sugar, and vanilla in a medium-size mixing bowl and beat with a hand-held electric mixer on low speed until blended, about 20 seconds.

Add the beaten egg, reduce the mixer speed to medium, and beat until blended, about 10 seconds. Stir in the flour mixture by hand; then stir in the chocolate chips.

4. Scoop 2-tablespoon quantities of the batter onto the prepared baking sheet, spacing the mounds 2½ to 3 inches apart. Bake the cookies until they are golden brown, 14 to 15 minutes.

5. Remove the baking sheet from the oven, place it on a wire rack, and let it cool for 5 minutes. Then use a metal spatula to transfer the cookies to the rack, and let them cool completely. (For storing information, see page 183.)

## variation

# Butternutter Crunch Cookies

**This variation** is laced with chunks of peanut butter instead of chocolate chips. If you like Butterfinger candy, you'll love these: Substitute ½ cup Butterfinger BBs for the chocolate chips.

# Chocolate Toffee Cookies

*Makes 6 large cookies; serves 3*

♦♦♦♦♦♦♦♦♦

**When Eleni, my** younger daughter, and I take a walk, we frequently end up heading towards the bakery down the street from our house that sells giant versions of this cookie. We both love them so much that we almost always share one on the way home. This cookie takes care of my two cookie cravings: chocolate chip and toffee, so I decided to develop a Small-Batch recipe. I use a large ice cream scoop or measuring cup to scoop these onto the baking sheet.

**4 ounces bittersweet or semisweet chocolate, chopped (about ¾ cup)**
**2 teaspoons unsalted butter**
**2 tablespoons all-purpose flour**
**¼ teaspoon baking powder**
**Pinch of salt**
**¼ cup plus 3 tablespoons sugar**
**1 large egg**
**½ teaspoon pure vanilla extract**
**1½ chocolate-covered toffee bars (such as Heath or Skor, 1.4-ounce size), coarsely chopped**

**PAN REQUIRED:**
**1 baking sheet**

**1.** Combine the chocolate and butter in a small microwave-safe bowl, and microwave on high power for 1 minute; then stir until the mixture is smooth. Let the chocolate mixture cool to lukewarm.

**2.** Place the flour, baking powder, and salt in a small bowl and whisk to blend well.

**3.** Place the sugar and egg in a medium-size mixing bowl and beat with a hand-held electric mixer on high speed until the mixture is thick and pale, 2 to 3 minutes. Beat in the chocolate mixture and the vanilla on high speed. Then reduce the mixer speed to low and beat in the flour mixture until blended, 20 to 30 seconds. Stir in the candy pieces with a wooden spoon. Cover the bowl and refrigerate the batter until it is firm, 20 to 30 minutes.

4. Place a rack in the center of the oven and preheat the oven to 350°F. Line a baking sheet with parchment paper.

5. Scoop ¼-cup quantities of the batter onto the parchment, spacing the cookies 3 inches apart. Using a spatula, press the cookies down to flatten them to ¾-inch thickness. Bake the cookies just until the tops are dry and cracked but the cookies are still soft to touch, 21 to 23 minutes.

6. Remove the baking sheet from the oven and slide the parchment onto a wire rack. Let the cookies cool completely on the parchment. Then use a metal spatula to lift them off the paper. (For storing information, see page 183.)

# Cream-Filled Chocolate Cookies

*Makes 6 filled cookies; serves 2 or 3*
◆◆◆◆◆◆◆◆◆

**I'm not going** to claim that these taste just like Oreos, but they are quite similar. The cookie is sweetly chocolate, crisp, and sturdy, and the filling is—dare I say—better than Oreos' because it is made with a little butter.

¼ **cup all-purpose flour**

**2 tablespoons plus 1 teaspoon unsweetened cocoa powder**

⅛ **teaspoon baking soda**

**Pinch of salt**

**About ¾ cup sugar**

**2 tablespoons unsalted butter, at room temperature**

2½ **teaspoons well-beaten egg or egg substitute**

**Vanilla Cream Filling (recipe follows)**

**PAN REQUIRED:**
**1 baking sheet**

1. Place a rack in the center of the oven and preheat the oven to 375°F. Line a baking sheet with parchment paper, and set it aside.

2. Place the flour, cocoa powder, baking soda, and salt in a small bowl and whisk to blend.

3. Place ¼ cup plus 2 teaspoons of the sugar, the butter, and the beaten egg in a medium-size mixing bowl and beat with a hand-held electric mixer

on low speed until blended, about 20 seconds. Increase the mixer speed to medium and beat until the mixture is light and fluffy, about 20 seconds. Add the flour mixture to the egg mixture and beat just until the dough is blended, 15 to 20 seconds.

**4.** Roll rounded teaspoonfuls of the dough in your hands to form 12 equal balls, and place them on the prepared baking sheet, spacing them 2 inches apart. Pour the remaining sugar (about 1/2 cup) into a small bowl. Dip the bottom of a drinking glass into the sugar, and press the sugar-coated glass onto a ball of dough to flatten it. Repeat with the remaining balls of dough, dipping the glass in the sugar before flattening each cookie. Bake the cookies until they are firm, 14 to 15 minutes.

**5.** Remove the baking sheet from the oven, place it on a wire rack, and let the cookies cool completely.

**6.** Spread 1½ teaspoons of the Vanilla Cream Filling over the flat side of half of the cookies. Place the remaining cookies on top, flat side down, gently pressing down on them to squeeze the filling out to the edges of the cookies. (For storing information, see page 183.)

# Vanilla Cream Filling

**This creamy filling** really benefits from the addition of butter and pure vanilla extract. It's also great sandwiched between store-bought vanilla wafers if you need a fast fix.

**MAKES ABOUT 3 TABLESPOONS**

1 tablespoon unsalted butter, at room temperature

1 tablespoon solid vegetable shortening

1/2 teaspoon milk

1/4 teaspoon pure vanilla extract

Pinch of salt

1/2 cup confectioners' sugar

Place the butter, shortening, milk, vanilla, and salt in a small bowl and mix with a fork until a soft, smooth paste forms. Add the confectioners' sugar and mix until the filling is well blended and smooth. (This may take up to 5 minutes.) Cover the bowl with plastic wrap and set it aside at room temperature until you are ready to use it.

## variation

# Espresso Cream Sandwich Cookies

**This is a variation** of Cream-Filled Chocolate Cookies (page 174) for coffee lovers: mocha-flavored cookies with a filling that tastes like a sweet caffè latte.

When you combine the sugar, butter, and egg in Step 3, add ¼ teaspoon instant espresso powder, and beat until it has dissolved in the mixture. When you are ready to make the filling, first stir a pinch of instant espresso powder into the milk; let it stand until the espresso dissolves.

# Mint Chocolate Wafer Cookies

*Makes 10 cookies; serves 2 or 3*
◆◆◆◆◆◆◆◆◆

**While I was** working on this book, our order of Girl Scout Thin Mints arrived. I decided it would be nice to be able to bake a small batch of them myself, any time I wanted, thereby keeping me from gobbling the major portion of a box the day it arrived. Although it's hard to duplicate a mass-produced cookie, these are very close. Now you won't have to wait another year for your Girl Scout cookies to be delivered!

¼ cup plus 1 tablespoon all-purpose
   flour
Pinch of baking soda
1 tablespoon plus 2½ teaspoons
   unsweetened cocoa powder

Pinch of salt
2 tablespoons unsalted butter,
   at room temperature
3 tablespoons sugar
2¼ teaspoons well-beaten egg or
   egg substitute
⅛ teaspoon pure vanilla extract
**Mint Chocolate Cookie Glaze**
   (recipe follows)

PAN REQUIRED:
1 baking sheet

1. Place the flour, baking soda, cocoa powder, and salt in a small bowl and whisk to blend.

2. Place the butter, sugar, beaten egg, and vanilla in a medium-size mixing bowl, and beat with a hand-

held electric mixer on low speed until blended, about 20 seconds. Increase the mixer speed to medium and beat until the butter mixture is well blended, about 20 seconds. Add the flour mixture to the butter mixture, reduce the mixer speed to low, and beat just until the dough is blended, 10 to 15 seconds.

**3.** Transfer the dough to a piece of plastic wrap and shape it into a 3-inch-long log, 1¾ inches in diameter. Wrap it well in the plastic wrap and refrigerate until it is well chilled, 3 to 4 hours or overnight.

**4.** Place a rack in the center of the oven and preheat the oven to 350°F. Line a baking sheet with parchment paper.

**5.** Cut the chilled dough into ¼-inch-thick slices and place them on the prepared baking sheet, spacing them ½ inch apart. Bake until the cookies are set and slightly firm on top, 8 to 10 minutes.

**6.** Remove the baking sheet from the oven and slide the parchment to a wire rack. Let them cool completely, then remove the cookies from the parchment with a metal spatula.

**7.** When you are ready to glaze the cookies, place a piece of waxed paper on a wire rack. Pour the hot glaze into a small bowl. Working with one cookie at a time, plunge the cookies into the glaze and turn them with a fork to coat both sides. Lift the cookies out with the fork and transfer them to the waxed paper. Place the wire rack, with the cookies on it, in the refrigerator until the chocolate is firm, about 15 minutes. (For storing information, see page 183.)

# Mint Chocolate Cookie Glaze

**This glaze tastes** just like the one on those Girl Scout cookies—smooth, dark, and minty.

**MAKES ⅓ CUP**

¾ **cup semisweet chocolate chips**
1 **tablespoon solid vegetable shortening**

¼ **teaspoon plus** ⅛ **teaspoon pure peppermint extract**

Combine all the ingredients in a small microwave-safe bowl and microwave on high power until the shortening is melted, 30 seconds. Stir until the glaze is smooth and use immediately.

# Irresistible Oatmeal Cookies

*Makes 8 cookies; serves 2 or 3*
◆◆◆◆◆◆◆◆

**Growing up, I** spent many a summer vacation week with my Aunt Cora in Winter Park, Florida, learning to bake. I'm still baking some of her recipes, such as this one, which was the first cookie I ever made. Aunt Cora's oatmeal cookies are chewy within but crisp on the outside—I think due to a bit more sugar than usual. (If you like your cookies really crisp, see the Note that follows the recipe.)

You can change the flavor by adding two tablespoons of chocolate or white chocolate chips to the batter. My mother makes them with dried cranberries or dried cherries, white chocolate chips, and chopped walnuts, and they are fabulous.

**4 tablespoons (1/2 stick) unsalted butter, at room temperature**

**1/3 cup sugar**

**1 teaspoon well-stirred sour cream**

**1 tablespoon well-beaten egg or egg substitute**

**1/2 teaspoon pure vanilla extract**

**1/4 cup plus 3 tablespoons all-purpose flour**

**1/8 teaspoon baking soda**

**1/4 teaspoon ground cinnamon (optional)**

**Pinch of salt**

**1/2 cup old-fashioned rolled oats**

**1/4 cup raisins**

**1/4 cup chopped pecans, toasted (optional; see Note, page 195)**

PAN REQUIRED:

**1 baking sheet**

## variation

# Peanut Butter Oatmeal Cookies

**These cookies** are softer than the Irresistible Oatmeal Cookies and remain mounded in shape.

Reduce the flour to 1/4 cup plus 2 tablespoons. Substitute 2 tablespoons of creamy peanut butter for

2 tablespoons of the butter. Omit the cinnamon. Substitute peanut butter chips or chocolate chips for the raisins, and chopped peanuts for the chopped pecans. Makes 6 to 8 cookies.

1. Preheat the oven to 350°F. Line a baking sheet with parchment paper, and set it aside.

2. Place the butter, sugar, and sour cream in a medium-size mixing bowl and beat with a hand-held electric mixer on medium speed until creamy, about 1 minute, scraping the bowl once or twice. Add the beaten egg and vanilla, and beat until the mixture is well blended, 30 to 45 seconds.

3. Place the flour, baking soda, cinnamon if using, and salt in a small bowl and whisk to blend. Add the flour mixture to the butter mixture and stir well with a wooden spoon. Stir in the oats, raisins, and pecans, if using.

4. Drop spoonfuls of the dough onto the prepared cookie sheet to make 8 equal-size mounds and space them 1½ to 2 inches apart (the cookies will spread out during baking). Bake the cookies until they are golden brown, about 15 minutes.

5. Remove the baking sheet from the oven, transfer the parchment to a wire rack, and let the cookies cool completely. Gently peel them off the parchment before serving. (For storing information, see page 183.)

NOTE: If you like your oatmeal cookies thin and crisp, omit the sour cream and reduce the flour to ¼ cup plus 2 tablespoons. Bake for 17 minutes.

# Big Blast Oatmeal Cookies

*Makes 2 large cookies; serves 2*

◆◆◆◆◆◆◆◆

One morning my then-two-year old insisted on having a "big

cookie" for breakfast. Normally cookies are not an A.M. option, but this looked to be a rule-breaker kind of day. So I dumped these together (literally, from the oatmeal box and the flour canister) and made them up on the spot. They were so good that I had to run to write down what I had done!

**3 tablespoons all-purpose flour**

**3 tablespoons old-fashioned rolled oats**

**3 tablespoons sugar**

**1/8 teaspoon baking soda**

**1/8 teaspoon salt**

**Pinch of ground cinnamon**

**1 1/2 tablespoons unsalted butter, at room temperature**

**1/4 teaspoon pure vanilla extract**

**1 tablespoon plus 1 teaspoon well-beaten egg or egg substitute**

**3 tablespoons raisins**

PAN REQUIRED:
**1 baking sheet**

1. Place a rack in the center of the oven and preheat the oven to 350°F. Line a baking sheet with parchment paper and set it aside.

2. Place the flour, oats, sugar, baking soda, salt, and cinnamon in a medium-size mixing bowl and stir with a fork to blend. Add the butter and vanilla, and blend with the fork until moist crumbs form. Add the beaten egg and blend it in with the fork, or with your fingers, until a stiff dough forms. Use your hands to mix in the raisins.

3. Divide the dough in half and place the halves 4 inches apart on the prepared baking sheet (the cookies will spread during baking). Bake the cookies until they are lightly browned, about 20 minutes.

4. Remove the baking sheet from the oven and transfer the parchment to a wire rack to cool for 15 minutes. Then gently peel the cookies off the parchment, place them on the rack, and let them cool completely. (For storing information, see box, facing page.)

# How to Store Cookies Once They're Baked

If you've made cookies for one or two people and still have more than you need, here's how you should take care of the leftovers until you're ready to eat them. If they're refrigerated, let them come to room temperature before serving. You can warm the soft cookies or bars in a 350°F oven for a minute or two for fresh-baked flavor.

**BROWNIES AND BARS:** Store the bars in the loaf pan in which they were baked (no need to keep the aluminum foil lining in it). Cover it with foil and store at room temperature for a day, or refrigerate up to 3 days.

**SOFT OR CHEWY COOKIES:** Place a piece of waxed paper on top of a larger sheet of aluminum foil and arrange the cookies in a single layer on it. Fold the waxed paper over the cookies and then securely seal the foil over it. Store at room temperature for a day, or refrigerate for up to 3 days.

**CRISP COOKIES:** In a dry climate, keep them in a container with a loose fitting lid, or loosely wrapped in wax paper, for a day or two. In a humid climate, keep them in a tightly closed container at room temperature for a day or two. Biscotti will keep for up to 3 days. If the cookies are glazed, store them between pieces of waxed paper in an airtight container.

**FILLED AND FROSTED COOKIES:** Place a piece of waxed paper on top of a larger sheet of aluminum foil and arrange the cookies in a single layer on it. Loosely drape the waxed paper over the cookies, bring the foil up and over the cookies, and just pinch the top edges together. Store at room temperature for a day, or refrigerate for up to 3 days.

# Oatmeal Tuiles

*Makes 4 cookies; serves 2*

◆◆◆◆◆◆◆◆◆

*Tuile* **is the** French word for a curved clay roofing tile, and it also refers to the most delicate of cookies, shaped like one of those tiles. Stir the batter before dropping it onto the baking sheet so the oats stay evenly suspended, and then watch the cookies closely while they are in the oven—they can burn in a wink.

**1 tablespoon unsalted butter, melted**

**2 tablespoons firmly packed light brown sugar**

**⅛ teaspoon salt**

**⅛ teaspoon ground nutmeg**

**Pinch of ground cinnamon**

**⅛ teaspoon pure almond extract**

**1 tablespoon lightly beaten egg white**

**1 tablespoon cake flour**

**2 tablespoons old-fashioned rolled oats**

**PAN REQUIRED:**
**1 baking sheet**

1. Place a rack in the center of the oven and preheat the oven to 425°F. Line a baking sheet with parchment paper and set it aside. Set aside a rolling pin and a metal spatula.

2. Place the butter, brown sugar, salt, nutmeg, cinnamon, and almond extract in a medium-size mixing bowl and mix with a wooden spoon until well blended. Add the egg white and cake flour, and stir with a whisk until the batter is smooth. Stir in the oats.

3. Spoon the batter into 4 equal rounds on the prepared baking sheet,

## FILLING *TUILE* CUPS

*uiles* can easily be molded to form serving cups for fruit and ice cream. Because you'll have to shape them quickly, have 4 molds ready to drape the hot cookies over: you can use oranges, lemons, ice cream scoops, or very small bowls.

After the *tuiles* have cooled, fill them with ice cream, sorbet, or fruit, and spoon a dessert sauce on the plate. Here are some combinations to try:

- Raspberries with Pineapple Crème Anglaise (page 391) or Passion Fruit Sauce (page 372)

- Chocolate sorbet with Mocha Mint Crème Anglaise (page 290) or Raspberry Sauce (page 248)

- Sliced bananas tossed with brown sugar, with Rich Caramel Sauce (page 259) or Bourbon Caramel Sauce (page 269)

- Orange segments with Orange Caramel Sauce (page 383)

- Strawberries with Milk Chocolate Sauce (page 251)

spacing them 4 inches apart. Moisten your fingers with water, and spread the batter out to form 3-inch rounds.

4. Bake the cookies until the edges turn golden brown, 4 to 5 minutes. Remove the baking sheet from the oven, and working quickly, use the spatula to transfer the cookies to the rolling pin, draping them over the pin. Let them cool completely on the rolling pin. When you remove them, they will retain the *tuile* shape. (For storing information, see page 183.)

# Chunky Peanut Butter Cookies

*Makes 8 cookies; serves 3 or 4*

◆◆◆◆◆◆◆◆◆

## I adore peanut butter

cookies. These are rich and crumbly, moist, chewy, and crunchy with peanuts all at the same time—just how a classic peanut butter cookie should be, complete with the criss-cross pattern on the top. If you like, you can press them out with the bottom of a glass that has been dipped in sugar.

⅓ cup plus 1 teaspoon all-purpose flour

Pinch of baking soda

Pinch of salt

3 tablespoons granulated sugar

1 tablespoon packed dark brown sugar

2 tablespoons unsalted butter, at room temperature

2 teaspoons well-beaten egg or egg substitute

¼ teaspoon pure vanilla extract

⅓ cup extra-chunky peanut butter

PAN REQUIRED:

1 baking sheet

1. Place the flour, baking soda, and salt in a small bowl and whisk to blend.

2. Place the granulated sugar, brown sugar, butter, beaten egg, and vanilla in a medium-size mixing bowl and beat with a hand-held electric mixer on low speed until blended, about 1 minute. Beat in the peanut butter until blended, about 20 seconds. Add

the flour mixture and beat on low speed until the dough is blended, about 30 seconds. Transfer the dough to a piece of plastic wrap and press it out to form a thick disk. Wrap it well in the plastic wrap and refrigerate until it is pliable, about 30 minutes.

**3.** Place a rack in the center of the oven and preheat the oven to 325°F. Set aside an ungreased baking sheet.

**4.** Shape the dough, by tablespoonfuls, into mounds on the baking sheet, spacing the mounds about 1 inch apart.

Using a fork, flatten each one to form a 1/3-inch-thick round, making grooves in the surface with the tines of the fork. Press the fork lightly in the opposite direction to make a crisscross pattern in the tops of the cookies. Bake the cookies until they are golden, about 13 minutes.

**5.** Remove the baking sheet from the oven and place it on a wire rack to cool for 5 minutes. Then use a spatula to transfer the cookies to the wire rack, and let them cool completely. (For storing information, see page 183.)

# Chocolate Ice Cream Peanut Butter Sandwiches

**Place a** Chunky Peanut Butter Cookie (page 186), smooth side up, on the center of a piece of heavy-duty aluminum foil. Scoop 2 to 3 tablespoons of slightly softened chocolate ice cream (or another flavor of your choice) onto the cookie and top it with a second cookie, smooth side down. Press the cookies together lightly and smooth the sides. Wrap the "sandwich" well in the aluminum foil and place it in the freezer. Repeat with the remaining cookies and ice cream, to make 4 sandwiches. Freeze the sandwich cookies for at least 3 hours.

To serve, unwrap the sandwiches and place them on dessert plates. Let them stand for 10 minutes for the ice cream to soften a bit. Then drizzle warm or room-temperature chocolate sauce over the sandwiches, and sprinkle chopped cocktail peanuts over them. Place each on a dessert plate and serve immediately, with a dessert fork.

# Outrageous Peanut Butter Cookies

*Makes 8 cookies; serves 3*
◆◆◆◆◆◆◆◆◆

**These are actually** triple-outrageous, with oats and a peanut/chocolate/caramel–loaded candy bar chopped and added to the dough. If you like rich, here you go!

¼ **cup all-purpose flour**

**Pinch of baking soda**

**Pinch of salt**

¼ **cup packed dark brown sugar**

**2 tablespoons unsalted butter, at room temperature**

**2 teaspoons well-beaten egg or egg substitute**

¼ **teaspoon pure vanilla extract**

⅓ **cup extra-chunky peanut butter**

1½ **tablespoons old-fashioned rolled oats**

**Half of a 1.8 to 2-ounce candy bar containing peanuts, peanut butter, chocolate, and caramel (such as NutRageous), cut into** ½-**inch cubes**

**Granulated sugar, for flattening the cookies**

PAN REQUIRED:
**1 baking sheet**

**1.** Place the flour, baking soda, and salt in a small bowl and whisk to blend.

**2.** Place the brown sugar, butter, beaten egg, and vanilla in a medium-size mixing bowl and beat with a hand-held electric mixer on low speed until blended, about 1 minute. Beat in the peanut butter until blended, about 20 seconds. Add the flour mixture, reduce the mixer speed to low, and beat until the dough is blended, about 30 seconds. Stir in the oats and the candy bar cubes.

3. Place a rack in the center of the oven and preheat the oven to 325°F. Line the baking sheet with aluminum foil, and set it aside.

4. Drop the dough by heaping table-spoonfuls onto the prepared baking sheet, spacing the mounds 1½ inches apart. Spoon about 2 tablespoons of granulated sugar into a shallow dish. Dip the bottom of a glass into the sugar and use it to slightly flatten one of the cookies. Repeat, dipping the glass in sugar before flattening each cookie. Place the baking sheet in the freezer to chill the cookies for 15 minutes.

5. Bake the cookies until they are golden, 15 to 20 minutes.

6. Remove the baking sheet from the oven and place it on a wire rack to cool until the cookies begin to firm, about 5 minutes. Then use a metal spatula to remove the cookies from the foil, place them on the rack, and let them cool completely. (For storing information, see page 183.)

# Shortbread Dainties

*Makes 5 cookies; serves 2*
◆◆◆◆◆◆◆◆◆

**These tender glazed** sugar cookies are subtly spiced with nutmeg. The dough holds its shape during baking, so this is a reliable recipe for cutting out cookie shapes. Both the plain milk glaze and the lemon glaze are delicious on the cookies; I drizzle them with a little of each.

**FOR THE COOKIES:**
1/2 **cup all-purpose flour**
**1 tablespoon plus 1 teaspoon cornstarch**
**Pinch of salt**
1/8 **teaspoon freshly grated nutmeg**
**4 tablespoons (1/2 stick) unsalted butter, at room temperature**
**3 tablespoons sugar**
**1 teaspoon pure vanilla extract**

**FOR THE GLAZES:**
1/2 **cup confectioners' sugar**
**About 1**1/2 **teaspoons whole milk**
**About 1**1/2 **teaspoons fresh lemon juice**

**PAN REQUIRED:**
**1 baking sheet**

**1.** Place a rack in the center of the oven and preheat the oven to 350°F. Set aside an ungreased baking sheet.

**2.** Place the flour, cornstarch, salt, and nutmeg in a medium-size mixing bowl and whisk to blend.

**3.** Place the butter, sugar, and vanilla in a small bowl and beat with a hand-held electric mixer on medium speed until fluffy, about 20 seconds. Add the flour mixture and mix it in with a fork until the dough comes together.

**4.** Turn the dough out onto a piece of waxed paper. Use your hands to gather the dough into a ball and flatten it into a disk. Cover the dough with another piece of waxed paper, and roll it out to ½-inch thickness. Cut out the cookies, using 2-inch cutters. Transfer the cookies to the ungreased baking sheet, spacing them ½ inch apart. Gather and reroll the scraps; then cut out additional cookies and transfer them to the baking sheet. Bake the cookies until they are firm to touch and just beginning to color, about 15 minutes.

**5.** Remove the baking sheet from the oven, and use a metal spatula to transfer the cookies to a wire rack. Let them cool completely.

**6. MAKE THE GLAZES:** Spoon ¼ cup confectioners' sugar into each of 2 small bowls. Add the milk to one bowl and the lemon juice to the other. Stir each until smooth. While the cookies are still on the wire rack, brush the desired glaze on each cookie, or drizzle the glaze on decoratively. Let the cookies dry completely on the rack, 2 to 3 hours. (For storing information, see page 183.)

# Lemon Lime Coolers

*Makes 6 cookies; serves 2 or 3*

◆◆◆◆◆◆◆◆◆

**These little round** cookies are similar to the ones you see in specialty food stores and mail-order catalogs. A packaged mix used for whiskey sours is what makes them tart; you'll find it in supermarkets and liquor stores. These buttery, tart, crumbly cookies melt in your mouth.

¼ **cup plus 2 teaspoons all-purpose flour**

½ **cup plus 1 tablespoon confectioners' sugar**

1 **teaspoon packaged powdered lemon-flavored bar mix (whiskey sour or margarita mix)**

2 **tablespoons unsalted butter, at room temperature**

¼ **teaspoon pure vanilla extract**

PAN REQUIRED:
**1 baking sheet**

1. Place the flour, 1 tablespoon of the confectioners' sugar, and the bar mix in a small bowl and whisk to blend. Add the butter and vanilla, and using a pastry blender or a fork, blend the dough well. Gather the dough into a ball and pat it into a disk. Wrap the dough in plastic wrap and refrigerate it for 30 minutes.

2. Place a rack in the center of the oven and preheat the oven to 375°F. Line a baking sheet with parchment paper.

3. With floured hands, roll level teaspoons of the dough to form ¾-inch balls and arrange them on the prepared baking sheet, spacing them 2 inches apart. Bake the cookies until they are pale gold, about 10 minutes.

4. While the cookies are baking, place the remaining ½ cup confectioners' sugar in a shallow bowl.

5. Remove the baking sheet from the oven and immediately transfer the hot cookies to the bowl of confectioners' sugar, gently rolling them to coat them completely with the sugar. Place them on a plate and let them cool completely. When they are cooled, roll them again in the confectioners' sugar. (For storing information, see page 183.)

# Pecan Snowball Cookies

*Makes 6 cookies; serves 2 or 3*

◆◆◆◆◆◆◆◆◆

**These little mounds** of crumbly, rich pecan shortbread have many names; they are sometimes called Mexican wedding cakes or Russian tea cakes. They are rolled twice in confectioners' sugar for a snowy, melt-in-your-mouth coating.

**About 1 cup confectioners' sugar**
**Pinch of baking powder**
**Pinch of salt**
**4 tablespoons (½ stick) unsalted butter, cut into pieces, at room temperature**
**¼ teaspoon pure vanilla extract**

**¼ cup plus 3 tablespoons all-purpose flour**
**¼ cup pecan pieces, lightly toasted (see box, facing page), finely chopped**

**PAN REQUIRED:**
**1 baking sheet**

1. Place ⅓ cup of the confectioners' sugar, the baking powder, and the salt in a medium-size mixing bowl and whisk to blend. Add the butter and vanilla, and beat with a hand-held electric mixer on low speed until well blended, about 1 minute. Mix in the flour with a wooden spoon. Then use a rubber spatula or your hands to knead in the pecans. Turn the mixture out onto a piece of heavy-duty plastic wrap. Press the dough out to form a thick disk, and wrap it up in the plastic wrap. Refrigerate for 1 hour, or up to 2 days.

## HOW TO TOAST NUTS

Toasting makes nuts more crisp and intensifies the flavor, bringing out their nutty best. You can toast most nuts in the oven or on the stovetop, following these methods. To toast hazelnuts, see page 203.

**OVEN METHOD:** Preheat the oven to 350°F. Place the shelled nuts in a single layer on an ungreased baking sheet. Bake until they are fragrant and lightly browned, 4 to 6 minutes if they are finely chopped, slivered, or sliced, or 7 to 10 minutes if they are whole or halves. Stir halfway through the baking time, and watch them closely to prevent burning. Cool the nuts completely before using.

**SKILLET METHOD:** Place the shelled nuts in a dry heavy skillet and toast over medium heat, stirring constantly, until they are fragrant and lightly browned, 3 minutes for finely chopped, slivered, or sliced, or 5 to 6 minutes if they are whole or halves. Cool the nuts completely before using.

**2.** Place a rack in the center of the oven and preheat the oven to 350°F. Line a baking sheet with parchment paper and set it aside.

**3.** Remove the dough from the refrigerator. With floured hands, roll spoonfuls of the dough into 2-inch balls and place them on the prepared baking sheet, spacing them 2 inches apart. Bake the cookies until the bottoms are golden brown, about 15 minutes.

**4.** While the cookies are baking, sift the remaining ⅔ cup confectioners' sugar into a pie plate.

**5.** Gently remove the cookies from the baking sheet and while they are still warm, roll them in the confectioners' sugar. Transfer the cookies to a wire rack and let them cool completely. Then roll the cookies in confectioners' sugar again. (For storing information, see page 183.)

# Cheesecake Toffee Drops

*Makes 6 cookies; serves 2 or 3*

◆◆◆◆◆◆◆◆◆

**Cream cheese keeps** these drop cookies moist and chewy, and the chopped chocolate-covered toffee in the batter makes them super-rich. If you'd rather keep them simple, stir in one quarter cup chopped walnuts instead of the candy bar.

⅓ **cup all-purpose flour**

⅛ **teaspoon baking soda**

**Pinch of salt**

¼ **cup firmly packed light brown sugar**

**2 tablespoons cream cheese, at room temperature**

**1 tablespoon unsalted butter, at room temperature**

**1 teaspoon well-beaten egg or egg substitute**

¼ **teaspoon pure vanilla extract**

¼ **cup chopped chocolate-covered toffee bar (such as Heath or Skor)**

**PAN REQUIRED:**
**1 baking sheet**

**1.** Place a rack in the center of the oven and preheat the oven to 300°F. Set aside an ungreased baking sheet.

**2.** Place the flour, baking soda, and salt in a small bowl and whisk to blend well.

**3.** Place the brown sugar, cream cheese, and butter in a medium-size mixing bowl and beat with a hand-held electric mixer on medium speed until smooth. Add the beaten egg and the vanilla, and beat on medium speed until the dough is lighter in texture, about 20 seconds. Scrape down the sides of the bowl and add the flour mixture. Beat on low speed just until the dry ingredients are blended in.

Then stir in the chocolate-covered toffee with a wooden spoon.

**4.** Drop the cookie batter by rounded tablespoonfuls onto the baking sheet, spacing them 1½ to 2 inches apart. Bake until the cookies appear dry and are golden, 20 to 25 minutes.

**5.** While the cookies are baking, lay a piece of waxed paper on a wire rack.

**6.** Remove the baking sheet from the oven and immediately transfer the cookies to the waxed paper. Let them cool completely. (For storing information, see page 183.)

# Coconut Almond White Chocolate Macaroons

*Makes 8 cookies; serves 2 or 3*

◆◆◆◆◆◆◆◆

**At first glance,** these bites appear to be light and airy—and they are. But the addition of toasted coconut, almonds, and white chocolate chips makes them more substantial than they look, and a bit chewy. This is a cookie that satisfies the desire for an indulgence with a very light touch. I think they are just right for enjoying with espresso or a glass of port.

½ **cup lightly packed sweetened flaked coconut**

**3 tablespoons slivered or chopped blanched almonds**

**White of 1 large egg, at room temperature**

⅛ **teaspoon cream of tartar**

**2 tablespoons sugar**

⅛ **teaspoon pure vanilla extract**

**Drop of pure almond extract**

**3 tablespoons white chocolate chips**

**PAN REQUIRED:**
**1 baking sheet**

1. Place a rack in the center of the oven and preheat the oven to 325°F. Line a baking sheet with parchment paper and set it aside.

2. Spread the coconut and almonds in a thin layer on a rimmed baking sheet and bake, stirring occasionally, until they are lightly browned, 12 to 15 minutes. Transfer the baking sheet to a wire rack and let the coconut and almonds cool completely. Keep the oven on.

3. Place the egg white and cream of tartar in a medium-size mixing bowl and beat with a hand-held electric mixer on high speed until soft peaks form, about 20 seconds. With the mixer running, gradually add the sugar, 1 tablespoon at a time, and the vanilla and almond extracts. Beat until stiff peaks form, 1 to 1½ minutes. Then gently fold in the toasted coconut, almonds, and white chocolate chips.

4. Spoon the macaroon mixture into 8 equal-size mounds on the prepared baking sheet, spacing them 2 inches apart. Bake until they appear dry, about 20 minutes.

5. Remove the baking sheet from the oven and slide the parchment paper onto a wire rack. Let the macaroons cool completely on the parchment. Then use a metal spatula to lift the macaroons off the paper. (For storing information, see page 183.)

# Chocolate Almond Biscotti

*Makes 8 cookies; serves 3*

**Biscotti are Italian** cookies that are baked as a flat log, then sliced and baked again. The crisp texture makes them perfect for dipping in sweet wine, coffee, milk, or tea. These biscotti are richly chocolate in flavor, studded with chopped toasted almonds, and dipped in white chocolate for an elegant contrast.

½ cup all-purpose flour, plus extra for the work surface

2 tablespoons Dutch-process cocoa powder

¼ teaspoon baking powder

Pinch of salt

1 ounce bittersweet or semisweet chocolate, finely chopped

2 tablespoons unsalted butter

¼ cup sugar

White of 1 large egg

¼ teaspoon pure vanilla extract

¼ teaspoon pure almond extract

¼ cup whole almonds (blanched or unblanched), lightly toasted (see page 195), coarsely chopped

2 ounces good-quality white chocolate (such as Baker's), finely chopped

PAN REQUIRED:
1 baking sheet

**1.** Place a rack in the center of the oven and preheat the oven to 350°F. Line a baking sheet with parchment paper and set it aside.

**2.** Place the flour, cocoa powder,

baking powder, and salt in a medium-size mixing bowl and whisk to blend.

**3.** Place the chocolate and butter in a small microwave-safe bowl and microwave on high power until the butter melts and the chocolate is soft, about 45 seconds. Stir the chocolate mixture until it is smooth; then stir in the sugar. Add the egg white and the vanilla and almond extracts, and whisk to blend. Add the chocolate mixture to the flour mixture, mixing well with a wooden spoon. Mix in the almonds. The dough will be soft. Scrape the dough into the center of the bowl, cover the bowl with plastic wrap, and refrigerate until it is firm enough to work with, 20 to 30 minutes.

**4.** Lightly flour a cutting board or work surface, and flour your hands. Transfer the dough to the board and form it into a $4\frac{1}{2}$ x $2\frac{1}{2}$ x 1 to $1\frac{1}{2}$-inch log. Place the log on the prepared baking sheet. Bake the biscotti log until it is firm, about 30 minutes.

**5.** Remove the baking sheet from the oven and use a spatula to gently transfer the log to a wire rack, leaving the parchment on the baking sheet. Let

the log cool completely, about 1 hour. Turn off the oven.

**6.** When the log is almost completely cool, preheat the oven to 325°F.

**7.** When the log is completely cool, transfer it to a cutting board. Carefully use a serrated knife to slice the log diagonally into 8 equal slices. Arrange them, cut side down, on the parchment-lined baking sheet and bake until they are dry and golden brown, 15 to 18 minutes.

**8.** Remove the baking sheet from the oven and using a thin spatula, turn the biscotti over. Continue baking until the biscotti are slightly dry, about 20 minutes.

**9.** Remove the baking sheet from the oven, and use a metal spatula to transfer the biscotti to the wire rack. Let them cool completely.

**10.** Place the white chocolate in a small microwave-safe bowl and microwave on medium power until it is glossy, about 45 seconds; then stir until smooth. Line the baking sheet with a clean piece of parchment or waxed paper. Carefully pick up a biscotti with tongs positioned at the sides of the cookie. Dip one entire side into the white chocolate, coating half of the cookie. Raise the tongs and turn the cookie over, grasp the uncoated part of the edges with your other hand, and lay the cookie on the parchment paper, coated side up. Repeat with the remaining biscotti. Refrigerate the biscotti until the white chocolate sets, about 30 minutes. (For storing information, see page 183.)

## variation
# Cherry Almond Chocolate Biscotti

Reduce the almonds in the Chocolate Almond Biscotti (page 199) to 2 tablespoons. Before wrapping and refrigerating the dough in Step 3, knead in 2 tablespoons dried cherries. Bake as directed. Instead of white chocolate, melt semisweet chocolate to coat the biscotti.

# Cinnamon Hazelnut Biscotti

*Makes 10 cookies; serves 3*
◆◆◆◆◆◆◆◆◆

## Cinnamon and hazelnut

aromas permeate the house when these are baking. A little cornmeal adds a slightly grainy texture to these superior biscotti. They are crunchy, with a sweet, rich flavor, and are delicious dunked in coffee.

¼ cup plus 3 tablespoons all-purpose flour

2 tablespoons yellow cornmeal

¼ teaspoon baking powder

Pinch of salt

⅛ teaspoon ground cinnamon

Yolk of 1 large egg

3 tablespoons sugar

2 tablespoons unsalted butter, melted and cooled

⅛ teaspoon pure vanilla extract

¼ cup hazelnuts, toasted (see box, facing page) and chopped

PAN REQUIRED:
1 baking sheet

1. Place a rack in the center of the oven and preheat the oven to 350°F. Line a baking sheet with parchment paper and set it aside.

2. Place the flour, cornmeal, baking powder, salt, and cinnamon in a medium-size mixing bowl and whisk to blend.

3. Place the egg yolk, sugar, melted butter, and vanilla in a small bowl and whisk to blend. Add the egg mixture to the flour mixture and stir until a stiff

dough forms. Using a wooden spoon or your hands, knead in the hazelnuts.

**4.** Lightly flour a cutting board or work surface, and flour your hands. Transfer the dough to the board and form it into a 6 x 2 x 1-inch log. Place the log on the prepared baking sheet. Bake the biscotti log until it has risen and spread to about double its size and is dry to the touch, about 30 minutes.

**5.** Remove the baking sheet from the oven and use a spatula to gently transfer the log to a wire rack, leaving the parchment on the baking sheet. Let the log cool completely, about 1 hour. Turn off the oven.

**6.** When the loaf is almost completely cool, preheat the oven to 325°F.

**7.** When the log is completely cool, transfer it to a cutting board. Carefully use a serrated knife to slice the log diagonally into 10 equal slices. Arrange them, cut side down, on the parchment-lined baking sheet, and bake until they are dry and golden brown, 15 to 18 minutes.

**8.** Remove the baking sheet from the oven and using a thin spatula, turn

## TOASTING HAZELNUTS

Oven-roasting the hazelnuts intensifies their flavor and makes them crisp. It also makes the skins easier to remove. To toast the nuts, preheat the oven to 275°F. Spread the nuts in a single layer in an ungreased shallow baking pan, and bake until the skins crack and the nuts turn light gold, 20 minutes. (You can roast them at 350°F for a shorter amount of time, 10 to 12 minutes, but they must be watched more closely. The nuts can darken and lose their mild sweet flavor in an instant.) Wrap the hot nuts in a clean terry-cloth towel and steam for 4 to 5 minutes; then rub vigorously to remove the remaining skin.

the biscotti over. Continue baking until the biscotti are slightly dry, about 10 minutes.

**9.** Remove the baking sheet from the oven and using a thin metal spatula, transfer the biscotti to the wire rack; let them cool completely. (For storing information, see page 183.)

# Moist Fudgy Brownies

*Makes 3 brownies; serves 3*

◆◆◆◆◆◆◆◆◆

**This Small-Batch** brownie is adapted from my family's recipe notebook, based on the original that I wrote down as my mom baked them. I grew up eating them and they are still what I make when one of us needs something rich, thick, and fudgy. They're so easy that you could be eating them in less than one hour.

**1½ tablespoons unsalted butter, at room temperature, plus more for greasing the pan**

**¾ ounce unsweetened chocolate, chopped (about 2½ tablespoons)**

**¼ cup plus 2 tablespoons sugar**

**1 tablespoon plus 2¼ teaspoons well-beaten egg or egg substitute**

**½ teaspoon pure vanilla extract**

**3 tablespoons plus 2 teaspoons all-purpose flour**

**⅛ teaspoon salt**

**¼ cup chopped pecans (optional)**

**PAN REQUIRED:**

**1 petite loaf pan (2-cup capacity, about 5 x 3 inches)**

**1.** Place a rack in the center of the oven and preheat the oven to 350°F. Lightly grease the loaf pan. Line the bottom of the loaf pan with a strip of aluminum foil to fit down the length and up the short sides, with enough extra length to extend over the edges by about 1½ inches. Lightly grease the foil, and set the pan aside.

**2.** Place the butter and the unsweetened chocolate in a medium-size microwave-safe bowl, and microwave on medium power until the chocolate is soft and the butter is melted, about 1 minute. Stir until the chocolate is smooth. Add the sugar and whisk well.

Then add the beaten egg and vanilla, and whisk until well blended. Add the flour and salt, and whisk well. Then fold in the pecans, if using. Spread the batter evenly in the prepared loaf pan.

**3.** Bake until a toothpick inserted in center comes out with moist crumbs attached, 28 to 30 minutes; the top will appear dry and will be starting to shrink from the edges of the pan. Do not overcook.

**4.** Remove the loaf pan from the oven, place it on a wire rack, and let the brownies cool completely in the pan. Use the edges of the foil to lift the brownies out of the pan. Remove the foil and cut the brownies into bars. (For storing information, see page 183.)

## variation

# Chocolate-Covered Cherry Brownies

**Top Moist Fudgy** Brownies with melted chocolate, marshmallows, and candied cherries, and serve them warm and gooey, with a fork.

Prepare the Moist Fudgy Brownies through Step 3. Bake until almost done, 27 minutes. Remove the loaf pan from the oven and immediately sprinkle 3 tablespoons of miniature marshmallows and 2 tablespoons of semisweet or milk chocolate chips evenly over the brownies. Return the loaf pan to the oven and bake for 2 minutes more. Remove the pan from the oven and sprinkle 2 tablespoons chopped candied cherries or chopped maraschino cherries evenly over the marshmallows. Let the brownies cool slightly in the pan, about 15 minutes, before lifting them out and cutting them into bars.

## variation

# Brownie Peanut Sundaes

**Prepare the** Moist Fudgy Brownies (page 204) through Step 2. Place the pan in the oven and bake for 28 minutes. Then immediately drizzle 3 tablespoons of Rich Caramel Sauce (page 259) over the brownies. Sprinkle 3 tablespoons semisweet or milk chocolate chips and 2 tablespoons chopped peanuts evenly over the brownies. Return the brownies to the oven and bake for 2 minutes more. Remove the pan from the oven and let the brownies cool in the pan until warm, about 15 minutes. Then lift them out of the baking pan, using the edges of the aluminum foil. Cut the warm brownies into 3 bars, and use a metal spatula to transfer them to dessert bowls. Top with ice cream, sliced bananas, and maraschino cherries.

# White Chocolate Blondies

*Makes 4 brownies; serves 2 to 4*

**These butterscotch bars** have all the compact moistness of a brownie, and they are particularly rich with white chocolate chips and toasted almonds. I like to give these as gifts—I chill them for about an hour, then cut them into tiny squares and nestle them in a small waxed-tissue-paper-lined gift box.

Unsalted butter, at room temperature, for greasing the loaf pan

½ cup all-purpose flour

¼ teaspoon baking powder

⅛ teaspoon salt

½ cup firmly packed light brown sugar

3 tablespoons well-beaten egg

1 tablespoon unsalted butter or margarine, melted

½ teaspoon pure vanilla extract

⅓ cup white chocolate chips

⅓ cup coarsely chopped almonds (blanched or unblanched), lightly toasted (see page 195)

PAN REQUIRED:

1 standard loaf pan (9 x 5 inches)

1. Place a rack in the center of the oven and preheat the oven to 350°F. Line the bottom of the loaf pan with a strip of aluminum foil to fit down the length and up the short sides, with enough extra length to extend over the edges by about 1½ inches. Lightly grease the foil, and set the pan aside.

2. Place the flour, baking powder, and salt in a medium-size mixing bowl and whisk to blend.

3. Place the brown sugar, egg, butter, and vanilla in a small bowl and whisk to blend. Add the egg mixture to the flour mixture and whisk until blended. Stir in the white chocolate chips and almonds. Spoon the batter into the prepared pan, and bake until the top is golden and dry, 22 to 23 minutes.

4. Remove the loaf pan from the oven and transfer it to a wire rack. Let the brownies cool completely in the pan. Then use the edges of the foil to lift out the brownies, and cut them into bars. (For storing information, see page 183.)

# Cherry Macadamia Bars

*Makes 6 bars; serves 3*
◆◆◆◆◆◆◆◆◆

**Layers of buttery** shortbread and fruit topped with nuts and coconut add up to bars that are so sturdy they are perfect to take on picnics and pack in lunchboxes. And they keep well, too!

### FOR THE FILLING:
**2 tablespoons dried sweet cherries**

**2 tablespoons red cherry preserves**

### FOR THE DOUGH AND TOPPING:
**Unsalted butter, at room temperature, or nonstick cooking spray, for greasing the loaf pan**

**1/2 cup all-purpose flour**

**3 tablespoons sugar**

**Pinch of salt**

**3 tablespoons unsalted butter, chilled, cut into 1/2-inch cubes**

**1/2 teaspoon pure vanilla extract**

**1 teaspoon well-beaten egg**

**2 tablespoons chopped macadamia nuts or sliced almonds**

**1 tablespoon packed sweetened flaked coconut**

### PAN REQUIRED:
**1 petite loaf pan (2-cup capacity, about 5 x 3 inches)**

**1.** MAKE THE FILLING: Place the dried cherries and cherry preserves in a small bowl, and stir well. Set the mixture aside.

**2.** Place a rack in the center of the oven and preheat the oven to 375°F. Line the bottom of the loaf pan with a strip of aluminum foil to fit down the length and up the short sides of the pan, with enough extra length to extend over the edges by 1½ inches. Lightly grease the foil, and set the pan aside.

**3. MAKE THE DOUGH:** Place the flour, sugar, and salt in a medium-size mixing bowl and whisk to blend. Add the butter cubes and vanilla, and cut them in with a pastry blender until the mixture forms small clumps. Measure out ¼ cup of the mixture, packing it into the measuring cup, and set it aside for the topping. Add the beaten egg to the remaining mixture in the bowl and mix well with a fork.

**4.** Spoon the dough into the prepared loaf pan and press it out evenly; then pierce it all over with a fork. Bake until the cookie loaf is golden, 15 minutes.

**5.** Remove the loaf pan from the oven and place it on a wire rack to cool for 15 minutes. (Keep the oven on.)

**6. MAKE THE TOPPING:** Place the reserved ¼ cup dough, the macadamia nuts, and the coconut in a small bowl. Mix with a fork to break up the dough and make a crumb topping.

## *variation*

# Apricot Coconut Macadamia Bars

**Substitute** chopped dried apricots and apricot preserves for the dried cherries and cherry preserves in the Cherry Macadamia Bars.

**7.** Spread the cherry filling over the baked crust, and then sprinkle the crumb topping evenly over the filling. Bake until the filling is bubbling and the topping is golden brown, 17 minutes.

**8.** Remove the loaf pan from the oven and transfer it to a wire rack. Let the cookie loaf cool completely in the pan, about 1 hour.

**9.** Use the foil overhang to lift the cookie loaf from the pan, and place it on a cutting board. Peel off the foil and cut the loaf in half lengthwise and then crosswise into thirds, to make 6 bars. (For storing information, see page 183.)

# Oatmeal Coconut Fruit Bars

*Makes 3 bars; serves 2*

◆◆◆◆◆◆◆◆◆

## These thick, chewy

oatmeal cookie bars are loaded with dried fruit and nuts for long-lasting energy. They are great for lunchboxes and perfect on-the-go snacks. They are my favorite energy boost when I'm out kayaking or hiking.

Unsalted butter, at room temperature, for greasing the pan

¼ cup plus 2 tablespoons old-fashioned rolled oats

3 tablespoons all-purpose flour

3 tablespoons packed dark brown sugar

3 tablespoons sweetened flaked coconut

2 tablespoons dried cherries

2 tablespoons finely chopped dried apricots

2 tablespoons chopped pecans

⅛ teaspoon baking powder

⅛ teaspoon salt

1½ tablespoons unsalted butter, melted and cooled

2 teaspoons well-beaten egg or egg substitute

¼ teaspoon pure vanilla extract

**PAN REQUIRED:**

**1 petite loaf pan (2-cup capacity, about 5 x 3 inches)**

1. Place a rack in the center of the oven and preheat the oven to 350°F. Line the bottom of the loaf pan with a strip of aluminum to fit down the length and up the short sides of the pan, with enough extra length to extend over the edges by 1½ inches. Lightly grease the foil, and set the pan aside.

2. Place the oats, flour, brown sugar, coconut, cherries, apricots, pecans, baking powder, and salt in a medium-size mixing bowl and toss to mix well.

3. Place the melted butter, beaten egg, and vanilla in a small bowl and beat with a fork to blend. Add the egg mixture to the oat mixture and stir just until blended. Spoon the batter into the prepared loaf pan and smooth the top. Bake until the cookie loaf is set and lightly browned, about 22 minutes.

4. Remove the pan from the oven and place it on a wire rack to cool for 10 minutes. Then use the edges of the foil to lift out the cookie loaf. Place the loaf

*variation*

# Triple Threat Bars

**Add chocolate** chips to the Oatmeal Coconut Fruit Bars and you have one that's triply hard to pass up.

Substitute ¼ cup semisweet or milk chocolate chips for the dried cherries and apricots.

on the rack and let it cool completely before cutting it into 3 bars. (For storing information, see page 183.)

# Chocolate Raspberry Oatmeal Squares

*Makes 3 bars; serves 2*

◆◆◆◆◆◆◆◆◆

**This is an elegant** bar cookie with a buttery oat crust on the bottom, layers of raspberry jam and melted chocolate, and an oat crumble topping. It is sophisticated but easy and quick to put together. When I decide to cook a special dinner for two at the last minute, I'll pull out this recipe and make them for dessert. Save the third bar for a treat for the next day if it isn't consumed with the others.

Unsalted butter, at room temperature, for greasing the loaf pan

⅓ cup all-purpose flour

⅓ cup old-fashioned rolled oats

3 tablespoons firmly packed light brown sugar

⅛ teaspoon baking powder

Pinch of salt

2½ tablespoons unsalted butter, chilled, cut into ½-inch pieces

3 tablespoons raspberry preserves

5 tablespoons semisweet chocolate chips

PAN REQUIRED:

1 petite loaf pan (2-cup capacity, about 5 x 3 inches)

**1.** Place a rack in the center of the oven and preheat the oven to 375°F. Line the bottom of the loaf pan with a strip of aluminum foil to fit down the length and up the short sides of the pan, with enough extra length to extend over the edges by 1½ inches. Lightly grease the foil, and set the pan aside.

**2.** Place the flour, oats, brown sugar, baking powder, and salt in a medium-size mixing bowl and whisk to blend. Cut in the butter, using a pastry blender or your fingers, until the mixture is crumbly. Set aside ¼ packed cup of the oat mixture for the topping. Press the remaining oat mixture in the bottom of the prepared pan. Bake until it appears dry and is starting to brown, 8 to 10 minutes. (It will not be fully baked.)

**3.** Remove the pan from the oven, transfer it to a wire rack, and let it cool completely, 30 minutes. (Keep the oven on.)

**4.** Spread the raspberry preserves evenly over the crust to within ¼ inch of the edges. Then sprinkle 2 tablespoons of the chocolate chips over the preserves. Sprinkle the reserved oat mixture over the chocolate chips, patting gently to make an even layer. Bake until the top is golden brown, 24 minutes.

**5.** Remove the loaf pan from the oven, transfer it to the wire rack, and let it cool completely.

**6.** Place the remaining 3 tablespoons of chocolate chips in a heavy-duty, self-seal plastic bag and microwave on medium power to melt the chocolate, 45 seconds. Seal the bag and knead the chocolate in the bag until it is smooth, and then push the chocolate into one corner of the bag. Snip off a tiny piece of the corner and, holding the bag over the oat topping, swirl the chocolate over the topping. Let it cool until the chocolate is set, about 30 minutes. Remove the cookie loaf from the pan, transfer to a cutting board, and cut into bars. (For storing information, see page 183.)

# Lemon Shortbread Squares

*Makes 3 bars; serves 2*

◆◆◆◆◆◆◆◆◆

## These old-fashioned

Southern favorites will brighten any occasion. Luscious lemon custard tops a buttery shortbread crust. For an elegant dinner, serve them on confectioners' sugar–dusted dessert plates with fresh raspberries or blueberries and maybe a tiny scoop of lemon sorbet.

### FOR THE CRUST:

Unsalted butter,
    at room temperature,
    for greasing the loaf pan

¼ cup all-purpose flour

3 tablespoons confectioners' sugar

1 teaspoon grated lemon zest

Pinch of salt

2 tablespoons (¼ stick) unsalted
    butter, chilled, diced

### FOR THE FILLING:

1 large egg

⅓ cup sugar

1 tablespoon all-purpose flour

1 tablespoon fresh lemon juice

1 teaspoon grated lemon zest

Pinch of salt

About 1 tablespoon confectioners'
    sugar

### PAN REQUIRED:

1 petite loaf pan (2-cup capacity,
    about 5 x 3 inches)

1. Place a rack in the center of the oven and preheat the oven to 350°F. Line the bottom of the loaf pan with a strip of aluminum foil that fits down

the length and up the short sides of the pan with enough extra length to extend over the edges by 1½ inches. Lightly grease the foil, and set the pan aside.

**2. MAKE THE CRUST:** Place the flour, confectioners' sugar, lemon zest, and salt in a medium-size mixing bowl. Add the butter pieces and cut them in with a pastry blender or fork until the mixture is crumbly. Press the mixture in an even layer into the bottom of the prepared loaf pan. Bake until the crust is beginning to brown, about 15 minutes. Remove the pan from the oven and set it aside. (Keep the oven on.)

**3. MAKE THE FILLING:** Place the egg, sugar, flour, lemon juice, lemon zest, and salt in a small bowl and whisk to

## variation
# Key Lime Coconut Squares

**The filling** for this variation tastes like key lime pie, and coconut adds a sweet crunch to the crust: Add 2 tablespoons sweetened flaked coconut to the flour mixture in Step 2. For the filling, use freshly squeezed key lime juice instead of the lemon juice.

blend well. Pour the filling over the warm crust. Bake until the filling is set, 20 minutes. Remove the pan from the oven and place it on a wire rack to cool completely, about 1½ hours.

**4.** Remove the shortbread crust from the pan using the aluminum foil handles and place it on a cutting board. Sift the confectioners' sugar over it, then cut into bars. (For storing information, see page 183.)

# CHAPTER 5

# Crumbly, Sweet, *and* Fruity: Cobblers, Crisps, Crumbles, *and* Shortcakes

**My husband's** father and mother were from Greece and, in typical Greek fashion, they always served fresh fruit for dessert. Although I enjoy a perfect peach just as much as they did, when it comes to dessert, I like my fruit a little dressy, perhaps cooked in sweet syrup, and maybe with a crunchy topping. In other words, I'm a fan of cobblers, crisps, crumbles, and short- cakes, and if you are too, you'll find the recipes in this chapter particularly appeal- ing. All have wonderful buttery crust, crumb toppings, or biscuits to sop up the sweet fruit juices. There are humble crisps with oat top- pings and sophisticated crisps with toppings of hazelnuts and amaretti cookies. All the basic cobblers are in this chapter—

berry, peach, and cherry—with delicious creamy sauces to drizzle over the top. They can be made in ovenproof bowls, small soufflé dishes, or any ovenproof ramekins you have. You can also layer them in large muffin cups and then scoop them out into serving bowls. All of these desserts are best eaten warm from the oven the day they are baked.

I'm always on the lookout for deep ceramic bowls for baking and serving cobblers and crisps. The bowl has to be deep so the cobbler will stay warm longer; it can't be shallow because those tend to be wide and don't perch well on the arms of my comfy sofa. I like to find two bowls of similar patterns so I can share the other serving that these recipes make, but if there is only one with the perfect shape, I'll use it.

Each shortcake recipe makes two single-size shortcakes, just right for the wonderful fillings and toppings in this chapter. From the classic plain shortcake biscuit to a cornmeal and milk chocolate version, you'll find one that suits your mood and your palate.

# Southern Peach Cobbler

## *with* Bourbon Cream

*Makes 2 cobblers; serves 2*

◆◆◆◆◆◆◆◆◆

**To this Southern** gal, there is nothing like peach cobbler in the summer, and summer comes early to Alabama. Peaches start showing up at local fruit stands and markets here in June, but even if you have to wait until July or August, they are worth the wait. The juicy, tart sweetness that bursts from a fresh peach makes this cobbler special.

But don't despair—though fresh peaches are more tender and flavorful than frozen peaches, frozen peaches are a good substitute when you can't get fresh ones. Serve the cobbler plain, with ice cream, or garnish it with Bourbon Cream and Candied Pecans to turn it into a truly spectacular dessert.

**Unsalted butter, at room temperature, for greasing the baking dishes**

**FOR THE FILLING:**
**3 ripe peaches, or 2 cups thawed frozen peaches**
**1/2 teaspoon fresh lemon juice**
**2 tablespoons firmly packed light brown sugar**
**1 teaspoon cornstarch**
**Pinch of ground cinnamon**

**FOR THE TOPPING AND FOR SERVING:**
**1/4 cup plus 2 tablespoons all-purpose flour**
**2 teaspoons granulated sugar**
**1/4 teaspoon baking powder**
**Pinch of salt**
**Pinch of ground cinnamon**

Pinch of ground nutmeg

1 tablespoon cold unsalted butter,
cut into pieces

2 tablespoons cold whipping (heavy)
cream

1/2 teaspoon granulated sugar

Bourbon Cream (recipe follows)

Candied Pecans (page 99; optional)

BAKING DISHES REQUIRED:

Two 1- to 1 1/2-cup ovenproof bowls
or ramekins, or one 2-cup soufflé
dish or casserole

1. Place a rack in the center of the oven and preheat the oven to 375°F. Lightly grease the baking dishes and set them aside.

2. MAKE THE FILLING: If you are using fresh peaches, peel them and cut them in half. Remove the pits and cut the pieces into 1/2-inch slices. Place the peaches and the lemon juice in a medium-size bowl, and toss to mix. (If using frozen peaches, omit the lemon juice.) Add the brown sugar, cornstarch, and cinnamon, and toss well to coat the peaches. Spoon the peaches and juices into the prepared baking dishes, dividing the filling evenly between them.

3. MAKE THE TOPPING: Place the flour, sugar, baking powder, salt, cinnamon, and nutmeg in a medium-size bowl and whisk to blend well. Add the butter pieces and toss to coat the butter with the flour mixture. Rub the mixture with your fingertips until the mixture is crumbly. Add the cream and toss with a fork just until the dough is combined.

4. Turn the dough out onto a lightly floured surface and knead it a few times to smooth it. Form the dough into a disk and roll it out, forming two 1/2-inch-thick pieces the shape and size of the top of the baking dishes. Place the dough pieces on top of the filling, and sprinkle each one with 1/4 tea-spoon of sugar. Bake until the top is golden brown and the juices are bubbling, 25 to 30 minutes.

5. Remove the dishes from the oven and let them cool on a wire rack for 15 minutes. Serve the cobbler warm, with the Bourbon Cream. If you are using them, sprinkle each serving with Candied Pecans.

# Bourbon Cream

**Dark brown sugar** and bourbon add Old South flavor to the whipped cream and a zing to the peach cobbler.

**MAKES ABOUT ⅔ CUP**

**⅓ cup cold whipping (heavy) cream**
**1 tablespoon firmly packed dark brown sugar**

**½ teaspoon bourbon**
**½ teaspoon pure vanilla extract**

Place the cream, brown sugar, bourbon, and vanilla in a medium-size mixing bowl and beat with a hand-held electric mixer on high speed until firm peaks form, 1½ to 2 minutes. Serve immediately.

# Flaky Cherry Cobbler

*Makes 2 cobblers; serves 2*

◆◆◆◆◆◆◆◆◆

**This old-fashioned** cobbler has a flaky biscuit topping that is tender, fluffy, and crisp on the top, just as it should be. Cherry cobbler is best during cherry season, but an excellent cobbler can be made throughout the year by using frozen sweet cherries. When using frozen cherries, measure them while they are frozen, let them thaw, and then drain them.

Unsalted butter, at room temperature,
for greasing the baking dishes

**FOR THE FILLING:**

2 cups fresh Bing cherries, pitted,
or frozen sweet cherries, thawed
and drained

1/8 teaspoon pure almond extract

2 tablespoons sugar

1 teaspoon cornstarch

**FOR THE TOPPING AND FOR SERVING:**

1/2 cup all-purpose flour

1 tablespoon plus 1 teaspoon sugar

1/8 teaspoon baking powder

1/8 teaspoon baking soda

1/8 teaspoon salt

1 tablespoon plus 2 teaspoons cold
unsalted butter, diced

2 1/2 tablespoons cold buttermilk

2 1/2 tablespoons cold whipping
(heavy) cream

Ice cream, sorbet, or topping of
choice (see page 224)

**BAKING DISHES REQUIRED:**

Two 1- to 1 1/2-cup ovenproof bowls
or ramekins, or one 2-cup soufflé
dish or casserole

1. Place a rack in the center of the
oven and preheat the oven to 375°F.
Lightly grease the baking dishes and
set them aside.

2. MAKE THE FILLING: Place the
cherries and the almond extract
in a medium-size mixing bowl, and toss
to mix. Add the sugar and cornstarch, and
toss to blend.
Transfer the cherry filling to the
prepared baking dishes, dividing it
evenly between them. Bake until the
filling is hot, 15 minutes.

3. MAKE THE TOPPING while the
filling is baking. Place the flour,
1 tablespoon of the sugar, the baking
powder, baking soda, and salt in a
medium-size mixing bowl and whisk
to blend well. Add the butter pieces
and toss to coat the butter with the
flour mixture. Rub the mixture with
your fingertips until it resembles
coarse meal.

4. Combine the buttermilk and cream
in a small bowl, and stir to blend.
Sprinkle the buttermilk mixture over
the crumb mixture, tossing it with a
fork until the dough comes together.

**5.** Drop the dough by rounded table-spoonfuls over the hot filling to cover it. Sprinkle the remaining 1 teaspoon of sugar evenly over the top. Bake until the topping is golden and cooked through, 23 to 25 minutes; a wooden toothpick inserted in the center of the topping should come out clean.

**6.** Remove the baking dishes from the oven and let them cool on a wire rack for 15 minutes. Serve warm, with your choice of ice cream or topping.

# Mixed Berry Cornmeal Cobbler

*Makes 2 cobblers; serves 2*

◆◆◆◆◆◆◆◆◆

**I always have** some frozen berries in my freezer so I can make this cobbler. It's super-quick—you don't even have to thaw the berries. Cornmeal adds a nice texture to the tender buttermilk biscuit topping, and it soaks up the berry juices nicely.

**Unsalted butter, at room temperature, for greasing the baking dishes**

**FOR THE FILLING:**
**1 cup mixed frozen unsweetened berries, such as blueberries, blackberries, raspberries, and strawberries (see Note)**
**1 tablespoon sugar**
**2 teaspoons all-purpose flour**
**1/2 teaspoon fresh lemon juice**

**FOR THE TOPPING AND FOR SERVING:**

¼ **cup all-purpose flour**

**1 tablespoon plus 1 teaspoon sugar**

**1 tablespoon yellow cornmeal**

¼ **teaspoon baking powder**

⅛ **teaspoon baking soda**

**Pinch of salt**

**2 teaspoons cold unsalted butter, diced**

**2 tablespoons buttermilk**

**Ice cream, sorbet, or topping of choice (see page 224)**

**BAKING DISHES REQUIRED:**

**Two 1- to 1½-cup ovenproof bowls or ramekins, or one 2-cup soufflé dish or casserole**

1. Place a rack in the center of the oven and preheat the oven to 400°F. Lightly grease the baking dishes and set them aside.

2. **MAKE THE FILLING:** Place the berries, sugar, flour, and lemon juice in a medium-size mixing bowl and toss to combine. Spoon the berry mixture into the prepared baking dishes, dividing it evenly between them.

3. **MAKE THE TOPPING:** Place the flour, sugar, cornmeal, baking powder, baking soda, and salt in a small bowl and whisk to blend well. Add the butter pieces and toss to coat the butter with the flour mixture. Rub the mixture with your fingertips, or cut the butter in with a pastry blender, until the mixture resembles coarse meal. Sprinkle the buttermilk over the flour mixture and toss briefly with a fork just until moist clumps form. Do not overmix. Spoon the topping evenly over the filling.

4. Bake until the topping is golden brown and the filling is bubbly, 15 to 20 minutes. Remove the baking dishes from the oven and let them cool on a wire rack for 15 minutes. Serve warm or at room temperature, with your choice of ice cream or topping.

NOTE: If you are using strawberries, quarter or slice them before measuring.

## Matching the Crumbly Sweet

Ice cream, sorbet, frozen yogurt, and any number of toppings described in this book pair wonderfully with the desserts in this chapter. So keep a selection of your favorite frozen flavors in the freezer ready for scooping over your freshly baked crumble or crisp. And don't forget the final flourish—a dollop of one of the many creamy toppings offered in this book. Here are some of my favorites.

**FLAKY CHERRY COBBLERS (page 220)**
Gourmet Vanilla Whipped Cream (page 231)

**MIXED BERRY CORNMEAL COBBLERS (page 222)**
Honey Crème Fraîche (page 231)
Vanilla Crème Fraîche (page 72)
Tipsy Vanilla Cream (page 231) made with Grand Marnier
Raspberry Whipped Cream (page 36)
Tapioca Sauce (page 234)

**HONEY APPLE OATMEAL CRISPS (page 226)**
Whipped Honey Cream (page 231)
Honey Crème Fraîche (page 231)

**STRAWBERRY AMARETTI CRISPS (page 228)**
Almond Dream Cream (page 231)
Tipsy Vanilla Cream, Spiked Cream, or Spiked Double Cream (page 231) made with amaretto

**ALMOND APPLE BLUEBERRY CRUMBLES (page 235)**
Almond Dream Cream (page 231)

**ALMOND PEACH BLACKBERRY CRUMBLES (page 235)**
Bourbon Cream (page 220)
Fruity Whipped Cream (page 231) made with blended peach yogurt

**ALMOND PLUM GRAPE CRUMBLES (page 235)**
Vanilla Crème Fraîche (page 72)
Gourmet Vanilla Whipped Cream (page 231)

## AND FRUITY DESSERTS WITH TOPPINGS

**ALMOND NECTARINE RASPBERRY CRUMBLES (page 235)**
Almond Dream Cream (page 231)
Screamin' Whipped Cream
  (page 231)
Tipsy Vanilla Cream (page 231)
  made with Chambord or
  Framboise
Spiked Whipped Cream (page 231)
  made with Chambord or
  Framboise
Raspberry Whipped Cream
  (page 36)

**ALMOND PINEAPPLE DATE CRUMBLES (page 235)**
Almond Dream Cream (page 231)
Screamin' Whipped Cream
  (page 231)
Tipsy Vanilla Cream (page 231)
  made with Tuaca (Italian
  liqueur of vanilla and citrus)
Spiked Whipped Cream (page 231)
  made with Bailey's Irish Cream

**ALMOND PEAR STRAWBERRY CRUMBLES (page 235)**
Gourmet Vanilla Whipped Cream
  (page 231)

Almond Dream Cream (page 231)
Screamin' Whipped Cream
  (page 231)
Tipsy Vanilla Cream (page 231)
  made with Poire William
  (pear brandy)
Spiked Whipped Cream (page 231)
  made with Poire William

**NECTARINE BLUEBERRY BUCKLES (page 237)**
Fruity Whipped Cream (page 231)
  made with blueberry yogurt
Orange Cream Topping (page 231)

**BERRY SLUMPS (page 239)**
Brown Sugar Cream (page 255)
Fruity Whipped Cream (page 231)

**GRAPE GRATIN WITH GINGER CRUNCH TOPPING (page 240)**
Screamin' Whipped
  Cream
  (page 231)
Almond Dream
  Cream
  (page 231)

# Honey Apple Oatmeal Crisps

*Makes 2 crisps; serves 2*

◆◆◆◆◆◆◆◆◆

**My children would** eat this dessert for breakfast every day, ice cream and all, if I let them. It's a delicious treat anytime of day and has a few healthy things going for it, too. Baked apples are sweetened with honey and topped with oatmeal-pecan streusel. If you are serving it for breakfast, top it with vanilla yogurt to make it a bit more credible as a morning meal.

**Unsalted butter, at room temperature, for greasing the baking dishes**

**FOR THE FILLING:**
**1½ cooking apples, such as Rome Beauty or Winesap**

**1½ teaspoons fresh lemon juice**
**2 tablespoons unsalted butter**
**2 tablespoons honey**
**1 teaspoon all-purpose flour**
**¼ teaspoon ground cinnamon**
**Pinch of salt**

**FOR THE TOPPING AND FOR SERVING:**
**2 tablespoons all-purpose flour**
**2 tablespoons firmly packed dark brown sugar**
**1 tablespoon cold unsalted butter or margarine, cut into pieces**
**3 tablespoons old-fashioned rolled oats**
**3 tablespoons chopped pecans, toasted (see page 195)**
**Ice cream or topping of choice (see page 224), or vanilla yogurt**

**BAKING DISHES REQUIRED:**

**Two 1- to 1½-cup ovenproof bowls or ramekins, or one 2-cup soufflé dish or casserole**

**1.** Place a rack in the center of the oven and preheat the oven to 375°F. Lightly grease the baking dishes and set them aside.

**2. MAKE THE FILLING:** Peel the apples, cut them in half, and remove the cores. Thinly slice the apples and place them in a mixing bowl. Add the lemon juice and toss to mix.

**3.** Melt the butter in a medium-size skillet over medium heat. Using a whisk, stir in the honey, flour, cinnamon, and salt, whisking until smooth. Add the apples and cook the mixture over medium heat, turning the apples gently, until they are just tender, 5 minutes.

**4.** Remove the skillet from the heat and spoon the apples and accumulated juices into the prepared baking dishes, dividing the apples evenly between them.

**5. MAKE THE TOPPING:** Place the flour and brown sugar in a small bowl, and whisk to blend well. Add the butter pieces and toss to coat the butter with the flour mixture. Rub the mixture with your fingertips until the mixture is crumbly. Mix in the oats and nuts. Sprinkle the mixture evenly over the apples. Bake until the topping is golden brown and the filling is hot, 20 minutes.

**6.** Remove the dishes from the oven and let them cool on a wire rack for 15 minutes. Serve the crisp warm or at room temperature, with your choice of ice cream or topping.

# Strawberry Amaretti Crisps

*Makes 1 crisp; serves 2*

◆◆◆◆◆◆◆◆

**Fresh sweet strawberries** make their own syrup when they are baked, and amaretti cookies make this topping extra crisp. It is a beautiful dessert, particularly when strawberries are truly in season and are juicy red inside and out. (If you get them when they are not at their peak and their centers are on the white side, the juices they give off will be watery and will taste less of strawberry.) Amaretti are Italian cookies made from ground almonds; they can be purchased in the specialty foods or cookie section of many large supermarkets and in specialty stores.

**Unsalted butter, at room temperature, for greasing the baking dish**

**FOR THE FRUIT:**

1½ **cups halved medium to large strawberries**

2 **tablespoons sugar**

1 **teaspoon cornstarch**

**Pinch of salt**

**FOR THE TOPPING AND FOR SERVING:**

¼ **cup all-purpose flour**

2 **tablespoons sugar**

¼ **teaspoon ground cinnamon**

2 **tablespoons unsalted butter at room temperature**

½ **cup crushed amaretti cookies, in coarse crumbs**

**Ice cream, sorbet, or topping of choice (see page 224)**

**BAKING DISH REQUIRED:**

**One 2- or 2½-cup shallow gratin dish, ovenproof soup bowl, or other baking dish**

1. Place a rack in the center of the oven and preheat the oven to 400°F. Lightly grease the baking dish.

2. **PREPARE THE FRUIT:** Arrange the strawberries in the baking dish. Place the sugar, cornstarch, and salt in a small bowl, and stir to blend well. Sprinkle the sugar mixture evenly over the strawberries.

3. **MAKE THE TOPPING:** Place the flour, sugar, and cinnamon in a small bowl, and whisk to blend well. Using your fingers or a fork, mix in the butter until moist crumbs form. Mix in the crumbled cookies. Sprinkle the topping evenly over the strawberries. Bake until the strawberry juice is thickened and the topping is browned, 13 to 15 minutes.

4. Remove the baking dish from the oven and let it cool on a wire rack for 15 minutes. Serve the crisp warm or at room temperature, with your choice of ice cream or topping.

# Fig and Hazelnut Crisps

*Makes 2 crisps; serves 2*

**♦♦♦♦♦♦♦♦♦**

**My neighbor has** a fig tree in her backyard and gives me a huge bowl of fresh figs every year. When they arrive, we have this dessert more than once that week. It's a showcase for beautiful figs in season, a grand dessert worthy of a fine meal. Sweetened with brown sugar and port, the figs are topped with buttery hazelnut streusel and baked until the figs are hot and the topping is brown.

**Unsalted butter, at room temperature, for greasing the baking dishes**

FOR THE FILLING:

**8 fresh figs**

**1 tablespoon port wine**

**2 tablespoons packed light brown sugar**

**2 tablespoons all-purpose flour**

**Pinch of salt**

**1½ tablespoons cold unsalted butter, diced**

**3 tablespoons chopped hazelnuts, toasted (see box, page 203)**

FOR THE SAUCE:

**¼ cup cold whipping (heavy) cream**

**2 teaspoons confectioners' sugar**

**2 tablespoons crème fraîche or sour cream**

BAKING DISHES REQUIRED:

**Two 1- to 1½-cup ovenproof bowls or ramekins, or one 2-cup soufflé dish or casserole**

1. Place a rack in the center of the oven and preheat the oven to 375°F. Lightly grease the baking dishes and set them aside.

2. MAKE THE FILLING: Cut the figs into quarters and place them in a small bowl. Add the port and 1 tablespoon of the brown sugar, and toss to combine. Arrange the figs in the prepared baking dishes, dividing them evenly between them.

3. Place the remaining 1 tablespoon brown sugar, the flour, and salt in a medium-size mixing bowl and whisk to blend well. Add the butter pieces and toss to coat the butter with the flour mixture. Rub the mixture with your fingertips until moist clumps form. Then rub in the hazelnuts. Spoon the topping evenly over the figs. Bake until the figs are hot and the topping is golden, 15 minutes.

4. Remove the baking dishes from the oven and let them cool on a wire rack for 15 minutes.

5. MAKE THE SAUCE: Place the cream and confectioners' sugar in a medium-size mixing bowl and beat with a hand-held electric mixer on high speed until firm peaks form. With the mixer on low speed, beat in the crème fraîche until blended, about 10 seconds.

6. Carefully spoon the crisps onto serving plates, using a spatula to place the topping attractively on the fruit. Add a dollop of sauce alongside.

# FLUFFY DESSERT TOPPINGS

Here are some quick and easy dessert toppings and sauces to dress up any cobbler, crisp, crumble, or shortcake:

HONEY CREME FRAICHE: Mix 1/3 cup of crème fraîche with 1 tablespoon of honey.

WHIPPED HONEY CREAM: Combine 1/2 cup of whipping cream with 1 tablespoon of honey, and whip to form firm peaks.

SPIKED CREAM: Combine 1/2 cup of whipping cream with 1 tablespoon of confectioners' sugar and 1 tablespoon of a liqueur of your choice, and whip to form medium-firm peaks.

SPIKED DOUBLE CREAM: Stir 2 tablespoons of crème fraîche or sour cream into the Spiked Cream.

TIPSY VANILLA CREAM: Soften 1/2 cup of vanilla ice cream and stir in 1 to 2 tablespoons of the liqueur of your choice. Do not refreeze.

FRUITY WHIPPED CREAM: Combine 1/2 cup of whipping cream with 1 tablespoon of confectioners' sugar, and whip to form firm peaks. Beat in 3 tablespoons of flavored yogurt.

SCREAMIN' WHIPPED CREAM: Combine 1/2 cup of whipping cream with 1/2 cup of softened ice cream, and whip until firm peaks form. Add 1/4 teaspoon of pure vanilla extract.

ORANGE CREAM TOPPING: Add 1/8 teaspoon of pure orange extract to Screamin' Whipped Cream.

ALMOND DREAM CREAM: Add 1/8 teaspoon of pure almond extract to Screamin' Whipped Cream.

GOURMET VANILLA WHIPPED CREAM: Combine 1/2 cup of whipping cream with 1 tablespoon of confectioners' sugar and 1/4 teaspoon of vanilla paste (see page 244), vanilla powder, or pure vanilla extract, and whip to form firm peaks.

# Strawberry Rhubarb Crumble

## *with* Tapioca Sauce

*Makes 2 crumbles; serves 2*

◆◆◆◆◆◆◆◆◆

## Crumbles have thick

golden crumb toppings that become crisp and buttery on top while remaining soft, but not gooey, underneath. This winning combination of strawberries and rhubarb is set off by its thick crumble topping and a creamy vanilla Tapioca Sauce, creating a bowlful of old-fashioned flavor.

**Unsalted butter, at room temperature, for greasing the baking dishes**

**FOR THE FILLING:**
**1 cup halved strawberries**

**¹/₂ cup ¹/₂-inch-thick slices fresh or frozen rhubarb**
**2 tablespoons sugar**
**2 teaspoons all-purpose flour**
**Small pinch of ground cloves**
**Pinch of salt**

**FOR THE TOPPING AND FOR SERVING:**
**3 tablespoons all-purpose flour**
**2 tablespoons sugar**
**Pinch of salt**
**2 tablespoons cold unsalted butter, diced**
**Tapioca Sauce (page 234)**

**BAKING DISHES REQUIRED:**
**Two 1- to 1¹/₂-cup ovenproof bowls or ramekins, or one 2-cup soufflé dish or casserole**

**1.** Place a rack in the center of the oven and preheat the oven to 350°F. Lightly grease the baking dishes and set them aside.

**2. MAKE THE FILLING:** Place the strawberries, rhubarb, sugar, flour, cloves, and salt in a medium-size mixing bowl, and toss to mix well. Spoon the mixture into the prepared baking dishes, dividing it evenly between them.

**3. MAKE THE TOPPING:** Place the flour, sugar, and salt in a small bowl and whisk to blend well. Add the butter pieces and toss to coat the butter with the flour mixture. Rub the mixture with your fingertips, or cut the butter in with a pastry blender, until you have coarse crumbs about ½ to ¾ inch in size, there is no loose flour, and the mixture looks pale yellow rather than white. Spoon the topping evenly over the filling.

**4.** Bake until the topping is pale gold and the fruit filling is bubbling, 30 minutes. Remove the baking dishes from the oven and let them cool on a wire rack for 10 to 15 minutes. Serve warm or at room temperature, with the Tapioca Sauce.

# Tapioca Sauce

**Old-fashioned** tapioca pudding consists of pearl-size tapioca, which has to be soaked overnight in water. This sauce uses quick-cooking tapioca, which is much smaller in size but nevertheless contributes wonderful texture. Crème fraîche adds a smooth, rich flavor that goes well with the tartness in the strawberry-rhubarb combination.

**MAKES ⅔ CUP**

**1 tablespoon quick-cooking tapioca**
**½ cup whole milk**
**1 large egg yolk, lightly beaten**
**1½ tablespoons sugar**
**Pinch of salt**
**½ teaspoon pure vanilla extract**
**3 tablespoons crème fraîche or**
**    sour cream**

**1.** Place the tapioca, milk, egg yolk, sugar, and salt in a small saucepan and whisk to mix well. Let the mixture stand for 5 minutes for the tapioca to absorb some of the liquid and begin to swell.

**2.** Bring the tapioca mixture to a simmer over medium-high heat, whisking constantly. Reduce the heat to medium-low and cook, stirring constantly, until it is slightly thickened, 30 to 40 seconds. Remove the saucepan from the heat and stir in the vanilla. Spoon the mixture into a bowl and cover it with plastic wrap. Refrigerate the sauce, stirring it frequently, until it is cool and thick, about 15 minutes.

**3.** Stir the crème fraîche into the sauce, and serve the sauce with the fruit crumble. (You can store any leftovers, covered, in the refrigerator for up to 2 days.)

# Almond Fruit Crumbles

*Makes 2 crumbles; serves 2*

◆◆◆◆◆◆◆◆◆◆

This is a do-it-yourself recipe: You pick one of the simple fruit pairs suggested on page 236, layer it with the almond crumble, then bake. Almond paste makes a moist crumb mixture; half of it bakes under the fruit to soak up the fruit juices and sweeten the fruit. Finally, sliced almonds are added to the rest of the crumb mixture to be sprinkled on top for crunch.

Unsalted butter, at room temperature, for greasing the baking dishes

FOR THE TOPPING:
¼ cup plus 2 tablespoons all-purpose flour
¼ cup firmly packed light brown sugar
3 tablespoons packed almond paste
Pinch of salt

2½ tablespoons cold unsalted butter, diced
3 tablespoons sliced or slivered almonds

FOR THE FILLING:
1 fruit combination (suggestions follow)
2 to 3 teaspoons sugar, to taste
Ice cream, sorbet, or topping of choice (see page 224)

BAKING DISHES REQUIRED:
Two 1- to 1½-cup ovenproof bowls or ramekins, or one 2-cup soufflé dish or casserole

1. Place a rack in the center of the oven and preheat the oven to 375°F. Lightly grease the baking dishes and set them aside.

2. MAKE THE TOPPING: Combine the flour, brown sugar, almond paste, and

salt in a food processor, and process until the almond paste is finely ground, about 45 seconds. Scrape down the sides of the bowl and add the butter pieces. Pulse until coarse crumbs form, 12 to 15 pulses. Transfer the crumb mixture to a bowl.

3. Scatter 2 tablespoons of the crumb mixture onto the bottom of each of the prepared baking dishes. Stir the almonds into the remaining crumb mixture and set it aside.

4. MAKE THE FILLING: Place the fruit in a medium-size mixing bowl and add sugar to taste. Spoon the fruit and accumulated juices over the crumb mixture. Sprinkle the almond crumb mixture evenly over the fruit. Bake until the fruit is tender and the top is golden brown, 20 to 23 minutes.

5. Remove the baking dishes from the oven and let them cool on a wire rack for 15 minutes. Serve warm or at room temperature, with your choice of ice cream or topping.

# Fruit Combinations

- 1 cup of diced peeled apple mixed with ½ cup of fresh or frozen unsweetened blueberries

- 1 cup of diced fresh or thawed frozen peaches, mixed with ½ cup of fresh or frozen unsweetened blackberries

- 1 cup of thinly sliced fresh plums mixed with ½ cup of halved seedless grapes

- 1 cup of diced fresh nectarines mixed with ½ of cup fresh or frozen unsweetened raspberries

- 1¼ cups of diced fresh or canned pineapple, drained, mixed with ¼ cup of diced fresh dates; use chopped macadamia nuts in place of almonds in the topping

- 1 cup of diced pears mixed with ½ cup of quartered strawberries and 1 teaspoon of grated orange zest

# Nectarine Blueberry Buckle

*Makes 2 buckles; serves 2*

◆◆◆◆◆◆◆◆◆

**A buckle is** a cake-like pudding, heavy with fruit, with a crumble topping. Baked all together, it is out of this world—not exactly elegant but definitely delicious. The combination of nectarines and blueberries makes this one especially appealing in the summer months.

Unsalted butter, at room temperature, for greasing the baking dish

FOR THE TOPPING:

2 tablespoons sugar

2 tablespoons all-purpose flour

⅛ teaspoon ground cinnamon

⅛ teaspoon ground nutmeg

1 tablespoon cold unsalted butter, diced

FOR THE BATTER AND FOR SERVING:

⅓ cup all-purpose flour

3 tablespoons sugar

Pinch of baking powder

⅛ teaspoon salt

1 large egg

¼ teaspoon pure vanilla extract

3 tablespoons unsalted butter, at room temperature

1 fresh, ripe nectarine, peeled, pitted, and thinly sliced

½ cup fresh or thawed frozen unsweetened blueberries

Ice cream, sorbet, or topping of choice (see page 224)

BAKING DISH REQUIRED:

One 2-cup casserole or soufflé dish

**1.** Place a rack in the center of the oven and preheat the oven to 350°F. Lightly grease the baking dish and set it aside.

**2. MAKE THE TOPPING:** Place the sugar, flour, cinnamon, and nutmeg in a small bowl and whisk to blend. Add the butter pieces and toss to coat the butter with the flour mixture. Rub the mixture with your fingertips until the lumps are no larger than small peas. Refrigerate the topping, covered, for 10 to 15 minutes.

**3. MAKE THE BATTER:** Place the flour, sugar, baking powder, and salt in a small bowl and whisk to blend.

**4.** Place the egg in a medium-size mixing bowl and beat with a hand-held electric mixer on low speed just until it is blended, 3 to 5 seconds. Measure out 1 tablespoon of the beaten egg and either discard or save the rest for another use. Add the vanilla and butter to the remaining egg in the bowl. Pour in the flour mixture. Beat on low speed until the dry ingredients are moistened, about 20 seconds. Increase the mixer speed to medium and beat until the batter is

well blended, 30 seconds. Scrape down the sides of the bowl, and fold in the nectarines and blueberries.

**5.** Spoon the batter into the prepared baking dish, and sprinkle the topping evenly over it. Bake the buckle until a toothpick inserted in the center comes out clean and the topping is golden brown, 35 to 38 minutes. Remove the baking dish from the oven and place it on a wire rack to cool. Serve warm or at room temperature, with your choice of ice cream or topping.

# Berry Slump

*Makes 2 slumps; serves 2*

◆◆◆◆◆◆◆◆◆

**In New England,** fruit desserts with a biscuit topping are called slumps, because the topping "slumps," or flattens, while it cooks. On Cape Cod, these desserts are even more picturesquely called grunts, because of the sounds that the biscuit-covered fruit makes as it bubbles on the stove. The topping is not as crisp as the one on a cobbler or crisp—it's more like a thin biscuit that absorbs most of the fruit juices. A slump isn't beautiful to look at, but it is *the* dessert to eat when curled up in front of a fire. You can mix up the biscuit topping in a flash and get the dessert in the oven in no time.

Unsalted butter, at room temperature, for greasing the baking dishes

**FOR THE FILLING:**

¾ cup fresh or frozen unsweetened blackberries

½ cup fresh or frozen unsweetened raspberries

2 tablespoons sugar

½ teaspoon quick-cooking tapioca

**FOR THE TOPPING AND FOR SERVING:**

½ cup all-purpose flour

1½ tablespoons sugar

¼ teaspoon baking powder

⅛ teaspoon salt

¼ cup whole milk

2 teaspoons unsalted butter, melted

Ice cream, sorbet, and topping of choice (see page 224)

**BAKING DISHES REQUIRED:**

Two 1- to 1½-cup ovenproof bowls or ramekins, or one 2-cup soufflé dish or casserole

1. Place a rack in the center of the oven and preheat the oven to 375°F. Lightly grease the baking dishes and set them aside.

2. MAKE THE FILLING: Place the berries, sugar, and tapioca in a mixing bowl, and toss to mix. Spoon the mixture into the prepared baking dishes, dividing it evenly between them.

3. MAKE THE TOPPING: Place the flour, sugar, baking powder, and salt in a medium-size mixing bowl and whisk to blend well. Add the milk and melted butter and whisk just until the batter is blended. Spoon the topping evenly over the berry mixture.

4. Bake until the topping is golden brown and the filling is hot, 22 to 25 minutes. Remove the baking dishes from the oven and let them cool on a wire rack for 15 minutes. Serve warm or at room temperature, with your choice of ice cream or topping.

# Grape Gratin

## *with* Ginger Crunch Topping

*Makes 1 gratin; serves 2*

◆◆◆◆◆◆◆◆◆

I always ate grapes out of hand until I discovered that they were a surprisingly flexible ingredient to cook with. Since that time, I've made dessert and meat sauces with grapes, stuffed pork with grapes, and baked with grapes. Grapes are, after all, one of those fruits that are fresh and tasty year-round.

This recipe is a great introduction to baking with grapes. The apricot preserves add a subtle tartness to the sauce, and the ginger nut topping is crisp and flavorful.

**Unsalted butter, at room temperature, for greasing the baking dish**

FOR THE FILLING:

**2 tablespoons apricot preserves**

**1 tablespoon sugar**

**1/2 teaspoon cornstarch**

**1 1/2 cups seedless red or green grapes, halved**

FOR THE TOPPING AND FOR SERVING:

**3 tablespoons old-fashioned rolled oats**

**2 tablespoons all-purpose flour**

**2 tablespoons packed light brown sugar**

**1 tablespoon chopped candied ginger**

**2 tablespoons chopped hazelnuts or almonds, lightly toasted (see pages 195 and 203)**

**2 tablespoons cold unsalted butter, diced**

**Ice cream, sorbet, or topping of choice (see page 224)**

BAKING DISH REQUIRED:

**One 2- to 2 1/2-cup shallow gratin dish, ovenproof soup bowl, or other baking dish**

1. Place a rack in the center of the oven and preheat the oven to 375°F. Lightly grease the baking dish and set it aside.

2. MAKE THE FILLING: Place the preserves, sugar, and cornstarch in a medium-size mixing bowl, and stir to blend. Mix in the grapes. Spoon the grape mixture into the prepared baking dish.

3. MAKE THE TOPPING: Place the oats in a food processor and process until they are coarsely ground. Add the flour, brown sugar, and ginger, and pulse until the ginger is finely chopped, 7 to 10 pulses. Sprinkle the nuts and butter pieces over the flour mixture, and pulse until coarse crumbs form, 8 to 10 pulses. Spoon the crumb mixture evenly over the grapes. Bake until the topping is golden brown and the grapes are tender, 20 to 25 minutes.

4. Remove the baking dish from the oven and let it cool on a wire rack for 15 minutes. Serve warm or at room temperature, with your choice of ice cream or topping.

# COOKING WITH GRAPES

To show you just how versatile grapes can be, here are a few quick dessert sauces that are delicious with shortcakes, pound cakes, angel food cakes, and cheesecakes.

**WARM GRAPE COMPOTE:** Place ½ cup of white grape juice, 2 tablespoons of sugar, and 1 tablespoon of white wine in a small saucepan. Bring to a boil over medium-high heat, stirring until the sugar melts. Reduce the heat to medium and boil, without stirring, until the syrup reduces to ¼ cup, 5 to 10 minutes. Stir in 1 cup of grapes of assorted colors—red, green, or blue-black—and simmer until they are hot, 2 to 3 minutes. Remove the saucepan from the heat, add 1 tablespoon of butter, and stir until it is incorporated. Serve warm or at room temperature.

**HONEY-SPICED GRAPES:** Place ⅓ cup of water, 1 tablespoon of sugar, 1 cinnamon stick (3 inches), 2 whole cardamom pods, and 3 whole cloves in a small saucepan. Bring to a simmer over medium heat, stirring until the sugar melts. Cover the pan, reduce the heat, and simmer to flavor the syrup, 15 minutes. Remove from the heat and allow to cool; then strain, discarding the spices. Stir 1 tablespoon of honey into the syrup and then 1 cup of assorted grapes—red, green, or blue-black. Serve at room temperature.

**HONEY MINT GRAPES:** Make the Honey Mint Syrup on page 91. Strain the syrup into a small saucepan, and add 1½ cups of assorted grapes—red, green, or blue-black. Bring the mixture to a simmer over medium heat. Simmer, uncovered, until the grapes are hot, 2 to 3 minutes, then remove the pan from the heat. Serve warm or at room temperature, garnished with fresh mint.

# Classic Vanilla Shortcakes

## *with* Fresh Strawberries and Lemon Cream

*Makes 2 shortcakes; serves 2*

◆◆◆◆◆◆◆◆◆

## Scone-like in texture,

these very tender shortcakes are fragrant with vanilla. They make a wonderful base for fresh, in-season strawberries. Bright lemon curd mixed into the whipped-cream topping offers a delicious contrast to the sweet shortcakes and strawberries.

**FOR THE SHORTCAKES:**

⅓ **cup plus 2 tablespoons cold whipping (heavy) cream**

¼ **teaspoon vanilla paste (see page 244), or ½ teaspoon pure vanilla extract**

⅔ **cup all-purpose flour**

1½ **tablespoons sugar**

½ **teaspoon baking powder**

¼ **teaspoon salt**

**FOR THE SAUCE:**

½ **cup sliced fresh, ripe strawberries**

**1 tablespoon sugar**

**FOR THE TOPPING AND GARNISH:**

¼ **cup cold whipping (heavy) cream**

**1 tablespoon store-bought lemon curd**

⅔ **cup sliced fresh, ripe strawberries**

**Fresh mint leaves, for garnish (optional)**

**PAN REQUIRED:**

**1 baking sheet**

1. Place a rack in the center of the oven and preheat the oven to 350°F. Line a baking sheet with parchment paper and set it aside.

2. **MAKE THE SHORTCAKES:** Place the cream and vanilla paste in a small bowl and stir to mix. Place the flour,

## A VANILLA PRIMER

People used to dismiss vanilla as being "plain," but anyone who has tested it recently won't share that opinion. Today spice companies are processing pure assertive vanilla beans into vanilla powder and paste as well as extracts. We are able to experience the creamy sweet-spicy nuances of vanilla as the powerful flavoring ingredient it is, and we have a choice of how we put that flavor into our foods.

*Madagascar bourbon pure vanilla powder* is made from vanilla beans grown on the island of Madagascar; it is in dry powder form, without sugar or alcohol. It's ideal for dissolving in hot or cold liquids, such as hot cocoa or coffee drinks, marinated fruits, quick breads, and white frostings or cooked meringues that you don't want to darken slightly, as happens with vanilla extract. One rounded teaspoon of vanilla powder has the flavor power of 1 teaspoon of pure vanilla extract.

*Madagascar bourbon pure vanilla bean paste* is a like jar of gold. The maker scrapes the vanilla beans for you and puts the seeds in a small jar. If I can see vanilla

sugar, baking powder, and salt in a medium-size mixing bowl and stir with a fork to blend. While you gently stir the flour mixture with a fork, gradually add the cream mixture; mix just until the dough barely holds together.

**3.** Using floured hands, divide the dough in half and gently form each half into a ball. Place the balls of dough on the prepared baking sheet, spacing them 3 inches apart. (They will spread out as they bake.) Bake the shortcakes until they are light golden brown, 28 minutes.

**4.** Remove the baking sheet from the oven, and slide the parchment paper, with the shortcakes on top, onto a wire rack. Allow them to cool completely.

bean seeds in a dessert, I know I will be greeted with an exotic vanilla flavor in the first spoonful. One teaspoon of vanilla paste equals 1 teaspoon of pure vanilla extract.

There is still plenty of decent vanilla extract available, but not all of it is created equal. Price may indicate how clean and powerful the vanilla flavor will be.

All vanilla extracts are made from vanilla beans steeped in alcohol and water. Some alcohols impart a harsh flavor if they are not aged—or mellowed—by the addition of sugar. Madagascar bourbon pure vanilla extract is developed from vanilla beans steeped in alcohol with little or no sugar, then it is aged to develop the flavors. It is pricier than a store brand been made from alcohol that has neither been aged before nor after production; sugar is added to take the edge off the alcohol and the extract can be shipped immediately to the retailer. Imitation vanilla extract is produced from synthetic vanillin—made from a by-product of paper-making or a coal-tar derivative—and is the most inexpensive flavoring of all.

**5.** MAKE THE SAUCE: Place the strawberries and sugar in a blender and puree until smooth. Set aside.

**6.** MAKE THE TOPPING: Place the cream in a medium-size mixing bowl and beat with an electric mixer on high speed until firm peaks form, 1 minute. Add the lemon curd and whisk to blend.

**7.** Pour the strawberry sauce on to 2 dessert plates, dividing it evenly between them. Place a shortcake on each plate, and spoon 1/3 cup of the sliced strawberries on top and around each shortcake. Top with the lemon cream, dividing it evenly between the shortcakes. Garnish with fresh mint, if desired, and serve immediately.

# Cornmeal Shortcakes Melba

*Makes 2 shortcakes; serves 2*
◆◆◆◆◆◆◆◆◆

**Poached peaches and** raspberry sauce are classic Peach Melba ingredients, and in this recipe they assert themselves in a beautiful shortcake. The fruit filling is gorgeous in color and the fresh flavors shine. The sour cream makes the shortcakes very light and tender, and the cornmeal gives them the texture that deliciously soaks up the sweet fruit juices and raspberry sauce.

**FOR THE SHORTCAKES:**

¼ cup plus 3 tablespoons
   all-purpose flour

1 tablespoon yellow cornmeal

1 tablespoon plus ½ teaspoon sugar

¼ teaspoon baking powder

⅛ teaspoon baking soda

⅛ teaspoon salt

1 tablespoon cold unsalted butter,
   diced

¼ cup sour cream

1 tablespoon whole milk

## FOR THE FRUIT FILLING:

**1½ cups sliced fresh or thawed frozen unsweetened peaches**

**½ teaspoon fresh lemon juice**

**2 tablespoons peach or apricot preserves, warmed**

**1 tablespoon sugar**

**½ cup fresh or thawed frozen unsweetened raspberries**

## FOR THE TOPPING AND FOR SERVING:

**⅓ cup cold whipping (heavy) cream**

**1 tablespoon confectioners' sugar**

**Raspberry Sauce (recipe follows)**

## PAN REQUIRED:

**1 baking sheet**

**1.** Place a rack in the center of the oven and preheat the oven to 400°F. Line the baking sheet with parchment paper and set it aside.

**2. MAKE THE SHORTCAKES:** Place the flour, cornmeal, 1 tablespoon of the sugar, the baking powder, baking soda, and salt in a medium-size bowl and whisk to blend. Add the butter pieces and toss to coat the butter with the flour mixture. Rub the mixture with your fingertips, or cut the butter in with a pastry blender, until the lumps are no larger than small peas.

Spoon the sour cream and milk over the crumb mixture, and toss with a fork just until the dough comes together.

**3.** Using floured hands, divide the dough in half and gently form each half into a ball. Place the balls of dough on the prepared baking sheet spaced 2 inches apart, and sprinkle the remaining ½ teaspoon of sugar evenly over them. Bake until the shortcakes are golden brown and a toothpick inserted in the center of one comes out clean, 15 to 18 minutes.

**4.** Remove the baking sheet from the oven and slide the parchment paper, with the shortcakes on top, onto a wire rack. Allow the shortcakes to cool to lukewarm.

**5. MAKE THE FRUIT FILLING:** Place the peaches and the lemon juice in a small bowl, and toss to combine. Add the melted preserves and the sugar, and toss to coat the peaches. Cover the bowl and set aside. (The raspberries will be added later.)

**6. MAKE THE TOPPING:** Place the whipping cream and confectioners' sugar in a medium-size mixing bowl and beat with a hand-held mixer on high speed until firm peaks form, 1 to 1½ minutes.

**7.** Just before you assemble the shortcakes, stir the raspberries into the fruit filling.

**8.** To serve, cut the shortcakes in half horizontally and place the bottom halves on serving plates. Spoon the fruit filling over the bottoms, and top with the sweetened whipped cream. Cover with the shortcake tops. Drizzle the Raspberry Sauce on and around the shortcakes.

# Raspberry Sauce

**Raspberry jam** and liqueur combine to make a puree full of flavor. It is a sauce you can use to make many desserts; it complements chocolate especially. I've served brownies with this sauce and whipped cream, and I've served the sauce with the White and Dark Chocolate Swirl Cheesecakes (page 356) and the Pavlovas (page 370). It is also elegant with fresh fruit and sorbet.

**MAKES ABOUT ½ CUP**

**1 cup fresh or undrained thawed frozen unsweetened raspberries**

**1 tablespoon raspberry jam or preserves or peach preserves**

**1 teaspoon raspberry-flavored liqueur (such as Chambord) or black-currant flavored liqueur (such as crème de cassis; optional)**

Place the raspberries, jam, and Chambord (if using) in a blender. If you are using fresh raspberries, add 1 tablespoon water. Blend until pureed. Use right away, or cover and refrigerate for up to 1 week.

# Milk Chocolate Raspberry Shortcakes
## *with* Milk Chocolate Sauce

*Makes 2 shortcakes; serves 2*

◆◆◆◆◆◆◆◆◆

**Raspberries and** chocolate are a sublime combination. Most recipes pair the luscious red berries with dark chocolate, but this is one dessert that is perfectly suited to milk chocolate. Both the shortcake and the sauce are pure sweet chocolate, which really sets off the raspberries.

**FOR THE SHORTCAKES:**

1/2 cup all-purpose flour

2 tablespoons sugar

2 teaspoons unsweetened cocoa powder

1/4 teaspoon baking powder

1/8 teaspoon baking soda

1/8 teaspoon salt

1 1/2 tablespoons cold unsalted butter, diced

1/2 ounce milk chocolate, finely chopped

2 to 3 tablespoons cold whipping (heavy) cream, or more as needed

**FOR THE FRUIT FILLING AND FOR SERVING:**

1 1/2 cups fresh raspberries

1 tablespoon granulated sugar

1 tablespoon raspberry liqueur, such as Chambord or Framboise (optional)

1/3 cup cold whipping (heavy) cream

1 tablespoon confectioners' sugar

Milk Chocolate Sauce (recipe follows)

**PAN REQUIRED:**
**1 baking sheet**

**1.** Place a rack in the center of the oven and preheat the oven to 400°F. Line a baking sheet with parchment paper and set it aside.

**2. MAKE THE SHORTCAKES:** Place the flour, sugar, cocoa powder, baking powder, baking soda, and salt in a medium-size mixing bowl and whisk to blend well. Add the butter pieces and toss to coat the butter with the flour mixture. Rub the mixture with your fingertips, or cut the butter in with a pastry blender, until the lumps are no larger than small peas. Stir in the chopped chocolate. Sprinkle 2 tablespoons of the cream over the crumb mixture and stir it lightly with a fork until the dough just holds together. (Add another tablespoon of cream, by teaspoonfuls, if the mixture is too dry.)

**3.** Using floured hands, divide the dough in half and gently form each half into a ball. Place the balls of dough on the prepared baking sheet 2 inches apart.

(The shortcakes will spread out during baking.) Bake the shortcakes until a toothpick inserted in the center of one comes out clean, about 17 minutes. Remove the baking sheet from the oven and slide the parchment, with the shortcakes on it, onto a wire rack to cool for 15 minutes.

**4. MAKE THE FRUIT FILLING:** while the shortcakes are cooling. Place ¼ cup of the raspberries, the sugar, and the liqueur if using in a small bowl, and mash the berries. Stir in the remaining whole raspberries.

**5.** Place the whipping cream and confectioners' sugar in a medium-size mixing bowl and beat with an electric mixer on high speed until stiff peaks form, about 1 minute.

**6.** To serve, cut the shortcakes in half horizontally and place the bottom halves on serving plates. Spoon the fruit and juices over the bottoms and top with the sweetened whipped cream. Prop the tops against the sides of the shortcakes. Drizzle the Milk Chocolate Sauce on the serving plates and the shortcakes.

# Milk Chocolate Sauce

**Milk chocolate** and raspberry liqueur make a sophisticated duo in this simple, creamy sauce. It is wonderful on pound cake, too.

**MAKES ABOUT ⅓ CUP**

¼ cup plus 1 tablespoon
  whipping (heavy) cream
1 ounce milk chocolate,
  chopped

2 teaspoons raspberry liqueur
  (such as Chambord or Framboise)

Place the cream in a small saucepan over high heat and bring to a boil. Remove the pan from the heat and add the chocolate and liqueur. Stir until the sauce is smooth. Serve the sauce hot or warm, or refrigerate, covered, for up to 1 week.

# Chocolate Flake Shortcakes

## *with* Minted Pears

*Makes 2 shortcakes; serves 2*

◆◆◆◆◆◆◆◆

**Chocolate and mint** turn poached pears into stars here. The pears are poached in sweet dessert wine flavored with fresh mint, then removed from the cooking liquid. Chocolate is then melted in the pear liquid to spoon over the chocolate-flecked short-cakes and pears. It is an unusual dessert.

**FOR THE SHORTCAKES:**

½ cup all-purpose flour

1 tablespoon plus ½ teaspoon sugar

¼ teaspoon baking powder

⅛ teaspoon baking soda

⅛ teaspoon salt

1 ounce bittersweet or semisweet
   chocolate, finely chopped

2 tablespoons cold unsalted butter,
   cut into ½-inch pieces

2 tablespoons plus 2 teaspoons
   cold buttermilk

**FOR THE FILLING:**

1 firm, ripe pear, such as Bosc, or
   slightly under-ripe softer pear,
   such as Anjou or Red Anjou

⅓ cup pear nectar

⅓ cup sweet dessert wine

2 tablespoons sugar

1 tablespoon packed fresh mint
   leaves

1 tablespoon whipping (heavy)
   cream

1 ounce bittersweet or semisweet
   chocolate, finely chopped

**FOR THE TOPPING:**

⅓ cup cold whipping (heavy) cream

1 tablespoon confectioners' sugar

**PAN REQUIRED:**

1 baking sheet

**1.** Place a rack in the center of the oven and preheat the oven to 400°F. Line the baking sheet with parchment paper.

**2. MAKE THE SHORTCAKES:** Place the flour, 1 tablespoon sugar, baking powder, baking soda, and salt in a food processor and process to blend, 2 to 3 seconds. Sprinkle the chocolate and butter pieces over the flour mixture and pulse until the butter pieces are no larger than very small peas, 22 to 23 pulses. Sprinkle the buttermilk evenly over the mixture and pulse just until moist clumps form, 5 or 6 pulses.

**3.** Turn the dough out onto a lightly floured work surface. Dust your hands with flour and gently form the dough into 2 halves. Pat out each half to form a 3-inch round. Place the shortcakes on the prepared baking sheet and sprinkle the remaining ½ teaspoon of sugar evenly over the tops. Bake the shortcakes until a toothpick inserted into the center of one comes out clean, about 15 minutes.

**4.** Remove the baking sheet from the oven and slide the parchment, with the shortcakes on it, onto a wire rack to cool.

**5. MAKE THE FILLING:** Peel and core the pears; cut them lengthwise into thin slices. Pour the pear nectar, wine, and sugar into a medium-size saucepan and add the mint. Stir to mix. Bring the mixture to a boil over medium-high heat, stirring constantly until the sugar melts. Add the pears, stirring them in gently, and cover the saucepan. Reduce the heat to medium-low and cook until the pear slices are just tender and translucent, 8 to 10 minutes. Use a slotted spoon to transfer the pears to a bowl, leaving the poaching liquid in the saucepan.

**6.** Add the cream to the poaching liquid. Increase the heat to medium-high and boil the mixture, uncovered, until it reduces to ¼ cup, 6 to 8 minutes. Remove the saucepan from the heat. Add the chopped chocolate, and whisk until the sauce is smooth.

**7. MAKE THE TOPPING:** Place the cream and confectioners' sugar in a small bowl, and beat with an electric mixer on high speed until firm peaks form.

**8.** To assemble the shortcakes, cut each one in half horizontally. Place each bottom half in a shallow serving bowl. Spoon the pears over them and top with the sweetened whipped cream. Place the shortcake tops on top of the pears, and drizzle the chocolate pear sauce over and around the shortcake stacks. Serve immediately.

# Coconut Shortcakes

## *with* Caramel Pineapple and Brown Sugar Cream

*Makes 2 shortcakes; serves 2*

**◆◆◆◆◆◆◆◆**

**Light the tiki** torches!
Flecked with toasted coconut,
these shortcakes are layered
with caramelized pineapple and
whipped cream flavored with
brown sugar and white chocolate.
If you are grilling outdoors, you
can grill the pineapple, then
add it to the caramelized sugar
in Step 6 and cook it for about
30 seconds, just to coat it with
the caramel.

**FOR THE BROWN SUGAR CREAM:**
**2 ounces imported white chocolate
(such as Lindt), chopped**

**1/2 cup cold whipping (heavy) cream**
**2 tablespoons packed dark
    brown sugar**
**1/4 teaspoon ground cinnamon**

**FOR THE SHORTCAKES:**
**1/2 cup all-purpose flour**
**2 tablespoons sweetened flaked
    coconut, lightly toasted
    (see page 24) and cooled**
**1 tablespoon plus 1/2 teaspoon
    granulated sugar**
**1/4 teaspoon baking powder**
**1/8 teaspoon baking soda**
**1/8 teaspoon salt**
**1 tablespoon cold unsalted butter,
    diced**
**1/4 cup sour cream**
**1 tablespoon whole milk**

**FOR THE FRUIT:**

**2 tablespoons packed dark brown sugar**

**2 teaspoons unsalted butter**

**4 fresh or canned drained pineapple slices (1/2 inch thick), quartered (see Note)**

**PAN REQUIRED:**

**1 baking sheet**

1. **MAKE THE BROWN SUGAR CREAM:** Place the white chocolate and 2 tablespoons of the cream in a small microwave-safe bowl and microwave on medium power until the white chocolate is soft, about 1 minute. Stir until smooth; then set it aside and allow to cool to room temperature, 30 to 45 minutes.

2. Place the remaining cream, the brown sugar, and the cinnamon in a medium-size mixing bowl and beat with an electric mixer on high speed until firm peaks form, about 1 minute. Pour in the white chocolate mixture and beat on high speed until well blended and fluffy, 20 to 30 seconds. (The brown sugar cream can be stored, covered, in the refrigerator for up to 4 hours.)

3. Place a rack in the center of the oven and preheat the oven to 400°F. Line a baking sheet with parchment paper and set it aside.

4. **MAKE THE SHORTCAKES:** Place the flour, coconut, 1 tablespoon of the sugar, baking powder, baking soda, and salt in a medium-size mixing bowl and whisk to blend well. Add the butter pieces and toss to coat the butter with the flour mixture. Rub the mixture with your fingertips, or cut the butter in with a pastry blender, until the lumps are no larger than small peas. Spoon the sour cream and milk over the crumb mixture, and toss the ingredients with a fork just until the dough comes together.

**5.** Using floured hands, divide the dough in half and gently form each half into a ball. Place the balls of dough on the prepared baking sheet 2 inches apart. (The shortcakes will spread out during baking.) Sprinkle the remaining ½ teaspoon of sugar evenly over them. Bake the shortcakes until they are golden brown and a toothpick inserted in the center of one comes out clean, 15 minutes.

**6.** Remove the baking sheet from the oven and slide the parchment, with the shortcakes on it, onto a wire rack to cool. (The shortcakes can be made up to 4 hours ahead; just warm them in a preheated 300°F oven for 10 minutes before serving. Cover and keep at room temperature.)

**7. PREPARE THE FRUIT:** Place the brown sugar and butter in a medium-size skillet over medium-high heat and bring to a simmer, stirring constantly. Continue to cook until the mixture turns a dark caramel color, about 2 minutes. Add the pineapple and cook, stirring gently, until the fruit is hot and glazed, about 2 minutes. Remove the skillet from the heat.

**8.** To serve, cut the shortcakes in half horizontally and place the bottom halves on serving plates. Spoon the fruit and juices over the bottoms, and top with some of the brown sugar cream. Prop the tops against the sides of the shortcakes, and spoon the rest of the Brown Sugar Cream on the side.

**NOTE:** If using canned pineapple, choose unsweetened or canned in light syrup.

# Pecan Shortcakes

## *with* Banana Cream and Caramel Sauce

*Makes 2 shortcakes; serves 2*

◆◆◆◆◆◆◆◆◆

**Both mashed and** sliced bananas are folded into whipped cream to make a luscious filling for these cake-like shortcakes. The homemade caramel sauce and candied pecans put this dessert over the top.

**FOR THE SHORTCAKES:**

⅔ cup all-purpose flour

1 tablespoon plus ½ teaspoon sugar

⅛ teaspoon baking powder

⅛ teaspoon baking soda

⅛ teaspoon salt

2 tablespoons cold unsalted butter, diced

3 tablespoons finely chopped pecans, toasted (see box, page 195)

3 tablespoons sour cream

Yolk of 1 large egg

¼ teaspoon pure vanilla extract

**FOR THE FILLING AND FOR SERVING:**

1 large ripe banana

1 teaspoon fresh lemon juice

2 teaspoons sugar

¼ cup whipping (heavy) cream

1 tablespoon confectioners' sugar

Rich Caramel Sauce (recipe follows), or ¼ cup store-bought caramel sauce and warmed Candied Pecans (optional; page 99)

**PAN REQUIRED:**

1 baking sheet

**1.** Place a rack in the center of the oven and preheat the oven to 400°F. Line the baking sheet with parchment paper and set it aside.

**2. MAKE THE SHORTCAKES:** Place the flour, 1 tablespoon of the sugar, the baking powder, baking soda, and salt in a medium-size mixing bowl and whisk to blend well. Add the butter pieces and toss to coat the butter with the flour mixture. Rub the mixture with your fingertips, or cut the butter in with a pastry blender, until the lumps are no larger than small peas. Mix in the pecans.

**3.** Place the sour cream, egg yolk, and vanilla in a medium-size mixing bowl, and whisk to blend. Add the sour cream mixture to the crumb mixture. Toss the ingredients with a fork just until the dough comes together.

**4.** Using floured hands, divide the dough in half and gently form each half into a ball. Place the balls of dough on the prepared baking sheet, spacing them 4 inches apart. Do not flatten them; they will spread out as they bake. Sprinkle the remaining 1/2 teaspoon of sugar evenly over the balls of dough. Bake the short-cakes until they are golden brown and a toothpick inserted into the center of one comes out clean, about 18 minutes.

**5.** Remove the baking sheet from the oven and slide the parchment, with the shortcakes on it, onto a wire rack. Let the shortcakes cool for 15 minutes.

**6. MAKE THE BANANA CREAM FILLING:** Peel the banana and slice it into a bowl. Add the lemon juice and toss (this prevents the banana from browning). Measure out half of the bananas and transfer that portion to another bowl. Cover the bowl and set it aside.

**7.** Mash the remaining banana mix-ture well, using a pastry blender or a potato masher. Stir in the 2 teaspoons sugar. Cover the mashed bananas and place them in the refrigerator.

**8.** Place the whipping cream and confectioners' sugar in a medium-size mixing bowl and beat with a hand-held electric mixer on high speed until firm peaks form. Fold in the banana puree and the sliced bananas.

**9.** To assemble the shortcakes, cut them in half horizontally. Place the bottom halves on serving plates and spoon the banana cream mixture on the bottoms, dividing it evenly between them. Replace the shortcake tops. Drizzle the plate and the shortcakes with the caramel sauce. Sprinkle with the candied pecans if using. Serve immediately.

# Rich Caramel Sauce

**A friend said** the right thing when she tasted this: "Who needs chocolate when you can eat homemade caramel sauce?" I agree— homemade caramel has a depth of flavor that makes it just as satisfying as chocolate.

**MAKES ½ CUP**

**½ cup sugar**
**¼ cup plus 2 tablespoons whipping (heavy) cream**

**1.** Combine the sugar and 2 tablespoons of water in a small saucepan over medium-high heat. Bring to a boil, stirring with a fork, and cook until the sugar dissolves, about 3 minutes. Reduce the heat to medium and cook, swirling the saucepan frequently, until the sugar syrup is golden amber in color, 7 to 9 minutes.

**2.** Remove the pan from the heat and gradually add the cream, stirring slowly and carefully—the caramel will sputter when the liquid is added. The sugar will seize and harden. Return the pan to the heat and continue cooking until the sugar melts again, about 2 minutes. Serve immediately, or store in a covered jar in the refrigerator for up to 1 week.

# CHAPTER 6

# Baked Puddings: I'd Rather Have Them for Supper

**Occasionally, all I** want to do for dinner is curl up with a soft blanket, a book, and a deep bowl of pudding warm from the oven. This chapter is dedicated to those of you who agree with me, even if you're able to hold off the pudding urge until dessert. Bread puddings, corn bread puddings, semolina puddings, pudding cakes—some are light in texture, and some are heartier, but none are heavy. All have wonderful flavor.

I learned to make bread pudding from a chef in New Orleans, where they know their bread pudding. Back in the 1980s I was a home economist for *Southern Living* magazine, giving cooking classes in cities around the South. Our Southern Living Cooking School director, Martha Johnston, took our school troupe to New Orleans to learn how to make bread pudding (as well as gumbo, étouffée, and jambalaya) in the *authentic* Southern way. Executive chef and cookbook author Terry Thompson-Anderson introduced me to the New Orleans style. One taste of the light, fluffy pudding bathed in its caramel-flavored bourbon sauce had me hooked.

When you start with just bread, eggs, milk, and vanilla, it seems only logical that you can add a multitude of ingredients to the mix. The bread doesn't have to be French or white; it can be brioche, English muffins, hearty country loaves, cinnamon raisin bread, and even corn bread. And the flavorings: banana pecan, pumpkin walnut, Goo Goo Clusters candy bar, carrot cake, butterscotch, cinnamon toast—even the popular chai. For the final touch, there's nothing better than a flavored whipped cream or a special sauce, such as the cream cheese hard sauce that goes with the Carrot Cake Bread Pudding, or the Tennessee Butterscotch Sauce that accompanies the Butterscotch Bread Pudding.

Not all of the puddings included here contain bread. There is a simple vanilla custard that is smooth and creamy and bursting with fresh berries. The Lemon Pudding Cake forms a layer of pudding underneath a soufflé-like cake as it bakes in the dish. Also in the lighter category are two puddings with unusual flavor combinations: The first is a semolina-based pudding, a firm yet delicate custard with a vanilla-orange-sherry-blueberry sauce, topped with an orange- and sherry-scented whipped cream. It is a perfectly beautiful ending for a summer meal. The second is a mocha pudding that rises like a soufflé and is complemented by a mocha crème anglaise accented with mint—out of this world.

Small-Batch baked puddings are cooked in individual ovenproof bowls or small baking dishes. In many cases they are unmolded onto the plate and drizzled with a sauce, but all of the puddings— even when served from the bowl— are as pretty to look at as they are delicious.

# Warm Chocolate Bread Pudding

*Makes 2 puddings; serves 2*

◆◆◆◆◆◆◆◆◆

## Dark, rich chocolate

custard soaks into egg bread for a
fluffy texture with deep flavor. This
is a luxurious pudding that is made
even more elegant served with fresh
raspberries alongside. Use brioche
or challah for the bread.

Unsalted butter, at room temperature,
  for greasing the ramekins
¾ cup half-and-half
2 ounces bittersweet or semisweet
  chocolate, chopped
1 large egg
3 tablespoons sugar
Pinch of salt
½ teaspoon pure vanilla extract
2 cups stale egg bread cubes
  (1-inch cubes)

Hot Chocolate Crème Anglaise
  (page 388), warmed

PANS REQUIRED:
Two 1-cup ramekins or custard
  cups
1 baking sheet

1. Place a rack in the center of the
oven and preheat the oven to 325°F.
Lightly grease the ramekins. Place
them on a baking sheet for easier
handling, and set it aside.

2. Pour the half-and-half into a small
saucepan and bring to a boil over
medium-high heat. Remove the pan
from the heat and add the chopped
chocolate, swirling the pan to immerse
the chocolate in the hot half-and-half.

## PROTECT THOSE FINGERS

The ramekins holding baked puddings can be very hot when you serve them. And although you place them on dessert plates, when you try to scoop pudding out without holding the ramekin in place, it will scoot around on its plate. Here's a suggestion to prevent it from scooting and also to protect those eager hands:

Fold two cloth dinner napkins (the larger the better) into quarters. Using tongs, place the hot ramekin in the center of the napkin. Fold the corners up the sides of the dish and secure the napkin with a large rubber band. The edges of the napkin will fan out around the dish and form a holder for the hot dessert. Place each ramekin on a serving plate. Now it's easy to dip into the hot pudding.

Let it stand until the chocolate softens, 1 minute. Then stir until the mixture is smooth.

**3.** Place the egg, sugar, salt, and vanilla in a medium-size bowl and whisk until the mixture is frothy, about 20 seconds. Continue whisking while you gradually pour in the chocolate cream. Add the bread cubes, pressing them down with a spatula to submerge them. Let the mixture stand, pressing on the bread occasionally to keep it submerged, until the bread is saturated, about 10 minutes.

**4.** Spoon the mixture into the prepared ramekins, dividing it evenly between them. Bake until the puddings are just set, about 30 minutes. Remove the baking sheet from the oven, transfer the ramekins to a wire rack, and let them cool for 10 minutes.

**5.** To serve, unmold the puddings: Run the tip of a sharp knife around the edge of the ramekins, and invert the puddings onto serving plates. Spoon the Hot Chocolate Crème Anglaise over the bread puddings.

# Banana Pecan Bread Pudding

## *with* Cane Syrup

*Makes 2 puddings; serves 2*

◆◆◆◆◆◆◆◆

## Mashed bananas and

toasted pecans make this bread pudding supremely Southern, even without the cane syrup.

I am the offspring of two Florida "crackers," and one thing I remember from childhood breakfasts and Sunday suppers is pouring cane syrup on my hotcakes. This richly flavored, distinctly Southern syrup is made by boiling down pure sugarcane juice until it is just the right thickness and color. It tastes like no other syrup. If you can't find a can or bottle of 100 percent cane syrup, you can order it on-line. My mother uses Steen's Cane Syrup in her pecan pies instead of dark corn syrup (and now I do too), and her pies are out of this world.

Unsalted butter, at room temperature, for greasing the ramekins

¼ cup cane syrup

1 large banana

1 large egg

½ cup whipping (heavy) cream

2 tablespoons packed light brown sugar

Pinch of salt

¼ teaspoon ground ginger

⅛ teaspoon ground cinnamon

½ teaspoon pure vanilla extract

1½ cups stale white bread cubes (½-inch cubes)

¼ cup chopped pecans, toasted (see page 195)

Whipped cream or vanilla or butter pecan ice cream, for serving

PANS REQUIRED:

Two 1-cup ramekins or custard cups

1 baking sheet

**1.** Place a rack in the center of the oven and preheat the oven to 350°F. Lightly grease the ramekins. Pour 2 tablespoons of the cane syrup into each ramekin, place the ramekins on a baking sheet, and set it aside.

**2.** Peel the banana and slice one third of it. Arrange the banana slices decoratively on the syrup in the ramekins.

Cover the ramekins with plastic wrap and set them aside while you prepare the pudding.

**3.** Cut the remaining two thirds of the banana into chunks, and place them in a food processor. Add the egg, cream, brown sugar, salt, ginger, cinnamon, and vanilla, and process until the mixture is smooth, about 15 seconds. Pour the mixture into a medium-size mixing bowl and stir in the bread cubes, pressing down on them to submerge them. Let the bread soak for 5 minutes. Then stir in the pecans.

**4.** Spoon the mixture into the ramekins, dividing it evenly between them. Bake until the puddings are firm and a knife inserted in the center of one comes out clean, 30 to 35 minutes. Remove the baking sheet from the oven, transfer the ramekins to a wire rack, and let them cool for 10 minutes.

**5.** To serve, unmold the puddings: Run a sharp knife around the edges of the ramekins, and invert the puddings onto individual plates. Pour any remaining cane syrup around the puddings. Serve warm, with whipped cream or ice cream.

# Chai Bread Pudding

*Makes 2 puddings; serves 2*

◆◆◆◆◆◆◆◆◆

**Now *this* is** my cup of tea. The tea and spices blend nicely with the half-and-half to make a delicious treat, with a flavor just like the popular Indian spiced tea. Serve it simply, with whipped cream.

**Unsalted butter, at room temperature, for greasing the ramekins**

**¾ cup half-and-half**

**1 tablespoon Darjeeling tea leaves**

**¼ cup sugar**

**⅛ teaspoon salt**

**⅛ teaspoon ground cinnamon**

**⅛ teaspoon ground cardamom**

**Pinch of ground cloves**

**1 large egg**

**Yolk of 1 large egg**

**2 cups stale egg bread (brioche or challah) cubes (½-inch cubes)**

**1½ tablespoons very finely minced crystallized ginger**

**Sweetened Whipped Cream (page 36), for serving**

**PANS REQUIRED:**

**Two 1-cup ramekins or custard cups**

**1 baking sheet**

**1.** Place a rack in the center of the oven and preheat the oven to 350°F. Lightly grease the ramekins. Place them on a baking sheet for easier handling, and set it aside.

**2.** Pour the half-and-half into a small saucepan and bring it to a boil over medium-high heat. Stir in the tea leaves; cover the saucepan and remove it from the heat. Let the tea steep for 5 minutes.

**3.** Place a fine-mesh sieve over a bowl and strain the half-and-half mixture through it. Discard the tea leaves.

## STALE BREAD = THE BEST BREAD PUDDING

Bread puddings were first made by inventive cooks who did not want to throw out old, dry bread. You'll find many recipes for bread pudding that call for day-old French bread; that's because French bread is made without fat, and fat is what gives bread its keeping quality. Therefore French bread is just the right stale texture the day after it is baked. Other bakery breads that contain fat may be fresh-tasting for more than one day, so you would want to make those bread puddings several days after the bread is baked.

Packaged sliced bread often stays fresh-tasting until the day it first displays mold. For that bread, you'll want to dry it out in the oven. (You can also dry a fresh loaf of bakery bread in the oven to use in bread pudding.) To dry bread, cut the bread into cubes, place them in a single layer on a baking sheet, and bake in a preheated 250°F oven for one hour.

4. Add the sugar, salt, cinnamon, cardamom, and cloves to the tea-infused cream, and whisk to blend well. Add the egg and egg yolk and whisk to blend well. Add the bread cubes and crystallized ginger, pressing down with a spatula to submerge them. Let the mixture stand, pressing on the bread occasionally to keep it submerged, until the bread is saturated, about 10 minutes.

5. Spoon the mixture into the prepared ramekins, dividing it evenly between them. Bake until puddings are puffed and set, about 35 minutes. Remove the baking sheet from the oven, transfer the ramekins to a wire rack, and let them cool for 15 minutes.

6. Top the puddings with Sweetened Whipped Cream and serve warm, in the ramekins.

# Pumpkin Walnut Brioche Pudding

## *with* Bourbon Caramel Sauce

*Makes 2 puddings; serves 2*

**This is so** tasty, you'll be tempted to serve it instead of pumpkin pie at Thanksgiving! It has pumpkin pie flavor in a moist, light bread pudding. Homemade caramel sauce, laced with bourbon, is just divine with it.

Unsalted butter, at room temperature, for greasing the ramekins

1/2 cup half-and-half

1/3 cup canned pumpkin puree (not pie filling)

1/4 cup packed dark brown sugar

1 large egg

1/2 teaspoon pumpkin pie spice

1/8 teaspoon ground ginger

1/2 teaspoon pure vanilla extract

2 cups stale egg bread (brioche or challah) cubes (1/2-inch cubes)

1/4 cup chopped walnuts

Bourbon Caramel Sauce (recipe follows)

**PANS REQUIRED:**

Two 1-cup ramekins or custard cups

1 baking sheet

**1.** Place a rack in the center of the oven and preheat the oven to 350°F. Lightly grease the ramekins. Place them on a baking sheet for easier handling, and set it aside.

**2.** Place the half-and-half, pumpkin, brown sugar, egg, pumpkin pie spice, ginger, and vanilla in a medium-size mixing bowl, and whisk to blend well. Stir in the bread cubes, pressing down on them with a spatula to submerge them. Let the mixture stand, pressing on the bread occasionally to keep it submerged, until the bread is saturated, about 10 minutes. Then stir in the walnuts.

**3.** Spoon the mixture into the prepared ramekins, dividing it evenly between them. Bake until the puddings are puffed and set, about 20 minutes. Remove the baking sheet from the oven, transfer the ramekins to a wire rack, and let them cool for 10 minutes.

**4.** To serve the puddings, unmold them: Run the tip of a sharp knife around the edge of the ramekins, and invert the puddings onto serving plates. Drizzle the Bourbon Caramel Sauce over the puddings, and serve warm.

# Bourbon Caramel Sauce

**Smooth and rich,** this sauce is a true luxury. It is just as wonderful over ice cream.

**MAKES ABOUT ½ CUP**

**2 tablespoons unsalted butter**

**¼ cup plus 2 tablespoons packed dark brown sugar**

**2 tablespoons whipping (heavy) cream**

**1 tablespoon bourbon**

Place the butter in a small saucepan over medium heat, and heat until melted. Stir in the brown sugar and cook, stirring constantly, until the sugar melts, about 5 minutes. Whisk in the cream and bring to a simmer. Simmer, uncovered, until the sauce has thickened slightly, about 5 minutes. Then whisk in the bourbon and remove the saucepan from the heat. Serve warm. (Store any leftover sauce in the refrigerator for up to 1 week; then warm it before you serve it.)

# Carrot Cake Bread Pudding

## *with* Cream Cheese Hard Sauce

*Makes 2 puddings; serves 2*

**As you might** imagine, in this unusual bread pudding—complete with grated carrots, pecans, pineapple, and, in the hard sauce that accompanies it, cream cheese— you'll find all the flavors of your favorite carrot cake.

Unsalted butter, at room temperature, for greasing the ramekins

2 cups stale white bread cubes (1/2-inch cubes)

1/3 cup grated carrots

1/4 cup plus 2 tablespoons chopped pecans, toasted (see page 195)

1/4 cup well-drained canned crushed pineapple, or 2 tablespoons pineapple and 2 tablespoons sweetened flaked coconut

1 large egg

Yolk of 1 large egg

1/4 cup sugar

1/8 teaspoon ground cinnamon

Pinch of salt

3/4 cup half-and-half

1/2 teaspoon pure vanilla extract

2 teaspoons unsalted butter,
 cut into small pieces

Cream Cheese Hard Sauce
 (recipe follows)

PANS REQUIRED:

Two 1-cup ramekins or custard cups,
 or 2 deep 1½- to 2-cup ovenproof
 bowls

1 baking sheet

1. Place a rack in the center of the oven and preheat the oven to 350°F. Lightly grease the ramekins. Place them on a baking sheet for easier handling, and set it aside.

2. Place the bread cubes, carrots, ¼ cup of the pecans, and the pineapple in a medium-size bowl and toss well.

3. Place the egg, egg yolk, sugar, cinnamon, salt, half-and-half, and vanilla in another medium-size mixing bowl, and whisk to blend. Pour this over the bread mixture, and mix gently but thoroughly. Let the mixture stand, pressing on the bread occasionally to keep it submerged, until the bread is saturated, about 10 minutes.

4. Spoon the mixture into the prepared baking dishes, dividing it evenly between them. Sprinkle the butter pieces evenly over the puddings. Bake until the puddings are set and golden brown, about 35 minutes. Remove the baking sheet from the oven, transfer the ramekins to a wire rack, and let them cool for 10 minutes.

5. To serve, unmold the puddings: Run the tip of a sharp knife around the edge of the ramekins, and invert the puddings onto serving plates. Serve warm, with the Cream Cheese Hard Sauce.

# Cream Cheese Hard Sauce

**It's not carrot cake** without cream cheese frosting, so I put cream cheese in the hard sauce that accompanies the bread pudding. Hard sauce is traditionally made by beating butter, confectioners' sugar, and brandy until it is fluffy and blended. By substituting cream cheese for part of the butter, the sauce tastes very much like cream cheese frosting but still has the texture of hard sauce. If you would rather not use brandy in the sauce, save the syrup or juice from the can of pineapple and substitute it for the brandy.

**MAKES ABOUT ½ CUP**

½ cup confectioners' sugar

2 tablespoons cream cheese, at room temperature

2 tablespoons unsalted butter, at room temperature

1 tablespoon brandy

Place all the ingredients in a small mixing bowl and beat with a hand-held electric mixer on medium speed until smooth and fluffy. Cover and refrigerate until chilled, about 30 minutes. (Store in the refrigerator in a covered container. It will keep for up to 4 days.)

# Goo Goo Bread Pudding

*Makes 2 puddings; serves 2*
◆◆◆◆◆◆◆◆◆

**Goo Goo Clusters,** made right here in the South, are good stuff and the inspiration for this bread pudding. These round "bars" are a layered concoction of caramel, marshmallow, and roasted peanuts, all coated in rich milk chocolate. This bread pudding is a salute to the only candy bar I'll indulge in, but it is not as sweet as the confection it's named for—really!

Unsalted butter, at room temperature, for greasing the ramekins
²/₃ cup half-and-half
¹/₃ cup plus ¼ cup milk chocolate chips

1 large egg
1 tablespoon sugar
1 teaspoon pure vanilla extract
1½ cups day-old French bread cubes (1-inch cubes)
¼ cup Rich Caramel Sauce (page 259) or store-bought caramel sundae syrup
¼ cup chopped pecans, lightly toasted (see page 195), or unsalted dry-roasted peanuts
¼ cup miniature marshmallows (optional)

**PANS REQUIRED:**
Two 1-cup ramekins or custard cups
1 baking sheet

1. Place a rack in the center of the oven and preheat the oven to 350°F. Lightly grease the ramekins. Place

them on a baking sheet for easier handling, and set it aside.

**2.** Pour the half-and-half into a small saucepan and bring it to a boil over medium-high heat. Remove the pan from the heat and add ⅓ cup of the chocolate chips, swirling the pan to immerse the chocolate in the hot half-and-half. Let it stand until the chocolate softens, 1 minute. Then stir until the mixture is smooth.

**3.** Place the egg, sugar, and vanilla in a medium-size mixing bowl and whisk until the mixture is frothy, about 20 seconds. Continue whisking while you gradually pour in the chocolate cream. Add the bread, pressing down on it with a spatula to submerge it. Let the mixture stand, pressing on the bread occasionally to keep it submerged, until the bread is saturated, about 10 minutes.

**4.** Spoon the mixture into the prepared ramekins, dividing it evenly between them. Bake until the puddings are just set, 30 to 35 minutes. Remove the baking sheet from the oven. Drizzle the caramel sauce over the puddings, and sprinkle them with the pecans and the marshmallows, if using. Return the baking sheet to the oven and bake until the caramel syrup is bubbling and the marshmallows are melted, about 1 minute.

**5.** Remove the baking sheet from the oven, transfer the ramekins to a wire rack, and let them cool for 10 minutes.

**6.** Place the remaining ¼ cup of chocolate chips in a microwave-safe bowl and microwave on medium power until soft, 45 to 55 seconds; then stir until the chocolate is smooth. Drizzle the melted chocolate over the puddings and serve them warm, in the ramekins.

# Butterscotch Bread Pudding

*Makes 2 puddings; serves 2*
◆◆◆◆◆◆◆◆◆

**This simple bread** pudding can be baked at a moment's notice—you probably already have all the ingredients on hand. The flavor comes from dark brown sugar and butter; it is an old-fashioned bread pudding full of flavor. When I'm after something truly ambrosial, I like to add a sprinkling of toffee bits, some banana slices, and a dollop of whipped cream to the bowl of pudding, then drizzle the sauce all over it.

Unsalted butter, at room temperature, for greasing the ramekins

¾ cup half-and-half or whole milk

¼ cup firmly packed dark brown sugar

1 tablespoon unsalted butter

Pinch of salt

1 large egg

White of 1 large egg

1 teaspoon pure vanilla extract

2 cups day-old "hearth-baked" bread cubes (½-inch cubes), such as ciabatta, country French, or country Italian

Tennessee Butterscotch Sauce (recipe follows)

Toffee bits, for serving (optional)

Sliced banana, for serving (optional)

Sweetened Whipped Cream (page 36), for serving (optional)

**PANS REQUIRED:**

Two 1-cup ramekins or custard cups

1 baking sheet

1. Place a rack in the center of the oven and preheat the oven to 350°F. Lightly grease the ramekins. Place them on a baking sheet for easier handling, and set it aside.

2. Place the half-and-half, brown sugar, butter, and salt in a small saucepan over medium-high heat and bring to a boil, stirring constantly, until the sugar melts, 4 to 5 minutes. Remove the pan from the heat.

3. Place the egg and the egg white in a medium-size mixing bowl and beat it lightly with a whisk. Gradually pour the hot cream mixture into the beaten egg, whisking vigorously as you pour, then stir in the vanilla. Add the bread to the cream mixture, pressing down with a spatula to submerge it. Let the mixture stand, pressing on the bread occasionally to keep it submerged, until the bread is saturated, about 10 minutes.

4. Spoon the pudding mixture into the prepared ramekins, dividing it evenly between them. Bake until the puddings are puffed and golden, about 35 minutes. Remove the baking sheet from the oven, transfer the ramekins to a wire rack, and let them cool for 10 minutes.

5. To serve, unmold the puddings: Run the tip of a sharp knife around the edge of the ramekins, and invert the puddings onto serving plates. Spoon the warm Tennessee Butterscotch Sauce over the puddings. If desired, sprinkle the puddings with toffee bits and arrange banana slices around them; then dollop with unsweetened whipped cream.

# Tennessee Butterscotch Sauce

**This thin, buttery** sauce is the right consistency to soak into the bread pudding, adding strong butterscotch flavor along with a Jack Daniel's zing.

**MAKES ½ CUP**

½ **cup sugar**

2 **tablespoons Jack Daniel's whiskey or bourbon whiskey**

1½ **tablespoons unsalted butter**

**1.** Place the sugar in a small saucepan over medium heat, and stir it slowly with a fork until the sugar melts and has turned an amber color, 20 to 25 minutes. Remove the saucepan from the heat and carefully pour 2 tablespoons of water and the Jack Daniel's down the side of the saucepan. The mixture will bubble furiously and steam, and the sugar will crystallize.

**2.** Return the saucepan to the heat and cook until the caramel dissolves, swirling the pan as it liquefies, about 5 minutes. Then remove the pan from the heat, add the butter, and stir until the sauce is smooth. Let the sauce cool slightly. (Covered, it will keep for up to 4 days in the refrigerator.)

# Cinnamon French Toast Pudding

*Makes 2 puddings; serves 2*
◆◆◆◆◆◆◆◆◆

**Like a bowl** of custard-soaked French toast, this pudding is a wonderful dessert, and also a great brunch dish. The bread cubes are tossed with cinnamon and sugar and toasted before they are soaked in the egg mixture, which gives the pudding a chunky texture. Warmed syrup is a perfect accompaniment at brunch. If you are serving it for dessert, either the syrup or Rich Caramel Sauce would be delicious; then consider adding a dollop of whipped cream.

Unsalted butter, at room temperature, for greasing the ramekins

**FOR THE BREAD:**

1 tablespoon sugar

1/8 teaspoon ground cinnamon

2 cups stale soft-crusted French bread or cinnamon raisin bread cubes (1/2-inch cubes)

2 tablespoons unsalted butter, melted

**FOR THE PUDDING:**

1 large egg

Yolk of 1 large egg

3/4 cup half-and-half or whole milk

1/4 cup sugar

1/4 teaspoon ground cinnamon

3/4 teaspoon pure vanilla extract

3 tablespoons raisins (optional)

Confectioners' sugar, for garnish

Maple syrup, cane syrup, or Rich Caramel Sauce (page 259), warmed

Sweetened Whipped Cream (page 36),
for serving (optional)

PANS REQUIRED:

Two 1-cup ramekins or custard cups,
or 2 deep 1½- to 2-cup ovenproof
bowls
1 baking sheet

1. Place a rack in the center of the
oven and preheat the oven to 350°F.
Lightly grease the ramekins. Place
them on a baking sheet for easier
handling, and set it aside.

2. PREPARE THE BREAD: Place the
sugar and cinnamon in a small bowl
and stir to mix. Spread out the bread
cubes on a rimmed baking sheet, and
drizzle the melted butter over them;
toss to coat the bread with the butter.
Sprinkle the cinnamon sugar over the
bread, and toss to coat the bread with
the cinnamon sugar. Bake the bread,
stirring the cubes once, until it is
lightly toasted, 12 to 15 minutes.
Remove the baking sheet from the
oven and let the bread cool completely,
15 to 20 minutes. Leave the oven on.

3. MAKE THE PUDDING: Place the
egg, egg yolk, half-and-half, sugar,
cinnamon, and vanilla in a medium-
size mixing bowl and whisk to blend.
Add the bread cubes and raisins, if
using, and stir to coat the bread with
the liquid. Press down on the bread
lightly with a spatula to submerge it.
Let the mixture stand, pressing on the
bread occasionally to keep it submerged,
until the bread is saturated, about
15 minutes.

4. Spoon the mixture into the prepared ramekins, dividing it evenly
between them. Bake until the puddings are puffed and set, about
35 minutes. Remove the baking
sheet from the oven, transfer the
ramekins to a wire rack, and let
them cool for 10 minutes.

5. To serve, unmold the puddings:
Run the tip of a sharp knife around
the edge of the ramekins, and invert
the puddings onto serving plates. Sift
confectioners' sugar
over them and serve
warm, with syrup
or caramel sauce
drizzled over
and around.
Add a dollop of
whipped cream,
if desired.

# Sweet Corn Bread Pudding

*Makes 2 puddings; serves 2*
◆◆◆◆◆◆◆◆◆

**Corn bread makes a** very moist, light bread pudding—a perfect dessert for a cold-weather meal of soup or stew. When we were in college at Virginia Tech, my friend Pam Hyler Stiles and I were regular customers at the diner on Main Street. We would walk in the door, and by the time we got to the counter in the back, there would be two tall milkshake glasses filled with crumbled hot homemade corn bread waiting for us. We'd pour in rich, thick buttermilk, sprinkle in some salt, and let the corn bread get good and soggy before we dove in with a soup spoon. That was my first corn bread pudding. This pudding has that old-fashioned flavor. That's because it's made with really good corn bread.

**Butter for greasing the ramekins**

FOR THE PUDDING:
**Old-Fashioned Corn Bread (page 306),
   torn into coarse crumbs**
**1 large egg**
**Yolk of 1 large egg**
**¼ cup whole milk**
**¼ cup buttermilk**
**¼ cup sugar**
**Pinch of salt**
**¼ teaspoon pure vanilla extract**
**¼ cup pecan pieces, toasted
   (see page 195)**

FOR THE CINNAMON SUGAR:

**1 teaspoon sugar**

**1/8 teaspoon of ground cinnamon**

**Maple syrup, warmed, for serving**

PANS REQUIRED:

**Two 1-cup ramekins or custard cups, or 2 deep 1 1/2- to 2-cup ovenproof bowls**

**1 baking sheet**

**1.** Place a rack in the center of the oven and preheat the oven to 350°F. Grease the ramekins with butter and place on a baking sheet.

**2.** MAKE THE PUDDING: Place the egg, egg yolk, milk, buttermilk, sugar, salt, and vanilla in a medium-size mixing bowl and whisk to blend well. Add the corn bread crumbs, pressing down with a spatula to submerge them. Let the mixture stand to allow the corn bread to absorb the liquid, 10 minutes. Then stir in the pecans.

**3.** MAKE THE CINNAMON SUGAR: Place the sugar and cinnamon in a small bowl, and stir to mix.

**4.** Spoon the pudding mixture into the ramekins, dividing it evenly between them. Sprinkle the cinnamon sugar evenly over the puddings. Bake until they are puffed and set, about 35 minutes. Remove the baking sheet from the oven, transfer the ramekins to a wire rack, and let the puddings cool for 10 minutes. Serve the puddings warm, in the ramekins, with maple syrup drizzled on top.

# Semolina Pudding

## *with* Blueberries and Orange Mascarpone Cream

*Makes 2 puddings; serves 2*
◆◆◆◆◆◆◆◆◆

**This creamy pudding** is lovely, with blueberries and pale orange cream—a perfect finale for a summertime dinner cooked on the grill. The sherry adds a subtle nutty flavor.

Unsalted butter, at room temperature, for greasing the ramekins

Semolina flour, for flouring the ramekins

**FOR THE BLUEBERRIES:**

2 tablespoons sugar

1 teaspoon cornstarch

1 cup fresh or thawed frozen blueberries

1 tablespoon cream sherry

1/2 teaspoon grated orange zest

**FOR THE PUDDING AND FOR SERVING:**

1 cup whole milk

Pinch of salt

3 tablespoons semolina flour

1/4 cup sugar

1 teaspoon cream sherry

1/4 teaspoon pure vanilla extract

⅛ teaspoon orange extract

1 large egg

Yolk of 1 large egg

Orange Mascarpone Cream
   (recipe follows)

PANS REQUIRED:

Two 1-cup ramekins or custard cups

**1.** Place a rack in the center of the oven and preheat the oven to 375°F. Lightly grease the ramekins and sprinkle them with semolina flour, tapping out the excess. Place them on a baking sheet for easier handling, and set it aside.

**2. PREPARE THE BLUEBERRIES:** Place the sugar and cornstarch in a small saucepan, and stir to mix. Add the blueberries, sherry, and orange zest, and stir well. Cook over medium heat, stirring frequently, until the sugar dissolves and the mixture is thickened, 3 to 4 minutes. Remove the pan from the heat and let the mixture cool while you prepare the pudding.

**3. MAKE THE PUDDING:** Place the milk and salt in a small saucepan over medium heat and bring to a simmer. Add the semolina flour in a thin stream, whisking constantly with a wire whisk so it doesn't form lumps. Cook, whisking constantly, until the semolina thickens and begins to pull away from the sides of the pan, about 2½ minutes. Remove the pan from the heat and stir in the sugar, sherry, and vanilla and orange extracts. Let the semolina mixture cool for 10 minutes.

**4.** Place the egg and egg yolk in a small bowl and whisk until frothy. Whisk in a little of the semolina mixture, then quickly whisk the egg mixture into the remaining semolina mixture. Pour it into the prepared ramekins, dividing it evenly between them. Bake until the puddings are lightly browned on top and are firm to the touch, about 27 minutes. Remove the baking sheet from the oven, transfer the ramekins to a wire rack, and let them cool for about 10 minutes.

**5.** To serve, unmold the puddings: Run the tip of a sharp knife around the edge of the ramekins, and invert the puddings onto serving plates. Spoon the blueberry mixture over the warm puddings, and place a spoonful of the Orange Mascarpone Cream on the side.

# Orange Mascarpone Cream

**Subtly scented** with orange and sherry, smooth whipped cream takes on creamy texture with the addition of the cheese.

**MAKES ¾ CUP**

**2 tablespoons mascarpone cheese**
**⅓ cup whipping (heavy) cream**
**1 tablespoon sugar**
**1 teaspoon grated orange zest**
**1 teaspoon cream sherry**

Place the cheese in a small bowl and beat with a hand-held electric mixer on high speed until it is fluffy and light, 20 to 30 seconds. Pour in the cream, sugar, orange zest, and sherry, and beat until the mixture holds firm peaks. (Store leftover whipped cream in a covered container in the refrigerator for up to 1 day, and serve it with pound cake or as a dip for gingersnaps.)

# Baked Berry Custard

*Makes 2 custard; serves 2*

◆◆◆◆◆◆◆◆◆

**A bowlful of** berries bound in a smooth, light custard describes this pudding. It is a wonderful no-fuss dessert that will not

overload you after dinner. And you can enjoy it anytime by keeping frozen berries in the freezer—you don't even need to thaw them.

Unsalted butter, at room temperature, for greasing the ramekins

Yolks of 2 large eggs

1 large egg

3 tablespoons sugar

¾ teaspoon pure vanilla extract

¾ cup half-and-half

1 tablespoon self-rising cornmeal mix or corn muffin mix

½ cup fresh or frozen blueberries

¼ cup fresh or frozen raspberries

Confectioners' sugar, for garnish

PANS REQUIRED:

Two 1-cup ramekins or custard cups

1 baking sheet

1. Place a rack in the center of the oven and preheat the oven to 350°F. Lightly grease the ramekins. Place them on a baking sheet for easier handling, and set it aside.

2. Place the egg yolks, egg, sugar, and vanilla in a small bowl and whisk to blend. Whisk in the half-and-half and cornmeal.

3. Place the blueberries and raspberries in the ramekins, dividing them evenly between them, and pour the half-and-half mixture over the top. Bake until the custards are just set, 12 to 15 minutes. Remove the baking sheet from the oven, transfer the ramekins to a wire rack, and let them cool for 10 minutes.

4. Just before serving, sift a little confectioners' sugar over each pudding. Serve the puddings warm, in the ramekins.

# Maple Hasty Pudding

*Makes 2 puddings; serves 2*

◆◆◆◆◆◆◆◆◆

**Hasty pudding dates** back to late-sixteenth-century England. The traditional ingredients vary, but it was generally a sweetened porridge made with flour, tapioca or oatmeal, and milk. In colonial America, cornmeal was cheap and readily available, so hasty pudding emerged in this country as a sweet cornmeal mush. It's sometimes called Indian pudding. I've updated the original recipe to include fruit and nuts, but it is still a comforting, easy baked pudding.

Unsalted butter, at room temperature, for greasing the soufflé dish

2 tablespoons whole milk

1 tablespoon unsalted butter, melted

½ teaspoon pure vanilla extract

¼ cup all-purpose flour

1 tablespoon plus 1 teaspoon yellow or white cornmeal

2 tablespoons firmly packed light brown sugar

½ teaspoon baking powder

⅛ teaspoon salt

½ teaspoon fresh lemon juice

1 firm ripe pear, such as Bosc

2 tablespoons pecan pieces

2 tablespoons dried blueberries or cherries

¼ cup maple syrup

Sweetened Whipped Cream (page 36) or vanilla ice cream, for serving

**PAN REQUIRED:**

**One 3-cup soufflé dish or casserole**

1. Place a rack in the center of the oven and preheat the oven to 325°F. Lightly grease the soufflé dish and set it aside.

**2.** Pour the milk, melted butter, and vanilla into a small bowl and whisk to blend.

**3.** Place the flour, cornmeal, brown sugar, baking powder, and salt in a medium-size mixing bowl and whisk to blend. Add the milk mixture and whisk just until the batter is smooth. Spoon the batter into the prepared soufflé dish. (The batter will be thick.)

**4.** Place the lemon juice in a small bowl. Peel, core, and dice the pear. Add it to the bowl and toss it with the lemon juice. Scatter the pears, pecans, and blueberries over the batter.

**5.** Pour the syrup and 2 tablespoons of water into a small saucepan and bring to a boil over medium heat. Remove the pan from the heat and pour the hot syrup evenly over the batter. Bake until a toothpick inserted into the pudding comes out clean, 25 to 30 minutes. Remove the pudding from the oven and place it on a wire rack to cool for 10 minutes.

**6.** To serve, spoon the warm pudding into individual bowls, and top with whipped cream or ice cream.

## variation

# Apple Cranberry Oatmeal Hasty Pudding

**Substitute** a Granny Smith apple for the pear, and dried cranberries for the blueberries.

Add 1½ tablespoons of rolled oats in addition to the all-purpose flour.

# Mocha Soufflé Pudding

## with Mocha Mint Crème Anglaise

*Makes 2 puddings; serves 2*

◆◆◆◆◆◆◆◆◆

**Whenever I serve** this to someone, a look of delight spreads across his or her face with the first bite. You may expect a hint of coffee in a chocolate dessert, but the touch of mint in the sauce is a pleasant surprise. A little unsweetened cocoa powder coupled with the melted chocolate gives the pudding a deep chocolate taste that is enhanced, not overpowered, by the espresso.

1 tablespoon unsalted butter, at room temperature, plus more for greasing the ramekins

4 tablespoons sugar

1 tablespoon all-purpose flour

1 teaspoon unsweetened cocoa powder

½ teaspoon instant espresso powder

¼ cup plus 2 tablespoons half-and-half

1½ ounces bittersweet or semisweet chocolate, finely chopped

1 teaspoon pure vanilla extract

1 large egg, separated

Boiling water, for the baking pan

¼ cup whipping (heavy) cream

Mocha Mint Crème Anglaise (recipe follows)

**PANS REQUIRED:**

**Two 1-cup ramekins or custard cups**

**1 baking pan**

1. Place a rack in the center of the oven and preheat the oven to 325°F. Lightly grease the ramekins. Place them in a larger baking pan and set it aside.

**2.** Place 3 tablespoons of the sugar, the flour, cocoa powder, and espresso powder in a medium-size mixing bowl and whisk to blend well.

**3.** Place the half-and-half, chocolate, and the 1 tablespoon butter in a small saucepan over medium-high heat, and stir constantly until the chocolate and butter melt and the mixture is smooth, 4 to 5 minutes. Remove the pan from the heat and stir in the vanilla. Whisk the chocolate mixture into the flour mixture until blended.

**4.** Place the egg yolk in a medium-size mixing bowl and beat it with a fork. Gradually whisk in the chocolate mixture.

**5.** Place the egg white and the remaining 1 tablespoon of sugar in a medium-size mixing bowl and beat with a hand-held electric mixer on high speed until stiff peaks form, 1 minute. Gradually and gently whisk in the chocolate mixture. Spoon the batter into the prepared ramekins, dividing it evenly between them.

**6.** Pour boiling water into the baking pan to come halfway up the sides of the ramekins. Place the baking pan in the oven and bake until the puddings are puffed and set and the tops are beginning to crack, about 25 minutes. Remove the baking pan from the oven, and use tongs to transfer the steamed puddings to a wire rack. Let them cool slightly.

**7.** Place the cream in a medium-size mixing bowl and beat with a hand-held electric mixer on high speed until firm peaks form.

**8.** To serve, spoon the Mocha Mint Crème Anglaise over the puddings in the ramekins and top with the whipped cream.

# Mocha Mint Crème Anglaise

**Chocolate-flavored** liqueur and espresso give this custard sauce a rich mocha flavor, which is kissed with a little mint liqueur. It is delicious with most anything chocolate; I've made it to serve with brownies bought at the bakery when I did not have time to bake a dessert.

**MAKES ABOUT ⅔ CUP**

Yolks of 2 large eggs
1 tablespoon sugar
⅓ cup half-and-half
⅛ teaspoon instant espresso powder
1 tablespoon crème de cacao
   (coffee liqueur)
½ teaspoon white crème de menthe
   (mint liqueur)

**1.** Fill a medium-size bowl with ice and water, and set it aside.

**2.** Place the egg yolks and sugar in a medium-size mixing bowl and beat with a hand-held electric mixer on medium speed until the mixture is thick and pale, about 2 minutes.

**3.** Place the half-and-half and espresso powder in a small saucepan and bring to a boil over medium-high heat. Remove the pan from the heat. Gradually pour half of the cream mixture over the beaten egg yolks, beating constantly with the electric mixer on low speed. Then beat in the remaining cream mixture and the liqueurs. Pour the mixture back in the saucepan, scraping the bowl with a rubber spatula. Cook over medium-low heat, whisking gently and constantly, until the mixture is thick enough to coat the back of a spoon, 4 to 5 minutes.

**4.** Place a small bowl in the bowl of ice water, and set a fine-mesh sieve over it. Pour the crème anglaise through the sieve into the bowl. Let the crème anglaise cool in the ice bath, stirring it occasionally, for 10 to 15 minutes to serve it at room temperature or 25 minutes to serve it chilled. (If you are not using it immediately, store it in an airtight container in the refrigerator for up to 1 day.)

# Brownie Surprise Pudding Cake

*Makes 2 pudding cakes; serves 2*
◆◆◆◆◆◆◆◆◆

**This pudding is** a perennial favorite that you find in many community cookbooks—the cake separates as it bakes, creating layers of pudding and cake. It is wonderful served warm, with a scoop of ice cream.

1/4 **cup all-purpose flour**

1/4 **cup granulated sugar**

**2 tablespoons plus 2 teaspoons unsweetened cocoa powder**

1/8 **teaspoon baking powder**

1/8 **teaspoon salt**

**2 tablespoons well-beaten egg**

1 1/2 **tablespoons unsalted butter, melted and cooled**

**2 tablespoons whole milk**

1/2 **teaspoon pure vanilla extract**

**2 tablespoons chopped walnuts**

**2 tablespoons miniature semisweet chocolate chips or chopped standard chocolate chips**

**3 tablespoons firmly packed light brown sugar**

1/3 **cup boiling water**

**Premium vanilla ice cream, for serving**

PANS REQUIRED:

**Two 1-cup ramekins or custard cups, or 2 deep 1 1/2- to 2-cup ovenproof bowls**

**1 baking sheet**

**1.** Place a rack in the center of the oven and preheat the oven to 350°F. Place the ramekins on a baking sheet for easier handling, and set it aside.

**2.** Place the flour, sugar, 1 tablespoon plus 1 teaspoon of the cocoa powder, the baking powder, and salt in a medium-size bowl and whisk to blend.

**3.** Place the beaten egg, butter, milk, and vanilla in another medium-size bowl, and whisk to blend well. Pour the flour mixture over the egg mixture, and stir with a wooden spoon just until the batter is combined. Stir in the walnuts and chocolate chips. Spoon the batter into the ramekins, dividing it evenly between them.

**4.** Place the remaining 1 tablespoon plus 1 teaspoon cocoa powder, the brown sugar, and the boiling water in a small bowl, and whisk to mix well. Pour the mixture over the batter in the ramekins. Bake the cakes until a toothpick inserted in the center of one comes out with a few crumbs clinging to it, about 20 minutes. Remove the baking sheet from the oven, transfer the ramekins to a wire rack, and let them cool for 10 minutes. Serve the cakes warm, in the ramekins, topped with scoops of ice cream if desired.

# Lemon Pudding Cake

## *with* Cherry Sauce

*Makes 2 pudding cakes; serves 2*

**While these pudding** cakes are baking, the batter separates, almost magically, creating two texturally different layers: a creamy pudding underneath a soufflé-like cake. The subtle lemon flavor is complemented by the sweet cherry sauce.

¼ **cup whole milk**

**1 tablespoon grated lemon zest**

**1 tablespoon plus 1 teaspoon unsalted butter, at room temperature, plus more for greasing the ramekins**

¼ **cup plus 1 tablespoon sugar**

**1 large egg, separated**

**Yolk of 1 large egg**

**2 tablespoons all-purpose flour**

**2 tablespoons plus 1 teaspoon fresh lemon juice**

½ **teaspoon pure vanilla extract**

**Boiling water, for the baking pan**

**Cherry Sauce (recipe follows)**

PANS REQUIRED:

**Two 1-cup ramekins or custard cups**

**1 baking pan**

1. Place a rack in the center of the oven and preheat the oven to 350°F. Lightly grease the ramekins and place them in a baking pan. Set it aside.

2. Place the milk and lemon zest in a small saucepan and bring to a boil over medium-high heat. Remove the pan from the heat and let the mixture cool completely, about 30 minutes.

3. Set a fine-mesh sieve over a bowl, and pour the cooled milk mixture through it. Discard the lemon zest and set the strained milk aside.

4. Place the butter, ¼ cup of the sugar, and the egg yolks in a medium-size mixing bowl and beat with a hand-held electric mixer on medium speed until the mixture is pale and fluffy, about 1 minute. Beat in the flour. Whisk in the infused milk, lemon juice, and vanilla.

5. Wash the mixer beaters and dry them thoroughly. Place the egg white in a medium-size mixing bowl and beat at high speed until soft peaks form, 20 to 30 seconds. Sprinkle the remaining 1 tablespoon of sugar over the egg whites and continue beating until the whites hold stiff peaks, 1½ to 2 minutes more. Gently fold the egg whites into the batter, making sure no streaks of egg white remain.

6. Spoon the batter into the prepared ramekins. Pour boiling water into the baking pan to reach halfway up the sides of the ramekins. Bake until small cracks appear on the tops of the cakes, about 22 minutes. Remove the baking pan from the oven, and using tongs, transfer the ramekins to a wire rack. Let them cool for 10 minutes.

7. Spoon the Cherry Sauce over the cakes in the ramekins; serve warm.

# Cherry Sauce

Using both cherries and cherry preserves doubles the flavor in this easy sauce. If you use fresh cherries, the sauce will be ruby colored; frozen cherries tend to be darker in color.

**MAKES ¼ CUP**

½ cup pitted fresh or drained,
    thawed frozen sweet cherries
2 tablespoons cherry preserves
½ teaspoon fresh lemon juice
Pinch of salt

1. Place the cherries, preserves, lemon juice, 1 tablespoon of water, and the salt in a blender and process until the mixture is pureed, 30 to 45 seconds. Place a fine-mesh sieve over a small saucepan and pour the mixture through it into the pan, pressing down hard on the solids to extract all the liquid. Scrape off the pulp that clings to the bottom of the sieve and add it to the pulp in the saucepan. Discard the solids.

2. Bring the mixture to a boil over medium-high heat. Boil, uncovered, until it reduces to ¼ cup, 3 to 4 minutes. Serve warm or at room temperature.

# Sweet *and* Savory Muffins *and* Breads

**I love being** able to bake scones, muffins, or biscuits in small batches in the morning. The aromas filling the kitchen are a fragrant wake-up call that always starts the day off right. I've included an enticing variety so you can try something new often. How about Apple Nut Oatmeal Muffins, Blueberry Granola Whole Wheat Muffins, Down Home Buttermilk Biscuits, or the more sophisticated Almond Cherry Scones and Chocolate Chip Cream Scones?

Quick breads, plain to fancy, are included in this chapter too. There's an Orange Date Nut Bread and a moist Sweet Potato Tea Bread that you can slice, butter, toast, and serve with morning coffee or as a snack at work. Chocolate Zucchini Breads and the not-to-be-missed Vanilla Spice Crumb Cakes are wonderful coffeecakes, perfect for your morning break. There are also savories to accompany dinner, such as Harvest Corn Bread Muffins with sage and popovers with or without cheese.

Did you ever wish you could bake a small loaf of yeast bread that serves two? Here you'll find small-size, bakery-worthy French loaves as well as Olive Bread, Herbed Cheese Bread, Country-Style Bread, and Whole Wheat Walnut Bread. All are made by conventional bread baking methods—and you will be able to eat them in one sitting!

# Happy Morning Muffins

*Makes 2 large muffins; serves 2*

◆◆◆◆◆◆◆◆

**You'll see variations** of these muffins in coffee shops all over the country. They are extremely moist and are loaded with all the ingredients you might find in carrot cake: carrots, pecans, raisins, and coconut. The cinnamon in the batter perfumes the kitchen with a warm fragrance that makes you want to sit down and stay for breakfast. (No wonder they are called "happy morning!") These are a Saturday ritual for me: I like to measure out the ingredients first thing in the morning, go have a workout, mix them up, bake the muffins while I shower, then sit down in a comfy chair with a muffin and a mug of steaming Viennese roast.

Unsalted butter, at room temperature, for greasing the muffin cups

½ cup all-purpose flour

¼ teaspoon baking powder

¼ teaspoon baking soda

⅛ teaspoon salt

½ teaspoon ground cinnamon

¼ cup plus 1 tablespoon sugar

1 medium egg

¼ cup vegetable oil

½ teaspoon pure vanilla extract

2 tablespoons grated peeled apple or lightly drained canned crushed pineapple

½ cup coarsely grated carrots

3 tablespoons chopped pecans, toasted (see page 195)

2 tablespoons raisins

1 tablespoon packed sweetened flaked coconut

**PAN REQUIRED:**

1 jumbo muffin pan (¾-cup capacity)

**1.** Place a rack in the center of the oven and preheat the oven to 350°F. Lightly grease only the bottoms of 2 jumbo muffin cups; then rub a little of the butter around the rim of each cup. (This will help them to form a more rounded top.) Set the muffin pan aside.

**2.** Place a large fine-mesh sieve over a medium-size mixing bowl. Place the flour, baking powder, baking soda, salt, and cinnamon in the sieve and sift the ingredients into the bowl.

**3.** Place the sugar, egg, oil, and vanilla in a small bowl and whisk to blend. Stir in the shredded apple. Add the apple mixture to the flour mixture all at once, and stir just until the dry ingredients are moistened. Then gently stir in the carrots, pecans, raisins, and coconut. Spoon the batter into the prepared muffin cups, dividing it evenly between them; they should be about three-quarters full. Fill the empty muffin cups halfway with water to prevent them from scorching.

**4.** Bake the muffins until a toothpick inserted in the center of one comes out clean, 30 to 33 minutes. Remove the muffin pan from the oven and place it on a wire rack to cool for 5 minutes. Carefully pour the water out of the empty muffin cups. Turn the muffins out of the cups and let them cool, upright, on the wire rack for at least 10 minutes before serving. Serve warm or at room temperature. (They are best eaten the day they are baked, but will keep for up to 1 day in a plastic bag at room temperature.)

NOTE: To make regular-size muffins, grease the bottoms and rims of 4 standard (1/2-cup) muffin cups. Spoon the batter into the cups, filling them about three-quarters full, and bake until a toothpick inserted in the center of one comes out clean, 15 to 18 minutes.

# Blueberry Granola Whole Wheat Muffins

*Makes 4 standard muffins; serves 2 or 3*

◆◆◆◆◆◆◆◆◆

**Blueberries are a** great source of antioxidants, fiber, and vitamins, and these muffins are just bursting with them. Add the fiber of granola and whole wheat, and you've got a supercharged muffin to kick-start your metabolism and keep you going through the morning. These are moist and full of texture, and subtly spiced with nutmeg.

Unsalted butter, at room temperature, for greasing the muffin cups

⅓ cup whole wheat flour

⅓ cup all-purpose flour

1 teaspoon baking powder

¼ teaspoon baking soda

Pinch of salt

Pinch of ground nutmeg

½ cup granola

¼ cup nonfat buttermilk

¼ cup firmly packed light brown sugar

1 medium egg

1 tablespoon vegetable oil

½ teaspoon pure vanilla extract

⅓ cup fresh or thawed frozen blueberries

PAN REQUIRED:

1 standard muffin pan (½-cup capacity)

1. Place a rack in the center of the oven and preheat the oven to 350°F. Lightly grease only the bottoms of

4 muffin cups; then rub a little of the butter around the rim of each cup. (This will help them to form a more rounded top.) Set the muffin pan aside.

2. Place a large fine-mesh sieve over a medium bowl. Place the whole wheat flour, all-purpose flour, baking powder, baking soda, salt, and nutmeg in the sieve, and sift the ingredients into the bowl. Mix in half of the granola.

3. Place the buttermilk, brown sugar, egg, oil, and vanilla in a medium-size mixing bowl and whisk to blend well, making sure that all the sugar lumps are dissolved. Add the buttermilk mixture to the flour mixture all at once, and stir just until the dry ingredients are moistened. Then gently stir in the blueberries. Spoon the batter into the prepared muffin cups, dividing it evenly among them; they should be

about three-quarters full. Sprinkle 1 tablespoon of the remaining granola evenly over the muffins; then gently pat the topping into the batter with your fingers. Fill the empty muffin cups halfway with water to prevent them from scorching.

4. Bake the muffins until a toothpick inserted in the center of one comes out clean, 15 to 18 minutes.

5. Remove the muffin pan from the oven and place it on a wire rack to cool for 5 minutes. Carefully pour the water out of the empty muffin cups. Turn the muffins out of the cups and let them cool, upright, on the wire rack for at least 5 minutes before serving. Serve warm or at room temperature. (They are best eaten the day they are made, but will keep for up to 1 day stored in a plastic bag at room temperature.)

## THOUGHTS ON THE YIELDS IN THIS CHAPTER

If the individual breads and muffins are small in size, I like to bake an extra 1 or 2 in case

seconds are in order. When they are baked in a jumbo muffin pan, generally 1 per serving is plenty.

# Cranberry Walnut Muffins

*Makes 3 standard muffins; serves 2*

**I like to pair** cardamom and cranberries; the sweet spice seems to soothe the cranberry's sharp taste a bit. And while these are baking, they fill the kitchen with a lovely cardamom scent. If you have a leftover muffin, take it with you to work for a midafternoon treat.

**FOR THE MUFFINS:**

Unsalted butter, at room temperature, for greasing the muffin cups

1/2 cup all-purpose flour

3/4 teaspoon baking powder

1/4 teaspoon salt

1/4 teaspoon ground cardamom or cinnamon

Yolk of 1 medium egg

3 tablespoons sugar

2 tablespoons whole milk

2 tablespoons vegetable oil

1/2 teaspoon pure vanilla extract

1/4 cup fresh or thawed frozen cranberries

3 tablespoons chopped walnuts

**FOR THE TOPPING:**

3/4 teaspoon sugar

Pinch of ground cardamom or cinnamon

**PAN REQUIRED:**

1 standard muffin pan (1/2-cup capacity)

**1.** Place a rack in the center of the oven and preheat the oven to 350°F. Lightly grease the bottoms (only) of

3 muffin cups; then rub a little of the butter around the rim of each cup. (This will help them to form a more rounded top.) Set the muffin pan aside.

**2.** Place a large fine-mesh sieve over a medium bowl. Place the flour, baking powder, salt, and cardamom in the sieve, and sift the ingredients into the bowl.

**3.** Place the egg yolk, sugar, milk, oil, and vanilla in a medium-size mixing bowl and whisk to blend. Add the egg mixture to the flour mixture all at once, and stir just until the dry ingredients are moistened. Then gently stir in the cranberries and walnuts. Spoon the batter into the prepared muffin cups, dividing it evenly among them; they should be about three-quarters full.

**4. MAKE THE TOPPING:** Place the sugar and the cardamom in a small bowl, and stir well.

**5.** Sprinkle the topping evenly over the muffins. Fill the empty muffin cups halfway with water to prevent them from scorching. Bake the muffins until a toothpick inserted into the center of one comes out clean, 18 to 20 minutes.

**6.** Remove the muffin pan from the oven and place it on a wire rack to cool for 5 minutes. Carefully pour the water out of the empty muffin cups. Turn the muffins out of the cups and let them cool, upright, on the wire rack for at least 10 minutes before serving. Serve warm or at room temperature. (They are best eaten the day they are baked, but will keep for up to 1 day in a plastic bag at room temperature.)

# Apple Nut Oatmeal Muffins

*Makes 3 standard muffins; serves 2 or 3*

◆◆◆◆◆◆◆◆

## Applesauce and oats

make these muffins moist and tender, and an oat-pecan streusel topping adds a crisp finish. They are not too sweet, which makes them a plus for breakfast or snack time. Because they are so moist, these muffins will last well through the day, so they are a great healthy addition to a lunchbox.

Unsalted butter, at room temperature, for greasing the muffin cups

**FOR THE STREUSEL TOPPING:**

2 tablespoons quick or old-fashioned rolled oats

2 tablespoons all-purpose flour

1 tablespoon packed light brown sugar

1 tablespoon cold unsalted butter, cut into bits

2 tablespoons chopped pecans

**FOR THE MUFFINS:**

¼ cup plus 2 tablespoons all-purpose flour

¼ cup quick or old-fashioned olled oats

3 tablespoons packed light brown sugar

1 teaspoon baking powder

¹/₈ teaspoon salt

2 tablespoons raisins

¹/₄ cup applesauce

2 tablespoons vegetable oil

Yolk of 1 medium egg

¹/₂ teaspoon pure vanilla extract

PAN REQUIRED:

1 standard muffin pan
   (¹/₂-cup capacity)

1. Place a rack in the center of the oven and preheat the oven to 400°F. Lightly grease only the bottoms of 3 muffin cups; then rub a little of the butter around the rim of each cup. (This will help them to form a more rounded top.) Set the muffin pan aside.

2. MAKE THE STREUSEL TOPPING: Combine the 2 tablespoons oats, 2 tablespoons flour, and brown sugar in a small bowl. Mix in the butter, using a fork or your fingertips, until the mixture is crumbly. Then mix in the pecans. Set the topping aside.

3. MAKE THE MUFFINS: Combine the flour, oats, brown sugar, baking powder, and salt in a medium-size mixing bowl, and stir to mix well. Add the raisins and toss to mix.

4. Place the applesauce, oil, egg yolk, and vanilla in a small bowl, and whisk to blend well. Add the applesauce mixture to the flour mixture all at once, and stir just until the dry ingredients are moistened. Spoon the batter evenly into the prepared muffin cups, dividing it evenly among them; they should be about two-thirds full. Sprinkle the streusel topping evenly over the muffins; then gently pat the topping into the batter with your fingers. Fill the empty muffin cups halfway with water to prevent them from scorching.

5. Bake the muffins until a toothpick inserted in the center of one comes out clean, 18 to 20 minutes.

6. Remove the muffin pan from the oven and place it on a wire rack to cool for 5 minutes. Carefully pour the water out of the empty muffin cups. Turn the muffins out of the cups and let them cool, upright, on the wire rack for at least 5 minutes before serving. Serve warm or at room temperature. (They are best eaten the day they are baked but will keep for up to 1 day in a plastic bag at room temperature.)

# Double Chocolate Bakeshop Muffins

*Makes 2 large muffins; serves 2*

◆◆◆◆◆◆◆◆◆

**When you have** to have chocolate in the morning, these are the perfect fix. The melted butter in the batter helps to make them rich and cake-like in flavor and texture, but they are not cupcake-sweet. If you eat them warm, the chocolate chips will be soft and gooey, for double the chocolate pleasure. Perfect with a glass of cold milk or a cup of hot cappuccino.

**Unsalted butter, at room temperature, for greasing the muffin cups**

**4 tablespoons (½ stick) unsalted butter, melted and cooled**

**2 tablespoons nonfat buttermilk**

**½ teaspoon pure vanilla extract**

**1 medium egg**

**¼ cup plus 2 tablespoons all-purpose flour**

**1 tablespoon plus 2 teaspoons unsweetened cocoa powder**

**¼ cup sugar**

**¾ teaspoon baking powder**

**⅛ teaspoon salt**

**¼ cup semisweet chocolate chips**

**PAN REQUIRED:**

**1 jumbo muffin pan (¾-cup capacity)**

1. Place a rack in the center of the oven and preheat the oven to 350°F. Lightly grease only the bottoms of

2 muffin cups; then rub a little of the butter around the rim of each cup. (This will help them to form a rounded top.) Set the muffin pan aside.

**2.** Place the melted butter, buttermilk, vanilla, and egg in a small bowl and whisk to blend. Set the mixture aside.

**3.** Place a large fine-mesh sieve over a medium bowl. Place the flour, cocoa powder, sugar, baking powder, and salt in the sieve, and sift the ingredients into the bowl. Toss in the chocolate chips. Add the buttermilk mixture all at once and stir just until the dry ingredients are moistened. Spoon the batter into the prepared muffin cups, dividing it evenly between them; they should be about three-quarters full. Fill the empty muffin cups halfway with water to prevent them from scorching.

**4.** Bake the muffins until a toothpick inserted into the center of one comes out clean, 25 to 30 minutes.

**5.** Remove the muffin pan from the oven and place it on a wire rack to cool for 5 minutes. Carefully pour the water out of the empty muffin cups. Turn the muffins out of the cups and let them cool, upright, on the wire rack for at least 10 minutes before serving. Serve warm or at room temperature. (They are best eaten the day they are baked but will keep for up to 1 day in a plastic bag at room temperature.)

NOTE: To make regular-size muffins, grease the bottoms and rims of 4 standard muffin cups. Spoon the batter into the cups, and bake as directed until a toothpick inserted in the center of one comes out clean, 15 to 18 minutes.

# Old-Fashioned Corn Bread

*Makes 2 large corn breads; serves 2*

◆◆◆◆◆◆◆◆◆

**I can't imagine** life without corn bread. For me it's like the perfect black dress—a basic. This slightly sweet version bakes up in a jiffy, meaning there's no reason you can't serve it fresh and warm whenever the mood strikes. Daily is best!

¹⁄₃ **cup buttermilk**

**2 teaspoons light or dark molasses**

**White of 1 large egg**

¹⁄₂ **cup yellow or white cornmeal**

**1 tablespoon sugar**

¹⁄₄ **teaspoon cream of tartar**

¹⁄₈ **teaspoon baking soda**

¹⁄₄ **teaspoon salt**

**3 teaspoons unsalted butter, melted**

**PAN REQUIRED:**

**1 jumbo muffin pan**
  (³⁄₄**-cup capacity)**

**1.** Place a rack in the center of the oven and preheat the oven to 450°F.

**2.** Place the buttermilk, molasses, and egg white in a small bowl and whisk to blend.

**3.** Place the cornmeal, sugar, cream of tartar, baking soda, and salt in a medium-size mixing bowl and whisk to mix well. Add the buttermilk mixture and whisk just until the batter is blended.

**4.** Place 1½ teaspoons of the melted butter in each of 2 muffin cups. Spoon the batter into the prepared muffin cups, dividing it evenly between them. Fill the empty muffin cups halfway with water to prevent them from scorching. Bake until the corn bread is crusty around the edges and springy to the touch, 9 to 10 minutes. Remove the muffin pan from the oven, and place it on a wire rack to cool for 5 minutes. Carefully pour the water out of the empty muffin cups. Turn the muffins out of the cups and serve hot or warm. (They are best eaten the day they are baked but will keep for up to 1 day in a plastic bag at room temperature.)

# Harvest Corn Bread Muffins

*Makes 3 standard muffins; serves 2*

**Another favorite** corn bread, these tender, moist muffins are savory with sage and fruity with dried cranberries. They are delicious with grilled or roasted pork or beef, and they are all you need to round out a salad lunch. They are also a nice alternative to stuffing or dressing for holiday dinners of roast turkey, lamb, or beef.

Unsalted butter, at room temperature,
   for greasing the muffin cups

¼ cup all-purpose flour

3 tablespoons yellow cornmeal

2 teaspoons sugar

¼ teaspoon baking powder

⅛ teaspoon baking soda

⅛ teaspoon salt

¼ teaspoon rubbed dried sage

3 tablespoons unsalted butter,
   melted and cooled

1 medium egg

3 tablespoons buttermilk

2 to 3 tablespoons dried cranberries,
   coarsely chopped

2 to 3 tablespoons chopped walnuts

PAN REQUIRED:

1 standard muffin pan
   (½-cup capacity)

1. Place a rack in the center of the oven and preheat the oven to 375°F. Lightly grease only the bottoms of 3 muffin cups; then rub a little of the butter around the rim of each cup. (This will help them to form a more rounded top.) Set the muffin pan aside.

2. Place the flour, cornmeal, sugar, baking powder, baking soda, salt, and sage in a medium-size mixing bowl and whisk to blend.

3. Place the butter, egg, and buttermilk in a small bowl and whisk to blend. Add the buttermilk mixture to the flour mixture, along with the dried cranberries and walnuts. Stir just until the dry ingredients are moistened. Spoon the batter into the prepared muffin cups, dividing it evenly among them; they should be about three-quarters full. Let the batter stand for 5 minutes. Fill the empty muffin cups halfway with water to prevent them from scorching.

4. Bake the muffins until the tops are pale golden and a toothpick inserted in the center of one comes out clean, about 15 minutes. Remove the muffin pan from the oven and place it on a wire rack to cool for 5 minutes. Carefully pour the water out of the empty muffin cups. Turn the muffins out of the pan and serve hot or warm. (They are best eaten the day they are baked, but will keep for up to 1 day in a plastic bag at room temperature.)

# FLAVORED WHIPPED BUTTERS

Creamy sweetened butter is a simple spread to make for biscuits and scones, and the slight effort it takes will garner rave reviews. All you do is beat the ingredients together in a small, deep bowl with a hand-held electric mixer on high speed until the mixture is lighter in color and fluffy, about one minute. You can store any leftovers in a covered container in the refrigerator for up to one week.

### WHIPPED ORANGE BUTTER:

**4 tablespoons (1/2 stick) unsalted butter, at room temperature**

**1 tablespoon confectioners' sugar**

**1 tablespoon fresh orange juice**

**1 tablespoon finely grated orange zest**

### SPICED HONEY BUTTER:

**4 tablespoons (1/2 stick) unsalted butter, at room temperature**

**2 tablespoons honey**

**1/4 teaspoon ground allspice or cinnamon**

### WHIPPED BERRY BUTTER:

**4 tablespoons (1/2 stick) unsalted butter, at room temperature**

**1/3 cup sliced strawberries, or whole raspberries or blueberries, mashed**

**2 teaspoons confectioners' sugar**

**1/4 teaspoon pure vanilla extract**

### WHIPPED MANGO BUTTER:

**4 tablespoons (1/2 stick) unsalted butter, at room temperature**

**1/3 cup finely chopped ripe mango**

**2 tablespoons honey**

### WHIPPED MAPLE BUTTER:

**4 tablespoons (1/2 stick) unsalted butter, at room temperature**

**2 tablespoons maple syrup**

**2 teaspoons packed light brown sugar**

# Almond Cherry Scones

*Makes 2 scones; serves 2*
◆◆◆◆◆◆◆◆◆

**My ideal scone** will always be the one that was delivered to my room with a pot of coffee at an inn in San Francisco. It was softball size, plain (no raisins or cherries or anything), just pure rich texture and a buttery sweet crisp crust. These scones are just as dreamy in texture as that one, but with a more sophisticated flavor. The almond paste makes them moist and slightly dense, and the dried cherries accentuate the sweet almond flavor.

¼ **cup boiling water**
2 **tablespoons dried tart cherries**
½ **cup all-purpose flour**
¾ **teaspoon baking powder**
⅛ **teaspoon salt**

2 **tablespoons almond paste**
1 **tablespoon sugar**
2 **tablespoons plus 2 teaspoons unsalted butter, at room temperature**
**Yolk of 1 medium egg**
1 **tablespoon half-and-half**

PAN REQUIRED:
1 **baking sheet**

**1.** Place a rack in the center of the oven and preheat the oven to 350°F.

**2.** Pour the boiling water into a small bowl and add the cherries. Let the mixture stand to soften the cherries, 10 to 15 minutes. Then drain the cherries, discarding the soaking liquid.

**3.** Place the flour, baking powder, and salt in a small bowl and whisk to blend.

**4.** Place the almond paste and sugar in a medium-size mixing bowl. Using a fork, mash the almond paste with the sugar. (This will make it a little easier to mix with the butter.) Add the butter, egg yolk, and half-and-half. Beat with a hand-held mixer on medium speed until the mixture is as smooth as possible, about 1 minute. (There may be a few lumps of almond paste left, but they should be very tiny.)

**5.** Add the creamed mixture and the cherries to the flour mixture, and stir with a fork just until the soft dough holds together. Using an ice cream scoop, scoop the dough into 2 equal mounds on the ungreased baking sheet, spacing them about 2 inches apart. (Alternatively, you can lightly flour your hands and form the dough into 2 balls, then place them on the baking sheet.)

**6.** Bake the scones for 15 minutes. Then reduce the oven temperature to 325°F and bake until they are pale golden brown, about 5 more minutes.

**7.** Remove the baking sheet from the oven and transfer the scones to a wire rack to cool. Serve them warm or at room temperature. (They are best eaten the day they are baked.)

# Cranberry Orange Oatmeal Scones

*Makes 2 scones; serves 2*

◆◆◆◆◆◆◆◆◆

**In the early part** of the twentieth century, Southern cooks put oatmeal in many bread products: muffins, yeast breads, even turkey dressing. The Quaker box was always in my grandmother's pantry, and I took notice of the way oats made her quick breads and yeast loaves moist and tasty. Not only was she adding nutrition but the oats added a special, almost nutty, flavor and a chewy texture. Here is a delicious scone that is moist, fragrant, tender, and slightly chewy. Substitute raisins for the dried cranberries if you wish.

2 tablespoons plus 2 teaspoons all-purpose flour, plus extra for the work surface

1 tablespoon plus 2 teaspoons sugar

½ teaspoon baking powder

⅛ teaspoon baking soda

¼ teaspoon salt

¼ teaspoon ground nutmeg

3 tablespoons plus 2 teaspoons cold unsalted butter, cut into bits

1 teaspoon finely grated orange zest

¼ cup plus 2 tablespoons old-fashioned rolled oats

3 tablespoons dried cranberries

2 tablespoons plus 2 teaspoons buttermilk

**PAN REQUIRED:**

**1 baking sheet**

1. Place a rack in the center of the oven and preheat the oven to 400°F.

2. Place the flour, sugar, baking powder, baking soda, salt, and nutmeg in a medium-size mixing bowl and whisk to blend.

3. Using a pastry blender, cut the butter pieces and the orange zest into the flour mixture until the remaining lumps are no larger than peas. Mix in the oats and dried cranberries. Sprinkle the buttermilk over the ingredients, and toss with a fork until the dough begins to hold together.

4. Sprinkle a little flour on a cutting board, and flour your hands. Turn the dough out onto the floured board and knead it until the oats adhere to the dough, about 6 times. Pat the dough into a rectangular shape and divide it in half. Form the two halves into disks 3 inches in diameter and 1 inch thick, and place them on the baking sheet. Bake for 15 minutes.

5. Remove the baking sheet from the oven and transfer the scones to a wire rack to cool. Serve warm or at room temperature. (They are best eaten the day they are baked.)

# Chocolate Chip Cream Scones

*Makes 3 scones; serves 2 or 3*
◆◆◆◆◆◆◆◆◆

## These are exceptional

in texture: very soft inside, with a tender crumb. When you eat them warm, the chocolate is soft and still melted and the scone is rich and extravagant. These are so good, I designed the recipe to make enough for a small brunch gathering. But if you have any left over and you want to heat them up later, wrap them in aluminum foil and reheat in a preheated 350°F oven for about five minutes.

**Unsalted butter, at room temperature, for greasing the baking sheet**

1 cup all-purpose flour, plus extra
    for the work surface

2 tablespoons plus ½ teaspoon sugar

1 teaspoon baking powder

¼ teaspoon salt

5 tablespoons cold unsalted butter,
    cut into ½-inch pieces

3 to 4 tablespoons semisweet
    chocolate chips

**Yolk of 1 medium egg**

¼ cup cold half-and-half

PAN REQUIRED:
**1 baking sheet**

**1.** Place a rack in the center of the oven and preheat the oven to 375°F. Lightly grease the baking sheet and set it aside.

**2.** Place the flour, 2 tablespoons of the sugar, the baking powder, and the salt in a medium-size mixing bowl and whisk to blend.

**3.** Sprinkle the butter pieces over the flour mixture, and cut the butter into the flour with a pastry blender until the remaining lumps are no larger than peas. Mix in the chocolate chips.

**4.** Place the egg yolk and half-and-half in a small bowl, and whisk to blend. Then pour the egg mixture over the flour mixture. Toss with a fork until a soft, moist dough just comes together.

**5.** Sprinkle a little flour on a cutting board, and put the dough on top. Flour your hands, and knead the dough gently 6 times. Pat the dough out to form a 1-inch-thick disk. Cut the disk into thirds with a sharp knife, and transfer the scones to the prepared baking sheet, spacing them 2 inches apart. Sprinkle the remaining ½ teaspoon sugar evenly over the tops of the scones. Bake the scones until they are golden on the bottom and just pale golden on top, 20 to 22 minutes.

**6.** Remove the baking sheet from the oven, and use a spatula to transfer the scones to a wire rack to cool. Serve warm or at room temperature. (They are best eaten the day they are baked.)

# Down Home Buttermilk Biscuits

*Makes 2 or 3 biscuits; serves 2*

◆◆◆◆◆◆◆◆◆

**I stay true** to my roots with biscuit baking. This is the way we Southerners like them: tangy and tender from buttermilk, not too thick, and buttery, crispy golden brown on the outside. The dough needs to be handled lightly so the gluten will not develop in the flour and make the biscuits tough. You can knead the Small-Batch dough in the bowl in which it is mixed; with such a small amount it is not necessary to knead it on a floured board. Rolling the biscuits out on a piece of waxed paper saves a bit of mess.

Most buttermilk nowadays is actually made from sweet milk—usually skim milk—to which lactic acid bacterial cultures are added. The cultures produce the tang that flavors baked breads. Cultured buttermilk tastes almost buttery to me because of its thick creaminess, and biscuits made with it will taste rich.

About 3 tablespoons unsalted
butter, melted

$1/2$ cup all-purpose flour, plus extra
for the work surface

$1/2$ teaspoon plus $1/8$ teaspoon
baking powder

$1/8$ teaspoon baking soda

$1/8$ teaspoon salt

$1/8$ teaspoon sugar

$1^1/2$ tablespoons cold unsalted
butter, cut into 12 pieces

3 to $3^1/2$ tablespoons cold
buttermilk

PAN REQUIRED:

1 baking sheet

1. Place a rack in the center of the oven and preheat the oven to 450°F. Brush 1 tablespoon of the melted butter over a 6-inch-square area on the baking sheet. Set the baking sheet aside.

2. Place a large fine-mesh sieve over a medium-size mixing bowl. Place the flour, baking powder, baking soda, salt, and sugar in the sieve and sift the ingredients into the bowl. Cut in the cold butter pieces with a pastry blender, or with a fork by dragging the tines of the fork through the flour and butter, pressing the tines

to the bottom of the bowl, until the remaining lumps are no larger than peas. Sprinkle 3 tablespoons of the buttermilk over the mixture and toss lightly with a fork just until the dough begins to hold together, just a few seconds. If necessary, sprinkle the remaining $1/2$ tablespoon buttermilk over the dough to make it hold together as a soft dough.

3. Flour your hands, and lightly knead the dough in the bowl 5 or 6 times. Sprinkle a teaspoon or two of flour on a piece of waxed paper or on a cutting board, and put the dough in the center. Pat the dough out to form a 5 x $2^1/2$-inch rectangle, about $1/2$ inch thick. Cut out 2 biscuits with a $2^1/2$-inch round cutter. If you wish, form the scraps into a third biscuit.

4. Place the biscuits on the buttered square on the baking sheet. Bake until the biscuits are golden, about 10 minutes.

5. Remove the baking sheet from the oven. For buttery tops, brush the hot biscuits lightly with the remaining 2 tablespoons melted butter. Serve immediately.

# Rustic Bacon Biscuits

*Makes 2 or 3 biscuits; serves 2*

◆◆◆◆◆◆◆◆◆

**These biscuits are** tender and fluffy and flaked with bits of bacon. They are always a hit, whether you split them and sandwich in a fried egg, slather them with peanut butter and jelly, serve them with a vegetable cheese omelet, or just grab one on the run to the office.

**2 thin slices (about 1 ounce) smoked bacon**

**1 tablespoon unsalted butter, melted**

**1/2 cup all-purpose flour**

**1/2 teaspoon baking powder**

**1/8 teaspoon baking soda**

**1/4 teaspoon salt**

**1 tablespoon cold unsalted butter, cut into 6 pieces**

**3 to 4 tablespoons cold whipping (heavy) cream**

**PAN REQUIRED:**

**1 baking sheet**

1. Place the bacon in a skillet over medium heat, and sauté until crisp. Transfer the bacon strips to paper towels and allow them to drain. Pour 1 1/2 teaspoons of the bacon drippings into a small bowl and freeze it until the drippings are solid, 10 to 15

minutes. Finely chop the cooked bacon and set it aside.

**2.** Place a rack in the center of the oven and preheat the oven to 450°F. Brush the melted butter over a 6-inch-square area on the baking sheet. Set the baking sheet aside.

**3.** Place a large fine-mesh sieve over a medium-size bowl. Place the flour, baking powder, baking soda, and salt in the sieve, and sift into the bowl. Scoop out the solid bacon drippings with a teaspoon, and drop them onto the dry ingredients. Add the butter pieces. Cut the drippings and butter into the flour mixture with a fork by dragging the tines of the fork through the flour, pressing the tines to the bottom of the bowl, until the remaining lumps are no larger than small peas. Toss in the chopped bacon. Sprinkle 3 tablespoons of the cream over the mixture, and toss lightly with the fork just until the dough begins to holds together. If necessary, sprinkle the remaining 1 tablespoon cream over the dough to make it hold together as a soft dough.

**4.** Flour your hands, and lightly knead the dough in the bowl 5 or 6

## variation

# Bacon Cheese Biscuits

**Reduce** the butter to 1½ teaspoons, finely diced. Add ¼ cup shredded sharp Cheddar cheese to the sifted flour mixture before cutting in the drippings and butter in Step 3.

times. Lightly flour a cutting board, place the dough on it, and pat the dough out to form a 5 x 2½-inch rectangle, about ½ inch thick. Cut out 2 biscuits with a 2½-inch round cutter. If you wish, form the scraps into a third biscuit.

**5.** Place the biscuits on the buttered square on the baking sheet. Bake until the biscuits are golden, 10 to 15 minutes.

**6.** Remove the baking sheet from the oven and serve hot or warm.

# Fast Food–Style Biscuits

*Makes 2 or 3 biscuits; serves 2*

◆◆◆◆◆◆◆◆◆

**I admit it**—if there were a Hardee's close to my home, I'd probably stop there on many a morning to pick up breakfast. I adored their melt-in-your-mouth biscuits years ago when I was working in *Southern Living* magazine's test kitchen. When my co-worker Peggy Smith declared one morning that she knew how to re-create Hardee's secret recipe, we went to work in the kitchen that instant. Now, years later, I've come up with a Small-Batch version.

2 tablespoons unsalted butter, melted

½ cup self-rising flour, plus extra for the work surface

2 tablespoons cold unsalted butter, cut into 12 pieces

3½ to 4 tablespoons cold whipping (heavy) cream

PAN REQUIRED:
1 baking sheet

1. Place a rack in the center of the oven and preheat the oven to 450°F. Brush 1 tablespoon of the melted butter over a 6-inch square area on the baking sheet. Set the baking sheet aside.

2. Place a large fine-mesh sieve over a medium-size bowl. Place the flour in the sieve and sift it into the bowl. Cut in the butter pieces with a fork by dragging the tines of the fork through

the flour and butter, pressing the tines to the bottom of the bowl, until the remaining lumps are no larger than peas. Sprinkle $3\frac{1}{2}$ tablespoons of the cream over the mixture, and toss lightly with the fork just until the dough begins to holds together. If necessary, sprinkle the remaining $\frac{1}{2}$ tablespoon cream over the dough to make it hold together as a soft dough.

**3.** Flour your hands, and lightly knead the dough in the bowl 5 or 6 times. Lightly flour a cutting board, place the dough on it, and pat the dough out to form a 5 x $2\frac{1}{2}$-inch rectangle, about $\frac{1}{2}$ inch thick. Cut out 2 biscuits with a $2\frac{1}{2}$-inch round cutter. If you wish, form the scraps into a third biscuit.

**4.** Place the biscuits on the buttered square on the baking sheet. Bake until they are golden, about 10 minutes.

**5.** Remove the baking sheet from the oven and serve, or wrap in a cloth napkin to stay warm. For buttery tops, brush the biscuits lightly with the remaining 1 tablespoon melted butter when you remove them from the oven. Serve hot or warm.

## A BISCUIT PRIMER

It's not difficult to make light, flaky biscuits. To start with, the butter that is cut into the flour needs to be finely diced (about $\frac{1}{4}$-inch), then refrigerated until it is cold. (I cut the butter and put it in the freezer while measuring out the rest of the ingredients.) Those tiny bits of cold butter help produce flaky biscuits when they hit the hot oven.

If you were to pour the liquid into the flour mixture all at once, as you do when preparing muffin batter, you would end up with a wet mess that does not at all resemble biscuit dough. Instead, use a spoon to sprinkle the liquid over the dry ingredients, and then lightly toss the dough together with a fork until it just starts to hold together. The flour will have a chance to absorb the liquid and make a nice, moist dough that will produce steam in the oven—encouraging the biscuits to rise higher and lighter.

# Angel Biscuits

*Makes 6 biscuits; serves 2 or 3*
◆◆◆◆◆◆◆◆◆

**Angel biscuits** are a tradition in my family for holiday brunches. They take more time than regular biscuits because they are made with yeast, but they are worth every bit of effort. The yeast roll flavor is there, but they have the density of a very fluffy biscuit. And these are not just for breakfast— serve the little gems with dinner, or split them and fill them with thin slices of country ham for cocktails. I never offer less than three biscuits per person; they are that good!

**2 tablespoons unsalted butter, at room temperature, cut into bits, plus more for greasing the baking sheet**

**1 medium egg, lightly beaten**

**1 cup commercial hot roll mix, plus 1½ teaspoons of the yeast packet (see box, page 325)**

**½ teaspoon baking powder**

**1 teaspoon sugar**

**About ½ cup all-purpose flour, plus extra for the work surface**

**2 tablespoons unsalted butter, melted**

**PAN REQUIRED:**

**1 baking sheet**

**1.** Lightly grease the baking sheet and set it aside.

**2.** Place the butter, egg, hot roll mix, yeast, baking powder, and sugar in a wide medium-size mixing bowl. Pour ¼ cup very hot water (120° to 130°F) over the ingredients; stir well with a wooden spoon until all the butter pieces have blended into the dough.

**3.** Sprinkle 3 tablespoons of the flour over the dough. Using a wooden spoon, knead the flour into the dough until the dough is no longer sticky; add more flour, by the tablespoon, if necessary. (To knead, pull the dough toward you with the wooden spoon and press it against the side of the bowl; then use the spoon to fold the dough away from you. Repeat the pulling and folding process until the flour is worked into the dough.) Then flour your hands and knead in 2 to 3 more tablespoons of flour until the dough is smooth and elastic, about 1 minute. Cover the bowl with a clean kitchen towel and let the dough rest for 5 minutes.

**4.** Sprinkle 2 to 3 tablespoons of flour on a cutting board, and place the dough in the center of the flour. Flour your hands, and pat the dough out to form a 1/2-inch-thick round. Using a 2 1/2-inch round cutter, cut out 3 biscuits. Reroll the scraps and cut out 2 more biscuits. Press the scraps together and cut out the remaining biscuit.

**5.** Place the biscuits on the prepared baking sheet, and brush the tops with some of the melted butter. Fold the biscuits in half, and then brush the unbuttered sides with the remaining melted butter. Cover the biscuits loosely with plastic wrap, and let them rise in a draft-free place for 1 1/2 to 2 hours.

**6.** Preheat the oven to 400°F.

**7.** Bake the biscuits until they are golden on top, 10 to 13 minutes.

**8.** Remove the baking sheet from the oven and place the biscuits in a tea towel–lined basket to serve. (If making the biscuits in advance, transfer them to a wire rack to cool. Place in a heavy-duty zip-lock bag and freeze for up to 1 week. Place biscuits in aluminum foil and warm in a 350°F oven for 5 minutes before serving.)

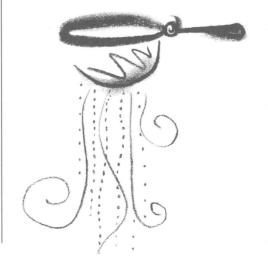

# Sunday Morning Sweet Rolls

*Makes 4 sweet rolls; serves 2*

◆◆◆◆◆◆◆◆◆

**These sweet rolls** are soft and gooey, spicy and sweet. I've discovered that a hot roll mix will bake up just a few yeast sweet rolls quickly with little mess, making these a treat you can enjoy often.

2 tablespoons unsalted butter, at room temperature, cut into bits, plus more for greasing the loaf pan

White of 1 large egg

1 cup hot roll mix, plus 1½ teaspoons of the yeast packet (see box, facing page)

2 teaspoons sugar

About ½ cup all-purpose flour, plus extra for the work surface

2 teaspoons unsalted butter, melted

2 tablespoons light brown sugar

½ teaspoon ground cinnamon

¼ teaspoon ground cardamom (optional)

Vanilla Milk Glaze (recipe follows)

PAN REQUIRED:

1 standard loaf pan (8 x 4 inches)

1. Lightly grease the bottom and sides of the loaf pan, and set it aside.

2. Place the butter, egg white, hot roll mix, yeast, and sugar in a wide medium-size mixing bowl. Pour ¼ cup hot water (120° to 130°F, or very hot to the touch) over the ingredients and stir well with a wooden spoon until all of the butter pieces have blended into the dough.

3. Flour your hands and sprinkle 3 to 4 tablespoons of flour over the dough. Knead the flour into the dough until it is no longer sticky, adding more flour, a tablespoon at a time, if necessary. Cover the bowl with a clean kitchen towel, and let the dough rest for about 5 minutes.

4. Sprinkle 2 to 3 tablespoons of flour on a cutting board, and place the dough on the flour. Flour your hands, and pat the dough out to form an 8 x 6-inch rectangle. Brush the top of the dough with the melted butter, and sprinkle it evenly with the brown sugar, cinnamon, and cardamom if using. Beginning with a short end, roll the dough up jelly-roll fashion. Cut the roll into 4 equal pieces. Place the

## HOT ROLL MIX

For recipes calling for hot roll mix, I use Pillsbury brand. It comes in a box with a separate aluminum foil yeast packet.

- It is important to bring the butter and egg white to room temperature for easier mixing.

- Store any hot roll mix you don't use in a self-seal plastic bag to use for your next craving; keep the remainder of the yeast in a small airtight jar in the refrigerator. Bring the hot roll mix mixture to room temperature before using it in a recipe.

- To encourage the sweet roll dough to rise, I put the unbaked rolls in the loaf pan on a small bowl filled with hot tap water, loosely cover the loaf pan with plastic wrap, then drape a clean kitchen towel over the loaf pan and bowl.

pieces, cut side up, in the prepared loaf pan. Cover the pan with a clean kitchen towel or plastic wrap, and let the dough rise in a warm, draft-free place for 30 minutes. (The dough will not quite double.)

**5.** Place a rack in the center of the oven and preheat the oven to 375°F.

**6.** Place the loaf pan in the oven and bake the rolls until they are golden brown, 15 to 20 minutes.

**7.** Place the loaf pan on a wire rack and let the rolls cool in the pan for 2 minutes; then transfer the rolls to a plate. Spoon the Vanilla Milk Glaze over the warm rolls, and serve warm or at room temperature. (They are best eaten the day they are baked.)

# Vanilla Milk Glaze

**Just a plain** glaze to cap off the sweet rolls' homemade flavor.

**MAKES ¼ CUP**

2 teaspoons whole milk, or more as
  needed
1½ teaspoons unsalted butter
½ cup confectioners' sugar
¼ teaspoon pure vanilla extract

Place the milk and butter in a small microwave-safe bowl and microwave on high power until the butter melts, 25 to 30 seconds. Stir in the confectioners' sugar and vanilla. If needed, stir in an additional teaspoon of milk to thin the glaze. If not using immediately, store in a covered container at room temperature for up to 1 hour, or refrigerated for up to 2 days.

# Honey Buns

*Makes 4 honey buns; serves 2*

◆◆◆◆◆◆◆◆◆

**These honey buns** have an old-fashioned, home-baked-bread flavor. They are far superior to the commercial varieties.

●

Unsalted butter, at room
  temperature, for greasing
  the loaf pan

**FOR THE TOPPING:**

2 teaspoons unsalted butter,
  at room temperature

3 tablespoons honey

3 tablespoons chopped pecans
  (optional)

**FOR THE FILLING:**

2 teaspoons unsalted butter,
  at room temperature

1 tablespoon honey

¼ teaspoon ground cinnamon

**FOR THE DOUGH:**

White of 1 large egg

2 tablespoons unsalted butter,
  cut into bits

1 cup hot roll mix, plus
  1½ teaspoons of the yeast
  packet (see box, page 325)

2 teaspoons sugar

About ½ cup all-purpose flour,
  plus extra for the work surface

**PAN REQUIRED:**

1 standard loaf pan (8 x 4 inches)

1. Lightly grease the bottom and sides of the loaf pan.

2. **MAKE THE TOPPING:** Place the butter, honey, and nuts, if using, in a small bowl, and stir to mix well. Spoon the mixture over the bottom of the prepared loaf pan, and set the pan aside.

**3.** **MAKE THE FILLING:** Place the butter, honey, and cinnamon in a small bowl, and stir to mix well. Set aside.

**4.** **MAKE THE DOUGH:** Place the egg white, butter, hot roll mix, yeast, and sugar in a wide medium-size mixing bowl. Pour ¼ cup hot water (120° to 130°F, or very hot to the touch) over the ingredients and stir well with a wooden spoon until all of the butter pieces have blended into the dough.

**5.** Flour your hands and sprinkle 3 to 4 tablespoons of flour over the dough. Knead the flour into the dough until it is no longer sticky, adding more flour, a tablespoon at a time, if necessary. Cover the bowl with a clean kitchen towel, and let the dough rest for about 5 minutes.

**6.** Sprinkle 2 to 3 tablespoons of flour on a cutting board, and place the dough on the flour. Flour your hands, and pat the dough out to form an 8 x 6-inch rectangle. Spread the honey filling evenly over the dough. Beginning with a short end, roll the dough up jelly-roll fashion. Cut the roll into 4 equal pieces. Place the pieces, cut side up, in the prepared loaf pan. Cover the pan with a clean kitchen towel or plastic wrap, and let the dough rise in a warm, draft-free place for 30 minutes. (The dough will not double.)

**7.** Place a rack in the center of the oven and preheat the oven to 375°F.

**8.** Place the loaf pan in the oven and bake the rolls until they are puffed and golden, about 15 minutes.

**9.** Remove the loaf pan from the oven and immediately invert the rolls, honey side up, onto a serving plate. Serve warm. (They are best eaten the day they are baked.)

# Whole Wheat Banana Bread

*Makes 1 small loaf; serves 2 to 3*

◆◆◆◆◆◆◆◆◆

**This banana bread** is every-thing you want it to be: moist, with lots of banana flavor and an almost chewy texture from the whole wheat flour. The mini loaf can be cut into five or six small slices, just the right size for two or three servings. It keeps well for a day or two. I like to butter and toast the slices for breakfast; my daughter spreads a little peanut butter on hers before toasting it.

Unsalted butter, at room temperature,
    for preparing the loaf pan
¼ cup plus 1 tablespoon all-purpose
    flour
¼ cup whole wheat flour

½ teaspoon baking powder
¼ teaspoon baking soda
⅛ teaspoon salt
½ cup mashed ripe banana
    (1 to 1½ bananas)
¼ cup plus 2 tablespoons packed
    light brown sugar
3 tablespoons vegetable oil
¾ teaspoon pure vanilla extract
Yolk of 1 medium egg
¼ cup chopped walnuts or pecans
    (optional)

PAN REQUIRED:

1 petite loaf pan (2-cup capacity,
    about 5 x 3 inches)

1. Place a rack in the center of the oven and preheat the oven to 350°F. Lightly grease the loaf pan and set it aside.

**2.** Place both flours, the baking powder, baking soda, and salt in a medium-size mixing bowl and whisk to blend.

**3.** Place the mashed banana, brown sugar, oil, vanilla, and egg yolk in a small bowl and whisk to blend. Add the banana mixture to the flour mixture all at once, and stir just until blended. Stir in the walnuts, if using.

**4.** Pour the batter into the prepared loaf pan, and bake until a toothpick inserted in the center comes out clean, 23 to 25 minutes.

**5.** Remove the pan from the oven and let it cool on a wire rack for 10 minutes. Then invert the pan over the rack, releasing the bread, and let the bread cool, upright, on the rack. Serve warm or at room temperature. (The loaf may be wrapped in aluminum foil, placed in a freezer bag, and frozen for up to 1 month. Store any leftovers, wrapped, at room temperature for up to 2 days.)

# Sweet Potato Tea Bread

*Makes 1 loaf; serves 2 or 3*

◆◆◆◆◆◆◆◆

**If you are one** of the many who eat sweet potatoes only on Thanksgiving, that's a shame, because they are an abundant source of beta-carotene and other nutrients in a small, tasty package. Sweet potatoes make breads and cakes very moist without adding a lot of fat to the batter. This loaf is ultra-moist, tender, and sweetly fragrant with pumpkin pie spice. It is a good gift bread because it has keeping power.

Unsalted butter, at room temperature, for greasing the pan

1/2 cup all-purpose flour, plus more for flouring the pan

1/4 teaspoon baking soda

1/8 teaspoon salt

1/4 teaspoon pumpkin pie spice

1/4 cup cold mashed sweet potatoes (about 1 small sweet potato, baked, peeled, and mashed)

1/4 cup sugar

2 tablespoons vegetable oil

1 tablespoon buttermilk

1/2 teaspoon pure vanilla extract

1 medium egg

PAN REQUIRED:

1 petite loaf pan (2-cup capacity, about 5 x 3 inches)

1. Place a rack in the center of the oven and preheat the oven to 350°F. Lightly grease the loaf pan and dust it with flour, tapping out the excess. Set the pan aside.

2. Place the flour, baking soda, salt, and pumpkin pie spice in a medium-size mixing bowl, and whisk to blend.

3. Place the sweet potatoes, sugar, oil, buttermilk, vanilla, and egg in a small bowl and whisk to blend. Add the sweet potato mixture to the flour mixture all at once, and stir just until the dry ingredients are moistened. Spoon the batter into the prepared loaf pan. Bake until a toothpick inserted in the center comes out clean, 26 to 30 minutes.

4. Remove the pan from the oven and let it cool on a wire rack for 15 minutes. Then invert the pan over the rack, releasing the bread, and let the bread cool completely on the rack, about 1 hour. Serve warm or at room temperature. (The loaf may be wrapped in aluminum foil, placed in a freezer bag, and frozen for up to 1 month. Store any leftovers, wrapped, at room temperature for up to 2 days.)

# Orange Date Nut Bread

*Makes 1 loaf; serves 2 or 3*
◆◆◆◆◆◆◆◆◆

**This date nut** bread is very dense and quite moist, with a subtle flavor of orange. If by chance there are leftovers, toast the slices the next day and spread them with butter or cream cheese for a sweet breakfast treat.

Unsalted butter, at room temperature, for greasing the can

¼ cup plus 3 tablespoons all-purpose flour, plus more for flouring the can

¼ cup whole milk

1 tablespoon frozen orange juice concentrate

⅓ cup chopped pitted dates

1 medium egg

3 tablespoons sugar

¼ teaspoon baking soda

⅛ teaspoon baking powder

⅛ teaspoon salt

3 tablespoons chopped walnuts

**PANS REQUIRED:**

**One 14- or 14.5-ounce can**
**1 baking sheet**

1. Place a rack in the center of the oven and preheat the oven to 350°F. Lightly grease the can and dust it with flour, tapping out the excess. Place the can on a baking sheet for easier handling, and set it aside.

2. Place the milk and orange juice concentrate in a small saucepan and bring to a boil over medium-high heat. Remove the pan from the heat and add the dates; let the mixture stand until cool. (The mixture will appear curdled.) Then beat in the egg with a fork.

3. Place the flour, sugar, baking soda, baking powder, and salt in a medium-size mixing bowl and whisk to blend.

**4.** Toss in the walnuts and add the date mixture to the flour mixture. Stir just until well blended. Spoon the batter into the prepared can, and bake until a toothpick inserted in the center comes out clean, 23 to 25 minutes.

**5.** Remove the baking sheet from the oven, transfer the can to a wire rack, and let it cool for 10 minutes. Run a thin, sharp knife around the edge of the can and invert it to release the bread. Place the bread on its side on the rack and let it cool completely. Serve at room temperature. (The loaf may be wrapped in aluminum foil, placed in a freezer bag, and frozen for up to 1 month. Store any leftovers, wrapped, at room temperature for up to 2 days.)

# Chocolate Zucchini Breads

*Makes 3 breads; serves 3*

**It's not the zucchini** that you'll taste in this bread, it's the specks of grated chocolate. The zucchini keeps the bread moist for a couple of days, so you can save one for tomorrow. The breads are delicious with a light brunch of omelet and fruit.

1 medium egg

¼ cup vegetable oil

½ cup sugar

½ teaspoon pure vanilla extract

½ cup grated unpeeled zucchini

¾ cup plus 2 tablespoons
all-purpose flour

½ teaspoon baking soda

¼ teaspoon baking powder

¼ teaspoon salt

¼ teaspoon ground cinnamon

1 ounce grated bittersweet
chocolate

¼ cup chopped walnuts

PAN REQUIRED:

1 jumbo muffin pan
(¾-cup capacity)

1. Preheat the oven to 350°F. Lightly grease only the bottoms of 3 muffin cups; then rub a little of the butter around the rim of each cup. (This will help them to form a more rounded top.) Set the muffin pan aside.

2. Place the egg, oil, sugar, and vanilla in a small bowl and whisk to blend. Stir in the zucchini.

3. Place the flour, baking soda, baking powder, salt, and cinnamon in a medium-size mixing bowl and whisk to blend. Add the chocolate and toss to mix. Add the zucchini mixture to the flour mixture all at once, and stir just until the dry ingredients are moistened. Fold in the walnuts.

4. Spoon the batter into the prepared muffin cups, dividing it evenly among them; they should be about three-quarters full. Fill the empty muffin cups halfway with water to prevent them from scorching.

5. Bake the breads until a toothpick inserted into the center of one comes out clean, about 18 minutes.

6. Remove the muffin pan from the oven and place it on a wire rack to cool for 10 minutes. Carefully pour the water out of the empty muffin cups. Remove the breads from the pan and let them cool, upright, on the rack. Serve warm or at room temperature. (The breads may be wrapped in aluminum foil, placed in a plastic freezer bag, and frozen for up to 1 month. Store any leftovers, wrapped, at room temperature for up to 2 days.)

# Vanilla Spice Crumb Cakes

*Makes 3 cakes; serves 2 or 3*
◆◆◆◆◆◆◆◆◆

**If you want** to lift a friend's spirits one morning, make a batch of these cakes. The cake is soft and fragrantly vanilla in flavor, with a thick crumb topping that browns to a crisp and remains moist where the topping meets the cake. It's just what you'd expect from an old-fashioned crumb cake.

Unsalted butter, at room
   temperature, for greasing the
   muffin pan
1 piece of vanilla bean (3 inches),
   or ½ teaspoon vanilla paste
3 tablespoons granulated sugar
3 tablespoons packed light brown
   sugar

⅔ cup plus 2 tablespoons
   all-purpose flour
⅛ teaspoon salt
¼ teaspoon ground nutmeg
3 tablespoons unsalted butter,
   at room temperature
¼ cup buttermilk
¼ teaspoon baking soda
White of 1 medium egg

PAN REQUIRED:
1 jumbo muffin pan (¾-cup capacity)

**1.** Preheat the oven to 350°F. Lightly grease only the bottoms of 3 muffin cups and set the muffin pan aside.

**2.** Split the vanilla bean lengthwise by slicing down one edge with the tip of a sharp knife. Open the bean and scrape the seeds into a medium-size mixing bowl. Add the granulated and brown sugars to the bowl, and mix well with a fork. Add the flour, salt, and nutmeg, and mix with the fork until well combined. Add the butter and mix with the fork, or with your fingertips, until the mixture is crumbly. Set aside ¼ cup of the crumb mixture for the topping.

**3.** Place the buttermilk and baking soda in a small bowl. Whisk in the egg white until it is well blended. Pour the buttermilk mixture over the remaining crumb mixture, and mix well with the fork until a batter is formed.

**4.** Spoon the batter into the prepared muffin cups, dividing it evenly among them. Sprinkle the reserved crumb mixture evenly over the batter and press it in lightly with your fingertips. Fill the empty muffin cups halfway with water to prevent them from scorching.

**5.** Bake the cakes until a toothpick inserted in the center of one comes out clean, about 15 minutes.

**6.** Remove the muffin pan from the oven and place it on a wire rack to cool for 5 minutes. Carefully pour the water out of the empty muffin cups. Turn the cakes out of the cups and let them cool, upright, on the wire rack for at least 10 minutes before serving. Serve warm or at room temperature. (The cakes may be wrapped in aluminum foil, placed in a plastic freezer bag, and frozen for up to 1 month. Store any leftovers, wrapped, at room temperature for up to 2 days.)

# Orange Tea Cakes

## *with* Honey Orange Glaze

*Makes 8 miniature tea cakes; serves 2 or 3*

◆◆◆◆◆◆◆◆◆

**Tea cakes take** many forms, from thick sugar cookies to tiny iced cakes. These glazed, slightly sticky one-bite morsels melt in your mouth. To serve them, put the cakes in decorative miniature paper baking cups.

Unsalted butter, at room
temperature, for greasing the
muffin cups

**FOR THE TEA CAKES:**
½ cup self-rising flour

2 teaspoons sugar

3 tablespoons unsalted butter,
melted and cooled

1 tablespoon whole milk

1 tablespoon frozen orange juice
concentrate, thawed

½ teaspoon pure vanilla extract

White of 1 medium egg

**FOR THE GLAZE:**
2 tablespoons honey

1 tablespoon frozen orange juice
concentrate, thawed

⅛ teaspoon ground cinnamon

**PAN REQUIRED:**
1 miniature muffin pan
(2-tablespoon capacity)

**1.** Place a rack in the center of the oven and preheat the oven to 350°F. Lightly grease 8 miniature muffin cups and set the pan aside.

**2. MAKE THE CAKES:** Place the flour and sugar in a medium-size mixing bowl, and stir to blend.

**3.** Place the melted butter, milk, orange juice concentrate, vanilla, and egg white in a small bowl, and whisk until blended. Add the milk mixture to the flour mixture, and stir just until the dry ingredients are moistened. Spoon the batter into the prepared muffin cups, dividing it evenly among them; they should be about three-quarters full. Fill the empty muffin cups halfway with water to prevent them from scorching.

**4.** Bake the cakes until they are beginning to brown around the edges and the tops are firm when lightly touched with a finger, about 12 minutes.

**5.** While the tea cakes are baking, prepare the glaze: Place the honey, orange juice concentrate, and cinnamon in a small bowl, and whisk to blend well.

**6.** When the tea cakes come out of the oven, carefully pour the water out of the empty muffin cups. Use a toothpick to poke 5 or 6 holes in the top of each cake, reaching all the way to the bottom. Using a teaspoon and working with one tea cake at a time, spread the glaze evenly over the cakes, lifting the edges to allow some of the syrup to flow to the bottom of the muffin cups. Let the tea cakes cool in the pan on a wire rack so they will soak up the glaze. Then turn them out onto a serving plate. Serve warm or at room temperature. If not serving on the same day, place on a plate, cover with plastic wrap, and store at room temperature for up to 1 day.

# Mini French Bread Boules

*Makes 2 loaves; serves 2*

**♦♦♦♦♦♦♦♦♦**

**These tasty little** loaves are so simple to put together that you may just find yourself making a batch daily. They are soft inside with a crisp crust, just like the ones you buy at the bakery. French bread is not the best keeper because it contains no fat—it is best served immediately after it has cooled.

¾ **cup plus 2 tablespoons bread**
   **flour, plus more as needed, and**
   **for dusting the work surface**

½ **teaspoon salt**

¼ **teaspoon rapid-rise yeast**

**Olive oil, for greasing the bowl**

**PAN REQUIRED:**
**1 baking sheet**

**1.** Place the bread flour, salt, and yeast in a food processor, and process for 3 seconds to blend. With the machine running, pour ¼ cup plus 3 tablespoons water through the feed tube; process until the dough holds together, about 20 seconds. The dough should be a sticky mass, and it should appear difficult to knead by hand. If the dough is too dry, add more water, a tablespoon at a time, processing for 5 seconds after each addition.

**2.** Lightly grease a medium-size mixing bowl with olive oil. Place the dough in the bowl and turn it to coat it with the oil. Cover the bowl loosely with plastic wrap, and let the dough rise at room temperature until it has nearly doubled in bulk, 2 to 3 hours.

**3.** Punch the dough down and let it rise again until nearly doubled in bulk, about 2 hours.

**4.** Sprinkle a cutting board or work surface with a little flour, place the dough on it, and cut the dough into 2 pieces. Shape the pieces into balls, sprinkling them with a little flour if necessary to make them easier to handle. Place the balls of dough on an ungreased baking sheet. Sprinkle a little flour over each round (to keep the plastic wrap from sticking), and cover them lightly with plastic wrap. Let the dough balls rise until nearly doubled in bulk, 1 to 1½ hours.

**5.** Place a rack in the center of the oven and preheat the oven to 400°F. To make a crisp crust, fill a clean spray bottle with water and spritz the inside of the oven with water just before you slide the bread into the oven.

**6.** Bake the bread rounds until golden and crusty, about 10 minutes. Remove the baking sheet from the oven or, if you like a crustier loaf, leave the bread in the oven with the door closed for 5 minutes after you have turned off the oven.

**7.** Transfer the bread to a wire rack to cool. Serve it warm or at room temperature.

# Herbed Cheese Bread

*Makes 1 loaf; serves 2*

**◆◆◆◆◆◆◆◆◆**

**This bread is** assertively flavored with cheese, herbs, and pepper—a nice choice with soup or salad. And the kitchen will smell wonderful while it is baking! To enable their flavor and fragrance to permeate the bread, finely crush the rosemary and thyme with a mortar and pestle, or grind them in a clean coffee grinder. The bread makes a delicious accompaniment to tomato-sauced dishes.

1¼ teaspoons active dry yeast

1½ teaspoons olive oil, plus extra for greasing the bowl and the baking sheet

¾ cup plus 2 tablespoons all-purpose flour, plus more as needed, and for dusting the work surface

¼ teaspoon salt

¼ teaspoon freshly ground black pepper

½ teaspoon finely crumbled dried rosemary

½ teaspoon minced fresh thyme

¼ cup freshly grated Parmesan cheese

¼ cup grated provolone cheese

PAN REQUIRED:

1 baking sheet

**1.** Pour ¼ cup plus 2 tablespoons warm water (110° to 115°F) into a medium-size mixing bowl, and sprinkle the yeast over the water. Stir to blend. Let the yeast mixture stand until it just begins to bubble, 5 minutes. Then add the oil, flour, salt,

pepper, rosemary, thyme, and cheeses. Stir until the dough is well combined.

**2.** Lightly flour a work surface and place the dough on it. Knead the dough until it is smooth and elastic, 5 to 7 minutes; add up to 3 or 4 more tablespoons of flour, as needed, to prevent the dough from sticking.

**3.** Lightly grease a medium-size mixing bowl with olive oil. Place the dough in it, and turn the dough to coat it with the oil. Cover the bowl loosely with plastic wrap, and let the dough rise in a warm, draft-free place until it is doubled in bulk, 1½ to 2 hours.

**4.** Punch down the dough on a lightly floured surface, and shape it to form a loaf about 4 inches long. Lightly oil a baking sheet and place the loaf on it. Cover the dough lightly with plastic wrap and let it rise in a warm, draft-free place until it is almost doubled in bulk, about 30 minutes.

**5.** While the dough is rising, place a rack in the center of the oven and preheat the oven to 400°F.

**6.** Bake the loaf until it is golden, about 25 minutes.

**7.** Remove the baking sheet from the oven, transfer the loaf to a wire rack, and let it cool. Serve the cheese bread warm or at room temperature. (The bread is best when eaten within 2 days. Store loosely wrapped at room temperature.)

# Country-Style Bread

*Makes 1 loaf; serves 2 or 3*
◆◆◆◆◆◆◆◆◆

**This is a rustic** loaf of crusty, coarse-textured bread. I cover slices of it with shredded sharp Cheddar, then tomato slices, and bake at 375°F until the cheese is runny and the tomatoes have released their juices. The bread doesn't actually toast, but it soaks up the delicious tomato juices wonderfully. It's also delicious torn into pieces and dunked into a dish of extra-virgin olive oil flavored with fresh cracked pepper and grated Parmesan cheese, and it's just right for making a roast beef sandwich or two. But tearing into the oven-warm loaf and smearing it with sweet butter is always a temptation.

**1¼ teaspoons active dry yeast**

**¾ teaspoon salt**

**¾ cup plus 2 tablespoons bread flour, plus extra for dusting the work surface**

**PAN REQUIRED:**
**1 baking sheet**

**1.** Pour ½ cup warm water (110° to 115°F) into a medium-size mixing bowl and sprinkle the yeast over the water; stir to blend. Let the mixture stand until it begins to bubble, 5 minutes. Then mix in the salt and ¾ cup of the flour. Using a flexible rubber spatula, knead the sticky mass in the bowl by lifting one side of the dough and folding it over the other, then pressing the dough down to the bottom of the bowl with the spatula. Work the remaining 2 tablespoons of flour into the dough, using the same technique, and continue kneading with the spatula until the dough is spongy, about 5 minutes.

**2.** Scrape down the sides of the bowl, and push the dough into a ball shape. Cover the bowl with a clean kitchen towel, and let the dough rise in a warm, draft-free place for 1 hour.

**3.** Using the spatula, stir down the dough. Cover the bowl with the towel and let the dough rise again until it is doubled in bulk, about 1 hour.

**4.** Sprinkle 3 to 4 tablespoons of flour over a cutting board or work surface. Place the dough on the flour and turn it over and over in the flour to form a round loaf. Sprinkle the dough with additional flour, a tablespoon at a time, if it is too sticky to shape.

**5.** Sprinkle flour on a baking sheet, covering an area double the size of the loaf. Place the dough on the flour, loosely cover it with plastic wrap, and let it rise until it is doubled in bulk, about 1 hour. (The dough will expand horizontally more than it will rise in height.)

**6.** Preheat the oven to 375°F.

**7.** Gently pull the plastic wrap off the dough. Fill a clean spray bottle with water and spritz the inside of the oven with water just before you slide in the bread. Bake the bread for 5 minutes. Spray the oven (not the bread) generously with water again. Bake the bread until it is golden and crusty, about 25 minutes, spraying the oven once more with water halfway through the baking time.

**8.** Remove the baking sheet from the oven, transfer the bread to a wire rack, and let it cool. Serve warm or at room temperature. (The bread is best eaten the day it is baked.)

# Olive Bread

*Makes 1 loaf; serves 2 or 3*
◆◆◆◆◆◆◆◆◆

**Olive oil keeps** this bread soft and tender and subtly underlines the flavor of the olives. The olives are quartered to make sure they are distributed throughout the bread, but you could halve them as is done in larger loaves. Substitute chopped walnuts for the olives to make a delicious walnut bread.

¾ cup plus 1½ tablespoons all-purpose flour, plus more as needed, and for dusting the work surface

½ teaspoon salt

½ teaspoon active dry yeast

Pinch of sugar

1½ teaspoons olive oil, plus extra for greasing the bowl

1 cup quartered pitted Kalamata olives or brine-cured green olives, patted dry

**PAN REQUIRED:**
**1 baking sheet**

1. Place the flour and salt in a medium-size mixing bowl and whisk to blend. Set it aside.

2. Pour ½ cup water into a microwave-safe bowl and microwave on high power until the water is very warm (105° to 115°F), 30 to 40 seconds. Sprinkle the yeast and sugar over the water, stirring to dissolve the yeast. Let the mixture stand until it is foamy, 5 minutes. Then stir in the oil. Gradually stir the yeast mixture into the flour mixture. The dough will be slightly sticky and rough.

**3.** Lightly flour a cutting board or work surface, and turn the dough out onto it. Knead the dough until it is smooth and elastic, 4 to 5 minutes. Add more flour, a tablespoon at a time, if the dough is sticky.

**4.** Lightly grease a medium-size mixing bowl with olive oil. Place the dough in the bowl and turn it to coat it with the oil. Cover the bowl with plastic wrap, then a clean kitchen towel. Let the dough rise in a warm, draft-free area until it is doubled in bulk, 1 to 1½ hours.

**5.** Dust a baking sheet with flour and set it aside.

**6.** Punch down the dough and turn it out onto a lightly floured cutting board or work surface. Press it out to form a ½-inch-thick rectangle. Sprinkle the olives evenly over the surface of the dough. Roll the dough up jelly-roll style, beginning with a short end. Knead the dough to distribute the olives evenly. Lightly flour your hands, and roll the dough back and forth until you have a 4-inch-long cylinder with tapered ends. Transfer the loaf to the prepared baking sheet and cover it with a clean kitchen towel. Let the loaf rise in a warm, draft-free area until it is doubled in bulk, about 1 hour.

**7.** Place a rack in the center of the oven and preheat the oven to 400°F. Fill a clean spray bottle with water.

**8.** Spray the hot oven walls with water. Then immediately place the baking sheet in the oven and bake until the loaf is golden and the bottom sounds hollow when tapped, 20 to 25 minutes.

**9.** Remove the baking sheet from the oven and transfer the olive bread to a wire rack to cool. Serve warm or at room temperature. (The bread is best eaten within 2 days. Store loosely wrapped at room temperature.)

# Whole Wheat Walnut Bread

*Makes 1 loaf; serves 2 or 3*
◆◆◆◆◆◆◆◆◆

**Whole wheat flour** makes this a robustly textured, dense loaf, and it is full of crunchy toasted walnuts. It is delicious served while it is still warm from the oven, accompanied by a dish of olive oil for dipping torn-off bites.

⅓ cup whole wheat flour
About ¾ cup bread flour
½ teaspoon salt
½ cup buttermilk
1 tablespoon plus 1 teaspoon
  unsalted butter, melted and cooled
  to lukewarm
1 teaspoon sugar
¾ teaspoon active dry yeast
⅓ cup coarsely chopped walnuts,
  toasted (see page 195)

**Olive oil, for greasing the bowl**

**PAN REQUIRED:**
**1 baking sheet**

**1.** Place the whole wheat flour, ⅓ cup of the bread flour, and the salt in a medium-size mixing bowl and whisk to blend. Set aside.

**2.** Place the buttermilk, melted butter, and sugar in a small microwave-safe bowl and stir to blend. Sprinkle the yeast over the mixture and stir to dissolve the yeast. Let the mixture stand until it begins to bubble, 5 minutes. Then microwave the mixture on high power until very warm (105° to 115°F), 35 to 50 seconds.

**3.** Pour the yeast mixture over the flour mixture, and stir until a sticky dough forms. Sprinkle 1 tablespoon of bread flour over the dough and stir it in.

**4.** Sprinkle 2 tablespoons of bread flour on a cutting board, and flour your hands. Turn the dough out onto the board and knead it until it is smooth and elastic, 4 to 5 minutes. Knead in up to 3 or 4 additional tablespoons of flour, 1 tablespoon at a time, to make a soft, but not too sticky, dough.

**5.** Lightly grease a medium-size mixing bowl with olive oil. Place the dough in the bowl, and turn it to coat it with the oil. Cover the bowl loosely with plastic wrap and let it rise in a warm, draft-free place until it is almost doubled in bulk, 1½ to 2 hours.

**6.** Meanwhile, sprinkle a little bread flour over a 5-inch round area on a baking sheet and set the baking sheet aside.

**7.** Punch down the dough, and turn it out onto a lightly floured cutting board or work surface. Press the dough out to form a ½-inch-thick rectangle. Sprinkle the walnuts evenly over the surface of the dough. Roll up the dough jelly-roll style, beginning with a short end. Knead the dough to distribute the walnuts evenly. Shape the dough into a round and put it on the prepared baking sheet. Cover it with a clean kitchen towel and let it rise in a warm, draft-free place until it is almost doubled in bulk, about 1 hour.

**8.** Place a rack in the center of the oven and preheat the oven to 375°F.

**9.** Place the baking sheet in the oven, and bake the bread until it is golden, 25 to 28 minutes.

**10.** Remove the baking sheet from the oven, transfer the bread to a wire rack, and let it cool. Serve warm or at room temperature. (The bread is best eaten within 2 days. Store loosely wrapped at room temperature.)

# Rosemary Focaccia

*Makes 1 small loaf; serves 2*

◆◆◆◆◆◆◆◆◆

**This herbed yeast** bread is about six inches in diameter, perfect for a dinner à deux. It also makes a delicious pizza crust for one or two: After the focaccia has baked for ten minutes, sprinkle it with about three-quarters cup grated mozzarella and/or provolone or Asiago cheese, add a layer of sliced plum tomatoes, and sprinkle with coarse salt. Then continue baking until the bread is crusty and the cheeses are melted, about five minutes.

**FOR THE BREAD:**

¼ teaspoon sugar

1⅛ teaspoons active dry yeast

1¼ cups bread flour, plus more as needed

1 teaspoon kosher salt

1 teaspoon minced fresh rosemary

2 tablespoons extra-virgin olive oil

Olive oil, for greasing the bowl and baking sheet

2 teaspoons yellow or white cornmeal, for dusting the baking sheet

**FOR THE TOPPING:**

1 tablespoon extra-virgin olive oil

2 tablespoons freshly grated Parmesan cheese

2 teaspoons crushed fresh rosemary

½ teaspoon kosher salt

**PAN REQUIRED:**

1 baking sheet

**1. MAKE THE BREAD:** Pour ½ cup of water into a small microwave-safe bowl and microwave on high power until the water is very warm (about 110°F), 30 to 40 seconds. Add the sugar and yeast, and stir until both dissolve. Set the mixture aside for 5 minutes. (The mixture will become slightly foamy.)

**2.** Place 1 cup of the bread flour, the salt, and the rosemary in a medium-size mixing bowl. Pour the yeast mixture and the olive oil into the bowl, and stir with a wooden spoon to make a sticky dough. Spread ¼ cup of the bread flour in the center of a cutting board, and turn the dough out onto the center of the flour. Flour your hands, and knead the dough until it is elastic and no longer sticky, about 5 minutes. If necessary, add another tablespoon or two of flour as you are kneading.

**3.** Grease a bowl with a teaspoon or two of olive oil, place the dough in the bowl, and turn it to grease it with the oil. Cover the bowl with a clean kitchen towel and let the dough rise in a warm, draft-free place until it is doubled in bulk, about 45 minutes.

**4.** Brush some olive oil over a 6-inch round area on the baking sheet, and sprinkle the cornmeal over the oil. Place the dough on the cornmeal and gently press it out to form a 6-inch round. Using your fingertip, make ½-inch-deep indentations 1 inch apart in the surface of the dough.

**5. ADD THE TOPPING:** Brush the olive oil over the dough, and sprinkle the cheese, crushed rosemary, and salt over it. Cover loosely with a piece of plastic wrap, and let the dough rest for 30 minutes.

**6.** Place a rack in the center of the oven and preheat the oven to 400°F.

**7.** Bake the focaccia until it is golden, 12 to 15 minutes.

**8.** Remove the baking sheet from the oven, transfer the focaccia to a wire rack, and let it cool for 5 minutes before cutting it into wedges. Serve warm or at room temperature. (It is best eaten the day it is baked.)

# Popovers

*Makes 2 popovers; serves 1 or 2*

**◆◆◆◆◆◆◆◆◆**

**There is no** leavening in crisp, airy popovers—eggs and the steam produced by the milk work to balloon them. It helps to have the egg and milk at room temperature so they will produce enough steam to rise high and evenly.

Serve the popovers right out of the oven with meats that have juices for the popovers to soak up. Or split the popovers and spread them with butter and jam for breakfast, or fill them with chicken salad or shrimp salad for lunch.

**2 teaspoons unsalted butter, melted**

**1 medium egg, at room temperature**

**¼ cup whole milk, at room temperature**

**¼ teaspoon sugar**

**⅛ teaspoon salt**

**¼ cup all-purpose flour**

**PAN REQUIRED:**

**1 standard muffin pan (½-cup capacity)**

**1.** Preheat the oven to 425°F. Pour ½ teaspoon of the melted butter into each of 2 muffin cups, and use your finger to spread it over the bottom and sides of the cups. Place the muffin pan in the oven while you quickly prepare the batter.

**2.** Place the remaining 1 teaspoon of melted butter, the egg, milk, sugar, and salt in a medium-size mixing bowl and whisk until well blended. Gradually add the flour, whisking until the mixture is smooth.

**3.** Remove the hot muffin pan from the oven and pour the batter into the prepared muffin cups, dividing it evenly between them. Fill the empty cups halfway with water to prevent them from scorching. Bake for 10 minutes. Then reduce the heat to 350°F and continue baking until the popovers are puffed and browned, about 15 minutes. Do not open the oven door until the popovers have baked for at least 25 minutes.

**4.** Remove the muffin pan from the oven. Loosen the popovers with the tip of a sharp knife, and remove them from the pan. Insert the tip of the knife into the side of each popover to let the steam escape. Serve immediately.

## variation

# Two to Try

## Parmesan Popovers:

Add 2 tablespoons finely grated Parmesan cheese to the milk mixture in Step 2. Then add the flour mixture and bake as directed.

## Yorkshire Popovers:

Instead of the butter, pour 1/2 to 1 teaspoon bacon drippings into each muffin cup. Heat the muffin pan just before pouring in the batter, as directed in Step 1.

# CHAPTER 8

# Valentine Specials

**The way to** someone's heart truly may be through their stomach. Whether you prepare the entree yourself, or get a little help from your favorite carry-out shop or restaurant, when it comes to dessert, I know that making a special effort to prepare a little fancy something wins a valentine's affections much quicker than a box of chocolates (unless they are homemade, of course). My language of love is often spoken through my homemade sweets.

But you don't have to save these grand desserts for Valentine's Day, and they don't need to be served to someone of Cupid's choosing. Here you will find all manner of delicious specialties: cream puffs, cloudlike soufflés,

silky cheesecakes, a chocolate torte that is pastry-shop elegant, cookie hearts topped with jam and fluffy meringue, miniature pavlovas (meringue tart shells) filled with luscious whipped cream and passion fruit, creamy flan, a napoleon layered with mousse and homemade caramel, and many complementary sauces.

The techniques are true to the full-size versions of these delights, and the flavors are divine. All are signature desserts that can be beautifully presented for any romantic occasion. Presentation, by the way, includes setting the scene: yes, candles (but not scented ones—you don't want to distract from the aroma of your wonderful cake); yes, subdued lighting (but

# BREAKFAST IN BED

Sentimental traditions make the heart grow fonder—a good reason to plan on serving breakfast in bed more often. Here are some suggestions:

- Honey Apple Oatmeal Crisp (page 226), served with a dish of vanilla yogurt. Roll up the newspaper, tie it with ribbon, and slip a flower in with it.

- Serve the Cinnamon French Toast Pudding (page 278) unmolded on a plate; sift confectioners' sugar over the bread pudding and drizzle the plate with maple syrup. Garnish the plate with fresh strawberries and a tiny bowl of confectioners' sugar for dipping.

- For the valentine who takes off for a run before breakfast, greet his or her return home with Blueberry Granola Whole Wheat Muffins (page 298) that have been baked in a heart-shaped muffin pan. Garnish the plate with small scoops of softened butter or cream cheese (formed with a melon baller). Accompany with turkey sausage and a tall glass of freshly squeezed pink grapefruit juice.

- Whole Wheat Banana Bread (page 329) is delicious served with an omelet filled with feta cheese, sautéed fresh spinach, and mushrooms.

- Sunday Morning Sweet Rolls (page 324) and Almond Cherry Scones (page 310) are delicious breads for special mornings. Add some fresh fruit and yogurt for a nourishing breakfast.

not so dark you can't see how attractive the dessert is); and, yes, a favorite CD playing in the background (but not so loud you can't hear the compliments your dessert will garner).

# Chocolate Walnut Tortes

*Makes 3 tortes; serves 3*

◆◆◆◆◆◆◆◆◆

## Loaded with ground

walnuts and rich chocolate flavor, these cakes are covered with a layer of fudgy chocolate that preserves the moist texture. A simple but elegant dessert, perfect to serve to yourself and your two favorite sweethearts.

3 tablespoons unsalted butter, at room temperature, plus more for greasing the cans

2 ounces premium-quality semisweet chocolate, finely chopped

1/2 cup walnut pieces

2 tablespoons all-purpose flour

1/4 cup sugar

2 large eggs, separated

1/2 teaspoon pure vanilla extract

Pinch of salt

Pinch of cream of tartar

Rich Ganache (recipe follows)

PANS REQUIRED:

Three 8-ounce cans (see page 6)

1 baking sheet

1. Place a rack in the center of the oven and preheat the oven to 375°F. Lightly grease the insides of the cans. Place the cans on a piece of parchment paper and trace around the circumfer-

ence. Cut out 3 rounds of parchment and line the cans with them. Place the prepared cans on a baking sheet for easier handling, and set it aside.

**2.** Place the chocolate in a small microwave-safe bowl, and microwave on medium power until it is glossy and beginning to melt, about 1 minute. Then stir until it is smooth. Let the chocolate cool.

**3.** Place the walnuts and the flour in a food processor and process until the walnuts are very finely ground but not oily, 10 to 15 seconds.

**4.** Place the 3 tablespoons butter and sugar in a medium-size mixing bowl and beat with a hand-held electric mixer on high speed until creamy. Add the egg yolks, one at a time, beating well after each addition. Beat in the vanilla with the last yolk. Reduce the mixer speed to low and beat in the melted chocolate until blended, 10 to 15 seconds. Using a wooden spoon, gently stir in the ground walnut mixture.

**5.** Wash the mixer beaters and dry them thoroughly. Place the egg whites, salt, and cream of tartar in a small bowl and beat with the mixer on high speed until the whites are shiny and hold stiff peaks when the mixer is turned off and the beaters are lifted, 1 to 1½ minutes. Fold the egg whites thoroughly but gently into the chocolate mixture in two batches.

**6.** Spoon the batter into the prepared cans, dividing it evenly among them. Bake the cakes until a toothpick inserted into the center of one comes out clean, about 20 minutes. Do not overbake; the cake should remain soft and moist in the center.

**7.** Remove the cans from the oven, place them on a wire rack, and let the cakes cool completely in the cans.

**8.** When the cakes have cooled, invert the cans over the wire rack to release the cakes. Peel off the parchment paper and place the cakes upright on the rack. Pour about 3 tablespoons of the lukewarm ganache over each cake, using a spatula to smooth the icing all over. Let the cakes stand until the ganache is firm, about 1 hour. The tortes will keep, covered, in the refrigerator for 2 to 3 days.

# Rich Ganache

**This is a classic** ganache that you pour on while it is lukewarm, resulting in a smooth finish on the cakes.

**MAKES ABOUT ½ CUP**

¼ **cup plus 2 tablespoons whipping (heavy) cream**

**5 ounces imported bittersweet chocolate (such as Lindt), finely chopped**

Pour the cream into a small saucepan and bring to a boil over medium-high heat. Immediately remove the pan from the heat and add the chocolate, swirling to submerge the chocolate in the hot cream. Let the mixture stand until the chocolate softens, 1 minute. Then stir with a whisk until the chocolate is melted and the mixture is smooth. Allow it to cool to lukewarm, about 1 hour. Then use immediately.

# White and Dark Chocolate Swirl Cheesecakes

*Makes 2 cheesecakes; serves 2*

◆◆◆◆◆◆◆◆◆

**Dark chocolate batter** is swirled with white chocolate batter to create these little cheese-cakes. For Valentine's Day, garnish them with fresh raspberries and edible rose petals.

**Unsalted butter, at room temperature, for greasing the cans**

FOR THE CRUST:
**½ cup crushed shortbread or chocolate wafer cookies**

**2 tablespoons sugar**

**2 tablespoons unsalted butter, melted**

FOR THE FILLING:
**⅓ cup semisweet chocolate chips**

**¼ cup white chocolate chips**

**4 ounces cream cheese, at room temperature**

**¼ cup sugar**

**1 large egg**

**2 tablespoons sour cream**

**½ teaspoon pure vanilla extract**

PANS REQUIRED:
**Two 8-ounce cans (see page 6)**

**1 baking sheet**

1. Place a rack in the center of the oven and preheat the oven to 325°F. Lightly grease the insides of the cans. Place the cans on a piece of parchment paper and trace around the circumference. Cut out 2 parchment rounds, and line the bottom of the cans with them. Cut out two 11 x 2-inch strips of parchment, and use them to line the inside of each can; the parchment

should reach the top of the cans. Place the cans on a baking sheet for easier handling, and set it aside.

2. MAKE THE CRUST: Place the crushed cookies and the sugar in a small bowl. Add the melted butter and toss with a fork until the crumbs are evenly moistened. Spoon the crumb mixture into the prepared cans, dividing it evenly. Gently press the crumb mixture down with your fingertips. Bake until the color of the crust begins to darken, 8 to 10 minutes.

3. Remove the baking sheet from the oven and transfer it with the cans onto a wire rack. Let the crusts cool while you prepare the cheesecake filling. Keep the oven on.

4. MAKE THE FILLING: Place the semisweet chocolate chips in a small

saucepan over low heat and heat until melted, then stir until smooth, about 1½ minutes. (Or place them in a microwave-safe bowl and microwave on medium power until melted, 40 to 60 seconds; then stir until smooth.) Melt the white chocolate chips in the same manner. Set the semisweet and white chocolate aside, separately, to cool.

**5.** Place the cream cheese and sugar in a medium-size mixing bowl and beat with a hand-held electric mixer on medium speed just until the mixture is smooth and creamy. Add the egg, reduce the mixer speed to low, and beat just until it is blended into the cream cheese mixture. Then beat in the sour cream and vanilla. Put ½ cup of the batter into another bowl, and beat in the melted white chocolate. Beat the semisweet chocolate into the remaining batter.

**6.** Measure out 1 tablespoon of the semisweet chocolate batter and set it aside. Spoon the remaining semisweet chocolate batter into the prepared crusts, dividing it evenly between them. Cover it evenly with the white chocolate batter. Use the tip of a knife to swirl the batters together.

**7.** Spoon half of the reserved 1 tablespoon semisweet chocolate batter on top of one of the cheesecakes and swirl it into the batter, barely dragging the knife tip through the top. Repeat the process with the rest of the semisweet chocolate batter and the remaining cheesecake. Return the cheesecakes to the oven on the baking sheet and bake until the cheesecakes are just set, 28 to 30 minutes.

**8.** Remove the baking sheet from the oven, transfer the cans to a wire rack, and let them cool completely. Then cover and refrigerate for 10 hours or overnight.

**9.** To serve, run a sharp knife around the sides of the cans to loosen the cheesecakes. Turn the cakes out, remove the parchment, and place them upright on serving plates. (The cheesecakes will keep, covered, in the refrigerator for 1 week.)

# Chèvre Cheesecakes

## *with* Honey-Anise-Ginger Syrup

*Makes 2 cheesecakes; serves 2*

◆◆◆◆◆◆◆◆◆

**These cheesecakes are** baked on top of a layer of spiced honey; then, like a flan, they are inverted so that the layer of honey smoothly coats their tops. Goat cheese adds a tangy depth of flavor to the creamy cheesecake filling.

**FOR THE HONEY-ANISE-GINGER SYRUP:**

¼ cup plus 2 tablespoons sage, basswood, or alfalfa honey

2 tablespoons sugar

6 whole star anise

4 quarter-size pieces of peeled fresh ginger

Unsalted butter, at room temperature, for greasing the soufflé dishes

**FOR THE FILLING:**

1 large egg

4 ounces mild fresh chèvre (goat cheese), at room temperature

3 ounces cream cheese, at room temperature

½ teaspoon pure vanilla extract

Boiling water, for the baking dish

Chopped natural, unsalted pistachios, for garnish

**PANS REQUIRED:**

Two 4 x 1⅜-inch tart pans with removable bottoms or two 1-cup soufflé dishes or ramekins

1 baking pan

1. **MAKE THE SYRUP:** Place the honey, sugar, star anise, ginger, and 2 tablespoons of water in a small heavy saucepan and bring to a boil over medium-high heat, stirring until

the sugar dissolves, $1\frac{1}{2}$ to 2 minutes. Remove the saucepan from the heat and let the syrup cool to room temperature, $1\frac{1}{2}$ to 2 hours.

**2.** Place a rack in the center of the oven and preheat the oven to 325°F. Lightly grease the tart pans. Wrap a piece of heavy-duty aluminum foil around the outside, including the bottom, of each tart pan. (Or lightly grease the soufflé dishes or ramekins.) Set aside the tart pans and a larger baking pan that will hold them.

**3.** Remove the star anise and the ginger from the cooled syrup, and place them in a small strainer set over the saucepan; allow the honey that clings to the spices to drip back into the saucepan.

**4. MAKE THE CHEESECAKE FILLING:** Place the egg, chèvre, cream cheese, vanilla, and $\frac{1}{4}$ cup of the honey-anise-syrup in a blender. Blend on high speed, stopping and scraping the sides of the blender as necessary, until the mixture is smooth and creamy, 20 to 30 seconds. Spoon the remaining honey syrup into the prepared tart pans, dividing it evenly between them. Pour the batter on top of the honey syrup, dividing it evenly between the pans. Scrape the batter that clings to the blender into the pans.

**5.** Place the tart pans in the larger baking pan, and pour boiling water into the pan to reach halfway up the sides of the tart pans. Place the pan in the oven and bake until the cheesecake custards are just set, about 30 minutes.

**6.** Remove the baking pan from the oven and, using tongs, carefully lift the tart pans from the water bath. Place them on a wire rack, and let them cool to room temperature. Then cover and refrigerate the tarts for at least 2 hours and up to 24 hours.

**7.** To serve, hold a hot, damp kitchen towel around the outside of the tart pans to loosen the honey syrup on the bottom. Then unmold the cheesecakes onto individual serving plates, pouring the loosened syrup over the cheese-cakes. Garnish with the chopped pistachios. (The cheesecakes will keep, unmolded in the refrigerator, for up to 2 days.)

# Cashew Calvados Caramel Cheesecakes

*Makes 2 cheesecakes; serves 2*
◆◆◆◆◆◆◆◆◆

**This heavenly** cheesecake has a thick, crunchy cashew crust and a creamy caramel filling and sauce flavored with Calvados (French apple brandy). The sophisticated flavor combination makes it an adults-only desert, very romantic served with cups of dark, rich coffee, or perhaps with a tiny glass more of Calvados.

Unsalted butter, at room temperature, for greasing the cans

**FOR THE CRUST:**

½ cup salted roasted cashews, plus more for garnish (optional)

2 tablespoons all-purpose flour

2 tablespoons packed light brown sugar

2 tablespoons unsalted butter, melted

**FOR THE FILLING:**

6 ounces cream cheese, at room temperature

6 tablespoons Calvados Caramel Sauce (recipe follows)

1 large egg

½ teaspoon pure vanilla extract

**PANS REQUIRED:**

Two 8-ounce cans (see page 6)

1 baking sheet

**1.** Place a rack in the center of the oven and preheat the oven to 325°F. Lightly grease the insides of the cans. Place the cans on a piece of parchment paper and trace around the circumference. Cut out 2 parchment rounds, and line the bottom of the cans with them. Cut out two 11 x 2-inch strips of parchment, and line the inside of each can with a strip; the strip should reach to the top of the can. Place the cans on a baking sheet for easier handling, and set it aside.

**2. MAKE THE CRUST:** Place the cashews, flour, brown sugar, and melted butter in a food processor and process until the cashews are finely ground. Spoon the mixture into the prepared cans, dividing it evenly between them. Gently press the mixture down with your fingertips. Bake until the crusts start to brown, about 12 minutes.

**3.** Remove the baking sheet from the oven and transfer it with the cans onto a wire rack. Let the crusts cool while you prepare the cheesecake filling.

**4. MAKE THE FILLING:** Place the cream cheese and 3 tablespoons of the Calvados Caramel Sauce in a medium-size mixing bowl and beat with a hand-held electric mixer on medium speed until smooth and blended, about 1 minute. Add the egg and vanilla, and beat just until the batter is blended, about 20 seconds. Spoon the batter into the tart shells, dividing it evenly between them.

**5.** Return the cheesecakes to the oven on the baking sheet and bake until they just set, 25 to 28 minutes.

**6.** Remove the baking sheet from the oven, transfer the cans to a wire rack, and let them cool completely. Then cover and refrigerate for 10 hours or overnight.

**7.** To serve, run a sharp knife around the sides of the cans to loosen the cheesecakes. Turn the cakes out, remove the parchment, and place them upright on serving plates. Spoon the remaining Calvados Caramel Sauce over each cheesecake and garnish with cashews, if using. (The cheesecakes will keep, unmolded, in the refrigerator for up to 1 week.)

# Calvados Caramel Sauce

This sauce is a perfect example of how compatible caramel is with so many other flavors. Calvados adds subtle apple flavor with a kick, and it pairs beautifully with cashews and cheesecake. If you use Cointreau instead of Calvados, you'll change the sauce's (and the cheesecake's) flavor to orange. Cointreau Caramel Sauce works well with the cheesecake, too. (For a nonalcoholic orange-flavored caramel sauce, see page 383.)

**MAKES ½ CUP**

½ cup sugar
¼ **cup whipping (heavy) cream**
**2 tablespoons Calvados**
   **(apple brandy)**
**Pinch of salt**

1. Combine the sugar and 2 tablespoons of water in a small saucepan and bring to boil over medium-high heat, stirring gently and constantly with a fork until the sugar melts. To eliminate the sugar crystals that may stick to the sides of the pot, either cover the pot for 15 seconds or brush the sides with a pastry brush that has been dipped in cold water. Cook until the sugar is just golden amber in color, about 4 minutes.

2. Immediately remove the pot from the heat and gradually pour in the cream, stirring slowly and carefully because the caramel will sputter when the liquid is added. Stir in the Calvados and salt and cook over low heat, stirring constantly with the fork, until the sauce is smooth and the caramel is dissolved, about 2 minutes. Let the sauce come to room temperature for serving.

# Chocolate-Glazed Raspberry Cheesecakes

*Makes 3 cheesecakes; serves 3*

◆◆◆◆◆◆◆◆◆

**I began making** raspberry cheesecakes for friends' birthdays, and they gained such delicious reputation that a neighborhood French restaurant asked me to make some for them! With its creamy-smooth, wildly raspberry red cheesecake layer, accentuated by a thin layer of luscious chocolate, it makes a terrific Valentine's Day dessert, too. Garnish the plates with fresh raspberries and pink rose petals if you're a true romantic. And, by the way, this recipe makes three cheesecakes, one extra in case your valentines are your mom and dad, or your spouse and a child. It's always best to have an extra one of these cakes.

**FOR THE RASPBERRY REDUCTION:**
2 cups (about 8 ounces) frozen unsweetened raspberries, thawed but not drained
¼ cup sugar

**FOR THE CANS AND CRUST:**
Unsalted butter, at room temperature, for greasing the cans
½ cup crushed chocolate wafers, such as Nabisco Famous (about 10 wafers)
1 teaspoon sugar
2 tablespoons unsalted butter, melted

**FOR THE CHEESECAKE FILLING:**

**1 package (8 ounces) cream cheese, at room temperature**

**¼ cup sugar**

**1 large egg**

**Yolk of 1 large egg**

**1 tablespoon whipping (heavy) cream**

**½ teaspoon pure vanilla extract**

**Rich Ganache (page 356), lukewarm**

**Fresh raspberries, for garnish**

**PANS REQUIRED:**

**Three 8-ounce cans (see page 6)**

**1 baking sheet**

**1. MAKE THE RASPBERRY REDUCTION:** Place a fine-mesh sieve over a small saucepan, and press the raspberries and juices through it. Press down hard on the solids to extract as much liquid as possible. Scrape off the pulp clinging to the outside bottom of the sieve and add it to the pulp in the saucepan. Stir in the sugar. Bring the mixture to a boil over

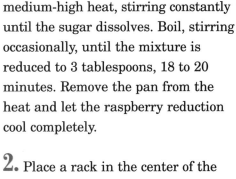

medium-high heat, stirring constantly until the sugar dissolves. Boil, stirring occasionally, until the mixture is reduced to 3 tablespoons, 18 to 20 minutes. Remove the pan from the heat and let the raspberry reduction cool completely.

**2.** Place a rack in the center of the oven and preheat the oven to 325°F. Lightly grease the insides of the cans. Place the cans on a piece of parchment paper and trace around the circumference. Cut out 3 parchment rounds and line the bottoms of the cans with them. Cut out three 11 x 2-inch strips of parchment, and line the inside of each can with a strip; the strip should reach to the top of the can. Place the cans on a baking sheet for easier handling, and set it aside.

**3. MAKE THE CRUST:** Place the crushed cookies and the sugar in a small bowl, and stir to mix. Add the melted butter and toss with a fork until the crumbs are evenly moistened. Spoon the crumb mixture into the prepared cans, dividing it evenly among them. Gently press down the crumb mixture with your fingertips. Bake for 10 minutes.

**4.** Remove the baking sheet from the oven and transfer it to a wire rack. Let the crusts cool with the cans on while you prepare the cheesecake filling. Keep the oven on.

**5. MAKE THE CHEESECAKE FILLING:** Place the cream cheese and sugar in a medium-size mixing bowl and beat with a hand-held electric mixer on medium speed just until the mixture is smooth and creamy, about 45 seconds. Add the egg and egg yolk, reduce the mixer speed to low, and beat just until they are blended into the cream cheese mixture, 15 to 20 seconds. Then beat in the cooled raspberry reduction, cream, and vanilla just until blended, 15 to 20 seconds. Spoon the batter into the crusts, dividing it evenly among them. Return the cheesecakes to the oven on the baking sheet and bake the cheesecakes until they are just set, 27 minutes.

**6.** Remove the baking sheet from the oven and transfer the cheesecakes to a wire rack. Let them cool completely in the cans. Then cover and refrigerate for 6 hours or overnight.

**7.** To serve, run a sharp knife around the insides of the cans to loosen the

## variation

# Raspberry Cheesecakes

**For a more** fruity version, try this: Use shortbread cookies instead of the chocolate wafers for the crust. Omit the ganache. Mix together 1/4 cup plus 2 tablespoons of sour cream and 1 tablespoon of sugar. Spread this over the cheesecakes during the last 5 minutes of baking time in Step 5.

cheesecakes. Gently turn the cakes out, remove the parchment, and place them upright on the wire rack. Spoon the ganache over the cheesecakes, and use a spatula to smooth it over the top and sides. Arrange fresh raspberries on the tops and refrigerate the cheesecakes until the ganache is just firm, about 20 minutes, then transfer to serving plates. (The cheesecakes will keep, loosely covered with plastic wrap, in the refrigerator for up to 4 days.)

# Apricot Meringue Cookie Tarts

*Makes 2 tarts; serves 2*

**Are they cookies?** Are they tarts? Buttery pecan-studded shortbread is cut into heart shapes, layered with jam, covered with fluffy meringue, and baked until golden. You'll need a knife and fork for these striking desserts, perfect for Valentine's Day or any romantic occasion.

**FOR THE PAN AND COOKIES:**

¼ cup all-purpose flour

2 tablespoons sugar

Pinch of salt

3 tablespoons unsalted butter, at room temperature, plus more for greasing the pan

3 tablespoons finely chopped pecans, toasted (see Note, page 195)

**FOR THE APRICOT LAYER:**

1 tablespoon plus 1 teaspoon apricot jam

**FOR THE MERINGUE:**

White of 1 large egg

3 tablespoons sugar

1 teaspoon very hot water (see Note)

Confectioners' sugar, for garnish

**PANS REQUIRED:**

1 standard loaf pan (8 x 4 inches)

1 baking sheet

**1.** Place a rack in the center of the oven and preheat the oven to 350°F. Line the bottom of the loaf pan with a strip of aluminum foil that fits down the length and up the short sides, with enough extra length to extend over the edges by about 1½ inches. Use butter to grease the foil. Set the pan aside. Cut out two 4-inch heart patterns from parchment paper to use for the cookies, and set them aside.

**2. MAKE THE COOKIES:** Place the flour, sugar, and salt in a medium-size mixing bowl and whisk to blend well. Using a fork or your fingertips, mix in the 3 tablespoons butter until the dough is well blended. Then mix in the pecans. Spoon the dough into the prepared loaf pan, pressing it to form an even layer.

**3.** Arrange the heart patterns on the dough, and trace around them

with the tip of a sharp knife, cutting through the dough. Remove the patterns. Bake the cookie loaf until it is lightly browned, about 25 minutes.

**4.** Remove the loaf pan from the oven, place it on a wire rack, and let the cookie loaf cool completely, about 1 hour.

**5.** Preheat the oven to 375°F.

**6.** Use the edges of the foil to lift the cookie loaf out of the pan, and place it on a cutting board. Using a sharp knife, cut through the score lines, cutting out the heart-shaped cookies. Lift the cookies off the foil and place them on a baking sheet. Crumble the remaining cookie loaf and set it aside.

**7.** Spread the apricot jam over the cookies, right to the edges.

**8. MAKE THE MERINGUE:** Place the egg white, sugar, and the very hot water in a medium-size mixing bowl and beat with a hand-held electric mixer on medium speed until frothy, about 15 seconds. Increase the mixer speed to high and beat until a stiff, glossy meringue forms, 45 to 60 seconds.

**9.** Spoon half of the meringue on each cookie. Use the back of a spoon to pull up the meringue, forming small peaks that curl over a bit. Place the baking sheet in the oven and bake until the meringue is golden brown, 20 to 25 minutes.

**10.** Remove the baking sheet from the oven, place it on a wire rack, and let it cool for 10 minutes. Then use a metal spatula to transfer the cookie tarts to the rack, and let them cool completely.

**11.** To serve, place the cookie tarts on serving plates and sift confectioners' sugar around them. Sprinkle the reserved cookie crumbs over the meringue and around the hearts.

**NOTE:** Don't use hot tap water for the meringue. While you're preparing the cooled cookies in Step 6, heat 1 cup of water in a saucepan over medium heat. When you're ready to make the meringue, spoon out a teaspoon of hot water. Then serve yourself a cup of tea.

## variation

# Sassy Meringue Cookie Tarts

**Changing** the choice of nuts for the cookie tart shortbread and matching a different jam to spread on top of the tarts will give you lots of delicious possibilities:

**RASPBERRY MERINGUE COOKIE TARTS:** Use walnuts and raspberry jam.

**BLUEBERRY MERINGUE COOKIE TARTS:** Use chopped toasted almonds and blueberry preserves. Stir a drop of pure almond extract into the blueberry preserves.

**CHERRY MERINGUE COOKIE TARTS:** Use chopped toasted macadamia nuts and cherry preserves.

# Pavlovas

## *with* Whipped Crème Fraîche and Passion Fruit Sauce

*Makes 2 tarts; serves 2*

**A pavlova is** a crisp baked meringue shell that is topped with whipped cream and fruit. "Pavs" (or at least their name) originated in Australia, where they are prepared in all manners and forms. The sweetened whipped cream here is fortified with crème fraîche for more body and a bit of tartness. A passion fruit puree is drizzled over the fruit to give the dessert a sweet-tart essence of flavor, not to mention spectacular color and a romantic association.

For fluffy, crisp shells, bake them on a dry, sunny day. When the air is damp, the sugar in the meringue absorbs the moisture and the meringue shells turn out limp and sticky. Even trying to dry them out in the oven will not solve the problem.

### FOR THE MERINGUES:
2 tablespoons plus
   2 teaspoons superfine sugar
   (see Note, page 74)
1/2 teaspoon cornstarch
White of 1 large egg
1/8 teaspoon cream of tartar
1/8 teaspoon white vinegar

### FOR THE FILLING AND SAUCE:
3 tablespoons cold whipping
   (heavy) cream

2 tablespoons crème fraîche or
  sour cream
1 tablespoon confectioners' sugar
¼ cup fresh blueberries
1 kiwi, peeled and sliced
Passion Fruit Sauce (recipe follows)

PAN REQUIRED:
1 baking sheet

**1.** Place a rack in the center of the oven and preheat the oven to 250°F. Line a baking sheet with parchment paper, and set it aside.

**2. MAKE THE MERINGUES:** Place the superfine sugar and cornstarch in a small bowl, and whisk to blend well.

**3.** Place the egg white, cream of tartar, and vinegar in a medium-size

mixing bowl and beat with a hand-held electric mixer on medium speed until foamy, 15 to 20 seconds. Increase the mixer speed to high and beat until soft peaks form, about 30 seconds. With the mixer running, gradually pour the sugar mixture over the egg whites in a slow stream. Beat until stiff, glossy peaks form, 45 to 60 seconds.

**4.** Spoon the meringue into 2 equal mounds on the prepared baking sheet, spacing them 6 inches apart. Use a spoon to make a 2-inch-diameter well in the center of each mound; the meringue mounds should be approximately 4 inches in diameter with 1-inch-high sides. Bake the meringue shells until they are crisp but still soft inside, 1 to 1¼ hours. (The meringues should not brown.) If the meringues are still not crisp after 1¼ hours, turn off the oven and let them cool in the oven for 1 hour.

**5.** Remove the baking sheet from the oven and use a metal spatula to gently transfer the meringue shells to a wire rack. Let them cool completely. (The meringues may stick if they are cooled on the paper.)

**6.** MAKE THE FILLING: Place the cream, crème fraîche, and confectioners' sugar in a medium-size mixing bowl and beat with a hand-held electric mixer on high speed until firm peaks form.

**7.** Place the meringue shells on serving plates, and spoon in the whipped cream dividing it evenly between them. Arrange the blueberries and kiwi on top, and spoon the Passion Fruit Sauce around the meringues.

# Passion Fruit Sauce

**This small tropical** fruit lends a distinctive sweet-tart flavor and an enchanting aroma to sauces and dessert fillings. Its golden flesh is filled with soft, edible seeds. Because the seeds are so full of flavor, this sauce is appealing even if you do not strain them out. Simply stir the orange juice and confectioners' sugar into the scooped-out flesh.

MAKES ¼ CUP

**2 or 3 passion fruits (see Note)**
**1 tablespoon fresh orange juice**
**2 teaspoons confectioners' sugar**

**1.** Place a fine-mesh sieve over a small bowl, and set it aside.

**2.** Cut the passion fruits in half, and use a teaspoon to scrape the seeds and pulp into a small bowl. Measure out ¼ cup of the pulp and seeds, and press it through the sieve, pressing down hard on the solids to extract all of the juice. (Or squeeze the pulp through cheesecloth into the bowl.) Stir the orange juice and confectioners' sugar into the strained passion fruit. (You can make this 1 day ahead and refrigerate it in a covered container.)

NOTE: If passion fruit is not available, you can make a sauce with guava nectar: Pour 6 tablespoons of store-bought guava nectar into a 2-cup microwave-safe bowl and microwave on high power until it is reduced to 3 tablespoons, 6 to 8 minutes. Stir in the confectioners' sugar and orange juice.

## WILD ABOUT PASSION FRUIT

The blunt little egg-shaped passion fruit is the crown jewel of tropical and temperate-climate fruits. The flavor is exotically perfumed, reminiscent of guava, honey, and lemon, and intensely concentrated. You can usually find passion fruits in the springtime in Latin American markets and some groceries. The most common variety sold in the U.S. has a dimpled, deep purple skin and golden-colored flesh. The interior of a passion fruit is made up of liquid-filled teardrop capsules that contain tiny dark seeds. To render the juice, cut the fruit in half and scoop out all of the pulp. Strain the pulp through a sieve. Two passion fruits should yield about 3 tablespoons of juice.

• Spoon Passion Fruit Sauce on Presto Pound Cake (page 83), Mini Génoises (page 78), or Angel Food Cake (page 73). Beat ¼ cup whipping cream with 1 tablespoon of the sauce to serve with the cake, too.

• Drizzle Passion Fruit Sauce on the Lemon Cornmeal Pound Cakes (page 88) instead of the Raspberry Coulis. Or swirl the two sauces together on the serving plates for a beautiful presentation.

• Spoon Passion Fruit Sauce over scoops of mango ice cream and serve with Chocolate Almond Biscotti (page 199)

• Prepare the Cream Puffs on page 377 and fill them with tropical fruit sorbet; then drizzle with Milk Chocolate Sauce (page 251) and Passion Fruit Sauce.

• Serve Passion Fruit Sauce with the Vanilla Bean Soufflés (page 389) or the Lemon Pudding Cakes (page 292).

# Peanut Butter Tarts

*Makes 2 tarts; serves 2*

◆◆◆◆◆◆◆◆◆

**You probably know** someone who is addicted to Reese's Peanut Butter Cups and would consider this tart absolute heaven. It is full of creamy peanut butter filling and is topped with a thick chocolate glaze. To garnish, stand shards of peanut brittle in the glaze for a bit of whimsy.

Unsalted butter, at room temperature, for greasing the tart pans

**FOR THE CRUST:**
⅔ cup crushed cream-filled chocolate wafer cookies (such as Oreos)
1 tablespoon unsalted butter, melted

**FOR THE FILLING:**
1 large egg
½ cup sugar
2 tablespoons creamy peanut butter
2 tablespoons sour cream
½ teaspoon pure vanilla extract

**FOR THE GLAZE AND GARNISH:**
1 tablespoon whipping (heavy) cream
1 teaspoon light corn syrup
1½ ounces semisweet chocolate, chopped
Peanut Brittle (recipe follows) or chopped peanuts, for garnish

**PANS REQUIRED:**

**Two 4 x 1⅜-inch tart pans with removable bottoms**

**1 baking sheet**

**1.** Place a rack in the center of the oven and preheat the oven to 325°F. Line the tart pans with aluminum foil, pressing the foil into the grooves of the pans. Lightly grease the foil. Place the tart pans on a baking sheet for easier handling, and set it aside.

**2. MAKE THE CRUST:** Place the crushed cookies and the melted butter in a food processor and process until the cookies are finely ground, about 45 seconds. Spread the cookie mixture on the bottom and up the sides of the prepared tart pans, pressing it firmly into the grooves of the pans. Bake the crusts until the color is beginning to deepen, 12 minutes.

**3.** Remove the baking sheet from the oven, transfer the tart pans to a wire rack, and let them cool while you prepare the filling. Keep the oven on.

**4. MAKE THE FILLING:** Place the egg, sugar, peanut butter, sour cream, and vanilla in a medium-size mixing bowl and whisk until smooth.

**5.** Spoon the filling into the prepared tart shells, dividing it evenly between them. Bake the tarts on the baking sheet until the filling is set in the center, about 15 minutes.

**6.** Remove the baking sheet from the oven, place the tart pans on a wire rack, and let them cool completely.

**7. MAKE THE GLAZE:** Place the cream and corn syrup in a small microwave-safe bowl and microwave on high power until boiling, 25 to 30 seconds. Add the chocolate and swirl the bowl to submerge the chocolate in the hot cream mixture. Let the mixture stand until the chocolate softens, about 1 minute. Then stir until the chocolate melts and the glaze is smooth. Let the glaze cool, stirring it occasionally, until it thickens slightly but is still spreadable, about 10 minutes.

**8.** Spoon the glaze over the tarts, spreading it right to the edges. Stand the shards of peanut brittle in the glaze, or sprinkle peanuts over the glaze. Refrigerate the tarts for 2 hours before serving. (The tarts will keep, covered, in the refrigerator for up to 3 days.)

# Peanut Brittle

**Thin sheets of** crisp caramel peanut candy add an appealing design when you stand them up in a dessert. You can also crush the homemade brittle and sprinkle it over the dessert.

**MAKES ABOUT ½ CUP PIECES**

**Nonstick cooking spray**
**¼ cup sugar**
**2 tablespoons unsalted dry-roasted peanuts**

**PAN REQUIRED:**
**1 baking sheet**

1. Mist a baking sheet with cooking spray and set it aside.

2. Place the sugar and 1 tablespoon of water in a small, heavy saucepan, and bring to a boil over medium-high heat, stirring with a fork until the sugar dissolves. Then boil, swirling the saucepan occasionally, until the syrup is a golden amber color, 3 to 4 minutes. Immediately remove the pan from the heat.

3. Working quickly, stir the peanuts into the caramel and then immediately pour the mixture onto the prepared baking sheet. Press the tip of a table knife into the edges of the caramel, nudging and stretching it gently in all directions to form a very thin sheet. Let the brittle cool completely, 10 minutes.

4. Break the brittle into irregular shards. (Store in an airtight container at room temperature for up to 2 days.)

# Cream Puffs

## *with* Coffee Ice Cream and Mocha Orange Sauce

*Makes 4 cream puffs; serves 2*

**Just because** a dessert is special doesn't mean that it has to be difficult to make. You can make cream puffs in a few minutes, even when it seems you have nothing on hand for dessert. If you have flour, sugar, and salt in the pantry and eggs and butter in the fridge, golden pastry shells can be baking within ten minutes. Cradling a delicious filling, the pastries will taste and look impressive. A simple scoop of ice cream and a spoonful of chocolate syrup is the quickest way to serve them. But be creative with the fillings and sauces. For example, here the rich chocolate sauce is flavored with orange, coffee, and a little cardamom. If you get hooked on these easy cream puffs, try some of the ice cream and sauce pairings described on page 378.

**3 tablespoons unsalted butter, cut into 1/2-inch pieces**

**1 teaspoon sugar**

**Pinch of salt**

**1/2 cup all-purpose flour**

**2 large eggs, at room temperature**

**Mocha Orange Sauce (recipe follows)**

**Coffee ice cream**

PAN REQUIRED:

**1 baking sheet**

**1.** Place a rack in the center of the oven and preheat the oven to 400°F. Line the baking sheet with parchment paper and set it aside.

**2.** Pour ½ cup water into a small, heavy saucepan and add the butter, sugar, and salt. Bring to a boil over high heat, stirring until the sugar dissolves. Reduce the heat to medium and add the flour. Cook, stirring constantly with a wooden spoon, until the dough pulls away from the sides of the pan, 20 seconds. Continue cooking, stirring constantly, for 20 seconds. Then remove the pan from the heat and let it cool, stirring constantly, for 5 minutes.

**3.** Pour the eggs into the flour mixture all at once, and beat well with a wooden spoon. The batter should be stiff enough to just hold soft peaks when the spoon is lifted. Spoon 4 equal-size mounds onto the prepared baking sheet, spacing them 3 inches apart. Bake the pastries for 10 minutes. Reduce the oven temperature to 325°F and bake for 15 minutes more.

**4.** Remove the baking sheet from the oven and use a skewer to pierce the side of each pastry to allow steam to escape. Return the baking sheet to the oven and continue to bake until the pastries are golden brown, 5 to 10 minutes. Then remove from the oven, transfer the parchment to a wire rack, and let the pastries cool completely.

## FILLING AND SAUCE COMBINATIONS

- Ben & Jerry's Cherry Garcia ice cream or cherry vanilla ice cream with Cherry Sauce (page 294)

- Mint chocolate chip ice cream with Mocha Mint Crème Anglaise (page 290)

- Praline or butter pecan ice cream with Rich or Bourbon Caramel Sauce (pages 259 and 269)

- Black raspberry ice cream or chocolate fudge frozen yogurt with Milk Chocolate Sauce (page 251)

**5.** To serve, cut the cream puffs in half horizontally (they will have hollow centers), fill the bottoms with small scoops of ice cream, and replace the tops. Place 2 filled cream puffs on each serving plate, and drizzle them with the Mocha Orange Sauce.

# Mocha Orange Sauce

**This thick, silky** sauce, with its complex yet harmonious flavors, is a perfect accompaniment for filled cream puffs.

**MAKES ABOUT ¼ CUP PLUS 2 TABLESPOONS**

**1 medium-size orange**
**⅓ cup whipping (heavy) cream**
**2 tablespoons sugar**
**¼ teaspoon instant coffee powder**
**⅛ teaspoon ground cardamom**
**2 ounces bittersweet or semisweet chocolate, chopped**

**1.** Using a small sharp knife or a vegetable peeler, remove the zest from the orange in strips. Scrape away any white pith that remains. Place the zest in a small saucepan and add the cream, sugar, coffee powder, and cardamom. Bring the mixture to a boil, stirring constantly until the sugar dissolves. Remove the saucepan from the heat and let it cool completely.

**2.** Place a fine-mesh sieve over a small bowl and strain the sauce, pressing down hard on the orange zest. Discard the zest and return the strained cream mixture to the saucepan.

**3.** Bring the cream to a boil over medium-high heat and immediately remove it from the heat. Add the chocolate and swirl the saucepan to submerge the chocolate in the hot cream. Let it stand until the chocolate softens, 1 minute. Then stir until the sauce is smooth. (Store the sauce in a covered container in the refrigerator for up to 2 days. Reheat in a microwave at medium power for 30 seconds and stir before using.)

# Pistachio Napoleons

## *with* Orange Mousse and Orange Caramel Sauce

*Makes 2 napoleons; serves 2*

◆◆◆◆◆◆◆◆◆◆

**These unusual** napoleons are prepared from phyllo stacks layered with pistachios and baked crisp. Layering the crisps with creamy orange mousse and topping them with Orange Caramel Sauce makes for a spectacular dessert—make sure you're really in love before preparing it! The pistachio crisps and the Orange Caramel Sauce can be made up to 6 hours ahead, but the mousse needs to be prepared just before serving. (Refrigerate the mousse, covered, for no longer than 1 hour in advance.) The crisps will be irregular triangles; stack them askew between layers of mousse.

**FOR THE PISTACHIO CRISPS:**

¼ **cup unsalted natural pistachios**

¼ **cup sugar**

½ **teaspoon grated orange zest**

2 **sheets frozen phyllo dough, thawed**

2 **tablespoons unsalted butter, melted**

**FOR THE ORANGE MOUSSE:**

**3 tablespoons orange marmalade**

**¹⁄₃ cup cold whipping (heavy)
cream**

**FOR SERVING:**

**Orange Caramel Sauce
(recipe follows)**

**2 to 3 tablespoons chopped
unsalted natural pistachios,
for garnish**

**PANS REQUIRED:**

**2 baking sheets**

1. **MAKE THE PISTACHIO CRISPS:**
Place a rack in the lower third of the
oven and preheat the oven to 350°F.
Line a baking sheet with parchment
paper, and set it aside.

2. Place the pistachios, sugar, and
orange zest in a food processor and
process until finely ground, about
15 seconds.

3. Cut each phyllo sheet crosswise
into 3 equal pieces; then stack the
pieces to make 2 stacks. Cover the
stacks with plastic wrap and then a
kitchen towel to keep the phyllo from
drying out while you work with it.

4. Place 1 piece of phyllo on the prepared baking sheet, and brush a little
of the melted butter over it. Sprinkle
1 quarter of the ground pistachio
mixture over the butter, and top with
another piece of the phyllo. Brush the
phyllo with butter and sprinkle with
1 quarter of the pistachio mixture.
Top with another piece of phyllo, pressing down on it gently, and brush it
with butter. Repeat the process with
the remaining phyllo, pistachio mixture, and butter to make 2 stacks.
Refrigerate the phyllo stacks on the
baking sheet for 10 minutes.

5. Remove the stacks from the refrigerator. While they are still on the baking
sheet, use a sharp knife to cut each
stack into 3 irregular triangular pieces
(see Note). Place a piece of parchment
paper over the stacks and weight the
stacks by placing another baking sheet
on top. Bake until the phyllo crisps are
golden, 14 to 15 minutes.

6. Remove the phyllo crisps from
the oven. Remove the top baking sheet
and carefully peel off the top parchment. Place the bottom baking sheet
on a wire rack and let the crisps cool
on the baking sheet. Cover loosely

with waxed paper and store at room temperature for up to 6 hours before serving.

**7. MAKE THE MOUSSE:** Heat the marmalade in a small saucepan until it is melted. Place a fine-mesh sieve over a small bowl, and strain the warmed marmalade through it, pressing down hard on the orange rind. Let the strained marmalade and the orange rind pieces cool separately. Then finely chop the orange rind.

**8.** Place the cream in a medium-size mixing bowl and beat with an electric mixer on high speed until stiff peaks form. Then beat in the strained marmalade and the chopped orange rind on high speed.

**9.** To assemble the napoleons, place a phyllo crisp (1 triangular stack) on each dessert plate, and top each one with about 1 quarter of the orange mousse. Repeat the layers of phyllo and mousse, and top with the remaining crisps. Drizzle the napoleons with the Orange Caramel Sauce, and sprinkle the chopped pistachios around the desserts.

**NOTE:** To cut the phyllo into 3 triangles, place the stack with the short end closest to you. Cut from the top left corner across the phyllo to the center of the long right side, then back across to the bottom left corner.

# Orange Caramel Sauce

## This smooth, orange-

scented caramel sauce is lighter in texture, but powerful in flavor. It is lovely on Pistachio Napoleons or spooned over a scoop of your favorite chocolate ice cream.

**MAKES ½ CUP PLUS 2 TABLESPOONS**

½ **cup sugar**

¼ **cup plus 2 tablespoons freshly squeezed tangelo, tangerine, navel orange, or blood orange juice**

2 **tablespoons whipping (heavy) cream**

1. Place the sugar and 2 tablespoons of the juice in a small saucepan and bring to a boil over medium-high heat, stirring with a fork until the sugar dissolves, about 3 minutes. Reduce the heat to medium and cook, swirling the saucepan frequently, until the sugar syrup is golden amber, about 9 minutes. Remove the saucepan from the heat and gradually add the remaining ¼ cup orange juice and the cream, stirring with a long-handled wooden spoon. (The caramel will sputter when the liquid is added.)

2. Return the saucepan to medium heat. Cook, stirring constantly, until the sauce is smooth again, about 2 minutes. Then remove the pan from the heat and let it cool to lukewarm, about 1 hour. Stir before using. (You can store any leftovers in a covered jar in the refrigerator for up to 1 week.)

# Chocolate Napoleons
## *with* Caramel Mousse

*Makes 2 napoleons; serves 2*
◆◆◆◆◆◆◆◆◆

**Here phyllo sheets** are sprinkled with sugar and cocoa to make chocolate crisps, which are then layered with luscious caramel mousse and drizzled with homemade caramel sauce and chocolate syrup. This makes a stunning presentation, rich in flavor with contrasting light textures, and will be a sure-fire hit with your heart's desire.

**FOR THE CHOCOLATE CRISPS:**

**2 tablespoons sugar**

**1 tablespoon unsweetened cocoa powder**

**2 sheets frozen phyllo dough, thawed**

**2 tablespoons unsalted butter, melted**

**FOR THE CARAMEL MOUSSE:**

**1/2 cup cold whipping (heavy) cream**

**3 1/2 tablespoons Rich Caramel Sauce (page 259)**

**FOR SERVING:**

**2 tablespoons Rich Caramel Sauce (page 259), warmed**

**2 tablespoons store-bought chocolate syrup**

**PANS REQUIRED:**

**2 baking sheets**

**1. MAKE THE CHOCOLATE CRISPS:** Place a rack in the lower third of the oven and preheat the oven to 350°F. Line a baking sheet with parchment paper, and set it aside.

**2.** Place the sugar and cocoa powder in a small bowl and whisk to blend well. Set the bowl aside.

**3.** Cut each phyllo sheet crosswise into 3 equal pieces; then stack the pieces to make 2 stacks. Cover the stacks with plastic wrap and then a kitchen towel to keep the phyllo from drying out while you work with it.

**4.** Place 1 piece of phyllo on the prepared baking sheet, and brush a little of the melted butter over it. Sprinkle 1 quarter of the cocoa-sugar mixture over the butter, and top with another piece of the phyllo. Brush the phyllo with butter and sprinkle with 1 quarter of the cocoa mixture. Top with another piece of phyllo, pressing down on it gently, and brush it with butter. Repeat the process with the remaining phyllo, cocoa-sugar mixture, and butter to make 2 stacks. Refrigerate the phyllo stacks for 10 minutes.

**5.** Remove the stacks from the refrigerator. While they are still on the baking sheet, use a sharp knife to cut each stack into 3 irregular triangular pieces (see Note, page 382). Place a piece of parchment paper over the stacks and weight the stacks by placing another baking sheet on top. Bake until the phyllo crisps are golden, 14 to 15 minutes.

**6.** Remove the phyllo crisps from the oven. Remove the top baking sheet and carefully peel off the top parchment. Place the bottom baking sheet on a wire rack and let the crisps cool on the baking sheet. The crisps can be prepared up to 6 hours in advance, covered loosely with waxed paper at room temperature.

**7. MAKE THE CARAMEL MOUSSE:** Place the cream in a medium-size mixing bowl and beat with a hand-held electric mixer on high speed until stiff peaks form, about 2 minutes. Then beat in the $3\frac{1}{2}$ tablespoons caramel sauce on high speed until well blended, 20 to 30 seconds.

**8.** To assemble the napoleons, place a phyllo crisp (1 triangular stack) on each dessert plate and top with a tablespoon of the caramel mousse. Repeat the layers of phyllo and mousse, and top with the remaining crisps. Drizzle each napoleon with a tablespoon of warm caramel sauce and a tablespoon of chocolate syrup.

# Double Hot Chocolate Soufflés

*Makes 2 soufflés; serves 2*
◆◆◆◆◆◆◆◆◆

**This soufflé is** a luscious combination of bittersweet and milk chocolate. Triple the dose by spooning Hot Chocolate Crème Anglaise into the center of the soufflés. To serve for Valentine's Day, cuddle the hot dishes in white or red cloth napkins to protect eager fingers, then place them on your best china dessert plates. For that extra touch, surround the soufflés on the plates with rose petals.

2 ounces premium-quality milk
    chocolate (such as Lindt),
    finely chopped

1/2 ounce bittersweet or semisweet
    chocolate, finely chopped

3 tablespoons whipping (heavy)
    cream

1 tablespoon sugar, plus more for
    preparing the soufflé dishes

2 teaspoons unsalted butter,
    at room temperature,
    plus more for greasing
    the soufflé dishes

1 teaspoon cognac (optional)

1/2 teaspoon pure vanilla extract

**Pinch of salt**

**1 large egg, separated**

**White of 1 large egg**

**Pinch of cream of tartar**

**Confectioners' sugar, for garnish**

**Hot Chocolate Crème Anglaise
    (page 388), for serving
    (optional)**

**BAKING DISHES REQUIRED:**

**Two 1-cup soufflé dishes**

**1 baking sheet**

**1.** MAKE COLLARS FOR THE SOUFFLE DISHES: Tear two 14- x 7-inch strips of aluminum foil and fold them over to make long, 3½-inch-wide strips. Wrap a foil strip around the outside of each soufflé dish, allowing it to extend 2 inches above the rim. Secure the foil strips with string. Place the soufflé dishes on a baking sheet for easier handling.

**2.** Place the milk chocolate, bittersweet chocolate, cream, 1 tablespoon sugar, and 2 teaspoons butter in a small, heavy saucepan over medium heat. Cook, stirring constantly, until the chocolate melts and the mixture is smooth, 3 to 5 minutes. Remove the pan from the heat and let the mixture cool to lukewarm, 20 to 30 minutes, then stir in the cognac (if using), vanilla, and salt.

**3.** Place a rack in the center of the oven and preheat the oven to 350°F. Lightly butter the soufflé dishes, completely covering the bottom and sides, and sprinkle the interior with sugar. Shake out the excess.

**4.** Add the egg yolk to the lukewarm chocolate mixture, and whisk to blend.

**5.** Place the egg whites and the cream of tartar in a medium-size mixing bowl and beat with a hand-held electric mixer on high speed until the whites are shiny and hold soft peaks, 60 to 80 seconds. Fold the egg whites into the chocolate mixture in two batches.

**6.** Spoon the mixture into the prepared soufflé dishes, dividing it evenly between them. Bake the soufflés until they are puffed and set, 20 minutes.

**7.** Remove the baking sheet from the oven and sift confectioners' sugar over the soufflés. Remove the foil strip and serve immediately, topped with spoonfuls of the Hot Chocolate Crème Anglaise, if desired.

# Hot Chocolate Crème Anglaise

## This luscious custard

sauce tastes just like a cup of rich hot cocoa, only thicker. It cooks up quickly and makes a nice topping for custards and puddings. Or, if you prefer, pour spoonfuls on small serving plates and place a couple of slices of Presto Pound Cake (page 83) on top. Garnish the cake with fresh blackberries or fresh raspberries.

**MAKES ¼ CUP**

¼ **cup half-and-half**
**Yolk of 1 large egg**
**1 tablespoon sugar**
**2 ounces imported milk chocolate (such as Lindt), finely chopped**
½ **teaspoon pure vanilla extract**

1. Pour the half-and-half into a small saucepan and bring it to a simmer over medium-high heat, 2½ to 3 minutes.

2. Meanwhile, place the egg yolk and sugar in a small bowl and whisk until the mixture is thick and pale, about 30 seconds.

3. Whisk about half of the hot half-and-half into the egg yolk mixture; then pour that back into the saucepan, whisking as you pour. Cook over medium heat, stirring constantly with a wooden spoon, until the mixture heavily coats the back of the spoon, about 2 minutes. Do not overcook. Remove the pan from the heat.

4. Add the milk chocolate and vanilla to the sauce and stir until smooth. Serve warm or at room temperature.

# Vanilla Bean Soufflé

*Makes 2 soufflés; serves 2*
◆◆◆◆◆◆◆◆◆

**For some,** the tropical floral flavor of vanilla romances the heart (and stomach). Never mind chocolate, vanilla is the dessert aroma of choice. If you agree, you'll love these fragrant soufflés. They get a wonderful depth of flavor from Tuaca, an Italian liqueur that tastes of vanilla, pineapple, and citrus. The individual soufflés rise quite high in the oven and fall rapidly, so call your guest to the table before you take the soufflés out of the oven.

½ cup half-and-half

1 piece of vanilla bean (2 inches), or ½ teaspoon vanilla paste

1 tablespoon all-purpose flour

3 tablespoons sugar, plus more for preparing the soufflé dishes

Pinch of salt

1 large egg, separated

1 teaspoon Tuaca liqueur, or ¼ teaspoon pure vanilla extract

Unsalted butter, at room temperature, for greasing the soufflé dishes

White of 1 large egg

Pinch of cream of tartar

Pineapple Crème Anglaise (page 391) or Hot Chocolate Crème Anglaise (page 388), for serving

BAKING DISHES REQUIRED:

Two 1-cup soufflé dishes

1 baking sheet

**1.** Pour the half-and-half into a small, heavy saucepan. Split the vanilla bean lengthwise and scrape the seeds into the saucepan, then drop in the split bean (or stir in the vanilla paste). Bring the mixture to a boil over medium-high heat, and immediately remove it from the heat. Cover the saucepan and let the cream cool to room temperature, about 1 hour. Remove the vanilla bean (if using) and discard it.

**2.** Place the flour, 2 tablespoons of the sugar, and the salt in a small bowl and whisk to blend well. Whisk the flour mixture into the cooled cream mixture (still in the saucepan), stirring until the mixture is smooth.

**3.** Return the saucepan to medium heat and cook the soufflé base, stirring, until thick and smooth, about 5 minutes. Remove the pan from the heat.

**4.** Stir the egg yolk and Tuaca into the soufflé base and transfer the mixture to a small bowl. Let it cool to room temperature, stirring it occasionally.

**5.** Place a rack in the center of the oven and preheat the oven to 350°F. Lightly grease the soufflé dishes, completely covering the bottom and sides, and sprinkle the interior with sugar. Shake out the excess.

**6. MAKE COLLARS FOR THE SOUFFLE DISHES:** Tear two 14- x 7-inch strips of aluminum foil and fold them over to make long 3½-inch-wide strips. Wrap a foil strip around the outside of each soufflé dish, allowing it to extend 2 inches above the rim. Secure the foil strips with string. Place the soufflé dishes on a baking sheet for easier handling.

**7.** Place the egg whites and cream of tartar in a medium-size mixing bowl and beat with a hand-held electric mixer on medium until foamy, about 20 seconds. Sprinkle the remaining 1 tablespoon of sugar over the egg whites, increase the mixer speed to high, and beat until they form stiff, glossy peaks, 1 to 1½ minutes. Fold the egg whites into the soufflé base in 2 batches.

**8.** Spoon the soufflé mixture into the prepared soufflé dishes, dividing it evenly between them. Bake the soufflés until they are puffed and golden brown on top, 28 minutes.

**9.** Remove the soufflés from the oven. Carefully remove the foil, wrap the soufflé dishes in napkins for safe handling, and serve immediately with the Pineapple Crème Anglaise (facing page) or the Hot Chocolate Crème Anglaise (page 388).

# Pineapple Crème Anglaise

**Pineapple juice gives** this custard sauce a light, fruity flavor that is a delicious accent to soufflés, cream puffs, and pound cake.

**MAKES ABOUT ¼ CUP**

¼ **cup pineapple juice, fresh or canned**
¼ **cup half-and-half**
**Yolk of 1 large egg**
**1 tablespoon sugar**
**1 teaspoon Tuaca liqueur, or ½ teaspoon pure vanilla extract**

**1.** Fill a medium-size bowl with ice and water, and set it aside.

**2.** Place the pineapple juice in a 2-cup microwave-safe bowl and microwave on high power until the juice reduces to 2 teaspoons, 5 to 6 minutes.

**3.** Pour the half-and-half and reduced pineapple juice into a small saucepan and cook, stirring occasionally, over medium-high heat until the mixture comes to a boil, 1 to 2 minutes.

**4.** Meanwhile, place the egg yolk and sugar in a small bowl and whisk until the mixture is thick and pale.

**5.** Whisk about half of the hot half-and-half mixture into the egg yolk mixture; then pour that back into the saucepan, whisking as you pour. Cook over medium heat, stirring constantly with a wooden spoon, until the mixture heavily coats the back of the spoon, about 2 minutes. Do not overcook. Remove the saucepan from the heat.

**6.** Stir the Tuaca into the sauce. Place a fine-mesh sieve over a small bowl, and strain the sauce through it. Place the small bowl in the bowl of ice water, and let the sauce cool, stirring it occasionally. Serve warm or at room temperature.

# Vanilla Banana Caramel Flans

*Makes 2 flans; serves 2*
◆◆◆◆◆◆◆◆◆

**I like a flan** that is more silky than creamy, so this one is made with half-and-half instead of heavy cream; the banana puree adds richness. The flavor is astonishingly intense and makes a sophisticated dessert. If you like, garnish the plate with slices of caramelized banana: Cut one or two bananas into long diagonal slices and toss them with a bit of lemon juice. Arrange them on a baking sheet, sprinkle with light brown sugar, and broil until the sugar melts; it will take about one minute.

½ cup plus 3 tablespoons sugar
1 very ripe banana
½ teaspoon fresh lemon juice
¾ cup half-and-half
2 large eggs
Yolk of 1 large egg
1 teaspoon pure vanilla extract
Boiling water, for the baking dish

PANS REQUIRED:
Two 1-cup soufflé dishes or ramekins
1 baking pan

1. Place a rack in the center of the oven and preheat the oven to 325°F. Set aside a baking pan that will hold the soufflé dishes. Place a fine-mesh sieve over a medium-size mixing bowl, and set it aside.

**2.** Pour ⅓ cup of water into a small saucepan, add ½ cup of the sugar, and bring to a boil over medium-high heat, stirring constantly until the sugar dissolves. Then boil, without stirring, until the color turns golden, 2 to 3 minutes. Reduce the heat to low and continue cooking until the color is a medium golden amber, 1 to 2 minutes.

**3.** Immediately remove the saucepan from the heat and spoon 1½ tablespoons of the caramel into each soufflé dish. Reserve the remaining caramel in the saucepan. Set the soufflé dishes aside.

**4.** Peel the banana and slice it into the saucepan. Add the lemon juice and mash the banana, caramel, and lemon juice together with a potato masher or a pastry blender. Add the half-and-half and the remaining 3 tablespoons of sugar. Place the pan over medium-high heat and bring the mixture to a boil. Cover the saucepan, reduce the heat, and simmer until the banana is cooked, 1 minute. Then remove the pan from the heat and strain the mixture through the sieve, pressing down hard on the banana to extract as much pulp as possible. Scrape off the pulp clinging to the outside bottom of the sieve and add it to the custard mixture in the bowl.

**5.** Whisk the eggs, egg yolk, and vanilla into the custard mixture, and pour the mixture evenly over the caramel in the soufflé dishes, dividing it evenly between them. Place the soufflé dishes in the baking pan and pour boiling water into the pan to reach halfway up the sides of the soufflé dishes. Place the baking pan in the oven and bake the flans until the centers are just set, 25 to 30 minutes.

**6.** Remove the baking pan from the oven and carefully lift the soufflé dishes from the pan with a metal spatula. Let the flans cool completely on a wire rack. Then cover them with plastic wrap and refrigerate until well chilled, 6 hours or overnight.

**7.** To serve, run a small sharp knife around the inside of the soufflé dishes to loosen the flans. Cover a soufflé dish with a dessert plate, and quickly invert the flan onto the plate. Pour the caramel mixture remaining in the soufflé dish over the flan. Repeat with the second flan. Serve immediately.

# Baked Raspberry Almond French Toast

*Makes 2 French toasts; serves 2*

◆◆◆◆◆◆◆◆◆

**When you have** an occasion to celebrate, this is the breakfast to start off the day: croissants spread with raspberry preserves, soaked in cinnamon-almond-flavored custard, then rolled in sliced almonds and baked golden brown. Serve them with warm honey or a sprinkling of confectioners' sugar, and top with fresh raspberries.

½ cup whole milk

1 large egg

2 tablespoons sugar

2 tablespoons amaretto
  (almond liqueur), or
  ½ teaspoon almond extract

¼ teaspoon ground cinnamon

⅛ teaspoon salt

3 tablespoons raspberry preserves

2 large store-bought croissants,
  cut in half horizontally

Unsalted butter, at room
  temperature, for greasing the
  baking sheet

¼ cup sliced almonds

1 tablespoon unsalted butter, melted

Honey, warmed, or confectioners'
  sugar, for garnish

Fresh raspberries, for garnish

PANS REQUIRED:

One shallow 1-quart baking dish

1 heavy baking sheet

**1.** Place the milk, egg, sugar, amaretto, cinnamon, and salt in the baking dish, and whisk to blend well.

**2.** Spread 1½ tablespoons of the raspberry preserves over the bottom half of each croissant. Replace the croissant tops and press them together. Place the filled croissants in the baking dish, turning to coat them with the custard. Let the croissants soak for 30 minutes to absorb the custard mixture, turning them often.

**3.** Place a rack in the center of the oven and preheat the oven to 325°F. Grease the baking sheet.

**4.** Place the almonds in a shallow bowl. Carefully remove the soaked croissants from the baking dish and coat both sides with the almonds. Place the coated croissants on the prepared baking sheet and brush the tops with the melted butter. (Discard any custard mixture left in the baking dish.) Bake until the croissants are puffed and browned and the custard is set, 25 to 27 minutes.

**5.** Remove the baking sheet from the oven and transfer the croissants to serving plates. Drizzle honey over them, or sift confectioners' sugar over them, and garnish with fresh raspberries.

# CHAPTER 9

# Holiday Goodies You Can't Live Without

**In my single** days I cooked a few Thanksgiving meals for just myself and a friend when we couldn't get home for the big dinner. In those days I never once considered leaving out the pumpkin pie. When the jubilation of the season took hold of my better judgment I also made pecan pie—much to my chagrin when faced with the leftovers the next day.

I call that My Life Before Small-Batch. Now if I cook dinner for two, I don't have three quarters of a full-size pumpkin pie left over, calling to me. By preparing Small-Batch pies, I can even justify the multi-indulgent joys of eating two different types with a holiday meal.

In this chapter you will find a wonderful mix of desserts that are fun to bake during the winter holidays. Some, like pecan pie and pies with mixed nuts, are expected. Others, like baklava loaded with caramel flavors, are not. Pumpkin is present not only in a classic pie but also in a cheesecake and a maple syrup–laced bread pudding. Candied cranberries sit atop a chocolate truffle-like tart—perfect for New Year's Eve. Eggnog flavors a crème brûlée and also pairs with cranberries for a breakfast pudding that is perfect for Christmas morning. There is a fruitcake that contains people-friendly fruits and nuts and chocolate, too. And we start off the chapter with sugar cookies, because they are a must for decorating for all holiday occasions.

## CRANBERRY CRYSTALS

This is a beautiful garnish for any holiday dessert, especially the Eggnog Crème Brûlèe on page 439. The crunchy coating around each single berry or cluster is gorgeous, with swirling strands of ruby spun sugar in between. Make this garnish no more than 1 hour before serving.

MAKES ⅓ CUP

⅓ cup fresh or thawed frozen cranberries

¼ cup sugar

1. Separate the cranberries on paper towels and allow them to dry thoroughly. Place the berries close together on a piece of nonstick aluminum foil or a buttered baking sheet.

2. Place the sugar and 2 teaspoons of water in a small saucepan and bring to a boil over medium heat, stirring constantly until the sugar melts, 3 to 4 minutes. Boil for 2 minutes without stirring, then pour the melted sugar evenly over the cranberries. Do not toss the berries. Working quickly and using 2 forks, separate the berries into single berries and clusters of 3, pulling the sugar between them into strands as you go. Let the crystal berries cool completely before using them as a garnish.

# Holiday Sugar Cookies

*Makes 8 to 10 cookies; serves 2 to 4*

◆◆◆◆◆◆◆◆◆

**If you have** a small family or you just want holiday cookies for yourself, this old-fashioned sugar cookie is the one to bake! They are buttery, crisp, and easy to make— these cookies don't spread and will always come out shaped just like the cutter you used. Decorate them with colored sugars before you bake them, or paint Royal Icing on them after they cool.

¼ **cup (½ stick) unsalted butter, at room temperature, plus more for greasing the baking sheet**

¼ **cup sugar**

**1 tablespoon well-beaten egg or egg substitute**

½ **teaspoon pure vanilla extract**

½ **cup plus 1 teaspoon all-purpose flour, plus more for the work surface**

¼ **teaspoon baking powder**

⅛ **teaspoon salt**

**Royal Icing (recipe follows)**

**Paste food colors of choice**

**Cookie decorations of choice (optional)**

PAN REQUIRED:
**1 baking sheet**

**1.** Place the butter and sugar in a medium-size mixing bowl and beat with a hand-held electric mixer on high speed until fluffy. Beat in the egg and vanilla. Sift the flour, baking powder, and salt together over the butter mixture. Reduce the mixer speed to low and beat until the dough is blended.

**2.** Sprinkle a little flour on a work surface, and scrape the dough out onto the floured surface. Flour your hands and knead the dough gently for 30 seconds. Then shape the dough into a disk and wrap it in plastic wrap. Refrigerate the dough until well chilled, 2 hours or up to 24 hours.

**3.** Place a rack in the center of the oven and preheat the oven to 350°F. Lightly grease the baking sheet and set it aside. Let the dough soften slightly at room temperature to make it easier to roll out, about 10 minutes.

**4.** Sprinkle a little flour on the work surface and place the dough in the center of it. Roll the dough out to ¼-inch thickness, lifting and turning it often and dusting the work surface lightly with flour to prevent sticking. Cut out the cookies using 2- or 3-inch cutters. Pull away the excess dough from around the cookies, and transfer the cookies to the prepared baking sheet, spacing them 1 inch apart. Gently reroll the dough scraps and cut out more cookies. Transfer them to the baking

sheet. Bake the cookies until they are beginning to brown, 10 to 11 minutes.

**5.** Remove the baking sheet from the oven and let the cookies cool on the baking sheet until just firm, about 5 minutes. Then use a metal spatula to transfer the cookies to a wire rack and let them cool completely.

**6.** Either leave the Royal Icing white or divide it among as many small bowls as you have food colors, and tint the icing as desired, using separate wooden picks to dip into each jar of food color and then into the bowls of icing. Stir the tinted icings well. If necessary, thin the icing with water, ¼ teaspoon at a time, until it is thin enough to brush over the cookies in a thin layer. Use a pastry brush to spread the icing over the cookies. If you like, decorate the tops with colored candy decorations while the icing is still wet. Or pipe contrasting colors of icing on the glazed cookies. Let the cookies dry on a wire rack until they are firm, at least 4 hours.

# Royal Icing

**Powdered egg whites** make this icing harden as it dries. They are quite safe to use uncooked and can be purchased in grocery stores across the country.

**MAKES ENOUGH ICING FOR 8 TO 10 COOKIES**

2¼ cups confectioners' sugar

1 tablespoon plus 1 teaspoon pasteurized powdered egg whites, such as Just Whites

Place the confectioners' sugar and powdered egg whites in a large bowl and whisk to blend well. Whisk in 3 tablespoons of water, stirring until the icing is very smooth. If necessary, adjust the thickness by whisking in additional water by teaspoonfuls, or additional confectioners' sugar by tablespoonfuls, until the icing is medium thick. Use the icing before it hardens, usually 15 to 30 minutes after it is made.

# Gingerbread Men

*Makes 4 cookies; serves 2*
◆◆◆◆◆◆◆◆◆

**Old-fashioned** gingerbread cookies make the kitchen smell wonderful, and this recipe has just the right blend of spices to make

sure that happens. The cookies are soft inside and have a concentrated yet not overly spicy flavor, and the dough is very easy to work with and holds its shape well during baking. After rolling out and cutting the dough, decorate the cookies with cinnamon candies, dried currants, licorice strips, mini chocolate chips, marshmallows, small jelly beans, and other candies.

½ cup plus 2 tablespoons all-purpose flour, plus extra for the work surface

⅛ teaspoon baking soda

Pinch of salt

¼ teaspoon plus ⅛ teaspoon ground ginger

Pinch of ground cinnamon

2 tablespoons sugar

2 tablespoons solid vegetable shortening

2 tablespoons light or dark molasses

1 teaspoon well-beaten egg or egg substitute

½ teaspoon white vinegar

Currants and cinnamon candies, for decorating

PAN REQUIRED:

1 baking sheet

A 4-inch gingerbread-man cutter

## THE MAKING OF A MAN

If you do not have a 4-inch gingerbread-man cutter, make your own pattern: Draw a figure that is 4 inches high and 2½ inches wide on parchment paper. Cut it out; lay it on the dough, and use the tip of a sharp knife to trace around the figure. Then lift off the pattern and repeat to make more cookies.

1. Place the flour, baking soda, salt, ginger, and cinnamon in a small bowl and whisk to blend.

2. Place the sugar, shortening, molasses, beaten egg, and vinegar in a medium-size mixing bowl. Beat with a hand-held electric mixer on low speed until blended, 20 seconds. Then increase the mixer speed to medium and beat until the mixture is smooth and creamy, about 30 seconds. Add the flour mixture and beat until the dough is well blended, about 15 seconds.

Transfer the dough to a piece of plastic wrap and shape it into a disk; wrap the dough well and refrigerate it for 2 hours or overnight.

**3.** Place a rack in the center of the oven and preheat the oven to 375°F. Set aside an ungreased baking sheet.

**4.** Generously flour a work surface. Roll out the dough to ⅛-inch thickness, sprinkling it with additional flour as necessary to keep it from sticking. Cut out cookies with a 4-inch gingerbread-man cutter, or trace around a pattern with the tip of a sharp knife. Use a floured metal spatula to lift the cookies and transfer them to the baking sheet. Press the currants into the dough to form the eyes, nose, and mouth of the gingerbread men, and press cinnamon into the bodies for buttons. Bake until the cookies are lightly browned, 8 minutes.

**5.** Remove the baking sheet from the oven and place it on a wire rack to cool for 2 minutes. Then use a metal spatula to transfer the cookies to a wire rack. Let them cool completely.

## variation
# Glazed Gingerbread Men

**Bake the** Gingerbread Men without decorating them. While they are cooling, combine ½ cup of confectioners' sugar, 1 tablespoon of water, and 1½ teaspoons of light corn syrup in a small bowl and mix well. When the cookies have cooled completely, spread this glaze over them, stirring the mixture before each dip of your brush. The glaze will take a while to set; press the decorations into the icing before it is dry. Let the cookies dry on the wire rack for at least 2 hours.

# Peppermint Candy Shortbread Cookies

*Makes 5 cookies; serves 2*
◆◆◆◆◆◆◆◆◆

**The very festive** finish for the baked Shortbread Dainties will definitely sweeten your disposition. Melted white chocolate is brushed on the tender cookies, then crushed peppermints are pressed into the warm glaze. I've used a small heart-shaped cutter to make cookie bites at Christmas and on Valentine's Day.

1 recipe Shortbread Dainties (page 191), baked and cooled

¼ cup good-quality white chocolate chips (such as Ghirardelli)

¼ teaspoon solid vegetable shortening

¼ cup crushed hard peppermint candy

**PAN REQUIRED:**

**1 baking sheet**

**1.** Arrange the cookies on a wire rack.

**2.** Place the white chocolate chips and vegetable shortening in a small microwave-safe bowl, and microwave on high power until the chocolate chips are partially melted, 45 seconds to 1 minute. Then stir the chocolate mixture until smooth.

**3.** Brush the white chocolate mixture over half of each cookie, and let the glaze cool but not set, 10 minutes. While it is still soft, sprinkle the crushed candy over the white chocolate. Let the cookies stand until the coating is hardened.

# Chocolate Orange Roulade

*Makes 1 cake; serves 2 or 3*
◆◆◆◆◆◆◆◆◆

## This miniature roulade

is a very rich, fragrantly chocolate dessert. Resembling the classic French Christmas dessert, *bûche de Noël,* the cake roll is tender, the classic ganache frosting has a superb, thick, fudgy texture that clings to the roll without being too stiff, and the glazed orange peel makes a festive garnish. Orange is a natural flavor ally for chocolate, in here it is present in the cake roll, the filling, the frosting, and as a garnish.

**FOR THE GLAZED ORANGE ZEST:**
**1 orange**
**¼ cup sugar**
**1½ teaspoons apple cider vinegar**

**FOR THE CAKE:**
**Unsalted butter, at room temperature, for greasing the pan**
**Yolk of 1 large egg**
**4 tablespoons granulated sugar**
**¼ teaspoon pure vanilla extract**
**1 tablespoon cake flour**
**2 teaspoons unsweetened cocoa powder**
**Pinch of salt**

½ teaspoon freshly grated
   orange zest

**Whites of 2 large eggs,
   at room temperature**

⅛ teaspoon cream of tartar

¼ **cup confectioners' sugar**

**FOR THE FILLING AND FROSTING:**
1½ **ounces bittersweet chocolate,
   finely chopped**

¼ **cup cold whipping (heavy) cream**

**1 tablespoon Grand Marnier,
   Cointreau, or orange juice**

**Rich Chocolate Orange Frosting
   (recipe follows)**

**PAN REQUIRED:**
**1 standard loaf pan
   (9 x 5 inches)**

**1.** **MAKE THE GLAZED ORANGE ZEST:**
Using a vegetable peeler, remove the
zest of the orange in strips, taking care
not to pick up the white pith. Turn the
strips over and gently scrape off any
remaining white pith with a small sharp
knife. Cut the zest into matchstick-size
slivers and place it in a small saucepan.
(Reserve ½ teaspoon for the cake
batter.) Add water to cover and bring
it to a boil over high heat. Immediately
drain the zest in a fine-mesh sieve and
rinse under cold water. Drain well.

**2.** Place the sugar, vinegar, and ⅓ cup
water in the same small saucepan,
and bring to a simmer over medium
heat, stirring constantly until the
sugar dissolves, 3 to 5 minutes. Add
the orange zest slivers and simmer,
uncovered, until they are translucent,
about 10 minutes. Drain the slivers
and spread them out on a piece of
aluminum foil to cool. (The glazed
orange zest can be made ahead; place
the zest in a covered container and
refrigerate.)

**3.** **MAKE THE CAKE:** Place a rack in
the center of the oven and preheat the
oven to 350°F. Grease the loaf pan and
line the bottom with parchment paper.
Set the pan aside.

**4.** Place the egg yolk, 3 tablespoons
of the sugar, and 2 teaspoons very hot
water in a medium-size mixing bowl.
Beat with a hand-held electric mixer
on high speed until the mixture is pale
and has thickened, 1½ to 2 minutes;
when you turn off the mixer and lift a
beater, a ribbon of egg mixture should
drizzle back onto the remainder in the
bowl and leave a "track" that sits on
the top before it sinks in. Beat in the
vanilla. Sift the flour, cocoa powder,

and salt together over the batter. Then add the zest and fold them all in gently but thoroughly with a rubber spatula.

**5.** Wash the mixer beaters and dry them thoroughly. Place the egg whites and cream of tartar in a medium-size mixing bowl and beat on medium speed until foamy, about 15 seconds. Sprinkle the remaining 1 tablespoon of granulated sugar over the egg whites and beat until soft peaks form, about 1¼ minutes. Fold the beaten whites into the yolk mixture, making sure no streaks of white remain.

**6.** Spoon the batter into the prepared pan, and smooth the top with a rubber spatula. Bake until a toothpick inserted in the center comes out clean, 12 to 13 minutes.

**7.** While the cake is baking, spread a clean kitchen towel on the counter and sift the confectioners' sugar onto an area the size of the baking pan. As soon as the cake is finished baking, invert the pan over the sugared area and lift off the pan; peel off the parchment paper.

**8.** Fold one end of the towel over a short end of the cake, and roll up the cake in the towel. Place the roll, seam side down, on a wire rack to cool.

**9. MAKE THE FILLING:** Put the chocolate in a microwave-safe bowl and microwave on high power until it is very glossy, 1 to 1½ minutes. Stir until it is smooth, and then let the chocolate cool to room temperature. The chocolate should be cooled but still soft.

**10.** Place the cream and Grand Marnier in a medium-size mixing bowl and beat with a hand-held electric mixer on high speed until stiff peaks form, about 1¼ minutes. Beat in the melted chocolate until blended, about 10 seconds.

**11.** When the cake has cooled, unroll it. Spread the filling on the cake to within 1 inch from the edges. Roll up the cake, using the towel to help (do not roll the towel into the cake). Place the cake roll, seam side down, on a serving platter and frost it with the Rich Chocolate Orange Frosting. Sprinkle the glazed orange zest over the cake. Let the cake stand for 1 hour before serving.

# Rich Chocolate Orange Frosting

**This is a classic** ganache frosting with a twist—an orange flavor supplied by a bit of Grand Marnier, Cointreau, or triple sec. You can heat it to make a silky fudge sauce perfect for ice cream, cake, or poached pears.

**MAKES 1½ CUPS**

½ **cup whipping (heavy) cream**
**Pinch of salt**
5 **ounces premium-quality bittersweet or semisweet chocolate, finely chopped**
3 **ounces premium-quality milk chocolate, finely chopped**
2 **tablespoons Grand Marnier, Cointreau, or triple sec**

Place the cream and salt in a medium-size microwave-safe bowl and microwave on high power until the cream reaches a boil, 1 to 1½ minutes. Add both chocolates and swirl to immerse the chocolate in the hot cream. Let the mixture stand until the chocolate is softened, 1 minute; then stir until smooth. Stir in the Grand Marnier and let the frosting cool to room temperature, stirring occasionally, 2 to 2½ hours (see Note). The frosting should be thick enough to spread. (Any leftover frosting can be stored in an airtight container for up to a week in the refrigerator; microwave the cold frosting on medium power until it is softened to the desired consistency. Stir well before using.)

**NOTE:** If you wish to cool the frosting quickly, put the mixture in a bowl and place the bowl in a bowl of ice cubes. Stir the frosting frequently until spreadably thick, 15 to 20 minutes.

# Lane Cake

*Makes 2 cakes; serves 2*

◆◆◆◆◆◆◆◆

**I think Lane cake** is a must at Christmas—the candied fruit in the filling is so festive. It is said that this cake originated in Alabama, right down the Interstate from where I live, and that it won a prize at the state fair for Emma Rylander Lane sometime at the end of the 19th century. The conventional version is especially popular in the South. Cake layers are stacked with a cooked bourbon custard full of nuts, candied fruit, and coconut, then the whole thing is covered in a meringue frosting. For this Small-Batch version, I've changed the frosting to an easy whipped cream, mascarpone, and bourbon mixture.

**FOR THE CAKE AND PANS:**

2 tablespoons plus 2 teaspoons unsalted butter, at room temperature, plus more for greasing the cans

½ cup plus 2 teaspoons sifted all-purpose flour, plus more for flouring the cans

White of 1 large egg

2 tablespoons plus 2 teaspoons whole milk

½ teaspoon pure vanilla extract

¼ cup sugar

¼ teaspoon baking powder

⅛ teaspoon salt

Pinch of ground nutmeg

**FOR THE FILLING AND FROSTING:**

Yolk of 1 large egg

2 tablespoons sugar

2 teaspoons unsalted butter, at room temperature

1 tablespoon bourbon

2 tablespoons chopped dried tart
  cherries, dried cranberries, or
  dried apricots

2 tablespoons (packed) sweetened
  flaked coconut

1 tablespoon finely chopped pecans

¼ ounce bittersweet or semisweet
  chocolate, finely chopped

Bourbon Cream Frosting
  (recipe follows)

PANS REQUIRED:

Two 14- or 14.5-ounce cans (see page 6)

1 baking sheet

1. Place a rack in the center of the oven and preheat the oven to 350°F. Grease and lightly flour the cans, tapping out the excess. Place the cans on a baking sheet for easier handling, and set it aside.

2. MAKE THE CAKES: Place the egg white, milk, and vanilla in a small bowl and whisk to mix.

3. Place the flour in a medium-size mixing bowl. Add the sugar, baking powder, salt, and nutmeg and whisk to combine. Add the 2 tablespoons plus 2 teaspoons butter and half of the milk mixture. Beat with a hand-held electric mixer on low speed until the dry ingredients are moistened, about 15 seconds.

Increase the speed to medium and beat until the batter is lightened, 30 seconds. Scrape down the sides of the bowl. Pour in the remaining milk mixture and beat at medium speed until the batter is well blended, 20 seconds.

4. Spoon the batter into the prepared cans, dividing it evenly between them. Bake the cakes until a toothpick inserted into the center of one comes out clean, about 25 minutes.

5. Remove the baking sheet from the oven, transfer the cans to a wire rack, and let them cool for 15 minutes. Then run a sharp knife around the edges of the cakes and remove them from the cans. Let the cakes cool upright on the rack. (The cakes can be made 1 day ahead. Wrap them in plastic wrap and store them at room temperature.)

6. MAKE THE FILLING: Place the egg yolk and sugar in a medium-size mixing bowl and beat with a hand-held electric mixer on medium speed until the mixture is thick and pale, about 1 minute. Reduce the mixer speed to low and beat in the butter just until blended, 10 seconds. Then stir in the bourbon and dried cherries.

**7.** Using a rubber spatula, transfer the mixture to a small saucepan. Cook the filling over medium-low heat, stirring it constantly with a wooden spoon, until the sugar is melted and the mixture is thick, 8 to 10 minutes. Remove the pan from the heat and stir in the coconut and pecans. Let the mixture cool to room temperature. Then stir in the chocolate.

**8.** Cut each cake in half horizontally. Place the bottom cake layers on serving plates, and spread half of the filling over the layers, dividing it evenly between them. Replace the top layers and spread the remaining filling on top, dividing it evenly between the 2 cakes. Spread the Bourbon Cream Frosting around the sides of both of the cakes.

# Bourbon Cream Frosting

**Lane cakes are** typically finished with a boiled frosting called seven-minute frosting. This lighter frosting is easier to make and adds distinctive Southern flavor to the cake.

**MAKES 1¼ CUPS**

**2 tablespoons mascarpone cheese or cream cheese, at room temperature**
**3 tablespoons confectioners' sugar**
**1 tablespoon bourbon**
**½ teaspoon pure vanilla extract**
**⅔ cup whipping (heavy) cream**

**1.** Place the mascarpone, 1 tablespoon of the confectioners' sugar, the bourbon, and the vanilla in a small bowl, and stir until smooth.

**2.** Place the cream and the remaining 2 tablespoons of confectioners' sugar in a medium-size mixing bowl and beat with a hand-held electric mixer on high speed until firm peaks form. Add the mascarpone mixture and beat just until the frosting is stiff enough to spread, about 10 seconds.

# Cranberry Pear Charlottes

*Makes 2 charlottes; serves 2*
◆◆◆◆◆◆◆◆◆

## Charlottes–molded

desserts with caramelized bread slices encasing a fruit filling— deserve a revival. The bread soaks up the fruit juices and caramelizes into a crisp yet soft crust that is unrecognizable as bread. Apple charlotte is the most familiar version, but a combination of pears and cranberries makes a fine charlotte, too, perfect for Thanksgiving, Hanukkah, Christmas, or any autumn or winter occasion. The delicate, vanilla-scented pear sabayon adds richness without making it a heavy dessert.

**FOR THE CRUST:**

**3 tablespoons unsalted butter**

**2 teaspoons sugar**

**1/8 teaspoon ground cinnamon**

**3 to 4 slices (1/4-inch-thick) of egg bread (brioche or challah)**

**FOR THE FILLING AND FOR SERVING:**

**1 1/2 firm, ripe pears, preferably Bosc**

**1 tablespoon unsalted butter**

**1 1/2 tablespoons sugar**

**1/8 teaspoon ground cinnamon**

**1/4 cup fresh or thawed frozen cranberries**

**1 tablespoon pear brandy (optional)**

**Vanilla Pear Sabayon Sauce (recipe follows)**

**PAN REQUIRED:**

**1 jumbo muffin pan (3/4-cup capacity)**

1. Place a rack in the center of the oven and preheat the oven to 375°F.

2. MAKE THE CRUST: Place the butter and sugar in a medium-size skillet over medium heat and cook, stirring constantly, until the butter has melted and the sugar has dissolved. Whisk in the cinnamon and remove the skillet from the heat.

3. Lay the bread on a cutting board, and using a 2-inch cookie cutter, cut out rounds of bread to fit the bottoms of 2 muffin cups. Cut the remaining bread into 1¾-inch strips to fit around the sides of the muffin cups. Discard the scraps. Brush one side of the bread pieces with the melted butter mixture. Arrange the rounds, buttered sides down, in the bottoms of 2 of the muffin cups. Arrange the strips around the sides of the muffin cups, buttered sides against the cups, to fit snugly and cover the sides completely, trimming them to fit. Set the muffin pan aside.

4. MAKE THE FILLING: Peel the pears and cut them into quarters. Remove the cores. Cut the quarters crosswise into thin slices.

5. Melt the butter in the same skillet over medium-high heat. Whisk in the sugar and cinnamon. Add the pears and stir to coat them with the butter mixture. Cook, stirring occasionally, until the pears are almost tender, about 2 minutes. Add the cranberries and pear brandy, if using, and cook for 2 minutes.

6. Pack the pear mixture into the prepared muffin cups, dividing it evenly between them. Fill the empty muffin cups halfway with water to prevent them from scorching. Bake until the bread is golden, about 20 minutes. Remove the muffin pan from the oven, place it on a wire rack, and let it cool for 10 minutes.

7. To serve, carefully pour the water from the empty muffin cups, and then invert the charlottes onto a baking sheet or cutting board. Use a spatula to lift them onto serving plates. Serve hot, with the Vanilla Pear Sabayon Sauce.

# Vanilla Pear Sabayon Sauce

**This sabayon** is scented with vanilla and pear brandy, then chilled and folded into whipped cream for a fluffy texture. Since it is made in a bowl above simmering water, be sure you use a saucepan that holds the bowl in place securely. Try it out before beginning.

**MAKES ABOUT ⅔ CUP**

2 large egg yolks

2 tablespoons sugar

1 piece vanilla bean (about ¼ of the bean), split lengthwise, or ¼ teaspoon vanilla paste

1 tablespoon pear brandy or pear nectar

¼ cup plus 2 tablespoons whipping (heavy) cream

**1.** Bring a saucepan half filled with water to a simmer, or bring water to a simmer in the bottom of a double boiler. Fill a larger bowl with ice and water, and set it aside.

**2.** Place the egg yolks and sugar in a medium-size metal bowl, or in the top of the double boiler, and whisk to blend. Scrape the vanilla bean seeds into the yolk mixture. Whisk in the pear brandy and 2 tablespoons of the cream. Set the bowl over the simmering water (do not let the bottom of the bowl touch the water) and cook, whisking constantly, until the mixture is frothy and thickened, 4 to 5 minutes. When you drag a spoon across the bottom of the saucepan, it should leave a trail of uncovered pan that lingers before the sabayon mixture fills it in.

**3.** Remove the bowl from the simmering water and place it in the bowl of ice water. Let the sabayon mixture cool, stirring it gently with a rubber spatula, until it is cold.

**4.** Place the remaining ¼ cup of cream in a medium-size mixing bowl and beat with a hand-held electric mixer on high speed until firm peaks form, about 1¼ minutes. Gently but thoroughly fold the whipped cream into the sabayon. Use immediately.

# A Fruitcake You Will Love

*Makes 2 fruitcakes, serves 2*

◆◆◆◆◆◆◆◆◆

## Here's a Small-Batch

version of the fruitcake I've given my family and friends in recent years. It's not your grandmother's fruitcake—it contains no lurid red and green candied fruit or unidentifiable ingredients that scare people away. Loaded with figs, toasted nuts, and chopped chocolate, and fragrant with ginger and orange, the cakes are soaked in hazelnut or almond liqueur and served with a liqueur-laced chocolate sauce.

### FOR THE CAKES:

**3 tablespoons plus 1 teaspoon unsalted butter, at room temperature, plus more for greasing the molds**

**2 tablespoons all-purpose flour, plus more for flouring the molds**

**1/2 cup blanched almonds, toasted (see page 195), cooled and chopped**

**1/4 cup diced dried Calimyrna figs**

1 ounce bittersweet or semisweet
chocolate, chopped

1 tablespoon plus 1 teaspoon finely
minced crystallized ginger

2 tablespoons plus 2 teaspoons
sugar

1 medium egg, or 3 tablespoons
well-beaten egg or egg substitute

2 teaspoons Frangelico (hazelnut
liqueur) or amaretto (almond
liqueur), plus additional for
soaking the cakes

1 teaspoon grated orange zest

2 tablespoons cake flour

⅛ teaspoon salt

FOR THE SAUCE:

1 ounce bittersweet or semisweet
chocolate, chopped

2 tablespoons whipping (heavy)
cream

2 teaspoons Frangelico or amaretto

PANS REQUIRED:

1 mini Bundt pan with six 1-cup
molds or 1 jumbo muffin pan
(¾-cup capacity)

1. MAKE THE CAKES: Place a rack in
the center of the oven and preheat the
oven to 300°F. Grease and lightly flour
2 of the Bundt molds or muffin cups,
tapping out the excess flour, and set
the pan aside.

2. Place the almonds, figs, chocolate,
and ginger in a small bowl and toss
to mix well. Set aside

3. Place the 3 tablespoons plus
1 teaspoon butter and the sugar in
a medium-size mixing bowl and beat
with a hand-held electric mixer on
medium speed until the mixture is
creamy, about 1 minute. Beat in the
egg, the 2 teaspoons Frangelico, and
the orange zest just until blended,
about 10 seconds. (The mixture will
look curdled.) Sift the 2 tablespoons
all-purpose flour, the cake flour, and
salt together over the batter. Beat the
flour mixture into the egg mixture on
low speed just until blended, 10 to
15 seconds. Then stir in the fruit and
nut mixture with a wooden spoon.

4. Spoon the batter into the prepared
molds, dividing it evenly between them.
Fill the empty Bundt or muffin cups
halfway with water to prevent them
from scorching. Bake the cakes until
a toothpick inserted near the center of
one comes out clean, 32 minutes for the
Bundt pan and 35 to 38 minutes for
the muffin pan. Remove the pan from
the oven and place it on a wire rack to
cool for 10 minutes. Carefully pour the

water out of the extra molds, and turn the cakes out onto a wire rack. Brush the molded sides with 2 tablespoons of the additional Frangelico while they are hot. Let the cakes cool completely.

**5.** Cut two 10-inch squares out of a double thickness of cheesecloth. Pour about ⅓ cup of the additional Frangelico into a small bowl. Dip one of the cheesecloth squares into the Frangelico and squeeze it out gently to remove some, but not all, of the liqueur. Wrap one of the cakes in the cheese-cloth, then in aluminum foil. Repeat the process with the other fruitcake. Put the wrapped fruitcakes in the refrigerator and chill them for at least 1 week and up to 2 weeks. If you like, unwrap the cheesecakes and brush them with additional liqueur after 3 days, then wrap them again in the cheesecloth and foil. Bring the cakes to room temperature before serving.

**6.** MAKE THE SAUCE: Place the chocolate, cream, and Frangelico in a small saucepan and warm over low heat until the chocolate melts and the sauce is smooth.

**7.** To serve, unwrap the cakes and place them on serving plates. Drizzle the cakes with the sauce.

# Cranberry Upside-Down Cake

*Makes 2 cakes; serves 2*

◆◆◆◆◆◆◆◆◆

## Tender yellow butter

cake is baked over orange-scented sweetened cranberries. When you invert it, the ruby-topped cake is dripping with sweet brown sugar–cranberry syrup. It is delicious served warm with vanilla ice cream, and make a wonderful Thanksgiving dessert for those who don't like pumpkin.

### FOR THE CRANBERRY MIXTURE:

1 tablespoon plus 1 teaspoon packed light brown sugar

1 tablespoon unsalted butter

2 teaspoons frozen cranberry juice concentrate or orange juice concentrate

1 teaspoon freshly grated orange zest

¼ teaspoon ground cinnamon

⅓ cup fresh or thawed frozen cranberries

### FOR THE CAKE AND FOR SERVING:

¼ cup whole milk

Yolk of 1 large egg

½ teaspoon pure vanilla extract

⅓ cup all-purpose flour

⅓ cup granulated sugar

⅛ teaspoon baking powder

⅛ teaspoon salt

2 tablespoons unsalted butter, at room temperature

Sweetened Whipped Cream (page 36) or vanilla ice cream, for serving

### PANS REQUIRED:

Two 8-ounce cans (see page 6)

1 baking sheet

1. Place a rack in the center of the oven and preheat the oven to 375°F.

2. Place one of the cans on a piece of parchment paper, and trace the circumference. Cut out 4 rounds of parchment, and line the bottoms of the cans with a double layer. Place the cans on a baking sheet for easier handling and set it aside.

3. **MAKE THE CRANBERRY MIXTURE:** Place the brown sugar, butter, juice concentrate, orange zest, and cinnamon in a small saucepan over medium heat and cook, stirring constantly, until the sugar dissolves and the liquid is bubbling, 3 to 5 minutes. Remove the pan from the heat and pour the mixture into a small bowl. Cover and refrigerate until the cranberry juice mixture is chilled, about 1 hour. Then stir in the cranberries and spoon the mixture into the prepared cans, dividing it evenly between them.

4. **MAKE THE CAKES:** Place the milk, egg yolk, and vanilla in a small bowl and whisk to blend.

5. Place the flour, sugar, baking powder, and salt in a medium-size mixing bowl, and whisk to blend. Add the butter and half of the egg mixture. Beat with a hand-held electric mixer on low speed until the dry ingredients are moistened, 10 to 20 seconds. Increase the mixer speed to medium and beat until the batter is lightened and has slightly increased in volume, 45 seconds. Scrape down the sides of the bowl. Pour in the remaining egg mixture and beat on medium speed until the batter is well blended and lightened, 20 seconds. Scrape down the sides of the bowl.

6. Spoon the batter over the cranberry mixture in the cans, dividing it evenly between them. Bake the cakes until a toothpick inserted in the center of one comes out clean, 15 to 20 minutes.

7. Remove the baking sheet from the oven, place the cans on a wire rack, and let them cool for 10 minutes. Then invert the cans over serving plates to release the cakes. Remove the parchment and serve the cakes warm, with whipped cream or ice cream.

# Pumpkin Maple Cheesecakes

*Makes 2 cheesecakes; serves 2*

◆◆◆◆◆◆◆◆◆

**Maple syrup in** the filling and in the sauce gives this pumpkin cheesecake rich flavor and makes it perfect for that most American of holidays, Thanksgiving. But you don't have to limit it to the last Thursday in November. It's a wonderful dessert throughout the fall and winter.

Cheesecakes are normally baked in springform pans, but the individual 4½-inch cheesecake pans are too shallow for me. Since my ideal is a New York–style cheesecake, which is taller than some, I find a 4-inch tart pan just the right fit for an individual cheesecake. Plus, the scalloped edge makes a pretty presentation.

**Unsalted butter, at room temperature, for greasing the tart pans**

**FOR THE CRUST:**

¼ cup chopped pecan pieces

¼ cup shortbread cookie crumbs

1 tablespoon granulated sugar

1 tablespoon plus 2 teaspoons unsalted butter, melted

**FOR THE FILLING:**

4 ounces cream cheese, at room temperature

¼ cup firmly packed light brown sugar

¼ cup canned pumpkin puree (not pumpkin pie filling)

1 teaspoon all-purpose flour

¼ teaspoon ground cinnamon

Pinch of ground nutmeg

Pinch of salt

1 tablespoon plus 2 teaspoons well-beaten egg or egg substitute

1 tablespoon pure maple syrup

1 tablespoon whipping (heavy) cream

**FOR THE SAUCE:**

⅓ cup whipping (heavy) cream

¼ cup pure maple syrup

Pecan halves, toasted (see page 195), for garnish

**PANS REQUIRED:**

Two 4 x 1⅜-inch tart pans with removable bottoms

1 baking sheet

**1.** Place a rack in the center of the oven and preheat the oven to 350°F. Lightly grease the tart pans and place them on a baking sheet for easier handling.

**2. MAKE THE CRUST:** Place the pecans, cookie crumbs, sugar, and melted butter in a food processor and process until the pecans are minced and the crust is blended, about 10 seconds. Press the mixture firmly into the bottom of the prepared tart pans. Bake until the crusts are lightly browned, about 8 minutes. Remove the baking sheet from the oven, transfer the tart pans to a wire rack, and let them cool to room temperature. Keep the oven on.

**3. MAKE THE FILLING:** Place the cream cheese and brown sugar in a medium-size mixing bowl and beat with a hand-held electric mixer on medium speed just until smooth, about 30 seconds. Add the pumpkin, flour, cinnamon, nutmeg, and salt, and beat just until blended, about 10 seconds. Reduce the mixer speed to low and beat in the egg, maple syrup, and cream just until the batter is smooth and blended, 10 to 15 seconds, taking care not to overbeat. Pour the filling into the tart shells, dividing it evenly between them. Bake the cheesecakes until they appear dry and have begun to brown, about 28 minutes.

**4.** Remove the baking sheet from the oven, transfer the tart pans to a wire rack, and let them cool completely. Cover and refrigerate the cheesecakes until well chilled, 2 hours or overnight.

**5. MAKE THE SAUCE:** Pour the cream and maple syrup into a small saucepan and bring to a boil over medium-high heat. Reduce the heat and boil gently until the sauce reduces slightly and thickens, 3 to 5 minutes. Let the sauce cool completely.

**6.** To serve, remove the cheesecakes from the tart pans and place them on serving plates. Drizzle the sauce over the cheesecakes and garnish with pecans. (The tarts and sauce can be prepared up to 1 day ahead; cover and refrigerate. Remove them from the refrigerator 1 hour before serving.)

# Praline Mango Cake

*Makes 2 cakes; serves 2*

◆◆◆◆◆◆◆◆◆

**I like to serve** this cake on Christmas morning, with fruit and coffee, but it makes a wonderful brunch dish on any holiday. Bright mango flavor and color permeate the cake, and when you invert it onto a plate, there is a buttery pecan streusel on top.

2 tablespoons unsalted butter or margarine, at room temperature, plus more for greasing the cans

½ cup all-purpose flour, plus more for flouring the cans

¼ cup plus 1 tablespoon firmly packed light brown sugar

1 tablespoon whipping (heavy) cream

⅓ cup finely chopped pecans

1 large egg

¼ cup plus 3 tablespoons granulated sugar

3 tablespoons vegetable oil

¼ cup pureed fresh or drained jarred mango

¼ teaspoon pure vanilla extract

⅛ teaspoon baking powder

⅛ teaspoon baking soda

¼ teaspoon salt

¼ teaspoon ground cinnamon

PANS REQUIRED:

**Two 8-ounce cans (see page 6)**

**1 baking sheet**

**1.** Place a rack in the center of the oven and preheat the oven to 350°F.

**2.** Grease and flour the cans, tapping out the excess. Place one of the cans on a piece of parchment or waxed paper, and trace the circumference. Cut out 4 rounds of parchment, and line the bottom of the cans with a double layer. Grease and flour the paper. Put the cans on a baking sheet for easier handling, and set it aside.

**3.** Place the brown sugar, the 2 tablespoons butter, and the cream in a small saucepan over medium heat and cook, stirring, until the butter melts and the sugar dissolves. Spoon the mixture into the prepared cans, dividing it evenly between them. Sprinkle the pecans evenly over the brown sugar mixture.

**4.** Place the egg, granulated sugar, oil, mango, and vanilla in a medium-size mixing bowl and beat with a hand-held electric mixer on medium speed until well blended, about 20 seconds.

**5.** Place the ½ cup flour, baking powder, baking soda, salt, and cinnamon in a small bowl and whisk to blend well. Add the flour mixture to the mango mixture and beat with the mixer on low speed just until the batter is blended, about 15 seconds. Spoon the batter over the pecans in the cans,

## variation

# Praline Pumpkin Cake

**Instead of** mango, you can make an equally moist and flavorful cake using pumpkin. Just substitute ¼ cup of pure pumpkin for the mango in the recipe, and add pumpkin pie spice instead of cinnamon.

dividing it evenly between the 2 cans. Bake the cakes until a toothpick inserted in the center of one comes out clean, about 37 minutes.

**6.** Remove the baking sheet from the oven, transfer the cans to a wire rack, and let cool for 5 minutes. Then run the tip of a sharp knife around the edge of the cakes and invert the cakes onto the racks. Let them cool, pecan side up, on the wire rack. Serve warm or at room temperature.

# Vanilla Cranberry Apple Pie

*Makes 2 pies; serves 2*
◆◆◆◆◆◆◆◆◆

**A baker can't** have too many apple pies to choose from. This one is a bit more sophisticated than most—perfect for Thanksgiving or any special dinner. The vanilla bean produces a wonderful fragrance and combines with the cinnamon to impart a velvety spice flavor in these pies; you'll love how the kitchen smells while they bake. The crisp oat crumb topping absorbs some of the juices where it meets the apple and cranberry filling, all the while remaining perfectly crunchy on top.

**2 partially baked Basic Pastry shells (page 159), baked in 4 x 1⅜-inch tart pans with removable bottoms, still in the pans**

**FOR THE CRUMB TOPPING:**

**3 tablespoons all-purpose flour**

**3 tablespoons quick-cooking oats**

**2 tablespoons plus 1 teaspoon firmly packed light brown sugar**

**Pinch of salt**

**1½ tablespoons unsalted butter, melted**

**FOR THE FILLING:**

**¼ cup granulated sugar**

**1½ teaspoons cornstarch**

**¼ teaspoon ground cinnamon**

**1 piece of vanilla bean (3 inches), split lengthwise (see Note)**

**1 medium-size Granny Smith apple**

¼ **cup fresh or thawed frozen cranberries**

**2 teaspoons unsalted butter, melted**

½ **teaspoon fresh lemon juice**

PANS REQUIRED:

**4 x 1⅜-inch tart pans with removable bottoms**

**1 baking sheet**

**1.** Place a rack in the center of the oven and preheat the oven to 400°F. Place the tart pans on a baking sheet and set it aside.

**2.** MAKE THE CRUMB TOPPING: Place the flour, oats, brown sugar, and salt in a medium-size bowl, and stir to blend. Add the melted butter and stir until the topping is well mixed. Cover and refrigerate until you are ready to bake the pie. (The crumb topping can be made 1 day ahead; cover and refrigerate.)

**3.** MAKE THE FILLING: Place the granulated sugar, cornstarch, and cinnamon in a medium-size mixing bowl, and whisk to blend. Slit open the vanilla bean and scrape the seeds into the bowl; toss the mixture well.

**4.** Peel the apple and cut it in half. Remove the core and place the halves,

cut sides down, on a cutting board. Cut each in half lengthwise, then cut them crosswise into ½-inch-thick slices. Add the apples, cranberries, melted butter, and lemon juice to the sugar mixture and toss to coat the apples with the mixture.

**5.** Spoon the filling into the tart shells, dividing it evenly between them. Sprinkle the topping evenly over the pies. Place the baking sheet in the oven and immediately reduce the oven temperature to 375°F. Bake the pies until the topping is golden brown and the filling is bubbling, about 27 minutes.

**6.** Remove the baking sheet from the oven, transfer the tart pans a wire rack, and let them cool. Serve the pies slightly warm or at room temperature.

NOTE: You can use 1 teaspoon vanilla paste instead of the vanilla bean.

# Petite Pear Tarte Tatin

*Makes 2 tarts; serves 2*

◆◆◆◆◆◆◆◆◆

**The classic Tarte Tatin** consists of caramelized apples baked with the crust on top (the tart is inverted before serving). It was popularized by the Tatin sisters in their restaurant near Orleans, France, in the early years of the 20th century. Since that time, it has become such a popular dessert that cooks have used the same method with pears, pineapple, and other fruits. The pear version is particularly good at Christmas, when pears are abundant and fresh. For special holiday flavor, the pears are dressed with candied ginger. For glorious seasonal color, top the tarts with Candied Cranberries.

**Unsalted butter, at room temperature, for greasing the tart pans**

**FOR THE PASTRY:**
**1 recipe Basic Sweet Pastry dough (page 163), prepared through Step 3**

**FOR THE FILLING AND FOR SERVING:**
1 firm, ripe pear, preferably Bosc
1 teaspoon fresh lemon juice
1 tablespoon unsalted butter
2 tablespoons sugar
1 tablespoon finely minced
    crystallized ginger
1 teaspoon amaretto (almond liqueur),
    or ¼ teaspoon pure almond
    extract
4 teaspoons sliced or slivered
    almonds, lightly toasted
    (see page 195)
Candied Cranberries (page 433)
Sweetened Whipped Cream
    (page 36), for serving (optional)

**PANS REQUIRED:**
Two 4½ x ¾-inch tart pans with
    removable bottoms
1 baking sheet

**1.** Place a rack in the center of the oven and preheat the oven to 425°F. Line the tart pans with aluminum foil to prevent them from leaking. Lightly grease the foil. Place the tart pans on a baking sheet for easier handling, and set it aside.

**2. MAKE THE PASTRY:** Roll out each chilled disk of dough between 2 pieces of waxed paper to form a 5-inch round. Refrigerate the pastry rounds while you prepare the filling.

**3. MAKE THE FILLING:** Peel the pear and cut it in half. Remove the core and cut the pear halves into ½-inch slices. Cut the slices in half crosswise. Place the lemon juice in a small bowl, add the pear pieces, and toss to mix.

**4.** Place the butter and sugar in a medium-size heavy skillet and bring to a simmer over medium heat, stirring constantly until the sugar melts. Add the pears and cook, stirring occasionally, until they are tender and the syrup is beginning to thicken, 5 to 8 minutes. Remove the skillet from the heat and stir in the ginger and the amaretto.

**5.** Sprinkle the almonds on the bottom of the prepared tart pans, dividing it evenly between them. Spoon the pears evenly over the almonds. Arrange a pastry round on top of each tart, tucking the edges in around the pears. Prick the top pastry with a fork in several places. Bake the tarts until the juices are bubbling and the crust is golden brown, 18 to 20 minutes.

**6.** Remove the baking sheet from the oven, transfer the tart pans to a wire rack, and let the tarts cool for at least 15 minutes.

**7.** Working with one at a time, invert a serving plate over a tart pan. Wearing oven mitts and keeping the plate firmly pressed against the pan, invert the tart onto the plate. Spoon a few Candied Cranberries on each tart and serve them warm, with Sweetened Whipped Cream, if desired. (The tarts can be prepared up to 1 day ahead. Let them cool completely in their pans; cover and refrigerate. Before serving, reheat them in a preheated 350°F oven for 10 minutes. Then invert them onto plates as described, and serve.)

# Brandy Caramel Pumpkin Pie

*Makes 2 pies; serves 2*

◆◆◆◆◆◆◆◆◆

**You won't believe** the silky, rich sweetness this caramel sauce adds to my favorite pumpkin pie, which is the perfect conclusion to a traditional Thanksgiving feast.

I couldn't resist adding the family secret ingredient, but if you don't wish to use brandy, you can substitute another tablespoon of whipping cream.

2 partially baked Basic Sweet
   Pastry shells (page 163), baked
   in 4 x 1⅜-inch tart pans with
   removable bottoms, still in
   the pans

½ cup canned pumpkin puree
   (not pumpkin pie filling)

3 tablespoons packed dark brown
   sugar

2 tablespoons Rich Caramel Sauce
   (page 259) or store-bought
   caramel sauce

1 teaspoon all-purpose flour

Pinch of salt

½ teaspoon pumpkin pie spice

3 tablespoons whipping (heavy)
   cream

3 tablespoons well-beaten egg or
   egg substitute

1 tablespoon brandy

PANS REQUIRED:

Two 4 x 1⅜-inch tart pans with
   removable bottoms

1 baking sheet

1. Place a rack in the center of the
oven and preheat the oven to 350°F.
Place the tart pans on a baking sheet
for easier handling.

2. Place the pumpkin, brown sugar,
caramel sauce, flour, salt, and pumpkin
pie spice in a medium-size mixing
bowl and whisk until smooth. Whisk
in the cream, egg, and brandy. Pour
the filling into the tart shells, dividing
it evenly between them. Bake the
pies until the filling is just set in the
center, 25 to 30 minutes.

3. Remove the baking sheet from
the oven and transfer the tart pans
to a wire rack. Let the tarts cool
completely before serving. Remove
them from the pans to serve. (The
tarts may be prepared up to 1 day
ahead; cover and refrigerate. Remove
them from the refrigerator 1 hour
before serving.)

# Southern Pecan Pie

*Makes 2 pies; serves 2*
◆◆◆◆◆◆◆◆◆

**Pecan pie is** another time-honored Thanksgiving dessert. I like my pie spiked, and if you do too, I recommend adding Southern Comfort to flavor the pie; it is sweeter than the more traditional bourbon, but has a similar mellow flavor. If you wish, you can use bourbon with an additional tablespoon of sugar. But if you make the pie with cane syrup rather than corn syrup, as my grandmother did and my mother does (and I do too), flavor it with bourbon (and don't add the extra sugar) because cane syrup is sweeter than corn syrup.

**FOR THE CRUSTS AND FILLING:**

2 partially baked Basic Pastry shells (page 159), baked in 4½ x 1⅜-inch tart pans with removable bottoms, still in the pans

⅓ cup plus 1 tablespoon granulated sugar

1 large egg

¼ cup dark or light corn syrup or cane syrup

1 tablespoon Southern Comfort or bourbon (optional)

2 teaspoons unsalted butter, melted

½ teaspoon pure vanilla extract

Pinch of salt

⅓ cup pecan halves

**FOR THE TOPPING:**

¼ cup cold whipping (heavy) cream

1 tablespoon confectioners' sugar

1 to 2 teaspoons Southern Comfort

½ teaspoon pure vanilla extract

**PANS REQUIRED:**

**Two 4 x 1⅜-inch tart pans with
removable bottoms**

**1 baking sheet**

**1.** Place a rack in the center of the
oven and preheat the oven to 350°F.
Place the tart pans on a baking sheet
for easier handling.

**2. MAKE THE FILLING:** Place the
sugar, egg, corn syrup, Southern
Comfort if using, melted butter, vanilla,
and salt in a medium-size mixing bowl
and whisk until smooth and blended.
Arrange the pecan halves in the tart
shells, dividing them evenly between
them, and then pour the filling evenly
over the pecans. Bake the pies until
they are set, about 30 minutes.

**3.** Remove the baking sheet from
the oven, transfer the tart pans to
a wire rack, and let them cool to
lukewarm.

**4. MAKE THE TOPPING:** Place
the cream, confectioners' sugar,
Southern Comfort, and vanilla in a
medium-size mixing bowl and beat
with a hand-held electric mixer on
high speed until stiff peaks form.
Remove the pies from their pans
and serve them lukewarm or at room
temperature, with the whipped cream
topping. (The pies can be prepared up
to 1 day ahead; cover and refrigerate.
Remove them from the refrigerator
2 hours before serving.)

# Candied Cranberry Chocolate Tart

*Makes 2 tarts; serves 2*

◆◆◆◆◆◆◆◆

**Extra crisp,** shortbread-like crusts filled with a rich chocolate cream and garnished with candied cranberries make this an elegant dessert—perfect for Christmas or Thanksgiving dinner. Crème de cassis adds a fruity flavor to the chocolate, but you can leave it out and get equally good-tasting results by adding another tablespoon of cream.

**3 tablespoons whipping (heavy) cream**

**3 ounces bittersweet or semisweet chocolate, chopped**

**1 tablespoon crème de cassis (black currant) or whipping (heavy) cream**

**2 fully baked Rich Sweet Pastry shells (page 165), baked in 4½ x ¾-inch tart pans with removable bottoms, still in the pans**

**Candied Cranberries (recipe follows)**

**PANS REQUIRED:**

**Two 4½ x ¾-inch tart pans with removable bottoms**

**1.** Pour the cream into a small saucepan and bring it to a simmer over medium-high heat. (Or pour the cream into a small microwave-safe bowl and microwave at high power until it simmers, 30 to 45 seconds.) Remove the cream from the heat and add the chocolate. Let it stand for the chocolate to soften, 1 minute. Then whisk the mixture until it is smooth. Whisk in the cassis. Pour the filling into the tart shells, dividing it evenly between them. Cover and refrigerate until the filling is firm, at least 2 hours and up to 24 hours.

**2.** Spoon the Candied Cranberries evenly over the filling, and drizzle

with the cranberry syrup that has accumulated around them. Refrigerate for 1 hour before serving. To remove the tarts from the pans, gently press the bottom of the pan up through the side. Use a metal spatula to lift the tarts off the bottoms.

# Candied Cranberries

**This beautifully colored,** sweet-tart fruit topping is also great with Pumpkin Maple Cheesecakes (page 419).

**MAKES ABOUT ½ CUP**

**Cooking spray**
**½ cup frozen cranberries**
**2 tablespoons sugar**

**1.** Place a rack in the center of the oven and preheat the oven to 425°F. Lightly mist a metal pie pan or cake pan with cooking spray.

**2.** Working quickly so the sugar does not dissolve, place the frozen cranberries in a medium-size bowl and sprinkle

the sugar over them. Toss to coat the cranberries with the sugar. Spread out the mixture on the prepared pie pan in a single layer. Bake until a few cranberries just begin to thaw, about 5 minutes. Remove the pie pan from the oven, and stir the berries and sugar gently with a wooden spoon. Return the pan to the oven and bake until the berries are thawed and most of the sugar is dissolved, 5 to 7 minutes.

**3.** Remove the pie pan from the oven and stir the berries and collected juices gently; let the mixture cool completely in the pan. If not using immediately, the mixture can stand, uncovered, at room temperature, up to 4 hours.

# Caramel Nut Tart

*Makes 2 tarts; serves 2*

◆◆◆◆◆◆◆◆◆

**These festive tarts** are chock-full of nuts tossed in a honey-butterscotch mixture that caramelizes as it bakes. The little tarts are elegant but easy to make, requiring few ingredients. They have become the impromptu dessert I rely on during the holidays. A drizzle of melted chocolate provides extra flair.

**2 fully baked Basic Pastry shells (page 159), baked in 4¹/₂ x ³/₄-inch tart pans with removable bottoms, still in the pans**

**¹/₄ cup pecan halves**

**¹/₄ cup walnut halves**

**¹/₄ cup blanched almonds**

**2 tablespoons unsalted butter**

**¹/₄ cup firmly packed light brown sugar**

**2 tablespoons honey**

**2 tablespoons whipping (heavy) cream**

**1 ounce good quality bittersweet, semisweet, or white chocolate (such as Lindt), finely chopped**

**PANS REQUIRED:**

**Two 4¹/₂ x ³/₄-inch tart pans with removable bottoms**

**1 baking sheet**

**1.** Place a rack in the center of the oven and preheat the oven to 350°F. Place the tart pans on a baking sheet for easier handling, and set it aside.

**2.** Coarsely chop the pecans, walnuts, and almonds.

**3.** Place the butter, brown sugar, and honey in a small saucepan and bring to a simmer over medium heat, stirring constantly. Simmer for 1 minute, then stir in the nuts and the cream. Let the nut mixture simmer for 30 seconds. Then spoon the filling into the tart shells, dividing it evenly between them. Bake the tarts until the filling is a few shades darker, about 15 minutes.

**4.** Remove the baking sheet from the oven, transfer the tart pans to a wire rack, and let them cool completely.

**5.** Place the chocolate in a small microwave-safe bowl and microwave on high power for 45 seconds; then stir until the chocolate is smooth. Dip the tines of a fork into the melted chocolate and drizzle it attractively over the tarts. Let the tarts stand at room temperature until the chocolate sets, about 1 hour. Serve the tarts at room temperature. (The tarts can be prepared 1 day ahead; cover and store at room temperature.)

# Pumpkin-Nut Bread Pudding

*Makes 2 puddings; serves 2*

◆◆◆◆◆◆◆◆◆

**This homespun bread** pudding, full of pumpkin flavor, is a great cold-weather dessert. It's just right to dress up a meal of Thanksgiving leftovers and it's easy to put together when you probably won't feel much like cooking. On the other hand, it's too good to keep only for Thanksgiving weekend.

**Unsalted butter, at room temperature, for greasing the muffin cups**

**¹/₃ cup half-and-half**

**¹/₃ cup canned pumpkin puree (not pumpkin pie filling)**

**3 tablespoons firmly packed dark brown sugar**

**1 tablespoon plus 1 teaspoon well-beaten egg or egg substitute**

**¹/₂ teaspoon pumpkin pie spice**

**¹/₂ teaspoon pure vanilla extract**

**1²/₃ cups stale egg bread (brioche or challah) cubes (¹/₂-inch cubes)**

**3 tablespoons chopped pecans, toasted (see page 195)**

**Rich Caramel Sauce (page 259) or store-bought caramel sauce, for serving**

**Sweetened Whipped Cream (page 36), for serving**

**PAN REQUIRED:**

**1 jumbo muffin pan (³/₄-cup capacity)**

**1.** Place a rack in the center of the oven and preheat the oven to 350°F. Lightly grease 2 of the muffin cups and set the pan aside.

**2.** Place the half-and-half, pumpkin, brown sugar, egg, pumpkin pie spice, and vanilla in a medium-size bowl and whisk to blend well. Mix in the bread

cubes and let the mixture stand for 15 minutes for the bread to soak up the custard. Then stir the pecans into the pudding mixture.

**3.** Spoon the mixture into the prepared muffin cups, dividing it evenly between them. Fill the empty muffin cups halfway with water to prevent them from scorching. Bake the puddings until a toothpick inserted in the center of one comes out clean, 30 to 35 minutes.

**4.** Remove the muffin pan from the oven, carefully pour the water out of the extra muffin cups, and turn out the bread puddings. Place them on serving plates and serve warm, topped with a drizzle of caramel sauce and a dollop of Sweetened Whipped Cream.

# Cranberry Eggnog Pudding

*Makes 1 pudding; serves 2 or 3*

◆◆◆◆◆◆◆◆◆

**Made from all** things richly Christmassy, this bread pudding is a perfect holiday dessert. Crumbled English muffins, cranberries, and toasted almonds are enrobed in sweet and creamy eggnog custard. It's a homey dessert—or a divine dish to serve for a holiday brunch, with thick slices of bacon or sausage and fresh orange sections on the side.

1 tablespoon unsalted butter
2 medium eggs, or ¼ cup plus
   2 tablespoons egg substitute
¾ cup plus 2 tablespoons
   store-bought eggnog
¼ cup whole milk

2 tablespoons unsalted butter, melted
Pinch of salt
¼ teaspoon ground nutmeg
2 English muffins
3 tablespoons fresh or thawed frozen
   cranberries
2 tablespoons light brown sugar
¼ cup cold whipping (heavy) cream

PAN REQUIRED:
1 standard loaf pan
   (8 x 4 inches)

1. Place the 1 tablespoon of butter in the loaf pan, and set the pan aside.

2. Place the eggs, ¾ cup of the eggnog, milk, melted butter, salt, and nutmeg in a medium-size mixing bowl. Crumble the English muffins and add them to the

eggnog mixture; stir in the cranberries. Stir the mixture, pressing down on the bread to submerge it in the liquid. Cover and refrigerate for 1 hour or overnight.

**3.** Place a rack in the center of the oven and preheat the oven to 350°F.

**4.** When the oven is hot, put the loaf pan in the oven and heat the pan until the butter melts. Remove the pan from the oven and pour in the pudding mixture. Cover the loaf pan with aluminum foil, and bake for 30 minutes.

**5.** Uncover the loaf pan and sprinkle the brown sugar over the top. Return the pudding to the oven, uncovered, and continue to bake for 8 minutes.

**6.** Remove the loaf pan from the oven and turn on the broiler. Broil the pudding 4 to 6 inches from the heat until the sugar on top caramelizes, about 1 minute.

**7.** Remove the loaf pan from the broiler and let it cool on a wire rack for 5 minutes.

**8.** While the pudding is cooling, place the cream in a medium-size mixing bowl and beat with a hand-held electric mixer on high speed until soft peaks form; stir in the remaining 2 tablespoons of eggnog.

**9.** To serve, spoon the pudding into deep bowls, and spoon the eggnog cream over the pudding.

# Eggnog Crème Brûlée

*Makes 2 custards; serves 2*

◆◆◆◆◆◆◆◆◆

**A creamy light** eggnog-flavored Crème Brûlée makes a perfect Christmas or New Year's Eve dessert—really for anytime during the holidays. Instead of broiling it to caramelize the sugar on the top, I get to use my favorite kitchen toy—a small propane torch. It is easier to get a perfect caramelized crust with a torch, but repeating the process for a large number of desserts can get tedious. So it is perfect for this Small-Batch version.

**Yolks of 3 large eggs**
**2 tablespoons sugar**
**1 piece (3 inches) of vanilla bean**
**  or 1 teaspoon vanilla paste**
**½ cup whole milk**
**¼ cup whipping (heavy) cream**

**2 pinches of ground nutmeg**
**1 teaspoon Bailey's Irish Cream**
**  (optional)**
**4 teaspoons firmly packed light**
**  brown sugar**
**Boiling water**

PANS REQUIRED:
**Two 1-cup ramekins or custard**
**  cups**
**1 baking pan**

**1.** Place a rack in the center of the oven and preheat the oven to 325°F. Place the ramekins in a larger baking pan, and set it aside.

**2.** Place the egg yolks and sugar in a medium-size mixing bowl and whisk until well blended. Slit open the vanilla bean and scrape the seeds into the yolk mixture. Gradually whisk in the milk, cream, nutmeg, and Bailey's

Irish Cream, if using. Pour the mixture into the ramekins, dividing it evenly between them. Pour enough boiling water into the baking pan to reach halfway up the sides of the ramekins. Carefully place the baking pan in the oven. Bake until the crème brûlées are set around the edge but still slightly jiggly in the very center, about 30 minutes.

**3.** Remove the baking pan from the oven and let the crème brûlées cool in the water in the baking pan for 30 minutes. Then use tongs to remove the ramekins from the water. Cover and refrigerate until well chilled, 6 hours or overnight. (The crème brûlées can be made 1 day ahead. Cover and refrigerate.)

**4.** About 2 hours before serving, place a rack in the top third of the oven and preheat the broiler.

**5.** Press the brown sugar through a small fine-mesh sieve over the custards, covering them evenly and completely. Broil the custards until the sugar bubbles and caramelizes, 1 to 2 minutes. Watch carefully— don't let the sugar burn. Remove the custards from the broiler and refrigerate them, uncovered, until the topping hardens, at least 2 hours and up to overnight. Serve cold.

# Conversion Table

## APPROXIMATE EQUIVALENTS

1 stick butter = 8 tbs = 4 oz = ½ cup
1 cup all-purpose presifted flour or dried
    bread crumbs = 5 oz
1 cup granulated sugar = 8 oz
1 cup (packed) brown sugar = 6 oz
1 cup confectioners' sugar = 4½ oz
1 cup honey or syrup = 12 oz
1 cup grated cheese = 4 oz
1 cup dried beans = 6 oz
1 large egg = about 2 oz or about 3 tbs
1 egg yolk = about 1 tbs
1 egg white = about 2 tbs

Please note that all conversions are approximate but close enough to be useful when converting from one system to another.

## WEIGHT CONVERSIONS

| US/UK | METRIC | US/UK | METRIC |
|---|---|---|---|
| ½ oz | 15 g | 7 oz | 200 g |
| 1 oz | 30 g | 8 oz | 250 g |
| 1½ oz | 45 g | 9 oz | 275 g |
| 2 oz | 60 g | 10 oz | 300 g |
| 2½ oz | 75 g | 11 oz | 325 g |
| 3 oz | 90 g | 12 oz | 350 g |
| 3½ oz | 100 g | 13 oz | 375 g |
| 4 oz | 125 g | 14 oz | 400 g |
| 5 oz | 150 g | 15 oz | 450 g |
| 6 oz | 175 g | 1 lb | 500 g |

## LIQUID CONVERSIONS

| U.S. | IMPERIAL | METRIC |
|---|---|---|
| 2 tbs | 1 fl oz | 30 ml |
| 3 tbs | 1½ fl oz | 45 ml |
| ¼ cup | 2 fl oz | 60 ml |
| ⅓ cup | 2½ fl oz | 75 ml |
| ⅓ cup + 1 tbs | 3 fl oz | 90 ml |
| ⅓ cup + 2 tbs | 3½ fl oz | 100 ml |
| ½ cup | 4 fl oz | 125 ml |
| ⅔ cup | 5 fl oz | 150 ml |
| ¾ cup | 6 fl oz | 175 ml |
| ¾ cup + 2 tbs | 7 fl oz | 200 ml |
| 1 cup | 8 fl oz | 250 ml |
| 1 cup + 2 tbs | 9 fl oz | 275 ml |
| 1¼ cups | 10 fl oz | 300 ml |
| 1⅓ cups | 11 fl oz | 325 ml |
| 1½ cups | 12 fl oz | 350 ml |
| 1⅔ cups | 13 fl oz | 375 ml |
| 1¾ cups | 14 fl oz | 400 ml |
| 1¾ cups + 2 tbs | 15 fl oz | 450 ml |
| 2 cups (1 pint) | 16 fl oz | 500 ml |
| 2½ cups | 20 fl oz (1 pint) | 600 ml |
| 3¾ cups | 1½ pints | 900 ml |
| 4 cups | 1¾ pints | 1 liter |

## OVEN TEMPERATURES

| °F | GAS MARK | °C | °F | GAS MARK | °C |
|---|---|---|---|---|---|
| 250 | ½ | 120 | 400 | 6 | 200 |
| 275 | 1 | 140 | 425 | 7 | 220 |
| 300 | 2 | 150 | 450 | 8 | 230 |
| 325 | 3 | 160 | 475 | 9 | 240 |
| 350 | 4 | 180 | 500 | 10 | 260 |
| 375 | 5 | 190 | | | |

Note: Reduce the temperature by 20°C (68°F) for fan-assisted ovens.

# Index